SCHAUM'S OUTLINE OF

THEORY AND PROBLEMS

OF

PROGRAMMING
WITH
STRUCTURED
BASIC

•

BYRON S. GOTTFRIED, Ph.D.
Professor of Industrial Engineering
University of Pittsburgh

SCHAUM'S OUTLINE SERIES
McGRAW-HILL, INC.

New York St. Louis San Francisco Auckland Bogotá Caracas
Lisbon London Madrid Mexico Milan Montreal
New Delhi Paris San Juan Singapore
Sydney Tokyo Toronto

To Marcia, Sharon, Gail and Susan

BYRON S. GOTTFRIED is a Professor of Industrial Engineering at the University of Pittsburgh. He received his Ph.D. from Case-Western Reserve University in 1962, and has been a member of the Pitt faculty since 1970. His primary interests are in the modeling and simulation of industrial processes. Dr. Gottfried also has active interests in computer graphics and computer programming languages. He is the author of several books, including three editions of *Programming with BASIC*, *Programming with C* and *Programming with Pascal* in the Schaum's Outline Series.

Schaum's Outline of Theory and Problems of
PROGRAMMING WITH STRUCTURED BASIC

7 8 9 QSR 5 4 3 2

ISBN 0-07-023899-5

Sponsoring Editor: John Aliano
Production Supervisor: Louise Karam
Editing Supervisors: Meg Tobin, Maureen Walker
Cover design by Amy E. Becker

Gottfried, Byron S., date
   Schaum's outline of theory and problems of programming with structured BASIC / Byron S. Gottfried.
      p.   cm. -- (Schaum's outline series)
   Includes index.
   ISBN 0-07-023899-5
   1. BASIC (Computer program language) 2. Structured programming.
I. Title.   II. Title: Outline of theory and problems of programming with structured BASIC.   III.
Title: Programming with structured BASIC.   IV. Series.
QA76.76.B3G68   1993
005.13'3--dc20   91-43808
                                                                                                        CIP

Preface

BASIC has been a popular programming language ever since it was first introduced in 1964. Its use has increased explosively, however, as a result of the proliferation of personal computers that occurred during the 1980s. Today, BASIC is the most popular of all programming languages. It is studied in high schools and colleges throughout the world, and remains the language of choice of most computer hobbyists.

As BASIC grew in popularity, it has also matured dramatically in terms of its capabilities. Many of the sophisticated, structured programming constructs that are present in other, newer programming languages have now been added to BASIC. In addition, the graphical user interfaces available on personal computers have brought about a vastly improved programming environment. As a result, BASIC has "grown up." Modern implementations of the language bear little resemblance to the simplistic language of the 1960s.

This book is intended as a replacement for my earlier *Schaum's Outline of Programming with BASIC*. It offers instruction in BASIC programming using the features found in contemporary, structured implementations of the language. Thus, the book stresses the development of programs that are logical, efficient and orderly. The reader is therefore exposed to the principles of good programming practice as well as the specific rules of BASIC.

The book concentrates on three implementations of structured BASIC: the 1987 ANSI standard, True BASIC and Microsoft's QuickBASIC/QBASIC. True BASIC is a popular personal computer implementation that adheres very closely to the 1987 ANSI standard. QuickBASIC, and its twin QBASIC, have personalities of their own. They are widely used on many personal computers.

One of my goals in writing this book is that it be easily understood. This enables the book to be attractive to a wide reader audience, ranging from high school students to practicing professionals. The book is particularly well suited to the advanced secondary or beginning college level, either as a textbook for a beginning programming course, as a supplementary text for a more comprehensive course in analytical techniques or as an effective self-study guide. For the most part, the required mathematical level does not go beyond high school algebra.

The material is organized in such a manner that the reader can write complete, though elementary, BASIC programs as soon as possible. It is very important that the reader write such programs and execute them on a computer concurrently with reading the text. This greatly enhances the beginning programmer's self-confidence and stimulates his or her interest in the subject. (Learning to program a computer is like learning to play the piano; it cannot be learned simply by studying a textbook!)

The text contains many examples. These include both comprehensive programming problems and simple illustrations that focus on specific programming constructs. In addition, sets of review questions, drill problems and programming problems are included at the end of each chapter. The review questions enable readers to test their recall of the material presented within the chapter. They also provide an effective chapter summary. Most of the drill problems and programming problems require no special mathematical or technological background. The student should solve as many of these problems as possible. (Answers to most of the drill problems are provided at the end of the text.) When using this book as a text in a programming course, it may also be advisable for the instructor to supplement the programming problems with additional assignments that reflect particular disciplinary interests.

The principal features of both True BASIC and QuickBASIC/QBASIC are summarized in five appendixes for the reader's convenience. This material should be used frequently for ready reference and quick recall. It will be particularly helpful when writing or debugging a new program.

Finally, readers who complete this book will have learned a great deal about general programming concepts as well as the specific rules of structured BASIC. In addition, they should be convinced that programming with structured BASIC is not only *easy*, but also *fun*.

BYRON S. GOTTFRIED

Contents

Chapter *1* **INTRODUCTORY CONCEPTS** 1

    1.1   Introduction to Computers 1
    1.2   Computer Characteristics 2
    1.3   Modes of Operation 5
    1.4   Types of Programming Languages 7
    1.5   Introduction to BASIC 8

Chapter *2* **GETTING STARTED WITH BASIC** 16

    2.1   Numeric Constants 16
    2.2   String Constants 17
    2.3   Variables 17
    2.4   Operators and Expressions 18
    2.5   Hierarchy of Operations 19
    2.6   Use of Parentheses 20
    2.7   Special Rules Concerning Numeric Expressions 20
    2.8   String Expressions 22
    2.9   Assigning Values: The LET Statement 22
   2.10   Reading Input: The INPUT Statement 23
   2.11   Printing Output: The PRINT Statement 25
   2.12   Adding Program Comments: The REM Statement 29
   2.13   The STOP and END Statements 30
   2.14   Library Functions 31

Chapter *3* **CREATING AND RUNNING A BASIC PROGRAM** 42

    3.1   Planning a BASIC Program 42
    3.2   Writing a BASIC Program 44
    3.3   Entering the Program Into the Computer 45
    3.4   Executing the Program 47
    3.5   Error Diagnostics 48
    3.6   Logical Debugging 50
    3.7   Other BASIC Programming Environments 54

Chapter *4* **CONTROL STRUCTURES** 62

    4.1   Relational Operators and Logical Expressions 62
    4.2   Logical Operators 63
    4.3   Conditional Execution: The IF-THEN Statement 65
    4.4   Conditional Execution: IF-THEN-ELSE Blocks 65
    4.5   Unconditional Looping: FOR-NEXT Structures 70
    4.6   Conditional Looping: DO-LOOP Structures 74
    4.7   Conditional Looping: WHILE-WEND Structures 77
    4.8   Nested Control Structures 78
    4.9   Selection: SELECT CASE Structures 85
   4.10   Line-Oriented Control Statements 92

Chapter 5 ARRAYS **105**

5.1   Defining an Array: The DIM Statement 105
5.2   Subscripted Variables 107
5.3   Initializing an Array: The DATA and READ Statements................... 113
5.4   Rereading Data: The RESTORE Statement....................................... 118

Chapter 6 FUNCTIONS AND SUBROUTINES **131**

6.1   Single-Line Functions: The DEF Statement...................................... 131
6.2   Multi-Line Functions... 136
6.3   External Functions 143
6.4   Subroutines... 150
6.5   Line-Oriented Subroutine Calls (GOSUB, ON-GOSUB)............. 157
6.6   External Subroutines 159
6.7   Recursion... 161

Chapter 7 SOME ADDITIONAL FEATURES OF BASIC................................. **181**

7.1   Additional Data Types... 181
7.2   More About Expressions.. 183
7.3   More About Statements 184
7.4   Clearing the Screen: The CLEAR and CLS Statements................. 186
7.5   Positioning the Cursor: The SET CURSOR and LOCATE Statements 186
7.6   More About Input 188
7.7   Formatted Output: The PRINT USING Statement 192
7.8   Some Additional Miscellaneous Commands 203

Chapter 8 DATA FILES... **214**

8.1   Data File Fundamentals... 214
8.2   Processing a Data File 215
8.3   Sequential Data Files... 216
8.4   File-Directed Device Output (Print Files) 227
8.5   Direct Data Files 227

Chapter 9 VECTORS AND MATRICES.. **248**

9.1   Vector and Matrix Operations 248
9.2   Matrix Input/Output.. 255
9.3   Special Matrices... 263
9.4   Changing Dimensions.. 270

Chapter 10 PROGRAMMING A PERSONAL COMPUTER................................ **288**

10.1 The Keyboard Function Keys 288
10.2 Other Programmable Input Devices.. 290
10.3 Use of Color and Sound 299

Chapter 11 INTRODUCTION TO COMPUTER GRAPHICS............................. **308**

11.1 Graphics Fundamentals.. 308

11.2 Points and Lines 309
11.3 Shapes...322
11.4 Animations 338
11.5 Character Graphics 346

Appendix *A* SUMMARY OF TRUE BASIC STATEMENTS..358

Appendix *B* SUMMARY OF TRUE BASIC FUNCTIONS...364

Appendix *C* SUMMARY OF QUICKBASIC STATEMENTS...367

Appendix *D* SUMMARY OF QUICKBASIC FUNCTIONS 374

Appendix *E* THE ASCII CHARACTER SET...377

ANSWERS TO SELECTED PROBLEMS 379

INDEX..413

Complete Programming Examples

The programming examples are listed in the order in which they first appear within the text. The examples vary from very simple to moderately complex. Multiple versions are presented for many of the programs, particularly the simpler programs.

1. *Area of a Circle* - Examples 1.6 - 1.8
2. *Roots of a Quadratic Equation* - Examples 3.1 - 3.4, 3.8, 3.9, 4.9
3. *Evaluating a Polynomial* - Example 3.7
4. *Averaging a List of Numbers* - Example 4.12
5. *Averaging a List of Positive Numbers* - Examples 4.13, 4.16, 4.17
6. *Solution of an Algebraic Equation* - Example 4.18
7   *Generation of Fibonacci Numbers and Search for Primes* - Examples 4.19, 7.8
8. *Calculating Depreciation* - Example 4.24
9. *Deviations About an Average* - Example 5.7
10. *Word Unscrambling* - Example 5.8
11. *Writing a String Backwards* - Example 5.9
12. *Reordering a List of Numbers* - Example 5.14
13. *Search for a Maximum* - Example 6.5
14. *Smallest of Three Numbers* - Example 6.7
15. *Simulation of a Game of Chance: Shooting Craps* - Examples 6.11, 6.14
16. *Smallest of Three Numbers* - Example 6.18
17. *Table Manipulation* - Examples 6.20, 6.21
18. *A Pig Latin Generator* - Example 6.22
19. *Calculating Factorials* - Example 6.27
20. *The Towers of Hanoi* - Example 6.28
21. *Programming a Screen Display (Nothing Can Go Wrong, Go Wrong . . .)* - Examples 7.11, 10.9
22. *Personal Finance (Compound Interest Calculations)* - Example 7.25
23. *Creating a Sequential Data File in QuickBASIC: Student Exam Scores* - Example 8.3
24. *Creating a Sequential Data File in True BASIC: Student Exam Scores* - Example 8.4
25. *Reading a Sequential Data File in QuickBASIC: Student Exam Scores* - Example 8.5
26. *Reading a Sequential Data File in True BASIC: Student Exam Scores* - Example 8.6
27. *Updating a Sequential Data File in QuickBASIC: Student Exam Scores* - Example 8.7
28. *Updating a Sequential Data File in True BASIC: Student Exam Scores* - Example 8.8
29. *Creating a Direct Data File in True BASIC: States and their Capitals* - Example 8.10
30. *Creating a Direct Data File in QuickBASIC: States and their Capitals* - Example 8.11
31. *Reading a Direct Data File in True BASIC: Locating State Capitals via Binary Search* - Example 8.12
32. *Reading a Direct Data File in QuickBASIC: Locating State Capitals via Binary Search* - Example 8.13
33. *Updating a Direct Data File in True BASIC: Baseball Team Records* - Example 8.14
34. *Updating a Direct Data File in QuickBASIC: Baseball Team Records* - Example 8.15
35. *Simultaneous Equations* - Example 9.25
36. *Least Squares Curve Fitting* - Example 9.30 (see also Example 11.9)
37. *Programming the Function Keys* - Example 10.1
38. *Programming a Light Pen* - Example 10.2
39. *Programming a Mouse* - Example 10.3
40. *Calibrating a Joystick* - Example 10.4
41. *Programming a Joystick* - Example 10.5
42. *Multicolored Text* - Example 10.6
43. *Programming a Speaker (A Siren)* - Example 10.8

44. *Random Points* - Example 11.5
45. *A Lightning Bolt* - Example 11.7
46. *Moving Lines (Kinetic Art)* - Example 11.8
47. *Linear Regression with Graphical Display* - Example 11.9
48. *Expanding Rectangles* - Example 11.11
49. *Random Blocks* - Example 11.13
50. *Expanding Circles* - Example 11.15
51. *A Filled Lightning Bolt* - Example 11.16
52. *A Pie Chart Generator* - Example 11.21
53. *Blimp with Animated Text* - Example 11.24
54. *Simulation of a Bouncing Ball* - Examples 11.25, 11.26
55. *A Game of Paddleball* - Example 11.27
56. *A Bar Chart Generator* - Examples 11.28, 11.29

Chapter 1

Introductory Concepts

BASIC (*B*eginner's *A*ll-purpose *S*ymbolic *I*nstruction *C*ode) is a popular, easily learned programming language that was first developed in the mid-1960s. In recent years BASIC has undergone extensive modifications, in order to provide the same structured programming features that are found in other popular programming languages. These newer versions of BASIC are often referred to as *structured BASIC*.

This book offers instruction in computer programming using the features found in these newer versions of BASIC. By studying this book you will learn the details of writing complete, structured programs in BASIC. The concepts are demonstrated in detail by the many sample problems included within the text.

1.1 INTRODUCTION TO COMPUTERS

Today's computers come in many different forms. They range from massive, multipurpose *mainframes* and *supercomputers* to desktop-size *personal computers*. Between these extremes is a vast middle ground of *minicomputers* and *workstations*. Large minicomputers approach mainframes in computing power, whereas workstations are powerful personal computers.

Mainframes and large minicomputers are used by many businesses, universities, hospitals and government agencies to carry out sophisticated scientific and business calculations. These computers are expensive (large computers can cost millions of dollars) and may require a sizeable staff of supporting personnel and a special, carefully controlled environment.

Personal computers, on the other hand, are small and inexpensive. In fact, portable, battery-powered personal computers smaller than a typewriter are now available. Personal computers are widely used in most schools and businesses and they are rapidly becoming common household items. Students typically use personal computers when learning to program with BASIC.

Figure 1.1 shows a student using a personal computer.

Fig. 1.1

Despite their small size and low cost, modern personal computers approach small minicomputers in computing power. They are now used for many applications that formerly required larger, more expensive computers. Moreover, their performance continues to improve dramatically as their cost continues to drop. The design of a personal computer permits a high level of interaction between the user and the computer. Most applications (e.g., word processors, graphics programs, spreadsheets and database management programs) are specifically designed to take advantage of this feature, thus providing the skilled user with a wide variety of creative tools to write, draw or carry out numerical computations. Applications involving high-resolution graphics are particularly common.

Many organizations connect personal computers to larger computers or to other personal computers, thus permitting their use either as stand-alone devices or as terminals within a computer *network*. Connections over telephone lines are particularly common. When viewed in this context, we see that personal computers often *complement*, rather than *replace*, the use of larger computers.

1.2 COMPUTER CHARACTERISTICS

All digital computers, regardless of their size, are basically electronic devices that can transmit, store, and manipulate *information* (i.e., *data*). Several different types of data can be processed by a computer. These include *numeric data*, *character data* (names, addresses, etc.), *graphic data* (charts, drawings, photographs, etc.), and *sound* (music, speech patterns, etc.). The two most common types, from the standpoint of a beginning programmer, are numeric data and character data. Scientific and technical applications are concerned primarily with numeric data, whereas business applications usually require processing of both numeric and character data.

To process a particular set of data, the computer must be given an appropriate set of instructions called a *program*. These instructions are entered into the computer and then stored in a portion of the computer's *memory*.

A stored program can be *executed* at any time. This causes the following things to happen.

1. A set of information, called the *input data*, will be entered into the computer (from the keyboard, a floppy disk, etc.) and stored in a portion of the computer's memory.

2. The input data will be processed to produce certain desired results, known as the *output data*.

3. The output data, and perhaps some of the input data, will be printed onto a sheet of paper or displayed on a *monitor* (a television receiver specially designed to display computer output).

This three-step procedure can be repeated many times if desired, thus causing a large quantity of data to be processed in rapid sequence. It should be understood, however, that each of these steps, particularly steps 2 and 3, can be lengthy and complicated.

Example 1.1

A computer has been programmed to calculate the area of a circle using the formula $a = \pi r^2$, given a numeric value for the radius r as input data. The following steps are required.

1. Read the numeric value for the radius of the circle.

2. Calculate the value of the area using the above formula. This value will be stored, along with the input data, in the computer's memory.

3. Print (display) the values of the radius and the corresponding area.

Each of these steps will require one or more instructions in a computer program.

The foregoing discussion illustrates two important characteristics of a digital computer: *memory* and *capability to be programmed*. A third important characteristic is its *speed and reliability*. We will say more about memory, speed, and reliability in the next few paragraphs. Programmability will be discussed at length throughout the remainder of this book.

Memory

Every piece of information stored within the computer's memory is encoded as some unique combination of zeros and ones. These zeros and ones are called *bits* (*binary digits*). Each bit is represented by an electronic device that is, in some sense, either "off" (zero) or "on" (one).

Small computers have memories that are organized into 8-bit multiples called *bytes*, as illustrated in Figure 1.2. Notice that the individual bits are numbered, beginning with 0 (for the rightmost bit) and extending to 7 (the leftmost bit). Normally, a single character (e.g., a letter, a single digit or a punctuation symbol) will occupy one byte of memory. An instruction may occupy 1, 2 or 3 bytes. A single numeric quantity may occupy 1 to 8 bytes, depending on its *precision* (i.e., the number of significant figures) and its *type* (integer, floating-point, etc.).

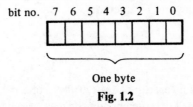

One byte

Fig. 1.2

The size of a computer's memory is usually expressed as some multiple of $2^{10} = 1024$ bytes. This is referred to as 1K. Small computers have memories whose sizes typically range from 64K to several megabytes, where 1 megabyte (1M) is equivalent to $2^{10} \times 2^{10} = 1024K$ bytes.

Example 1.2

The memory of a small personal computer has a capacity of 256K bytes. Thus, as many as $256 \times 1024 = 262{,}144$ characters and/or instructions can be stored in the computer's memory. If the entire memory is used to represent character data (which is actually quite unlikely), then over 3200 names and addresses can be stored within the computer at any one time, assuming 80 characters for each name and address.

If the memory is used to represent numeric data rather than names and addresses, then over 65,000 individual numbers can be stored at any one time, assuming each numeric quantity requires 4 bytes of memory.

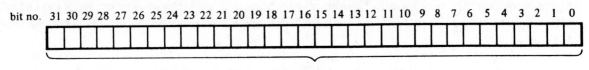

One 32-bit word

Fig. 1.3

Large computers have memories that are organized into *words* rather than bytes. Each word will consist of a relatively large number of bits - typically 32 or 36. The bit-wise organization of a 32-bit word is illustrated in Figure 1.3. Notice that the bits are numbered, beginning with 0 (for the right-most bit) and extending to 31 (the left-most bit).

Figure 1.4 shows the same 32-bit word organized into 4 consecutive bytes. The bytes are numbered in the same manner as the individual bits, ranging from 0 (for the right-most byte) to 3 (the left-most byte).

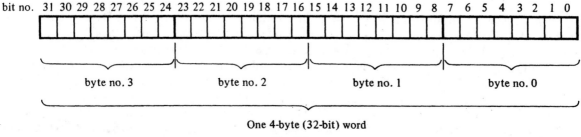

One 4-byte (32-bit) word

Fig. 1.4

The use of a 32- or a 36-bit word permits one numeric quantity, or a small *group* of characters (typically 4 or 5), to be represented within a single word of memory. Large computers commonly have several million words (i.e., several megawords) of memory.

Example 1.3

The memory of a large computer has a capacity of 2M (2048K) words, which is equivalent to 2048 x 1024 = 2,097,152 words. If the entire memory is used to represent numeric data (which is unlikely), then more than 2 million numbers can be stored within the computer at any one time, assuming each numeric quantity requires one word of memory.

If the memory is used to represent characters rather than numeric data, then about 8 million characters can be stored at any one time, based upon 4 characters per word. This is more than enough memory to store the contents of an entire book.

Most computers also employ *auxiliary storage devices* (e.g., magnetic tapes, disks, optical memory devices) in addition to their primary memories. These devices typically range from 20 or 40 megabytes for a small computer to several hundred megawords for a large computer. Moreover, they allow information to be recorded permanently, since they can often be physically disconnected from the computer and stored when not in use. However, the access time (i.e., the time required to store or retrieve information) is considerably greater for these auxiliary devices than for the computer's primary memory.

Speed and Reliability

Because of its extremely high speed, a computer can carry out calculations within minutes that might require many days, and perhaps even months or years, if carried out by hand. For example, the end-of-semester grades for all students in a large university can typically be processed in just a few minutes on a large computer.

The time required to carry out simple computational tasks, such as adding two numbers, is usually expressed in terms of *microseconds* (1 μsec = 10^{-6} sec) or *nanoseconds* (1 $nsec$ = 10^{-3} μsec = 10^{-9} sec). Thus, if a computer can add two numbers in 10 nanoseconds (typical of a modern medium-speed computer), 100 million (10^8) additions will be carried out in one second.

This very high speed is accompanied by an equally high level of reliability. Thus, computers never make mistakes of their own accord. Highly publicized "computer errors," such as a person's receiving a tax refund of several million dollars, are the result of programming errors or data entry errors rather than errors caused by the computer itself.

1.3 MODES OF OPERATION

There are two different ways that a large computer can be shared by many different users. These are the *batch mode* and the *interactive mode*. Each has its own advantages for certain types of problems.

Batch Processing

In *batch processing*, a number of jobs are entered into the computer, stored internally, and then processed sequentially. (A *job* refers to a computer program and its associated sets of input data.) After the job is processed, the output, along with a listing of the computer program, is printed on multiple sheets of paper by a high-speed printer. Typically, the user will pick up the printed output at some convenient time, after the job has been processed.

In *classical batch processing*, the program and the data are recorded on *punched cards*. This information is read into the computer by means of a mechanical card reader and then processed. In the early days of computing all jobs were processed in this manner. Fortunately, this mode of operation is now obsolete.

Modern batch processing is generally tied into a timesharing system (see below). Thus, the program and the data are typed into the computer via a *timesharing terminal* or a personal computer acting as a terminal. The information is then stored within the computer's memory and processed in its proper sequence. This form of batch processing is preferable to classical batch processing, since it eliminates the need for punched cards and allows the input information (program and data) to be edited while it is being entered.

Large quantities of information (both programs and data) can be transmitted into and out of the computer very quickly in batch processing. Furthermore, the user need not be present while the job is being processed. Therefore, this mode of operation is well-suited to jobs that require large amounts of computer time or are physically lengthy. On the other hand, the total time required for a job to be processed in this manner may vary from several minutes to several hours, even though the job may have required only a second or two of actual computer time. (Each job must wait its turn before it can be read, processed, and printed out.) Thus, batch processing is undesirable when processing small, simple jobs that must be returned as quickly as possible (as, for example, when learning computer programming).

Timesharing

Timesharing allows many different users to use a single computer simultaneously. Generally, the host computer is a mainframe or a large minicomputer. The various users communicate with the computer through their own individual terminals. In a modern timesharing network, personal computers are often used as timesharing terminals. Since the host computer operates much faster than a human sitting at a terminal, one large computer can support many terminals at essentially the same time. Therefore, each user will be unaware of the presence of any other users, and will seem to have the host computer at his or her own disposal.

An individual timesharing terminal may be wired directly to the host computer, or it may be connected to the computer over telephone lines, a microwave circuit, or even an earth satellite. Thus, the terminal can be located far — perhaps hundreds of miles — from its host computer. Systems in which personal computers are connected to large mainframes over telephone lines are particularly common. Such systems make use of *modems* (i.e., *mod*ulator/*dem*odulator devices) to convert the digitized computer signals into analog telephone signals and vice versa. Through such an arrangement a person working at home, on his or her own personal computer, can easily access a remote computer at school or at the office.

Timesharing is best suited for processing relatively simple jobs that do not require extensive data transmission or large amounts of computer time. Many applications that arise in schools and commercial offices have these characteristics. Such applications can be processed quickly, easily, and at minimum expense using timesharing.

Example 1.4

A major university has a computer timesharing capability consisting of 200 hard-wired timesharing terminals and 80 additional telephone connections. The timesharing terminals are located at various places around the campus and are wired directly to a large mainframe computer. Each terminal is able to transmit information to or from the central computer at a maximum speed of 960 characters per second.

The telephone connections allow students who are not on campus to connect their personal computers to the central computer. Each personal computer can transmit data to or from the central computer at a maximum speed of 240 characters per second. Thus, all 280 terminals and personal computers can interact with the central computer at the same time, though each student will be unaware that others are simultaneously sharing the computer.

Interactive Computing

Interactive computing is a type of computing environment that originated with commercial timesharing systems and has been refined by the widespread use of personal computers. In an interactive computing environment, the user and the computer interact with each other during the computational session. Thus, the user may periodically be asked to provide certain information that will determine what subsequent actions are to be taken by the computer and vice versa.

Example 1.5

A student wishes to use a personal computer to calculate the radius of a circle whose area has a value of 100. A program is available that will calculate the area of a circle, given the radius. (Note that this is just the opposite of what the student wishes to do.) This program isn't exactly what is needed, but it does allow the student to obtain an answer by trial and error. The procedure will be to guess a value for the radius and then calculate a corresponding area. This trial-and-error procedure continues until the student has found a value for the radius that yields an area sufficiently close to 100.

Once the program execution begins, the message

```
Radius = ?
```

is displayed. The student then enters a value for the radius. Let us assume that the student enters a value of 5 for the radius. The computer will respond by displaying

```
Area = 78.5398

Do you wish to repeat the calculation?
```

The student then types either yes or no. If the student types yes, the message

```
Radius = ?
```

again appears, and the entire procedure is repeated. If the student types no, the message

```
Goodbye
```

is displayed and the computation is terminated.

Shown below is a printed copy of the information displayed during a typical interactive session using the program described above. In this session, an approximate value of $r = 5.6$ was determined after only three calculations. The information typed by the student is underlined.

```
Radius = ? 5
Area = 78.5398

Do you wish to repeat the calculation? yes

Radius = ? 6
Area = 113.097

Do you wish to repeat the calculation? yes

Radius = ? 5.6
Area = 98.5204

Do you wish to repeat the calculation? no

Goodbye
```

Notice the manner in which the student and the computer appear to be conversing with one another. Also, note that the student waits until he or she sees the calculated value of the area before deciding whether or not to carry out another calculation. If another calculation is initiated, the new value for the radius supplied by the student will depend on the previously calculated results.

Programs designed for interactive computing environments are sometimes said to be *conversational* in nature. Computerized games are excellent examples of such interactive applications. This includes fast-action, graphical arcade games, even though the user's responses may be reflexive rather than numeric or verbal.

1.4 TYPES OF PROGRAMMING LANGUAGES

Many different languages can be used to program a computer. The most basic of these is *machine language* — a collection of very detailed, cryptic instructions that control the computer's internal circuitry. This is the natural dialect of the computer. Very few computer programs are actually written in machine language, however, for two significant reasons: first, because machine language is very cumbersome to work with; and second, because every different type of computer has its own unique instruction set. Thus, a machine-language program written for one type of computer cannot be run on a different type of computer without significant alterations.

Usually, a computer program will be written in some *high-level* language, whose instruction set is more compatible with human languages and human thought processes. Most of these are *general-purpose* languages such as BASIC, C, Pascal and Fortran. There are also various *special-purpose* languages whose instruction sets are specifically designed for some particular type of application. Some common examples are LISP, a *list-processing* language that is widely used for artificial intelligence applications, and CSMP and SIMAN, two different types of special-purpose *simulation* languages.

As a rule, a single instruction in a high-level language will be equivalent to several instructions in machine language. This greatly simplifies the task of writing complete, correct programs. Furthermore, the rules for programming in a particular high-level language are much the same for all computers, so that a program written for one computer can generally be run on many different computers with little or no alteration. Thus, we see that a high-level language offers three significant advantages over machine language: *simplicity, uniformity* and *portability* (i.e., machine independence).

A program that is written in a high-level language must, however, be translated into machine language before it can be executed. This is known as *compilation* or *interpretation*, depending on how it is carried out. (Compilers translate the entire program into machine language before executing any of the instructions. Interpreters, on the other hand, proceed through a program by translating and then executing single instructions or small groups of instructions.) In either case, the translation is carried out automatically within the computer. In fact, inexperienced programmers may not even be aware that this process is taking place, since they typically see only their original high-level program, the input data, and the calculated results. Most implementations of BASIC operate as interpreters, though compilers are becoming increasingly common.

A compiler or interpreter is itself a computer program. It accepts a program written in a high-level language (e.g., BASIC) as input, and generates a corresponding machine-language program as output. The original high-level program is called the *source* program, and the resulting machine-language program is called the *object* program. Every computer must have its own compiler or interpreter for a particular high-level language.

It is generally more convenient to develop a new program using an interpreter rather than a compiler. Once an error-free program has been developed, however, a compiled version will normally execute much faster than an interpreted version. The reasons for this are beyond the scope of our present discussion.

1.5 INTRODUCTION TO BASIC

BASIC is a general-purpose, easy-to-use programming language. Its instructions consist of terms that resemble algebraic expressions, augmented by certain English keywords such as IF, THEN, FOR, DO, SELECT, INPUT, and PRINT. Other high-level languages have similar features, though they tend to be more complicated to use. Hence, BASIC is particularly well-suited for persons learning to program for the first time. In fact, most high schools and many junior high schools now provide instruction in BASIC programming.

The use of BASIC is by no means restricted, however, to elementary programming exercises. It is often used for more advanced applications in business, science, engineering and mathematics. Moreover, BASIC is the principal language that is used with personal computers (PCs). Thus, BASIC is used for many novel applications, such as computer games that require the use of graphics and sound enhancements. We will see a representative sampling of these different types of programming applications in the examples included within this book.

History of BASIC

BASIC was originally developed in 1964 at Dartmouth College by John Kemeny and Thomas Kurtz. At that time all computing was carried out on mainframe computers using batch processing. Fortran, Algol and COBOL were the standard programming languages. The original BASIC was much easier to use than any of these languages, however, and it could be run interactively in a timesharing environment. Thus, BASIC provided a radical improvement in the way computing was carried out at that time.

Interactive computing environments became popular during the 1970s, as many commercial timesharing services became available. BASIC was adopted as a standard programming language by most of these timesharing services. It was also available on a variety of minicomputers, which were being installed at many schools and small businesses. As a result, BASIC became very popular and thousands of computer users became proficient BASIC programmers.

The advent of the personal computer in the late 1970s caused an explosive growth in the use of BASIC. A version of BASIC quickly became available for practically every personal computer. In fact, many personal computers contained a BASIC interpreter within the computer's hardware (in a read-only memory chip). This practice that still continues, though it is less common than it once was.

Of particular significance was a small hardware-resident BASIC interpreter written by Paul Allen and William Gates, the founders of Microsoft Corporation. This simple BASIC interpreter was supplied with many early personal computers. It later evolved into a succession of more comprehensive implementations of BASIC, known collectively as Microsoft BASIC. QuickBASIC and QBASIC are current, state-of-the-art versions of Microsoft BASIC (they differ only in that QuickBASIC can produce compiled object code, whereas QBASIC is strictly an interpreter). Earlier versions were called GW-BASIC (by Microsoft) and BASICA (by IBM). The availability of Microsoft BASIC, in its many variations, contributed significantly to the widespread acceptance of personal computers as viable computing devices.

As BASIC became available on many different computers, its implementations began to differ markedly from the language originally introduced by Kemeny and Kurtz. Many of the features found in other programming languages were added to BASIC. This included *structured* programming features, which permitted BASIC programs to be written in a logical, orderly manner. Thus, the language continued to grow in an uncoordinated manner, as determined by the inclinations of commercial software developers.

In 1987 the American National Standards Institute (ANSI) issued a comprehensive standard for the BASIC language.[*] This standard includes structured programming features and is representative of contemporary programming practice. True BASIC, a PC-based version of BASIC developed by Kemeny and Kurtz, follows the 1987 ANSI standard very closely. However, some of the features provided in the ANSI standard conflict with other commercial implementations of the language. Moreover, many commercial versions of BASIC include additional features that are not defined in the ANSI standard.

In the personal computer marketplace, the competition between various computer manufacturers and different software vendors has discouraged any realistic attempts at standardization. Most versions of BASIC written for personal computers are highly enhanced with special features customized for the hardware capabilities of their host computers. For example, there are special instructions for creating graphic displays, for generating sounds, and for interacting with various peripheral devices, such as disk drives, printers, pointing devices and keyboard function keys. Also, modern PC versions of BASIC provide complete programming environments, including pull-down menus and dialog boxes, support for pointing devices (the most popular of which is the *mouse*), screen editors and interactive debuggers. Fortunately, however, the various implementations of BASIC include many grammatical similarities, so that a program written for one version of BASIC can usually be modified for another version of BASIC without undue effort.

This book describes the commonly used features of BASIC, beginning with the most elementary features and progressing to more specialized material, including features designed specifically for personal computers. Structured programming concepts are emphasized throughout the text. The examples draw heavily from Microsoft QuickBASIC and from True BASIC. The reader who has mastered this material should have little difficulty in utilizing the features found in any particular version of BASIC, or in altering programs so that they will run under different versions of the language or on different computers.

---

[*]*American National Standard for Information Systems - Programming Languages - Full BASIC*, ANSI X3.113-1987, American National Standards Institute, New York, 1987.

Structure of a BASIC Program

Each instruction in a BASIC program is written as a separate *statement*. Thus, a complete BASIC program will be composed of a sequence of statements. These statements will be executed in the order in which they appear unless a deliberate "jump" (i.e., a transfer of control) is indicated.

The following rules are suggested by the 1987 ANSI standard:

1. Every statement must begin on a separate line. A line can be as long as 132 characters.

2. Every line must begin with a *line number* — a positive integer not exceeding 50000.

3. No two lines can have the same line number.

4. Successive statements must have increasing line numbers.

5. Blank spaces may be inserted freely in order to improve the readability of the statement. (Some minor restrictions on the use of blank spaces will be discussed later.)

Example 1.6 Area of a Circle

Shown below is a simple BASIC program to calculate the area of a circle whose radius is specified. This program is written in accordance with the 1987 ANSI standard. The logic used to carry out the computation has already been discussed in Example 1.1, though the program is so elementary that its logical basis can be determined simply by inspection.

```
10 REM PROGRAM TO CALCULATE THE AREA OF A CIRCLE - VERSION 1
20 PRINT "Radius = ";                    !prompt for input data
30 INPUT radius                          !enter the input data
40 LET area = 3.14159 * radius ^ 2       !calculate the result
50 PRINT "Area ="; area                  !display the result
60 END
```

We see that the program consists of six statements, each of which appears on a separate line. Every statement has its own line number. The line numbers increase successively, by 10s, from the beginning to the end of the program. Lines 20 through 50 each contain an *in-line comment* that explains the purpose of the statement.

The first statement (10 REM...) is a program heading. The second statement (20 PRINT "Radius = ";) generates a message prompting the user for the required input data, whereas the third statement (30 INPUT radius) causes a value of the radius to be entered from the keyboard. The fourth statement (40 LET area = 3.14159 * radius ^ 2) causes the area to be evaluated. The fifth statement (50 PRINT "Area ="; area) causes the calculated value of the area to be displayed on an output device (a monitor or a printer). Finally, the last statement (60 END) identifies the end of the program.

Notice the symbols used in line 40 to represent arithmetic operations. Multiplication is indicated by an asterisk (*), and an upward-pointing arrow (^) is used to raise a quantity to a power. (This last operation is called *exponentiation*. The symbol used to indicate exponentiation is properly called a *circumflex*, though it is usually referred to as the exponentiation operator.) The remaining arithmetic operations, addition, subtraction and division, are represented in BASIC by a plus sign (+), a minus sign (−) and a slash(/), respectively.

Shown below is a typical interactive session that illustrates what happens when this program is executed.

```
Radius = ? 5
Area = 78.53975
```

The question mark is generated automatically by the INPUT statement on line 30. Following the question mark is the value of the radius (5) supplied by the user. The user's response is underlined for clarity. (We will follow this convention throughout the book.) The next line shows the corresponding area (78.53975), as determined by the program.

The use of line numbers requires some additional discussion. In early versions of BASIC, line numbers were used in order to transfer control within a program (i.e., to jump from one place to another). The 1987 ANSI standard retained the use of line numbers in order to maintain compatibility with older versions of the language. However, modern structured programming practices avoid such jumps within a program. Hence, most contemporary implementations of BASIC do not require line numbers; in fact, their use is strongly discouraged. We will therefore avoid the use of line numbers in the remaining examples within this book.

Example 1.7

The following listing shows another version of the program given in Example 1.6. This version does not contain line numbers. Also, the initial remark (i.e., the program heading) is written as an in-line comment, and the remaining in-line comments have been removed. (Though the use of in-line comments is generally encouraged, the appearance of a comment on almost every line is excessive, particularly in very elementary programs.)

```
!PROGRAM TO CALCULATE THE AREA OF A CIRCLE - VERSION 2 (no line numbers)
PRINT "Radius = ";
INPUT radius
LET area = 3.14159 * radius ^ 2
PRINT "Area ="; area
END
```

This program will generate the same interactive dialog as that shown in Example 1.6

Example 1.8

Shown below is still another program for calculating the area of a circle. In fact, this program calculates the area of several different circles. The program is designed to continue executing until the user enters a value of 0 for the radius.

```
REM PROGRAM TO CALCULATE THE AREA OF A CIRCLE - VERSION 3
PRINT "Radius = ";
INPUT radius
DO WHILE radius > 0                    'begin loop
   LET area = 3.14159 * radius ^ 2
   PRINT "Area ="; area
   PRINT
   PRINT "Radius = ";
   INPUT radius
LOOP                                   'end loop
END
```

This program contains a loop structure that will execute repeatedly, until a value of 0 is detected for the radius. During each pass through the loop, a value for area is calculated corresponding to the current value entered for radius. A new value is then entered for radius, and the process is repeated as often as the user may desire.

Notice that the statements within the loop are indented, so that the loop structure is readily identifiable. The use of indentation is not essential, though it should be done as a matter of good programming practice.

This type of loop structure is defined in the 1987 ANSI standard and is supported by most contemporary versions of BASIC. We will discuss loops in greater detail in Chap. 4.

When the program is executed an interactive session is generated, such as that shown below. The user's responses are underlined. Notice that the computation continues until the user supplies a value of 0 for the radius.

```
Radius = ? 3
Area = 28.27431

Radius = ? 5
Area = 78.53975

Radius = ? 0
```

Some Advantages of BASIC

1. BASIC is easy to learn and fun to use. Any well-organized person can learn to program in BASIC. A formal background in computer science or mathematics is not necessary.

2. BASIC is very flexible, allowing the programmer to develop new programs and to alter existing programs with relatively little effort.

3. BASIC is particularly well-suited for use in an interactive environment. This includes both dedicated applications on personal computers and timesharing applications on larger computers.

4. BASIC is universally available on both large and small computers. It has become the principal programming language for most personal computer applications.

5. The commonly used features of BASIC are relatively standard, though there are some differences between one version of BASIC and another. Most BASIC programs can be adapted to a variety of different computers without major modifications.

Review Questions

1.1   What is a mainframe computer? Where can mainframes be found? What are they generally used for?

1.2   What is a personal computer? How do personal computers differ from mainframe computers?

1.3   What is a supercomputer? A minicomputer? A workstation? How do these computers differ from one another? How do they differ from mainframes and personal computers?

1.4   Name four different types of data.

1.5   What is meant by a computer program? What, in general, happens when a computer program is executed?

1.6   What is computer memory? What kinds of information are stored in a computer's memory?

1.7   What is a bit? What is a byte? What is the difference between a byte and a word of memory?

1.8   What terms are used to describe the size of a computer's memory? What are some typical memory sizes?

1.9   Name some typical auxiliary storage devices. How do devices of this type differ from the computer's main memory?

1.10   What time units are used to express the speed with which elementary tasks are carried out by a computer?

1.11   What is the difference between batch processing and timesharing? What are the relative advantages and disadvantages of each?

1.12   What is meant by interactive computing? For what types of applications is interactive computing best suited?

1.13   What is machine language? How does machine language differ from high-level languages?

1.14   Name some commonly used high-level languages. What are the advantages of using high-level languages?

1.15   What is meant by compilation? What is meant by interpretation? How do these two processes differ?

1.16   What is a source program? An object program? Why are these concepts important?

1.17   What does the acronym "BASIC" stand for?

1.18   What are the general characteristics of the BASIC language?

1.19   Where was BASIC originally developed and by whom was it developed?

1.20   To what extent do individual versions of BASIC differ from one another? Has the language been standardized?

1.21   What is a BASIC statement? In what order must the statements appear in a BASIC program?

1.22   Summarize five rules that apply to all BASIC programs, as suggested by the 1987 ANSI standard.

1.23   In BASIC, what symbols are used to indicate addition, subtraction, multiplication and division? What symbol is used to represent exponentiation?

1.24   What is the purpose of line numbers in a BASIC program? In contemporary practice, do BASIC programs include line numbers?

1.25   Summarize the principal advantages of BASIC.

Problems

1.26   Several elementary BASIC programs are presented below. Explain the purpose of each program.

```
(a)  INPUT A, B, C, D, E
     LET SUM = A + B + C + D + E
     PRINT SUM
     END
```

```
(b)  PRINT "Length = ";
     INPUT L
     PRINT "Width = ";
     INPUT W
     LET A = L * W
     PRINT "Area ="; A
     END
```

```
(c)  PRINT "Base = ";
     INPUT B
     DO UNTIL B <= 0
        PRINT "Height = ";
        INPUT H
        PRINT "Area =";(B * H) / 2
        PRINT
        PRINT "Base = ";
        INPUT B
     LOOP
     PRINT "Bye, have a nice day!"
     END

(d)  PRINT "Enter values for a, b and c below:"
     INPUT a, b, c
     LET root = (b ^ 2 - 4 * a * c) ^ .5
     LET x1 = (-b + root) / (2 * a)
     LET x2 = (-b - root) / (2 * a)
     PRINT "x1 =";x1, "x2 =";x2
     END

(e)  PRINT "Enter values for U and V below:"
     INPUT U, V
     LET W = U + V
     LET X = U - V
     LET Y = U * V
     LET Z = U / V
     PRINT "W ="; W, "X ="; X
     PRINT "Y ="; Y, "Z ="; Z
     END

(f)  PRINT "Length = ";
     INPUT L
     DO
     PRINT "Width = ";
        INPUT W
        PRINT "Area ="; L * W
        PRINT
        PRINT "Length = ";
        INPUT L
     LOOP UNTIL L <= 0
     END

(g)  PRINT "X = ";
     INPUT X
     DO
        PRINT "Y ="; 1 + X + ( X ^ 2) / 2 + (X ^ 3) / 6
        PRINT
        PRINT "X = ";
        INPUT X
     LOOP WHILE X > 0
     END
```

1.27　Modify the program shown in Example 1.8 (AREA OF A CIRCLE - VERSION 3) in the following ways.

　　(*a*)　When the program first begins execution, generate the message

```
AREAS OF CIRCLES - To STOP, Enter 0 for the Radius
```

　　(*b*)　At the end of the interactive session, generate the message

```
GOODBYE, Have a Nice Day!
```

　　Hint: add a PRINT statement to generate each message.

1.28　Write an elementary BASIC problem for each of the situations described below.

　　(*a*)　Calculate the radius of a circle whose area is known [see Example 1.5].

　　(*b*)　Calculate the product of five given numbers [see Problem 1.26(*a*)].

　　(*c*)　Calculate the length of a rectangle whose area and width are known [see Problem 1.26(*b*)].

　　(*d*)　Calculate the circumference of a circle whose radius is known [see Examples 1.5 and 1.7].

　　(*e*)　Calculate the hypotenuse of a right triangle whose base and height are given [see Problem 1.26(*c*)].

　　(*f*)　Evaluate the formula

$$w = (u - v) / (u + v)$$

　　　　where *u* and *v* are given [see Problem 1.26(*e*)].

　　(*g*)　Evaluate the formula

$$y = 100(1 + x + 2x^2 + 3x^3)$$

　　　　where *x* is specified [see Problem 1.26(*g*)].

1.29　Shown below is a BASIC program to calculate the area and perimeter of a rectangle and the length of the diagonal. Some of the statements are written incorrectly. Identify all errors.

```
INPUT L, W
LET A = L * W              LET P = 2 (L + W)
D = (L ^ 2 = W ^ 2) ^.5
PRINT A, P, X
```

Chapter 2

Getting Started with BASIC

In this chapter we will consider several fundamental features of BASIC, such as numbers, variables and expressions. We will then consider six commonly used BASIC statements, which allow us to assign data, to read and display data, to add remarks to a program, to stop the program execution and to designate the (physical) end of a program. We will also discuss the use of library functions, which simplify various mathematical and string manipulation operations. After completing this chapter, you will be able to write simple BASIC programs of your own for a variety of problem situations.

2.1 NUMERIC CONSTANTS

Numeric quantities are referred to in BASIC as *numeric constants*. Numeric constants can be expressed three different ways: as *integer quantities* (whole numbers without a decimal point), as *fixed-point quantities* (numbers that contain a decimal point) or as *floating-point quantities* (numbers that include an exponent). The following rules apply to numeric constants:

1. Commas cannot appear anywhere in a numeric constant.

2. A numeric constant can be preceded by a + or a − sign. The constant is understood to be positive if a sign does not appear.

3. A numeric constant can be written with an exponent (i.e., as a floating-point number) if desired. Exponential notation is similar to scientific notation, except that the base 10 is replaced by the letter E. Thus, the quantity 1.2×10^{-3} could be written in BASIC as $1.2E-3$. The exponent itself can be either positive or negative, but it cannot contain a decimal point.

4. Most versions of BASIC allow a numeric constant to have at least seven significant figures.

5. Typically, the magnitude of a numeric constant can be as large as 10^{38} and as small as 10^{-38}. These limiting values vary, however, from one version of BASIC to another. A value of zero is also permissible.

Example 2.1

Several BASIC numeric constants are shown below. Note that each quantity (each row) can be written in several different ways.

0	+0	-0	
1	+1	0.1E+1	10E-1
-5280	-5.28E+3	-.528E4	-52.8E2
+1492	1492	1.492E+3	+14.92E2
-.0000613	-6.13E-5	-613E-7	-0.613E-4
3000000	3E6	3E+6	0.3E7

2.2 STRING CONSTANTS

A *string constant* is a sequence of characters (i.e., letters, numbers and certain special characters, such as +, -, /, *, =, $, ., etc.), enclosed in quotation marks. Blank spaces can be included within a string. A quotation mark can also be placed within a string, but it must be written as *two adjacent* quotation marks (see the last line in the example below).

The maximum number of characters that can be included in a string constant will vary from one version of BASIC to another. Most versions of BASIC permit at least 255 characters (excluding the quotation marks). Some allow as many as 32,767 characters, which, for all practical purposes, can be considered infinite.

String constants are used to represent nonnumeric information, such as names, addresses, etc. They are also used to label numeric output and to display text messages. We will see many applications of string constants throughout this book.

Example 2.2

Several string constants are shown below.

```
"SANTA CLAUS"                      "Please type a value for C:"
"$19.95"                           "Welcome to the 21st Century"
"X1 = "                            "3730425"
"The answer is "                   "Do you wish to try again?"
"The professor said, ""Please don't snore in class"" "
```

2.3 VARIABLES

A *variable* is a name that represents a numeric quantity or a string. A variable name must begin with a letter. Additional characters may be letters or digits. Some versions of BASIC also permit certain other characters, such as the underscore (_) or period (.) to be included in a variable name. In addition, every *string variable* must *end* with a dollar sign ($).

Example 2.3

Several numeric variables are shown below.

```
A          AREA          X          xmax          C3          Radius
```

Here are several string variables. Notice the dollar sign at the end of each variable name.

```
A$          NAME$          X$          C3$          address$
```

Most versions of BASIC permit a variable name to contain as many as 31 characters.* Some implementations permit variable names to be even longer, though this is rarely necessary in practice. In fact, the use of lengthy variable names is generally discouraged.

Every version of BASIC includes certain *reserved words* (also called *keywords*) that have predefined meanings. These reserved words *cannot* be used as variable names. Some commonly used reserved words

---

*Early versions of BASIC restricted the names of numeric variables to a single letter or a single letter followed by an inter (e.g., X, X2). String variable names were restricted to a single letter followed by a dollar sign, or a single letter followed by an integer followed by a dollar sign (e.g., A$, A2$).

in shown in Table 2.1. Some of these reserved words represent *statements*, others represent *library functions*. Consult the programmer's reference manual for your particular version of BASIC to determine the complete list of reserved words.

TABLE 2.1   COMMON RESERVED WORDS

ABS	ELSE	NEXT	STOP
ASC	END	PRINT	SUB
ATN	EXP	RANDOMIZE	TAB
CALL	FOR	READ	TAN
CASE	IF	REM	THEN
CHR$	INPUT	RESTORE	TO
COS	INT	RND	UCASE$
DATA	LCASE$	SELECT	UNTIL
DEF	LET	SGN	USING
DIM	LOG	SIN	WHILE
DO	LOOP	SQR	WRITE

2.4 OPERATORS AND EXPRESSIONS

In BASIC special symbols, called *arithmetic operators*, are used to indicate arithmetic operations such as addition, subtraction, multiplication, division and exponentiation. These operators are used to connect numeric constants and numeric variables, thus forming *numeric expressions*.

The standard arithmetic operators are

Addition: +   (plus sign)

Subtraction: −   (minus sign)

Multiplication: *   (asterisk)

Division: /   (slash)

Exponentiation: ^   (caret, or upward-pointing arrow)

When arithmetic operators appear within an arithmetic expression, the indicated operations are carried out on the individual terms within the expression, resulting in a single numeric value. Thus, *a numeric expression represents a specific numeric quantity.*

Example 2.4

Several numeric expressions are presented below.

```
J + 1                          count + 1
A + B - C                      first + second - third
3.14159 * R ^ 2                3.14159 * radius ^ 2
4 * pi * r ^ 3 / 3             4 * PI * RADIUS ^ 3 / 3
b ^ 2 - (4 * a * c)            (2 * x - 3 * y) / (u + v)
```

Each expression represents a numeric quantity. Thus, if the variables A, B and C represent the quantities 2, 5 and 3, respectively, the expression A + B - C will represent the quantity 4.

Many versions of BASIC include two additional arithmetic operators: integer division (\) and integer remainder (MOD). In integer division, each of the two given numbers is first *rounded* to an integer; the division is then carried out on the rounded values and the resulting quotient is truncated to an integer. The integer remainder operation provides the remainder resulting from an integer division.

Example 2.5

The results of several ordinary division, integer division and integer remainder operations are shown below.

```
13 / 5 = 2.6              13 \ 5 = 2              13 MOD 5 = 3
8.6 / 2.7 = 3.185185      8.6 \ 2.7 = 3          8.6 MOD 2.7 = 0
8.3 / 2.7 = 3.074074      8.3 \ 2.7 = 2          8.3 MOD 2.7 = 2
8.3 / 2.2 = 3.772727      8.3 \ 2.2 = 4          8.3 MOD 2.2 = 0
```

A numeric expression can be composed of a single numeric constant or a single numeric variable as well as some combination of constants, variables and operators. In any event, *every numeric variable that appears in a numeric expression must be assigned a specific numeric value before it can appear in the expression.* Otherwise, the expression could not be evaluated to yield a specific numeric result.

2.5 HIERARCHY OF OPERATIONS

Questions in meaning may arise when several operators appear in an expression. For example, does the expression 2 * X - 3 * Y correspond to the algebraic term $(2x) - (3y)$ or to $2(x - 3y)$? Similarly, does A / B * C correspond to $a/(bc)$ or to $(a/b)c$? These questions are answered by the hierarchy of operations and the order of execution within each hierarchical group.

The hierarchy of operations is

1. *Exponentiation.* All exponentiation operations are performed first.

2. *Multiplication and division.* These operations are carried out after all exponentiation operations have been performed. Multiplication does not necessarily precede division.

3. *Integer division.* In those versions of BASIC that include this operation, integer division operations are carried out after all multiplication and (ordinary) division operations.

4. *Integer remainder.* In those versions of BASIC that include integer division, integer remainder operations are carried out after all integer divisions operations.

5. *Addition and subtraction.* These operations are the last to be carried out. Addition does not necessarily precede subtraction.

Within a given hierarchical group, the operations are carried out from left to right.

Example 2.6

The numeric expression

```
A / B * C
```

is equivalent to the mathematical expression $(a / b) c$, since the operations are carried out from left to right.

Similarly, the expression

```
B ^ 2 - 4 * A * C
```

is equivalent to the mathematical expression $b^2 - (4 a c)$. In this case the quantity B ^ 2 is formed initially, followed by the product 4 * A * C [first 4 * A, then (4 * A) * C]. The subtraction is performed last, resulting in the quantity (B ^ 2) − (4 * A * C).

A more extensive listing of the BASIC operators and their respective hierarchical ordering is given in Chap. 4 (see Sec. 4.2).

2.6 USE OF PARENTHESES

We may wish to alter the normal hierarchy of operations in a numeric expression. This is easily accomplished by inserting pairs of parentheses at the proper places within the expression. The operations within the innermost pair of parentheses will then be performed first, followed by the operations within the second innermost pair, and so on. Within a given pair of parentheses, the natural hierarchy of operations will apply unless specifically altered by other pairs of parentheses embedded inside the given pair.

Remember always to use *pairs* of parentheses. A careless imbalance of right and left parentheses is a common error among beginning programmers.

Example 2.7

Suppose we want to evaluate the algebraic term

$$[2(a + b)^2 + (3c)^2]^{m/(n+1)}$$

A BASIC expression corresponding to this algebraic term is

```
(2 * (A + B) ^ 2 + (3 * C) ^ 2) ^ (M / (N + 1))
```

If there is some uncertainty in the order in which the operations are carried out, we can introduce additional pairs of parentheses, giving

```
((2 * ((A + B) ^ 2)) + ((3 * C) ^ 2)) ^ (M / (N + 1))
```

Both expressions are correct. The first expression may be preferable, however, since it is less cluttered with parentheses and therefore easier to read.

2.7 SPECIAL RULES CONCERNING NUMERIC EXPRESSIONS

Special problems can arise if an expression is not correctly written. Such problems can be avoided by applying the following rules.

1. Preceding a variable by a minus sign is equivalent to multiplication by −1.

Example 2.8

The numeric expression

        -X ^ N

is equivalent to $-(X ^ N)$ or $-1 * (X ^ N)$, since exponentiation has precedence over multiplication. Hence, if X and N are assigned values of 3 and 2, respectively, then -X ^ N will yield a value of -9.

2. Except for the condition just described, operations cannot be implied.

Example 2.9

The algebraic expression $2(x_1 + 3x_2)$ must be written in BASIC as

        2 * (X1 + 3 * X2)

Note that the multiplication operators must be shown explicitly. Thus, the expressions 2 (X1 + 3 * X2) and 2 * (X1 + 3 X2) are incorrect.

3. In an expression involving exponentiation, a negative quantity can be raised to a power only if the exponent is an integer. (Do not confuse the exponent in a *numeric expression* with the exponent that is a part of a *floating-point constant*.)

   To understand this restriction, we must see how exponentiation is carried out. If the exponent is an *integer* quantity, the quantity to be exponentiated is multiplied by itself an appropriate number of times.

   On the other hand, suppose the exponent is *not* an integer quantity. The procedure with a noninteger exponent is to compute the *logarithm* of the quantity being exponentiated, multiply this logarithm by the exponent, and then compute the antilog. Since the logarithm of a negative number is not defined, we see that the operation is invalid if the quantity being exponentiated is negative.

Example 2.10

Consider the expression

        (C1 + C2) ^ 3

The quantity represented by (C1 + C2) is multiplied by itself twice, thus forming the cubic expression. It does not matter whether the quantity (C1 + C2) is positive or negative.

   On the other hand, the expression

        (B ^ 2 — 4 * A * C) ^ .5

will be valid only if (B ^ 2 — 4 * A * C) represents a positive quantity.

   Finally, consider what happens when either A or N in the expression A^N is zero. If N has a value of zero, then A^N will be assigned a value of 1, regardless of the value of A. If A has a value of zero and N is nonzero, however, A^N will be evaluated as zero.

We will say more about numeric expressions in Chap. 7. In particular, we will see what happens when a numeric expression involves mixed data types (see Sec. 7.2).

2.8 STRING EXPRESSIONS

Numeric operations cannot be performed on string constants or string variables. However, most versions of BASIC allow strings and string variables to be *concatenated* (i.e., combined, one behind the other). The 1987 ANSI standard defines the ampersand (&) as a string concatenation operator, though some versions of BASIC use the plus sign for this purpose.

Example 2.11

Suppose the string variables X$ and Y$ have been assigned the following values:

```
X$ = "TEN"
Y$ = "THOUSAND"
```

Then the string expression

```
X$ & " " & Y$ & " DOLLARS"
```

will cause the three individual strings to be concatenated, resulting in the single string

```
TEN THOUSAND DOLLARS
```

In Microsoft BASIC, the string expression would be written as

```
X$ + " " + Y$ + " DOLLARS"
```

rather than as shown above.

2.9 ASSIGNING VALUES: THE LET STATEMENT

The LET statement is used to assign a numeric or string value to a variable. We *define* a particular variable in a program by establishing its value in this manner.

A LET statement is composed of the keyword LET, followed by an assignment term that resembles a mathematical equation. The assignment term must consist of a variable, an equal sign and an expression.

Example 2.12

Shown below are several unrelated LET statements.

```
LET X = 12.5
LET CONST = X
LET AREA = 3.141593 * RADIUS ^ 2
LET N$ = "Name: "
LET TEMP$ = N$
LET STR$ = FIRST$ + LAST$
```

In each statement, the value of the expression on the right of the equal sign is assigned to the variable on the left.

The variable on the left of the equal sign and the term on the right must always be of the same type (either numeric or string). Thus, a numeric value cannot be assigned to a string variable and vice versa.

It is important to understand the difference between the assignment term that appears in the LET statement and an algebraic equation. Many LET statements look like algebraic equations. On the other hand, there are certain kinds of assignments that would make no sense if viewed as algebraic equations.

Example 2.13

Consider the following LET statement.

```
LET J = J + 1
```

The assignment term $J = J + 1$ obviously does not correspond to an algebraic equation, since the equation $j=j+1$ makes no sense. What we are doing here is to increase the value of the numeric variable J by one unit. Thus, the assignment term is entirely logical if we interpret it as follows: add 1 to the value represented by the variable J and assign this new value to J. The new value of J will replace the old value. This operation is known as *incrementing*.

Some versions of BASIC allow greater flexibility in writing LET statements than others. For example, in Microsoft BASIC, it is possible to assign the same value to two or more variables in a single LET statement. Moreover, the keyword LET can be omitted in many versions of BASIC. Microsoft BASIC and True BASIC both support this feature.

Example 2.14

The following assignment statements would be permitted in *some* versions of BASIC.

```
LET A = B = C = 5.089
area = length * width
X1 = X2 = (a + b) / (c + d)
LET A$ = K$ = "TERMINATE"
```

Notice that the first, third and fourth statements involve multiple assignments. Also, the keyword LET has been omitted from the second and third statements.

2.10 READING INPUT: THE INPUT STATEMENT

The INPUT statement is used to enter numeric or string data into the computer during program execution. The statement consists of the keyword INPUT followed by a list of variables. Both numeric and string variables can be included in the list. The variables must be separated by commas.

Example 2.15

Several typical input statements are shown below:

```
INPUT A, B, C
INPUT N$, M$, X, FACTOR
INPUT P(I), Q(I), T$(I)
```

The first statement will cause three numeric values to be entered into the computer and assigned to the variables A, B and C, respectively. The second statement will cause two strings, followed by two numeric values, to be entered into the computer and assigned to N$, M$, X and FACTOR. The third statement will cause two numeric values and a string to be entered into the computer and assigned to P(I), Q(I) and T$(I).

The variables appearing in the last statement are called *subscripted variables*. We will discuss subscripted variables in Chap. 5.

When an INPUT statement is encountered during program execution, a question mark (?) appears on the output device indicating a request for data. Normally the question mark appears at the beginning of a new line. Further execution of the program will then be suspended until the requested data have been supplied.

Once the question mark appears, the person using the program must supply the requested information by entering the appropriate data into the computer. The data will then be transmitted to the computer's memory and program execution will resume. Thus, the INPUT statement is well suited for conversational-mode programming.

The following rules must be observed when entering the required input data:

1. The data items must correspond in number and in type to the variables listed in the INPUT statement (i.e., numbers must be supplied for numeric variables, strings for string variables). Extra data items will be ignored.

2. The data items must be separated by commas.

3. The data items can consist only of numbers and strings. Expressions are not permitted.

4. If a string contains commas or begins with a blank space, it *must* be enclosed in quotation marks. Other strings may be enclosed in quotation marks if desired.

Example 2.16

Suppose the following statement is encountered during the execution of a BASIC program:

```
INPUT hours, rate, date$
```

This statement will cause a question mark to be printed at the beginning of a new line on the output device. Further program execution will then be suspended until the user enters the requested values for hours, rate and date$.

Suppose the appropriate input values are 20, 5.50, and January 20, 1993. The user would then enter the required input data, in response to the question mark, as shown below.

```
? 20,5.5,"January 20, 1993"
```

The user's entries are underlined.

The INPUT statement is widely used in BASIC. It is especially useful in programs that are interactive in nature. We will see some variations in the use of the INPUT statement in Chap. 7 (see Sec. 7.6).

2.11 PRINTING OUTPUT: THE PRINT STATEMENT

The PRINT statement is used to transmit numeric values or strings from the computer's memory to the output device, thus causing the data to be displayed on the output device. The statement consists of the keyword PRINT followed by a list of output items. The output items can be numeric constants, expressions or strings. Successive items must be separated by either commas or semicolons.

Example 2.17

Several typical PRINT statements are shown below.

```
PRINT A, B, C
PRINT "X ="; X, "Y ="; Y
PRINT "Name: "; N$, "Address: "; A$
PRINT
PRINT Customer$, 5 * XMAX ^ 2 / 2
PRINT I, U(I) + V(I), P$(I) + Q$(I)
```

The first statement will cause the values of A, B and C to be displayed. In the second statement, the values of X and Y are displayed with accompanying labels (a label will precede each numeric value). Similarly, the third statement will cause the strings represented by the variables N$ and A$ to be displayed with accompanying labels.

The fourth statement is an empty PRINT statement, resulting in a blank line on the output device. Finally, the last two statements illustrate the use of expressions within a PRINT statement.

The variables U(I), V(I), P$(I) and Q$(I) appearing in the last statement are called *subscripted variables*. We will discuss subscripted variables in Chap. 5.

The following rules must be observed when writing a PRINT statement.

Line Spacing

1. Each PRINT statement begins a new line of output (an exception is discussed in rules 5 and 6 below). However, a single PRINT statement can generate several lines of output if the list of data items is lengthy.

Example 2.18

The PRINT statement

```
PRINT C1, C2, C3, C4, C5, C6, C7, C8
```

will cause eight different numeric values to be displayed on the output device, with several blank spaces between successive values. However, each line has enough room for only five values. Therefore, the values of C1 through C5 will be displayed on the first line, and the values of C6 through C8 will be displayed on the second line.

Suppose, for example, that C1 through C8 represent the following values:

C1 = 3	C2 = −12	C3 = 6.5	C4 = 5000
C5 = 0	C6 = 0.0047	C7 = −8	C8 = 7.2E−15

The output will typically appear as follows:

```
3              -12         6.5          5000         0
  .0047        -8          7.2E-15
```

The exact appearance may vary somewhat from one version of BASIC to another.

2. If a PRINT statement does not contain any data items, a blank line will appear. This is a useful way to control the appearance of the output data.

Example 2.19

The PRINT statements

```
PRINT C1, C2, C3, C4
PRINT
PRINT C5, C6, C7, C8
```

will cause the values of C1 through C4 to be printed on one line and C5 through C8 on another line, with a blank line between them.

If C1 through C8 have the same values as in Example 2.18, then the output resulting from the above three PRINT statements will typically appear as follows:

```
3              -12         6.5          5000

0              .0047       -8           7.2E-15
```

Significant Figures

3. The appearance of numeric output (i.e., number of significant figures, inclusion of an exponent, etc.) will vary somewhat from one version of BASIC to another. Typically, an integer or a fixed-point quantity containing seven or fewer digits will be displayed as such. If the quantity exceeds seven digits, it will be displayed as a floating-point constant (with an exponent).

Example 2.20

Suppose a BASIC program contains the variables A, B, C, D, E and F, which have been assigned the following values:

```
A = 1234567          D = 0.000012345
B = 123456789        E = −1234.5
C = −0.001234        F = 1234567.89
```

The statements

```
PRINT A, B, C
PRINT D, E, F
```

would then generate the following two lines of output:

```
1234567         1.234568E+08 -0.001234
1.2345E+05      -1234.5          1.234568E+06
```

Strings

4.   String constants must be enclosed in quotation marks. (See Example 2.21 below.)

Spacing of Output Items Within a Line

5.   If the data items in the output list are separated by commas, each line of output will be divided into several (typically, five) zones of equal length. One output value will be printed in each zone.

Example 2.21

A BASIC program contains the statement

```
PRINT "Name", N$, X, (C1 + C2) / 2
```

If the variables are assigned the values

```
N$ = Susan                C1 = 7
X  = 39                   C2 = 11
```

then the above PRINT statement will generate the following line of output:

```
Name            Susan           39              9
```

Other illustrations of the use of commas as separators within a PRINT statement are shown in Examples 2.18, 2.19 and 2.20.

If a comma follows the *last* item in the data list, then the next output quantity (i.e., the first output quantity in a subsequent PRINT statement) will be displayed on the same line, providing sufficient space is available. (Note that this produces an exception to rule 1 discussed earlier.)

Example 2.22

A BASIC program contains the following PRINT statements

```
PRINT A, B, C,
PRINT D, E, F
```

(Notice the comma after the variable C.) When the program is executed, the values of A, B, C, D and E will be displayed on one line, followed by the value of F on the next line.

If A, B, C, D, E and F have been assigned the same numerical values as in Example 2.20, the output will appear as follows:

```
1234567        1.234568E+08 -0.001234      1.2345E+05      -1234.5
1.234568E+06
```

(Compare with the results in Example 2.20.)

Several consecutive commas can appear if desired. The effect of each comma is to move to the start of the next print zone. This allows the individual data items to be spaced widely apart when they are displayed.

Example 2.23

A BASIC program contains the statements

```
PRINT A, B, C, D, E
PRINT F,,,,G
```

Suppose the variables have been assigned the following values:

```
A = 1           C = 3           E = 5           G = 7
B = 2           D = 4           F = 6
```

When the program is executed, the output will then appear as follows:

```
1               2               3               4               5
6                                                               7
```

6. If semicolons rather than commas are used to separate numeric data items in an output list, then the output values will be spaced more closely together. The particular spacing will depend on the number of digits or characters in each output item. By using semicolons in this manner it is possible to display more than five output quantities on each line.

Example 2.24

A BASIC program contains the statement

```
PRINT A1; A2; A3; A4; A5; A6; A7; A8
```

Suppose the variables have been assigned the following values:

```
A1 = 11                      A5 = 15
A2 = 12                      A6 = 16
A3 = 13                      A7 = 17
A4 = 14                      A8 = 18
```

Then the above PRINT statement will generate the following line of output:

```
11   12   13   14   15   16   17   18
```

If a semicolon follows a string constant or a string variable in an output list, then the string will be printed without any trailing spaces and the next output item will be printed immediately beyond the string.

Example 2.25

A BASIC program contains the following statement:

```
PRINT "X ="; X, "Y =";Y
```

If the variables are assigned the values X = 12 and Y = −5, this statement will generate the following output :

```
X = 12            Y =-5
```

In many BASIC programs, an INPUT statement is preceded by a PRINT statement that contains a string constant. The purpose of the PRINT statement is to display a message prompting the user for the required input data. If the string constant is followed by a semicolon, then the question mark generated by the INPUT statement will appear at the end of the message rather than the beginning of the next line.

Example 2.26

A BASIC program has been written to compute the area and circumference of a circle. The first step in executing the program is to enter a value for the radius. Hence, the program will contain the statements

```
PRINT "Radius = ";
INPUT radius
```

These two statements will cause the following prompt to be displayed on the output device:

```
Radius = ?
```

The user then enters a value for the radius, as illustrated in Example 1.5.

Note that the semicolon at the end of the PRINT statement will cause the next output item (in this case, the question mark) to appear on the same line as the last output item.

In Chap. 7 we will see how displayed data can be *formatted*, thus providing greater control over the appearance of the output (see Sec. 7.7).

2.12 ADDING PROGRAM COMMENTS: THE REM STATEMENT

The REM (REMARK) statement is used to add comments (remarks) to a BASIC program. This statement consists of the keyword REM, followed by a textual message. REM statements can be inserted anywhere in a BASIC program. They have no effect on the program execution.

Example 2.27

Here is a typical REM statement.

```
REM PROGRAM TO CALCULATE THE ROOTS OF A QUADRATIC EQUATION
```

This statement might be a heading for a program that calculates the roots of a quadratic equation. The comment will appear only in the program listing; it will *not* be displayed as a part of the output when the program is executed.

REM statements are listed with all other statements in a BASIC program, in the correct sequential order. Thus they offer the programmer a convenient means to *document* a program (i.e., to provide a program heading, to identify important variables, and to distinguish between major logical segments of a program). We will see numerous illustrations of the use of REM statements in subsequent examples in this book.

Sometimes it is desirable to add an *in-line* comment at the end of an executable statement, rather than as a separate statement. Most versions of BASIC allow this, provided the comment is preceded by some special character. Some versions of BASIC use an exclamation mark (!) for this purpose, whereas other versions of the language use an apostrophe ('). The exclamation mark is recommended by the 1987 ANSI standard.

Example 2.28

A BASIC program includes the following statements:

```
!PROGRAM TO CALCULATE THE ROOTS OF A QUADRATIC EQUATION
. . . . .
LET X1 = (-b + root) / (2 * a)    !calculate the first root
LET X2 = (-b - root) / (2 * a)    !calculate the second root
```

Each statement includes a comment that begins with an exclamation mark. Notice that the entire first statement is a comment, though it does *not* make use of the keyword REM. Thus, we see another way to add full-line comments to a program.

Some versions of BASIC require that each comment begin with an apostrophe rather than an exclamation mark. For example, in Microsoft BASIC, the above statements would be written as

```
'PROGRAM TO CALCULATE THE ROOTS OF A QUADRATIC EQUATION
. . . . .
LET X1 = (-b + root) / (2 * a)    'calculate the first root
LET X2 = (-b - root) / (2 * a)    'calculate the second root
```

2.13 THE STOP AND END STATEMENTS

The STOP statement is used to terminate the execution at any point in the program. The statement consists simply of the keyword STOP. The END statement, on the other hand, indicates the *physical* end of a BASIC program. This statement consists of the keyword END.

It is important to understand the distinction between the STOP and END statements. The STOP statement can appear *anywhere* in a BASIC program except at the very end. Multiple STOP statements may appear in the same program (though modern programming practice tends to avoid the use of the STOP statement, as shown later in this book). The END statement, however, *cannot* appear anywhere *except* at the end of the program; hence, it cannot appear more than once in any program.

The 1987 ANSI standard requires that every BASIC program end with an END statement, though some versions of BASIC ignore this requirement. If END does appear, it must be placed at the end of the program and it must have the highest line number (if line numbers appear in the program).

2.14 LIBRARY FUNCTIONS

BASIC contains a set of *library functions* (also called *built-in functions, standard functions* or *elementary functions*) that provide a quick and easy way to carry out many mathematical operations, to manipulate strings, and to perform certain logical operations. These library functions are prewritten routines that are included as an integral part of the language. They may be used in place of variables within an expression or a statement.

Table 2.2 presents several commonly used library functions. These and many others are available in most versions of BASIC.

Table 2.2 Commonly Used Library Functions

Function	Application	Description
ABS	LET Y = ABS(X)	Return the absolute value of x; $y = |x|$.
CHR$	LET Y$ = CHR$(N)	Return the character whose numerically encoded value is n. For example, in the ASCII character set, CHR$(65) = "A".
COS	LET Y = COS(X)	Return the cosine of x (x must be in radians).
EXP	LET Y = EXP(X)	Return the value of e to the x power; $y = e^x$.
INT	LET Y = INT(X)	Return the largest integer that algebraically does not exceed x. For example, INT(-1.9) = -2.
LCASE$	LET Y$ = LCASE$(X$)	Return the lowercase equivalent of X$.
LEN	LET Y = LEN(X$)	Return the length (number of characters) of X$.
LOG	LET Y = LOG(X)	Return the natural logarithm of x; $y = \log_e(x), x > 0$.
RND	LET Y = RND	Return a random number, uniformly distributed within the interval $0 \le y < 1$.
SIN	LET Y = SIN(X)	Return the sine of x (x must be in radians).
SGN	LET Y = SGN(X)	Determine the sign of x; ($y = +1$ if x is positive, $y = 0$ if $x = 0$, and $y = -1$ if x is negative).
SQR	LET Y = SQR(X)	Return the square root of x; $y = \sqrt{x}, x > 0$.
STR$	LET Y$ = STR$(X)	Return a string whose characters comprise the value of x. For example, STR$(-2.50) = "-2.50".
TAB	PRINT TAB(N); X	Causes the value of x to be displayed at column number n. (Left column is considered column 1.)
TAN	LET Y = TAN(X)	Return the tangent of x (x must be in radians).
UCASE$	LET Y$ = UCASE(X$)	Return the uppercase equivalent of X$.
VAL	LET Y = VAL(X$)	Return a numeric value corresponding to the string X$, written as a number. For example, VAL("-2.50") = -2.5.

Note: The symbol e represents the base of the natural (Naperian) system of logarithms. It is an irrational number whose approximate value is 2.718282.

A library function is accessed simply by stating its name, followed by whatever information must be supplied to the function, enclosed in parentheses. A numeric quantity or string that is passed to a function in this manner is called an *argument*. Once the library function has been accessed, the desired operation will be carried out automatically. The function will then return the desired value.

Example 2.29

Suppose we wanted to calculate the square root of the value represented by the expression `area / 3.14159`, using the library function SQR. To do so, we could write

```
LET radius = SQR(area / 3.141593)
```

Notice that SQR's argument is the numeric expression (`area / 3.141593`).
Of course, we could have written

```
LET radius = (area / 3.141593) ^ 0.5
```

The library function is not required in this situation — it is merely used for convenience. In many situations, however (such as calculating the log of a number, or calculating the length of a string), the use of library functions may be the only straightforward way to carry out the calculation.

Most of the functions listed in Table 2.2 have a straightforward interpretation. A few, however, require some additional explanation. The next several examples should clarify any confusion.

Example 2.30

The INT function can be confusing, particularly with negative arguments. The values resulting from several typical function calls are shown below.

```
INT(2.3) = 2                    INT(-2.3) = -3
INT(2.7) = 2                    INT(-2.7) = -3
```

Remember that INT produces a value whose magnitude is equal to or *smaller* than its argument if the argument is *positive*, and equal to or *larger* than its argument if the argument is *negative*.

Some functions, such as LOG and SQR, require positive arguments. If any such function is supplied a negative argument, an error message will be generated when an attempt is made to evaluate the function.

Example 2.31

A BASIC program contains the statements

```
LET X = -2.7
. . . . .
PRINT SQR(X)        (Notice the negative value assigned to X.)
```

When the program is executed, the following error message will be displayed :

```
SQR of negative number
```

The execution will then cease.
Similarly, the statement

```
PRINT LOG(X)
```

will produce the following error message when the program is executed:

```
LOG of number <= 0
```

All string functions accept one or more strings as arguments. However, some string functions return a string, whereas others return a numeric value.

Example 2.32

A simple BASIC program is presented below.

```
LET city$ = "New York, NY"
PRINT city$
PRINT LEN(city$)
PRINT LCASE$(city$)
PRINT UCASE$(city$)
```

Execution of this program results in the following output:

```
New York, NY
 12
new york, ny
NEW YORK, NY
```

The TAB function permits the programmer to specify the exact positioning of each output item listed in a PRINT statement. This allows more control over the spacing of output data than the methods described in Sec. 2.11. Each time the TAB function appears in an output list, the cursor or print head will move to the right until the specified column has been reached. (The leftmost column is considered column 1). If the cursor is already positioned beyond (i.e., to the right of) the specified column, the TAB function will be ignored.

Example 2.33

Suppose we want to display the values of A, B and C on a single line, with the first value beginning in column 9, the second in column 29 and the third in column 47. This can be accomplished by writing

```
PRINT TAB(9); A; TAB(29); B; TAB(47); C
```

(Note that positive values will be displayed one additional column to the right, because a blank space representing the sign will appear in the designated TAB column. Thus, if A has a value of 5, the 5 will appear in column 10.)

Now consider the statement

```
PRINT "Name and Address: "; TAB(12); customer$
```

In this example the TAB function will be ignored, since the string "Name and Address: " extends beyond column 12. (To be precise, the string occupies the first 18 columns, therefore extending to column 19).

On the other hand, if the statement had been written

```
PRINT "Name and Address: "; TAB(24); customer$
```

then the string represented by `customer$` would begin in column 24, as indicated by the TAB function.

The use of library functions is not confined to LET or PRINT statements — a library function may appear wherever a constant or a variable might ordinarily be present. Moreover, the arguments need not be constants or simple variables. Subscripted variables and expressions (which may include references to other functions) can be used as valid function arguments. Truncation will be performed automatically, if necessary, for those functions that require integer-valued arguments (as, for example, the TAB function).

We will encounter additional library functions elsewhere in this book, in conjunction with features to be discussed in later chapters.

Review Questions

2.1   Name three different types of numeric constants.

2.2   Summarize the rules for writing numeric constants.

2.3   Present a detailed comparison between a number written in scientific notation and a number written in BASIC as a floating-point constant.

2.4   What is a string constant? What is the purpose of a string constant?

2.5   With your version of BASIC, what is the maximum permissible length of a string constant?

2.6   Summarize the rules for writing numeric and string variables.

2.7   With your version of BASIC, what is the maximum permissible length of a variable name?

2.8   What are reserved words (keywords)? Can a reserved word be used as a variable name?

2.9   What arithmetic operators are available in BASIC? What is their natural hierarchy? In what order are operations carried out within a hierarchical group?

2.10 What is a numeric expression? What does a numeric expression represent?

2.11 How can the natural hierarchy of operations be altered within a numeric expression?

2.12 Describe a particular problem that can arise in exponentiation operations. Give a reason for the problem and describe how the problem can be avoided.

2.13 What is a string expression? How do string expressions differ from numeric expressions?

2.14 What operations can be carried out on strings?

2.15 What is the purpose of the LET statement?

2.16 Summarize the rules for writing a LET statement.

2.17 Discuss the similarities and differences between a LET statement and an algebraic equation.

2.18 In what ways are the rules for writing a LET statement relaxed in some versions of BASIC?

2.19   What is the purpose of the INPUT statement?

2.20   What happens when an INPUT statement is encountered during the execution of a BASIC program?

2.21   Summarize the rules for writing an INPUT statement.

2.22   What is the purpose of the PRINT statement?

2.23   Summarize the rules that apply to each of the following aspects of the PRINT statement:
   (*a*)   The generation and spacing of lines of output.
   (*b*)   The appearance of numeric output and the maximum number of significant figures.
   (*c*)   The treatment of strings.
   (*d*)   The spacing of numeric quantities and strings within a line of output.

2.24   In what way is a PRINT statement used in conjunction with an INPUT statement to read data into the computer?

2.25   What is the purpose of the REM statement? What rules govern its use?

2.26   How can comments be added to a BASIC program without using the REM statement? Describe how this is accomplished for your particular version of BASIC.

2.27   What is the purpose of the END statement? What are the rules associated with its use?

2.28   What are library functions? What useful purpose do they serve?

2.29   What other names are sometimes used for library functions?

2.30   Name several of the more common library functions. State the purpose of each.

2.31   What is an argument? Do all library functions require arguments?

2.32   What happens if a negative value is supplied to a library function that requires a positive argument?

2.33   How is a library function used in a BASIC program?

2.34   What is the purpose of the INT function? What does the INT function return if it receives a negative argument?

2.35   What is the purpose of the LEN, LCASE$, UCASE$ and POS functions? What type of arguments do these functions require?

2.36   What is the purpose of the TAB function? In which statement is it used?

2.37   Can a library function accept an expression as an argument? Can it accept a reference to another library function as an argument?

Problems

2.38   Answer the following questions for your particular version of BASIC.

(a) How many significant figures can be included in a numeric constant?

(b) What is the largest permissible floating-point constant? What is the smallest, disregarding zero?

(c) How many characters can be included in a string constant?

(d) How many characters can be included in a variable name?

(e) Are all of the reserved words shown in Table 2.1 supported? If not, which words are not supported?

(f) What arithmetic operators are available, besides addition, subtraction, multiplication, division and exponentiation?

(g) How is string concatenation carried out?

(h) How are in-line comments written?

(i) Does your version of BASIC support all of the features defined in the 1987 ANSI standard? If not, does it support most of the features?

2.39 Express each of the following quantities as a numeric constant.

(a) 7,350

(b) −12

(c) 10^6

(d) $-2,053.18 \times 10^3$

(e) 0.00008291

(f) 9.563×10^{12}

(g) 1/6

2.40 Each of the following numeric constants is written incorrectly. Identify the errors.

(a) `7,104`

(b) `-+4920`

(c) `2.665E+42`

(d) `0.333333333333`

(e) `4.63E-0.8`

2.41 Each of the following items represents a string constant. Identify which, if any, are written incorrectly.

(a) `"July 4, 1776"`

(b) `"2 + 5 = 7"`

(c) `Another game?`

(d) `"75.50"`

(e) `"Divide "X" by 100"`

(f) `"One hundred twenty-nine and 73/100 dollars"`

(g) `"Programming with BASIC isn't difficult`

2.42   Identify which of the following numeric variables are written incorrectly.

   (*a*)   `xmax`   (*f*)   `Y.3`

   (*b*)   `QBAR`   (*g*)   `ANSWER?`

   (*c*)   `BIG C`   (*h*)   `root1`

   (*d*)   `BIG_C`   (*i*)   `input`

   (*e*)   `#space`   (*j*)   `input3`

2.43   Identify which of the following string variables are written incorrectly.

   (*a*)   `Name$`   (*d*)   `Acct_No$`

   (*b*)   `Address`   (*e*)   `input$`

   (*c*)   `Name$3`

2.44   Write a numeric expression that corresponds to each of the following algebraic formulas.

   (*a*) $3x + 5$ (*e*) $(u + v)^{k-1}$

   (*b*) $i + j - 2$ (*f*) $(4t)^{1/6}$

   (*c*) $x^2 + y^2$ (*g*) $t^{(n+1)}$

   (*d*) $(x+y)^2$ (*h*) $(x + 3)^{1/k}$

2.45   Determine the value of each of the following expressions.

   (*a*)   17 / 3   (*g*)   7.1 / 1.3

   (*b*)   17 \ 3   (*h*)   7.1 \ 1.3

   (*c*)   17 MOD 3   (*i*)   7.1 MOD 1.3

   (*d*)   7.8 / 1.8   (*j*)   7.1 / 1.8

   (*e*)   7.8 \ 1.8   (*k*)   7.1 \ 1.8

   (*f*)   7.8 MOD 1.8   (*l*)   7.1 MOD 1.8

2.46   Write a string concatenation expression to join each of the following groups of strings.

   (*a*)   `A$, B$  and  C$`

   (*b*)   `name$, street$ and city$`, with a blank space between each string

   (*c*)   `"Hello, " and NAME$`

2.47   Write a LET statement for each of the following situations.

(a) Assign a value of 2.54 to the variable C.

(b) Assign a value of 12 to the variable xmin.

(c) Assign the value represented by the variable N to the variable NSTAR.

(d) Assign the string "January 31" to the variable DATE$.

(e) Assign the string represented by the variable STR$ to the variable TSTR$.

(f) Assign the value represented by the expression (A ^ 2 + B ^ 2 + C ^ 2) to the variable squares.

(g) Increase the value assigned to the variable count by 0.01.

(h) Assign the value represented by the expression (I + J) to the variable I.

(i) Assign the string "PITTSBURGH, PA." to the variable city$.

(j) Assign the value of the expression X / (A + B - C) to the variable F_STAR.

(k) Decrease the value assigned to the variable K by 2.

(l) Double the value assigned to the variable prize.

2.48   Write a LET statement that corresponds to each of the following algebraic equations.

(a) $z = (x/y) + 3$

(b) $z = x/(y + 3)$

(c) $w = (u + v)/(s + t)$

(d) $f = [2ab/(c + 1) - t/(3(p + q))]^{1/3}$

(e) $y = (a_1 - a_2 x + a_3 x^2 - a_4 x^3 + a_5 x^4)/(c_1 - c_2 x + c_3 x^2 - c_4 x^3)$

(f) $P = Ai(1 + i)^n/[(1 + i)^n - 1]$

2.49   What particular difficulty might be experienced in executing the statement

         LET X = (Y - Z) ^ 0.25

2.50   Consider the statement

         LET P = -Q ^ 4

If $Q = 2$, what value will be assigned to P?

2.51 Consider the statement

    LET P = Q ^ 4

If Q = −2, what value will be assigned to P? (Compare with the answer to the previous problem.)

2.52 Write an appropriate statement, or group of statements, for each situation described below.

(a) Enter numeric values for A, B and C, followed by a string value for HEADING$. All of the data are to be entered on one line.

(b) Enter numeric values for A, B and C on one line, and a string value for HEADING$ on the next line.

(c) Enter numeric values for A and B on one line, and a numeric value for C followed by a string value for HEADING$ on the next line.

(d) Display the values of C1, C2, C3, C4 and C5 all on one line.

(e) Display the values of A, B and C on one line and the values of X, Y and Z on another line, with a blank line separating them.

(f) Display the values of A, B, C, X, Y and Z all on one line, spaced as closely as possible.

(g) Display the values of X, Y and Z on one line. Precede each numeric value with an appropriate label.

(h) Display the values of N$ and N next to one another, followed by the value of the expression A ^ 2 + B ^ 2.

(i) Display the strings "LEFT" and "RIGHT" on the same line, near the left and right edges.

(j) Display a message saying

    Enter NUMBER OF ITEMS and COST PER ITEM below:

Then enter the requested data on the next line.

(k) Display the message Roots of Simultaneous Equations on one line, near the center.

(l) Display a message indicating a request for the numeric value of Const, then enter a numeric value for Const.

(m) Display the values of NAME$ and SSN$ on separate lines, with a blank line between them. Label the items NAME and SOCIAL SECURITY NUMBER, respectively.

2.53 Show how the input data should be entered in each of the following situations.

(a) INPUT A, B, C, N$

    where A = 4.83 x 10^{-3} B = −537   C = 941.55   N$ = Boston

(b) INPUT N$, A
     INPUT B, C

where the variables have the same values as in part (a).

(c) INPUT city$, v1, v2

where city$ = Boston, MA   v1 = -8.05   v2 = 350

(d) INPUT c1$, c2$, c3$

where C1$ = New York   C2$ = Chicago   C3$ = San Francisco

(e) INPUT P, P$, Q, Q$

where P = 2,770,543   P$ = July 4, 1776   Q = 48.8×10^9 Q$ = Philadelphia, PA

2.54 Show how the output will appear in each of the following situations.

(a) PRINT "Name: ", name$, pay, tax, net

where name$ = George Smith   pay = 7000   tax = 1500   net = 5500

(b) PRINT "Name: "; name$; pay; tax; net

where the variables have the same values as in part (a).

(c) PRINT A1, B1, C1, D1
     PRINT A2, B2, C2, D2

where   A1 = 3   A2 = 5
             B1 = 6   B2 = 10
             C1 = 9   C2 = 15
             D1 = 12   D2 = 20

(d) PRINT A1; B1; C1; D1;
     PRINT A2; B2; C2; D2

where the variables have the same values as in part (c).

(e) PRINT A1 + B1; D2 / C2; (A1 * B2) / (B2 * C2)

where the variables have the same values as in part (c).

2.55 In each of the following cases, show how the comment (or remark) can be placed in a BASIC program.

(a) Add the program heading AREA AND CIRCUMFERENCE OF A CIRCLE

(b) Add the program heading AVERAGING OF AIR POLLUTION DATA

(c) Add the comments AREA and CIRCUMFERENCE to the statements

```
LET A = PI * R ^ 2
LET C= 2 * PI * R
```

    (d) Insert the remark `LOOP TO CALCULATE CUMULATIVE SUM`

    (e) Add the comment `CALCULATE AN AVERAGE VALUE` to the statement

```
LET avg = sum / n
```

2.56 Obtain a list of library functions for your particular version of BASIC. Are all of the functions shown in Table 2.2 available? Do you recognize other important, commonly used functions?

2.57 Write LET statements that correspond to each of the following algebraic equations.

    (a) $w = \log_e (v)$ (d) $r = (p + q)^{1/2}$

    (b) $p = q\,e^{-qt}$ (e) $y = a\,e^{bx} \sin cx$

    (c) $w = ||u - v| - |u + v||$ (f) $y = (|\sin x - \cos x|)^{1/2}$

2.58 Write a BASIC statement for each of the following situations.

    (a) Determine the sign of the quantity $(ab - cd) / (f + g)$.

    (b) Determine if the value of the variable N is even or odd, assuming that N has a positive integer value. (*Hint:* Compare the value of N / 2 with the truncated value of N / 2.)

    (c) In problem (b) above, what will happen if N has a negative integer value?

    (d) Determine the largest integer that algebraically does not exceed z, where $z = x^2 - y^2$. Assign this integer to the variable I.

    (e) In problem (d) above, if $x = 2.5$ and $y = 6.3$, what value will be assigned to I?

    (f) Display the following on one line: `"X= "`, followed by the value of the variable X; `"Y= "`, followed by the value of Y; and `"Z= "`, followed by the value of Z. Begin in columns 4, 28 and 52, respectively.

    (g) Display the values of X$, X, Y$ and Y on one line. Let the string represented by X$ begin in column 10, followed immediately by the value of X. Similarly, let Y$ begin in column 50, followed immediately by Y.

2.59 Determine the result of each of the following expressions. Assume that the variable N$ has been assigned the string `"1600 Pennsylvania Avenue"`.

    (a) `LEN(N$)`   (d) `STR$(1/5)`

    (b) `UCASE$(N$)`   (e) `VAL("1.25")`

    (c) `LCASE$(N$)`

Chapter 3

Creating and Running a BASIC Program

By now we have learned enough about BASIC to write complete, though simple, BASIC programs. We therefore pause briefly from our coverage of new features and devote some attention to the planning, writing and execution of a BASIC program. We will also consider methods for detecting and correcting the different types of errors that can occur in improperly written programs.

Our attention will be directed primarily toward the use of Microsoft's QuickBASIC on an IBM-type personal computer. We emphasize this particular version of BASIC because it is a complete state-of-the-art, structured BASIC programming environment, though it is not entirely compatible with the 1987 ANSI standard. It is representative of contemporary BASIC usage on many different computers. An interpreter-only version, called QBASIC, is included as a part of Microsoft's widely used MS-DOS operating system.

We will also describe the use of True BASIC, which is another state-of-the-art, structured implementation of BASIC that very closely parallels the new ANSI standard.

3.1 PLANNING A BASIC PROGRAM

When developing a new program, the overall program strategy should be completely planned out before beginning any detailed programming. This allows you to concentrate on the general program logic, without being concerned with the syntactic details of the individual instructions. Once the overall program strategy has been clearly established, the details associated with the individual program statements can be considered. Such an approach is generally referred to as "top-down" programming. With large programs, this entire process might be repeated several times, with more programming detail added at each stage.

Top-down program organization is normally carried out by developing an informal outline, consisting of phrases or sentences that are part English and part BASIC. In the initial stages of program development, the amount of actual BASIC is minimal, consisting only of keywords that suggest various BASIC instructions. Additional detail is provided by descriptive English phrases. As the program begins to take shape, the English phrases are replaced by specific BASIC statements or groups of statements.

Example 3.1 Roots of a Quadratic Equation

Suppose we wish to calculate the roots of the quadratic equation $ax^2 + bx + c = 0$, using the well-known formulas

$$x_1 = \frac{-b + (b^2 - 4ac)^{1/2}}{2a}$$

$$x_2 = \frac{-b - (b^2 - 4ac)^{1/2}}{2a}$$

where the values of a, b and c are known. Let us assume that the values of a, b and c are such that $b^2 - 4ac$ will always be positive. Therefore we need not worry about attempting to calculate the square root of a negative number.

We will enter the values for a, b and c interactively. That is, each numeric value will be entered in response to an appropriate on-screen *prompt*. We will also label the output, so that the meaning of each value is clearly understood.

The overall steps to be followed are as follows:

1. Read numeric values for a, b and c.

2. Calculate a value for $(b^2 - 4ac)^{1/2}$.

3. Calculate values for x_1 and x_2, using the above formulas.

4. Display the values for x_1 and x_2.

5. Stop.

Each of these steps appears very simple when viewed from the top. However, some of these steps can be broken down further to facilitate the actual programming. In particular, the data input step involves an interactive dialog generated by pairs of PRINT and INPUT statements, as explained in Chap. 2 (see Example 2.26). The remaining steps can be written in terms of BASIC keywords interspersed with descriptive English phrases.

Here is a more detailed form of the outline.

1. Enter the values for a, b and c interactively, in response to program-generated prompts.

    (a) Generate (PRINT) a prompt for a, then INPUT a value for a.

    (b) Generate (PRINT) a prompt for b, then INPUT a value for b.

    (c) Generate (PRINT) a prompt for c, then INPUT a value for c.

2. Evaluate $(b^2 - 4ac)^{1/2}$ as follows:

    LET *root* = SQR$(b^2 - 4ac)$

3. Calculate values for x_1 and x_2 using the following formulas:

    (a) LET $x_1 = (-b + root)/2a$

    (b) LET $x_2 = (-b - root)/2a$

4. Display (PRINT) the values for x_1 and x_2, with appropriate labels.

5. Stop program execution by specifying the END of the program.

This last outline contains more detail than is necessary for a program this simple, though detailed outlines of this type are very helpful when planning more complex programs.

We will consider the detailed development and implementation of this program in Examples 3.2, 3.3 and 3.4.

Another method that can be used to develop a BASIC program is the "bottom-up" approach. This method may be useful for programs that make use of independent program modules. The bottom-up approach involves the detailed development of these program modules early in the overall planning process. The overall program development is then based upon the known characteristics of these individual modules.

In practice, we often use both approaches: top-down for the overall program planning, and bottom-up with respect to independent program modules. Note, however, that the individual modules may themselves be developed using the top-down approach.

3.2 WRITING A BASIC PROGRAM

Once an overall program strategy has been formulated and a program outline has been written, attention can be given to the detailed development of the actual BASIC program. At this point the emphasis becomes one of translating each step of the program outline into one or more equivalent BASIC statements. This should be a straightforward activity provided the overall program strategy has been developed carefully and in sufficient detail.

It should be understood, however, that there is more to writing a good BASIC program than simply arranging the individual statements in the correct order. Attention should also be given to including certain additional features that will improve the readability of the program and its resulting output. These features include the arrangement of the statements into logical groups, the use of indentation, the use of comments, and the generation of clearly labeled output. We will include these features, as needed, in the programming examples that appear throughout the remainder of this book.

Example 3.2 Roots of a Quadratic Equation

Presented below is a complete QuickBASIC program corresponding to the second outline presented in Example 3.1. Step 1 is implemented by means of a series PRINT and INPUT statements. Steps 2 and 3 are carried out using LET statements. Steps 4 and 5 are implemented using a PRINT statement and an END statement, respectively.

Notice that comments are included in the program, using both the REM statement and the method based on the use of apostrophes.

```
REM *** ROOTS OF A QUADRATIC EQUATION ***
PRINT "a = ";
INPUT a
PRINT "b = ";
INPUT b
PRINT "c = ";
INPUT c
LET root = SQR(b ^ 2 - 4 * a * c)
LET x1 = (-b + root) / (2 * a)          'calculate the first root
LET x2 = (-b - root) / (2 * a)          'calculate the second root
PRINT "x1 ="; x1; TAB(20); "x2 ="; x2
END
```

This program is short, simple and logically straightforward. Thus, we did not have to concern ourselves with the arrangement of the statements into logical groups, or the use of indentation. There are, however, some other desirable features that might have been included. For example, we might want to execute the program repetitively, for several different sets of input data. Or, we might have added error traps, preventing the user from processing input data resulting in negative values of $b^2 - 4ac$. We will see how such features can be added as we progress through the remainder of this book.

3.3 ENTERING THE PROGRAM INTO THE COMPUTER

Once the program has been written, it must be entered into the computer before it can be executed. In older versions of BASIC this was done by typing the program into the computer on a line-by-line basis. Editing changes were made using the backspace key for the current line being entered, or by deleting and retyping a line once it had already been entered into the computer.

Most contemporary versions of BASIC include a full-screen *editor* that is used for this purpose. The editor is generally integrated into the software package. Thus, to access the editor, you must first enter the BASIC programming environment. The manner with which this is accomplished varies from one implementation of BASIC to another.

Consider, for example, Microsoft QuickBASIC, as implemented on a personal computer using Microsoft's MS-DOS operating system. To enter QuickBASIC, simply type QB at the system prompt. This results in the full-screen display shown in Fig. 3.1.

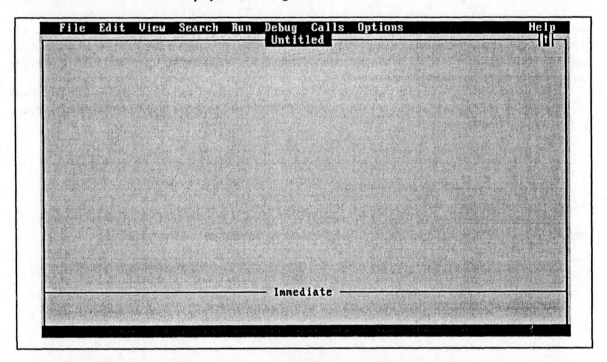

Fig. 3.1

The first line in this figure is a *menu bar*. Selecting one of the items in the menu bar (e.g., File, Edit, View, etc.) will cause a *drop-down menu* to appear, with a number of choices related to the menu bar selection. For example, the File menu includes choices that allow you to open a program (i.e., to retrieve a program), to save a program or to exit from QuickBASIC. We will discuss certain of these menu items later in this chapter.

The large clear space beneath the menu bar represents an *editing area* where a new program can be entered or an existing program can be displayed. Portions of the program listed in this area can be changed, deleted, copied or moved to another part of the program. Some of these changes are made directly in the editing area, while others are made by *highlighting* (i.e., marking) a part of the program and then moving or deleting the highlighted material using the selections provided in the Edit menu.

The smaller clear space, beneath the line labeled Immediate, is an area where individual statements such as PRINT can be executed immediately, independent of the program listed in the editing area. The Immediate area can be removed by selecting the small vertical arrow at the upper right corner of the screen, beneath Help. (Usually a pointing device, such as a *mouse*, is used to select a menu item. This is accomplished by moving the cursor over the desired item and then "clicking" on the item; i.e., pressing a button on the pointing device.)

The bottom line contains a copyright notice when QuickBASIC is first activated. Once a menu item is highlighted, however, the copyright notice will disappear and the line will contain a brief explanation of the selected menu item. We will see examples of this later in this chapter.

To enter a new program in QuickBASIC, you simply type the program into the editing area on a line-by-line basis and press the ENTER key at the end of each line. To edit a line, use the mouse or the cursor movement (arrow) keys to locate the beginning of the edit area. Then use the BACKSPACE or DELETE keys to remove unwanted characters. You may also insert additional characters, as required.

You may delete one or more lines simply by highlighting the lines and then selecting Cut from the Edit menu. One or more lines can also be copied or moved to another location using the Copy or Paste selections in the Edit menu. Detailed editing instructions are provided in the QuickBASIC User's Manual.

Once the program has been entered correctly, it should be saved on an auxiliary memory device before it is executed. In QuickBASIC, this is accomplished by selecting Save As from the File menu and then supplying a program name, such as ROOTS.BAS. Once the program has been saved and a name has been provided, it may again be saved at a later time (with, for example, any recent editing changes) simply by selecting Save from the File menu.

A program that has been saved can later be recalled by selecting Load File from the File menu and then supplying the program name. A printed copy of the current program may be obtained by selecting Print from the File menu.

Example 3.3 Roots of a Quadratic Equation

Suppose you have entered the BASIC program shown in Example 3.2 into an IBM-type personal computer using QuickBASIC. After all typing corrections have been made, the screen will appear as shown in Fig. 3.2.

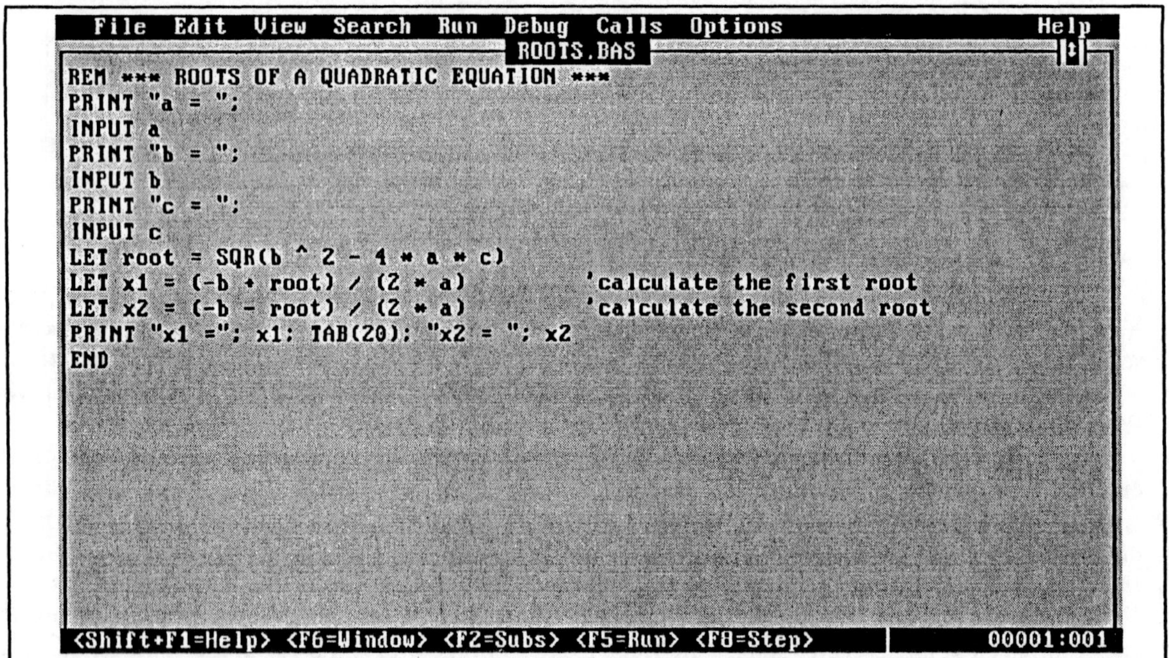

Fig. 3.2

In order to save the program, select Save As from the File menu, as shown in Fig. 3.3. Once you press the ENTER key a dialog box will appear, prompting you for the name of the program being saved. You will then respond by entering a program name, such as ROOTS.BAS (this is not shown). You may then conclude the session by selecting Exit from the File menu.

```
 File  Edit  View   Search  Run  Debug  Calls  Options              Help
                              ROOTS.BAS                                 ↕
 New Program         │UADRATIC EQUATION ***
  pen Program...
  erge...
  ave
 Save  s...
 Sa e All
  reate File...      │ - 4 * a * c)
  oad File...        │ / (2 * a)          'calculate the first root
  nload File...      │ / (2 * a)          'calculate the second root
                     │B(20): "x2 = "; x2
  rint...
 OS Shell

 E it


 F1=Help │ Removes currently loaded program from memory │      00001:001
```

Fig. 3.3

3.4 EXECUTING THE PROGRAM

Once the program has been entered into the computer, edited and saved, it can be executed by selecting Start from the Run menu. (If this is a new QuickBASIC session, it will be necessary to load the program before it can be executed. This is accomplished by selecting Open Program from the File menu.) The program will then begin execution, prompting for input as required. If the program executes correctly the results will be displayed as they are generated, in accordance with the program's PRINT statements.

Example 3.4 Roots of a Quadratic Equation

Suppose you have reentered QuickBASIC after concluding the session described in Example 3.3. You begin by loading ROOTS.BAS into the computer's memory (select Open Program from the File menu). In order to execute the program after it has been loaded, select Start from the Run menu, as shown in Fig. 3.4. The QuickBASIC screen will then clear and a conventional interactive dialog will begin. After the execution has been completed, you may press any key to return to the QuickBASIC environment.

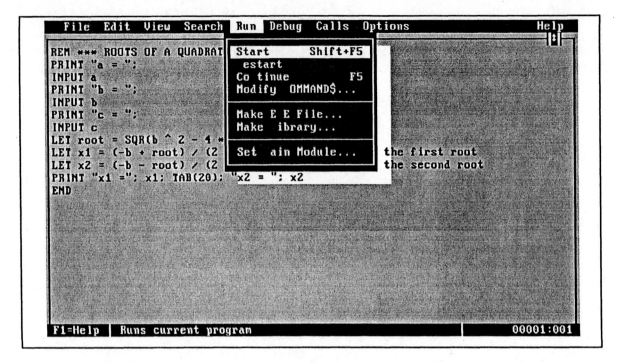

```
   File   Edit   View   Search   Run  Debug  Calls  Options                    Help

REM *** ROOTS OF A QUADRAT    Start        Shift+F5
PRINT "a = ";                  estart
INPUT a                       Co tinue          F5
PRINT "b = ";                 Modify  OMMAND$...
INPUT b
PRINT "c = ";                 Make E E File...
INPUT c                       Make  ibrary...
LET root = SQR(b ^ 2 - 4 *
LET x1 = (-b + root) / (2     Set  ain Module...    the first root
LET x2 = (-b - root) / (2                           the second root
PRINT "x1 =": x1: TAB(20); "x2 = ": x2
END




F1=Help  | Runs current program                              00001:001
```

Fig. 3.4

A typical interactive session is is shown below.

```
a = ? 2
b = ? 5
c = ? 3
x1 =-1                x2 =-1.5
```

Thus, we see that $x_1 = -1$ and $x_2 = -1.5$ when $a = 2$, $b = 5$ and $c = 3$. (The computed results are shown in a separate window.)

In this case, the program executed without any difficulties. Things do not always go this smoothly, however, as we will see in Examples 3.5 and 3.6.

3.5 ERROR DIAGNOSTICS

Programming errors often remain undetected until an attempt is made to compile (or interpret) the program. Once the RUN command has been issued, however, the presence of *syntactic* (or *grammatical*) errors will become readily apparent, since these errors will prevent the program from compiling successfully. Some particularly common errors of this type are misspelled keywords, references to undefined variables, right- and left-hand parentheses that do not balance, incorrect punctuation, etc.

Most implementations of BASIC will generate diagnostic messages when syntactic errors are detected while attempting to compile a program. The meaning of these diagnostic messages is not always straightforward, but the messages are nevertheless helpful in identifying the nature and location of the errors.

Example 3.5 Syntactic Errors

A version of ROOTS.BAS containing several syntactic errors is shown below. (There are 3 errors; can you find them?)

```
REM *** ROOTS OF A QUADRATIC EQUATION ***
PRINT "a = ";
INPUT a
PRINR "b = ";
INPUT b
PRINT "c = ";
INPUT c
LET root = SQR(d ^ 2 - 4 * a * c)
LET x1 = (-b + root) / (2 * a)          'calculate the first root
LET x2 = (-b - root) / (2 * a          'calculate the second root
PRINT "x1 ="; x1; TAB(20); "x2 ="; x2
END
```

When an attempt is made to compile the program in QuickBASIC, the following error message is generated.

```
Expected: end-of-statement
```

The cursor is then placed at the end of the statement that contains the error; i.e.,

```
PRINR "b = ";
```

(Note that the keyword PRINT is misspelled.)

When this error is corrected and another attempt is made to compile the program, the following error message is generated.

```
Expected: )
```

Now the cursor is placed on the apostrophe (i.e., at the beginning of the comment) in the statement

```
LET x2 = (-b - root) / (2 * a          'calculate the second root
```

The difficulty with this statement is the missing right parenthesis at the end. The program compiled successfully once this last error was corrected.

Execution errors are also very common. Such errors occur during the execution of programs that are free of syntactic errors. Some common execution errors are a reference to a nonexistent variable, the generation of an excessively large number (exceeding the largest permissible number that can be stored in the computer), division by zero, and attempting to compute the logarithm or the square root of a negative number. Diagnostic messages are usually generated in situations of this type, making it easy to identify and correct the source of error. Such diagnostics are sometimes called *execution* diagnostics, to distinguish them from the *syntactic* diagnostics or *compilation* diagnostics described earlier.

Example 3.6 Execution Errors

In this example we see what happens when we attempt to execute the previous version of ROOTS.BAS after a successful compilation.

In the first attempt to execute the program with the values $a = 1$, $b = 2$ and $c = 3$, the following message was obtained.

```
Illegal function call
```

Also, the entire statement

```
LET root = SQR(d ^ 2 - 4 * a * c)
```

was highlighted, indicating that this statement was the source of error. The problem in this case is the reference to the nonexistent variable d within the parentheses. This variable should have been b rather than d.

Once this error was corrected, another attempt was made to execute the program using the same input values. The error message

```
Illegal function call
```

was again obtained, though for a different reason. Now the problem is the choice of input values, which result in the value -8 for the quantity $b^2 - 4ac$. Since this value is negative, its square root cannot be calculated. The program cannot continue its execution beyond this point. Hence, calculated values for x_1 and x_2 do not appear on the screen.

In the next attempt to execute the program using the input values $a = 10^{-30}$, $b = 10^{10}$, $c = 10^{36}$, a numerical overflow occurred in the calculation of x_1. Hence the following message appeared on the screen beneath the input data.

```
Overflow
```

Notice that this diagnostic message does not indicate where the overflow occurred. Some additional effort is required to determine that the difficulty arises in the calculation of x_1 (see Example 3.8).

3.6 LOGICAL DEBUGGING

We have just seen that syntactic errors and execution errors usually result in the generation of error messages when the program is compiled and executed. Errors of this type are usually easy to find and correct, even if the error messages are unclear. Much more subtle, however, are *logical* errors. Here the program correctly conveys the programmer's instructions, free of syntactic errors, but the programmer has supplied the computer with instructions that are logically incorrect. Such errors can be very difficult to detect, since the output resulting from a logically incorrect program may appear to be error-free. Moreover, logical errors are often hard to find even when they are known to exist (as, for example, when the computed output is obviously incorrect). Thus, a good bit of probing may be required in order to find and correct errors of this type. Such probing is known as *logical debugging*.

Detecting Errors

The first step in attacking logical errors is to find out if they are present. This can sometimes be accomplished by testing a new program with data that will yield a known answer. If the correct results are *not* obtained, then the program obviously contains errors. If the correct results *are* obtained, however, you cannot be absolutely certain that the program is error free, since some errors cause incorrect results only under certain circumstances (as, for example, with certain values of the input data or with certain program options). Therefore, a new program should receive thorough testing before it is considered to be error free. This is especially true of complicated programs or programs that will be used extensively by others.

Sometimes a calculation will have to be carried out by hand (with the aid of a calculator) in order to obtain a known answer. For some problems, however, the amount of work involved in carrying out a hand calculation is prohibitive, since a calculation that requires a few minutes of computer time may require *several weeks* to solve by hand. Therefore, a sample calculation cannot always be developed to test a new program. The logical debugging of such programs can be particularly difficult, though you can often detect the presence of logical errors by studying the computed results carefully to see if they are reasonable.

Correcting Errors

Once you have established that a program contains a logical error, some resourcefulness and ingenuity may be required to find the error. Error detection should always begin with a thorough review of each logical group of statements within the program. Knowing that an error exists somewhere, you can often spot the error by carefully inspecting the program. If the error cannot be found, it sometimes helps to set the program aside for a while. This is especially true if you are experiencing some fatigue or frustration; it is not unusual for a tired, tense programmer to miss an obvious error the first time around.

If you cannot locate an error by inspection, you should modify the program to print out certain intermediate results and then rerun it. This technique is referred to as *tracing*. The source of error often becomes evident once you examine these intermediate calculations carefully. In particular, you can usually identify the specific area within the program where things begin to go wrong. The greater the amount of intermediate output, the more likely you are to pinpoint the source of error.

Sometimes an error simply cannot be located, despite the most elaborate debugging techniques. On such occasions you may suspect some difficulty that is beyond your control, such as a hardware problem or an error in the BASIC compiler or interpreter. In most cases, however, the problem turns out to be some subtle error in the program logic. Thus, you should resist the temptation to blame the computer and not continue to look for that elusive programming error. Although hardware problems do occur *on rare occasions*, they usually produce very bizarre results, such as the computer "dying" or spewing out unintelligible characters. Also, errors occasionally turn up in a new compiler or interpreter, though they are usually corrected after the compiler (or interpreter) has been in use for a short period of time.

Finally, you should recognize that some logical errors are inescapable in computer programming, though a conscientious programmer will make every attempt to minimize their occurrence. You should therefore anticipate the need for some logical debugging when writing realistic, meaningful programs.

Example 3.7 Evaluating a Polynomial

A student has written a QuickBASIC program to evaluate the formula

$$y = [(x-1)/x] + [(x-1)/x]^2/2 + [(x-1)/x]^3/3 + [(x-1)/x]^4/4 + [(x-1)/x]^5/5$$

To simplify the programming, the student has defined a new variable, u, as

$$u = [(x-1)/x]$$

so that the formula becomes

$$y = u + u^2/2 + u^3/3 + u^4/4 + u^5/5$$

Here is the student's BASIC program, called POLY.BAS.

```
REM *** Program to evaluate an algebraic formula ***
PRINT "x = ";
INPUT x
LET u = x - 1 / x
LET y = u + (u / 2) ^ 2 + (u / 3) ^ 3 + (u / 4) ^ 4 + (u / 5) ^ 5
PRINT "y =";y
END
```

The student suspects that y should have a value of about 0.7 when $x = 2$. However, the following results are obtained when the program is loaded and executed using QuickBASIC.

```
x = ? 2
y = 2.209705
```

Since the calculated value of y differs from the value expected, it is apparent that the program contains logical errors that must be found and corrected.

After inspecting the program carefully, the student realized that the first LET statement is incorrect. The statement should have been written as

```
LET u = (x - 1) / x
```

The student corrected the program and reran it, again using the value of $x = 2$. The resulting output,

```
y = .5673838
```

indicates that a logical error is still present.

After some additional study, the student discovered that the second LET statement is also incorrect. This statement should be written as

```
LET y = u + u ^ 2 / 2 + u ^ 3 / 3 + u ^ 4 / 4 + u ^ 5 / 5
```

The program was then modified and rerun, resulting in the output

```
y = .6885417
```

which now appears correct.

Debugging Aids

Most contemporary versions of BASIC include special debugging features that facilitate the detection of errors. For example, they may allow the execution of the program to be suspended at designated places, called *breakpoints*, revealing the values of certain program variables or expressions (called *watch variables* or *watch expressions*) at the time the execution is suspended. They may also allow the execution of a program to be suspended whenever a watch expression becomes true. The place where this occurs is known as a *watchpoint*. By monitoring the values of watch expressions at carefully selected breakpoints and watchpoints, it is easier to determine where and when an error originates.

QuickBASIC, for example, includes a debugger within the QuickBASIC environment. The debugger is activated by selecting Debug from the main menu bar. This causes a drop-down menu containing the various debugger selections to appear. Fig. 3.5 shows the debugger menu, with the Add Watch selection highlighted.

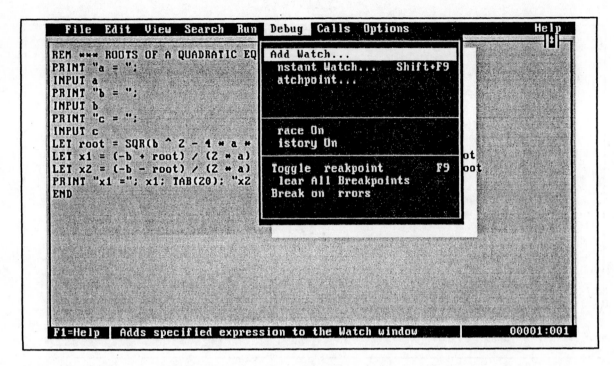

Fig. 3.5

Example 3.8 Roots of a Quadratic Equation

In Example 3.6 we saw that an overflow occurred during the execution of the program ROOTS.BAS when the values $a = 10^{-30}$, $b = 10^{10}$ and $c = 10^{36}$ were entered as input data. We stated that the source of the problem was the calculation of x_1, but we did not say how this conclusion was obtained. Let us now use the QuickBASIC debugger to establish this conclusion.

We first load ROOTS.BAS into the QuickBASIC environment, as in Example 3.3 (see Fig. 3.2). We then activate the debugger and carry out the following steps.

1. Set root, x1 and x2 as watch variables. This is done by selecting Add Watch three different times from the Debug menu.

2. Set the second LET statement (LET x1 = ...) as a breakpoint. To do so, we move the cursor to this statement and then select Toggle Breakpoint from the Debug menu.

3. Select Start from the Run menu. Then enter the input values in response to the program prompts.

The program will stop at the designated breakpoint, showing the values of the watch variables root, x1 and x2 at the top of the screen. At this point only the first LET statement will have been executed. Thus, only the watch variable root will show a nonzero value (in this case, 1e+10, which is a rounded value). We then press the function key F8 (as indicated by the help line at the bottom of the screen) to execute the next instruction. This results in an overflow message, indicating that the overflow occurred in the evaluation of x1. A value of zero is still shown for x1, but now it is after an attempt was made to calculate a nonzero value. Pressing F8 once more results in another overflow message, this time in attempting to evaluate x2.

Figure 3.6 shows the appearance of the screen after the first overflow message. Notice the area at the top of the screen, where the current values of the watch variables are shown. Also, notice that the breakpoint (the second LET statement) is shown highlighted.

```
  File   Edit   View   Search   Run  Debug  Calls  Options                      Help
  ROOTS.BAS root:   1E+10
  ROOTS.BAS x1:   0
  ROOTS.BAS x2:   0
━━━━━━━━━━━━━━━━━━━━━━━━━━━━ ROOTS.BAS ━━━━━━━━━━━━━━━━━━━━━━━━━━━━━━━━━━━━━━━━━━━━
REM *** ROOTS OF A QUADRATIC EQUATION ***
PRINT "a = ";
INPUT a
PRINT "b = ";
INPUT b
PRINT "c = ";
INPUT c
LET root = SQR(b ^ 2 - 4 * a * c)

LET x2 = (-b - root) / (2 * a)              'calculate the second root
PRINT "x1 ="; x1; TAB(20); "x2 = "; x2
END




<Shift+F1=Help> <F5=Continue> <F9=Toggle Bkpt> <F8=Step>              00009:001
```

Fig. 3.6

3.7 OTHER BASIC PROGRAMMING ENVIRONMENTS

So far our emphasis in this chapter has been on Microsoft QuickBASIC. We have chosen QuickBASIC because of its support of structured programming concepts, its widespread use and its excellent user interface. There are, however, other implementations of structured BASIC commercially available. Some are command driven, while others provide complete programming environments. Moreover, irrespective of the user interface, they may include features that are considerably different than those found in QuickBASIC. We will discuss one in particular, since it closely follows the 1987 ANSI standard and is used elsewhere in this book.

True BASIC

True BASIC is a modern, PC-based implementation of BASIC that retains the flavor and character of earlier versions of the language. (This is not surprising, since it was developed by John Kemeny and Thomas Kurtz, the originators of BASIC.) True BASIC differs considerably from QuickBASIC and the other dialects of Microsoft BASIC. Of particular significance is a high level of compatibility between True BASIC and the 1987 ANSI standard. Thus, True BASIC can be expected to become increasingly popular as interest in the 1987 ANSI standard intensifies.

True BASIC is supported by a relatively simple menu-driven user interface, though it does include a number of helpful editing and debugging features. It also makes use of a split screen. The upper portion of the screen is used to list and edit the program while the lower portion is used to issue commands (such as LIST, RUN, etc.) and to view calculated results. Most of the commands can also be selected from the main menu bar. True BASIC also includes a number of helpful editing and debugging features.

To enter True BASIC, type "Hello" at the system prompt. This results in the full-screen display shown in Fig. 3.7. (Compare with Fig. 3.1, which shows the opening screen for Microsoft QuickBASIC.)

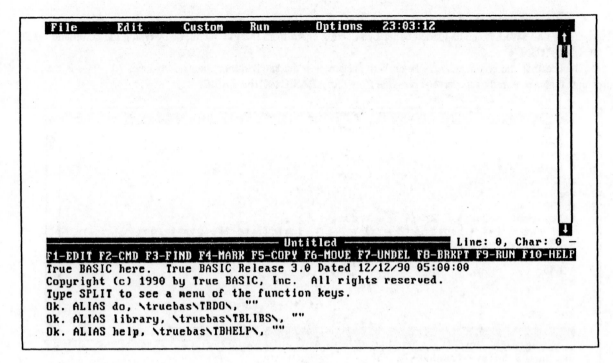

```
  File      Edit      Custom     Run       Options    23:03:12                    ↑
                                                                                  ▮
                                                                                  │
                                                                                  │
                                                                                  │
                                                                                  │
                                                                                  │
                                                                                  │
                                                                                  │
                                                                                  ↓
══════════════════════════ Untitled ═══════════════════ Line: 0, Char: 0 ═
F1-EDIT F2-CMD F3-FIND F4-MARK F5-COPY F6-MOVE F7-UNDEL F8-BRKPT F9-RUN F10-HELP
True BASIC here.  True BASIC Release 3.0 Dated 12/12/90 05:00:00
Copyright (c) 1990 by True BASIC, Inc.  All rights reserved.
Type SPLIT to see a menu of the function keys.
Ok. ALIAS do, \truebas\TBDO\, ""
Ok. ALIAS library, \truebas\TBLIBS\, ""
Ok. ALIAS help, \truebas\TBHELP\, ""
```

Fig. 3.7

The first line is a *menu bar*, which permits access to True BASIC's drop-down menus. These menus can be accessed either from the keyboard or with a mouse, by highlighting and then clicking on a particular selection.

Beneath the menu bar is the *editing area*, where BASIC programs are entered on a line-by-line basis. Some limited editing, such as editing or deleting characters and marking lines for movement or deletion, is permitted directly within this area. More extensive editing, such as moving or deleting blocks of lines, requires the use of the function keys or the features within the Edit menu.

At the bottom of the screen is the *command area*, where commands such as Load, Save, Run, Bye, etc. can be issued. These commands are vestiges of early versions of BASIC. The same actions can be carried out by selecting various features from the drop-down menus. The interactive dialog resulting from a program execution also takes place within the command area. A copyright notice appears in this area when True BASIC is first initiated.

Separating the editing area from the command area is a two-line *split bar*. The first line of the split bar contains the program name. The second line, which can be turned off, summarizes the use of the function keys.

To enter a new True BASIC program, you simply type the program into the edit area on a line-by-line basis. An existing program is entered by selecting the Open feature from the File menu, or by typing Old, followed by the program name, in the command area. Other file management procedures (e.g., Save, Print, etc.) can be selected from the File menu, as in QuickBASIC, or can be initiated from the command area with an appropriate system command (e.g., Save, List, etc.).

Example 3.9 Roots of a Quadratic Equation via True BASIC

Figure 3.8 illustrates the use of True BASIC with our familiar program ROOTS.BAS, which we first saw in Example 3.2. (The program is now called ROOTS.TRU, to conform to the True BASIC naming convention.) The upper portion of the screen shows a listing of the program, after is has been loaded into memory. The program can be typed directly into the upper portion of the screen on a line-by-line basis, if it is new. If the program has been entered previously and saved, it can be loaded either by selecting Open from the File menu, or by typing the command OLD ROOTS.TRU

Notice that the comments now begin with exclamation marks (!) rather than apostrophes ('). This is the only change that is required to convert the program from QuickBASIC to True BASIC.

```
 File        Edit       Custom      Run        Options     23:05:03
■ REM *** ROOTS OF A QUADRATIC EQUATION ***                                ↑
■ PRINT "a = ";
■ INPUT a
■ PRINT "b = ";
■ INPUT b
■ PRINT "c = ";
■ INPUT c
■ LET root = SQR(b ^ 2 - 4 * a * c)
■ LET x1 = (-b + root) / (2 * a)          !calculate the first root
■ LET x2 = (-b - root) / (2 * a)          !calculate the second root
■ PRINT "x1 ="; x1; TAB(20); "x2 = "; x2
■ END
■                                                                          ↓
 ───────────────────────────── ROOTS.TRU ─────────── Line: 0, Char: 0 ─
F1-EDIT F2-CMD F3-FIND F4-MARK F5-COPY F6-MOVE F7-UNDEL F8-BRKPT F9-RUN F10-HELP
Ok. ALIAS help, \truebas\TBHELP\, ""
Ok. colors from cfile
Ok. split
Ok. rem echo to history.out
Ok. old ROOTS.TRU
Ok.
```

Fig. 3.8

```
 File        Edit       Custom      Run        Options     23:07:55
 New      N │ OTS OF A QUADRATIC EQUATION ***                               ↑
 Open     O │ ";
 Switch   L │
 Close    W │ ";
            │
 Save     S │ ";
 Save As  Z │
 Unsave   H │   SQR(b ^ 2 - 4 * a * c)
            │ -b + root) / (2 * a)          !calculate the first root
 Print    P │ -b - root) / (2 * a)          !calculate the second root
            │ ="; x1; TAB(20); "x2 = "; x2
 Quit     Q │
                                                                           ↓
 ───────────────────────────── ROOTS.TRU ─────────── Line: 1, Char: 1 ─
F1-EDIT F2-CMD F3-FIND F4-MARK F5-COPY F6-MOVE F7-UNDEL F8-BRKPT F9-RUN F10-HELP
Ok. ALIAS help, \truebas\TBHELP\, ""
Ok. colors from cfile
Ok. split
Ok. rem echo to history.out
Ok. old ROOTS.TRU
Ok.
```

Fig. 3.9

Figure 3.9 shows the File menu superimposed over the edit area. The Save As feature is highlighted. Selecting this feature will allow the current program to be saved under a new name.

Figure 3.10 shows what happens when this program is executed for the values $a = 2$, $b = 5$ and $c = 3$. (Program execution is initiated either by selecting Run from the Run menu, or by typing Run in the command area.) The interactive dialog is shown in the command area, followed by the resulting values of $x_1 = -1$ and $x_2 = -1.5$.

```
 File      Edit      Custom     Run       Options   23:10:49
■ REM *** ROOTS OF A QUADRATIC EQUATION ***
■ PRINT "a = ";
■ INPUT a
■ PRINT "b = ";
■ INPUT b
■ PRINT "c = ";
■ INPUT c
■ LET root = SQR(b ^ 2 - 4 * a * c)
■ LET x1 = (-b + root) / (2 * a)          !calculate the first root
■ LET x2 = (-b - root) / (2 * a)          !calculate the second root
■ PRINT "x1 ="; x1; TAB(20); "x2 = "; x2
■ END
■

━━━━━━━━━━━━━━━━━━━━━━━━ ROOTS.TRU ━━━━━━━━━━━━━━━ Line: 1, Char: 1 ━
F1-EDIT F2-CMD F3-FIND F4-MARK F5-COPY F6-MOVE F7-UNDEL F8-BRKPT F9-RUN F10-HELP
Ok. run
a = ? 2
b = ? 5
c = ? 3
x1 =-1                x2 = -1.5
Ok.
```

Fig. 3.10

This discussion is intended only to present a general overview of True BASIC. The reader is referred to the True BASIC reference manuals for additional information about this excellent system.

Finally, it should be understood that there are other high-quality, contemporary implementations of BASIC available, intended both for personal computers and for larger computers. We are not necessarily expressing preferences in this book. Moreover, future releases of all programming languages undergo refinements as the languages continue to evolve. Thus, certain of the details presented in this chapter will undoubtedly change in the years ahead.

Review Questions

3.1   What is meant by "top-down" programming? What are its advantages? How is it carried out?

3.2   What is meant by "bottom-up" programming? How does it differ from top-down programming?

3.3   What are menu bars? What are drop-down menus? How can menu bars and drop-down menus be accessed?

3.4   What is a syntactic error? What is an execution error? How do syntactic errors and execution errors differ?

3.5   Name some common syntactic errors. Name some common execution errors.

3.6   What is a logical error? How do logical errors differ from syntactic and execution errors?

3.7   What are diagnostic messages?

3.8   What is the difference between syntactic diagnostics and execution diagnostics? Name some situations in which each type of diagnostic message would be generated.

3.9   What is meant by logical debugging? Name some logical debugging procedures.

3.10   What is meant by tracing? In what way is tracing useful?

3.11   What are breakpoints? What are watch expressions? What are watchpoints? What useful purposes are served by breakpoints, watch expressions and watchpoints?

Problems

The following questions are concerned with information gathering rather than actual problem solving.

3.12   If personal computers are used at your particular school or office, obtain answers to the following questions.

   (a)   Exactly what equipment is available (printers, auxiliary memory devices, etc.)?

   (b)   What operating system is available?

   (c)   How are programs saved, displayed, and transferred from one memory device to another?

   (d)   What version of BASIC is available on your computer? How is it accessed?

   (e)   How is the editor accessed? How are normal editing functions (e.g., insert, delete, etc.) carried out?

   (f)   How is an existing BASIC program loaded into the computer's memory? How is a program listed? How is a program saved? How is a program executed?

   (g)   What is the cost of one complete personal computer system? What is the cost of a BASIC interpreter or compiler?

3.13   If timesharing is used at your particular school or office, obtain answers to the following questions.

   (a)   Are video display terminals (monitors) available? Are hard-copy terminals available?

   (b)   How is a terminal turned on or off?

   (c)   How is a single character deleted from a typed line before it is transmitted to the computer? How is an entire line deleted?

   (d)   How is a typed line transmitted to the computer?

   (e)   Can a hard copy of your timesharing session be obtained? If so, how?

   (f)   Is a telephone dial-up required to establish a connection with the computer? If so, what is the dial-up procedure?

(g)	How do you log on and log off your computer?

(h)	Can your timesharing terminal be operated in a local mode (i.e., as a stand-alone device, independent of the host computer)? If so, how is this done?

(i)	How is BASIC accessed?

(j)	What editor or editors are available on your system? How are normal editing functions (e.g., insert, delete, etc.) carried out?

(k)	How is an existing BASIC program loaded into the computer's memory? How is a program listed? How is a program saved? How is a program executed?

(l)	How much does it cost to use your particular timesharing system?

Programming Problems

3.14	Enter the program given in Example 1.6 into the computer, making any necessary modifications that may be required by your particular version of BASIC. Be sure to correct any typing errors. List the program, correct any apparent errors, and save it when you are sure it is correct. Execute the program, using several different values for the radius. Verify that the computed answers are correct by comparing them with hand calculations.

3.15	Enter, edit and execute the programs given in Examples 1.7 and 1.8. Verify that they run correctly with your particular version of BASIC.

3.16	Enter, edit and execute a few of the programs given in Problem 1.26. Verify that they run correctly with your particular version of BASIC.

3.17	Example 3.2 presents a BASIC program for determining the real roots of a quadratic equation. Enter this program into the computer and save it. Then execute the program using several different sets of input data. Verify that the calculated results are correct by comparing them with hand calculations.

3.18	Repeat Problem 3.17 using input data that will generate execution diagnostics, as illustrated in Example 3.6. Be sure you understand the cause and the meaning of each diagnostic message.

3.19	Write a complete BASIC program for each of the following problem situations.

(a)	Display HELLO! in the middle of a line.

(b)	Have the computer print

```
Hi, What's your name?
```

on one line. The user then enters his or her name immediately after the question mark. The computer then skips two lines and prints the following two lines.

```
Welcome, (name)!
Let's be friends!
```

3.20 Write an interactive BASIC program for each of the following problem situations.

(a) A temperature reading, in Fahrenheit degrees, is to be read into the computer and converted into Celsius degrees, using the expression

$$^\circ C = (5/9)\,(^\circ F - 32)$$

(b) A piggy bank contains n_1 half-dollars, n_2 quarters, n_3 dimes, n_4 nickels and n_5 pennies. How much money is in the bank, in terms of dollars?

3.21 Develop an outline then write a complete BASIC program for each of the following problems. Write each program in such a manner that it can be used to process several sets of data sequentially. Be sure that all output data is clearly labeled.

(a) Calculate the volume and area of a sphere using the expressions

$$V = 4\pi r^3/3, \quad A = 4\pi r^2$$

where r is the radius of the sphere.

(b) The pressure, volume and temperature of a mass of air are related by the expression

$$PV = 0.37m(T + 460)$$

where P = pressure, pounds per square inch
V = volume, cubic feet
m = mass of air, pounds
T = temperature, $^\circ F$

If an automobile tire containing 2 cubic feet of air is inflated to 28 pounds per square inch at room temperature, how much air is in the tire?

(c) If a, b and c represent the three sides of a triangle, then the area of the triangle is

$$A = [\,s\,(s - a)\,(s - b)\,(s - c)\,]^{1/2}$$

where $s = (a + b + c)/2$. Also, the radius of the *largest inscribed* circle is given by

$$r_i = A/s$$

and the radius of the *smallest circumscribed* circle is

$$r_c = abc/(4A)$$

Calculate the area of the triangle, the area of the largest inscribed circle and the area of the smallest circumscribed circle for each of the following sets of data:

a:	11.88	5.55	10.00	13.75	12.00	20.42	7.17	173.67
b:	8.06	4.54	10.00	9.89	8.00	27.24	2.97	87.38
c:	12.75	7.56	10.00	11.42	12.00	31.59	6.66	139.01

(d) Suppose that P dollars are invested at an annual interest rate of i (expressed as a decimal). If the interest is reinvested, after n years the total amount of money, F, can be determined as follows:

$$F = P(1+i)^n.$$

This is known as the *law of compound interest*.

If \$5000 is invested at 6%, compounded annually, how much money will have accumulated after 10 years?

If the interest is compounded quarterly rather than annually, the above equation must be changed to read

$$F = P(1+i/4)^{4n}$$

If the same \$5000 is invested at the rate of 6%, compounded quarterly, how much will have accumulated after 10 years? Compare this answer with the result obtained earlier, for interest compounded annually.

(e) The increase in population of a bacteria culture with time is directly proportional to the size of the population. Thus the larger the population, the faster the bacteria will increase in number. Mathematically the population at any time can be expressed as

$$P = P_0[1 + ct + (ct)^2/2 + (ct)^3/6 + \ldots + (ct)^n/n!]$$

where $t =$ time in hours beyond a reference time
$P_0 =$ bacteria population at the reference time
$P =$ bacteria population at time t
$c =$ an experimental constant

Calculate the population multiplication factor (P/P_0) at 2, 5, 10, 20 and 50 hours beyond the reference time, assuming $c=0.0289$. Include the first 10 terms of the series (i.e., let $n=9$).

3.22 Write an interactive BASIC program that will accept a string from the keyboard and will then display the following:

(a) On the first line, display the original string, followed by a numerical value indicating the number of characters in the string.

(b) On the second line, display a new string consisting of the original string in lower-case letters, followed by the original string in upper-case letters. Do not insert any blank spaces within this new string. (Example: if the original string is New York, then the new string will appear as new yorkNEW YORK.)

Chapter 4

Control Structures

In most of the BASIC programs that we have encountered so far, the statements were executed in the same order in which they appeared within the program. Each statement was executed once and once only. Programs of this type are unrealistically simple, since they do not include any logical control structures. In particular, such programs do not include tests to determine if various conditions are true or false; they do not require that one or more statements be executed on a selective basis, depending on the outcome of a true/false test; and they do not require that certain groups of statements be executed repeatedly. However, virtually all programs that are of some practical interest make extensive use of features such as these.

For example, many programs require that a logical test be carried out at some particular point within the program. An action will then be taken whose exact nature depends upon the outcome of the logical test. This is known as *conditional execution*.

Or, a program may require that a group of instructions be executed repeatedly, until some particular condition has been satisfied. This is known as *looping*. Sometimes the number of passes through the loop will be known in advance (*unconditional* looping). In other situations the looping action will continue indefinitely, until some logical condition has been satisfied (*conditional* looping).

And finally, there is a special kind of conditional execution in which one group of statements is selected from several available groups, depending on the value of an expression. This is sometimes called *selection*.

All of these operations can be carried out using the various control structures in BASIC. How this is accomplished will be the subject of this chapter. We will see that the use of these statements allows us to write programs that are much more interesting than those considered earlier.

4.1 RELATIONAL OPERATORS AND LOGICAL EXPRESSIONS

In order to carry out conditional branching operations in BASIC we must be able to express conditions of equality and inequality. To do so, we make use of the following *relational operators*:

Equal:	=
Not equal:	<>
Less than:	<
Less than or equal to:	<=
Greater than:	>
Greater than or equal to:	>=

These operators are used to compare numeric quantities (i.e., constants, numeric variables or numeric expressions) or strings, thus forming *logical expressions* that are either *true* or *false*. The *operands* within a logical expression must be of the same type; i.e., both must be numeric or both must be strings.

Example 4.1

Several logical expressions involving numeric quantities are shown below. Each logical expression will be either true or false, depending on the value assigned to the numeric variables.

```
X = 27
error <= abs(x1 - x2)
C < sqr(A + B)
profit > (gross - taxes)
FLAG <> CUTOFF
i >= j - 2
```

Thus, the first expression will be true if X has been assigned a value of 27; otherwise, the expression will be false. Similarly, the second expression will be true if the value assigned to error does not exceed the absolute value of the numeric expression x1 - x2, and so on. Notice that the second and third expressions involve the use of library functions.

Strings can be tested for equality or inequality, in much the same manner as numeric quantities. However, string expressions involving operators <, <=, > and >= refer to alphabetical ordering; that is, these operators are interpreted as "comes before" or "comes after" rather than "less than" or "greater than." The actual alphabetic ordering is determined by the system used to encode the characters (as, for example, the ASCII character set).

String comparisons are carried out on a character-by-character basis, from left to right. Upper-case characters precede lower-case characters. Blank spaces precede nonblank characters. If one string is shorter than the other and all of its characters are the same as the corresponding characters in the longer string, the shorter string is considered to precede the longer string. Thus, car precedes far, DOG precedes dog, cat precedes cats, and so on.

Example 4.2

Several logical expressions involving strings are presented below. Each logical expression will be either true or false, depending on the particular strings that are assigned to the string variables.

```
NAME$ = "Smith"
char$ <> "w"
target$ < city$
```

The first expression will be true if the string assigned to NAME$ is "Smith"; otherwise, the expression will be false. Similarly, the second expression will be true if the string assigned to char$ is not "w", and the last expression will be true if the string assigned to target$ comes earlier in the alphabet than the string assigned to city$. Thus, if target$ represents "Philadelphia" and city$ represents "Pittsburgh", the expression will be true.

4.2 LOGICAL OPERATORS

In addition to the relational operators, BASIC also contains the *logical operators* AND, OR and NOT. The first two operators (AND and OR) are used to combine logical expressions, thus forming more complex logical expressions. The last operator (NOT) is used to reverse (*negate*) the value of a logical expression (e.g., from true to false).

Some versions of BASIC (e.g., Microsoft BASIC) include the additional logical operators XOR (exclusive OR), EQV (equivalent) and IMP (implies). Briefly, when used to connect two logical expressions, XOR will result in a condition that is true only if one expression is true and the other is false; EQV will result in a condition that is true if both expressions have the same logical value (either both true or both false); and IMP will result in a true condition unless the first expression is true and the second is false. Since these three logical operands are not generally used in introductory level programs, we will not discuss them further in this text.

Example 4.3

Shown below are several logical expressions that make use of logical operators.

```
X = 27 AND NAME$ = "Smith"
X > 0 AND NAME$ <= "Smith"
C < sqr(A + B) OR FLAG <> CUTOFF
NOT(NAME$ = "Smith") AND (ACCOUNT$ = "CURRENT")
```

The first two logical expressions will be true only if *both* logical operands are true. Thus, the first logical expression will be true if the numeric value assigned to X is 27 and the string assigned to NAME$ is "Smith". (Note that the first logical operand involves numeric quantities whereas the second involves strings.) Similarly, the second logical expression will be true if the numeric value assigned to X exceeds zero and the string assigned to NAME$ precedes "Smith".

The third logical expression will be true if *either* logical operand is true; i.e., if the numeric value assigned to C is less than the square root of (A + B), or the value assigned to FLAG differs from the value assigned to CUTOFF.

The last logical expression involves both NOT and AND. In this case, the logical expression will be true only if the string assigned to NAME$ is *not* "Smith", and the string assigned to ACCOUNT$ *is* "CURRENT". Notice that the NOT operator has reversed (negated) the condition for which the first operand will be true.

The complete hierarchy of arithmetic, relational and logical operators is as follows:

	Operation	*Operator*
1.	Exponentiation	^
2.	Negation (i.e., preceding a numeric quantity with a minus sign)	—
3.	Multiplication and division	* /
4.	Integer division	\
5.	Integer remainder	MOD
6.	Addition and subtraction	+ —
7.	Relationals	= <> < <= > >=
8.	Logical NOT	NOT
9.	Logical AND	AND
10.	Logical OR	OR
11.	Logical XOR	XOR
12.	Logical EQV	EQV
13.	Logical IMP	IMP

Within a given hierarchical group, the operations are carried out from left to right. The natural hierarchy can be altered, however, by using parentheses, as described in Sec. 2.6. In particular, note that parentheses can be used with logical expressions, just as they are used with arithmetic expressions.

Example 4.4

Consider the logical expression

```
BALANCE > 0 OR FLAG = 1 AND ACCOUNT$ = "REGULAR"
```

This expression is equivalent to

```
BALANCE > 0 OR (FLAG = 1 AND ACCOUNT$ = "REGULAR")
```

Thus, the expression will be true if either BALANCE has been assigned a value greater than 0, or FLAG has been assigned a value of 1 and ACCOUNT$ has been assigned the string "REGULAR".

On the other hand, the logical expression

```
(BALANCE > 0 OR FLAG = 1) AND ACCOUNT$ = "REGULAR"
```

has a different interpretation. Now the expression will be true only if either BALANCE has been assigned a value greater than 0 or FLAG has been assigned a value of 1, and in addition, ACCOUNT$ has been assigned the string "REGULAR".

Note that the first logical expression can be satisfied simply if BALANCE > 0 is true. However, the second logical expression requires that *two* conditions be true; ACCOUNT$ = "REGULAR" must be true, and one or both of the remaining conditions must also be true (either BALANCE > 0 or FLAG = 1).

4.3 CONDITIONAL EXECUTION: THE IF - THEN STATEMENT

The IF - THEN statement is used to execute a single statement on a conditional basis. The statement is written as

IF *logical expression* THEN *executable statement*

The *executable statement* will be executed only if the *logical expression* is true. Otherwise, the statement following IF - THEN will be executed next.

Example 4.5

A typical situation utilizing an IF - THEN statement is shown below.

```
IF x < 0 THEN LET x = 0
PRINT x
```

This example causes negative values of x to be set to zero prior to printing. Note that the LET statement is executed only if the logical expression x < 0 is true.

Here is another typical IF - THEN statement.

```
IF x < 0 THEN PRINT x
```

In this situation the value of x will be printed only if it is negative (i.e., the PRINT statement will be executed only if the logical expression x < 0 is true).

The IF - THEN statement can also be used to execute *multiple* statements conditionally. This is a special type of IF - THEN - ELSE block, as described below.

4.4 CONDITIONAL EXECUTION: IF - THEN - ELSE BLOCKS

An IF - THEN - ELSE block permits one of two different groups of executable statements to be executed, depending on the outcome of a logical test. Thus, it permits a much broader form of conditional execution than is available with a single IF - THEN statement. (This is a relatively new feature in BASIC. It is supported by the 1987 ANSI standard, but it is not available in most older versions of the language.)

In general terms, an IF - THEN - ELSE block is written as

```
IF logical expression THEN
     . . . . . . . . .
     executable statements
     . . . . . . . . .
ELSE
     . . . . . . . . .
     executable statements
     . . . . . . . . .
END IF
```

If the *logical expression* is true, then the first group of *executable statements* will be executed. Otherwise, the second group of *executable statements* will be executed. Thus, one group of executable statements will always be executed. Note that IF - THEN, ELSE and END IF are separate statements that are used together to create a complete IF - THEN - ELSE block.

The executable statements are usually indented with respect to the IF - THEN, ELSE and END IF statements, so that the structure of the block is readily identifiable. This is not a rigid syntactical requirement, but it is considered to be good programming practice and is strongly encouraged.

Example 4.6

A typical IF - THEN - ELSE block is shown below. This block allows us to calculate either the area of a circle or the area of a rectangle, depending on the string that is assigned to the variable `form$`.

```
IF (form$ = "circle") THEN          'circle
   INPUT radius
   LET area = 3.141593 * radius ^ 2
ELSE                                 'rectangle
   INPUT length, width
   LET area = length * width
END IF
PRINT "Area ="; area
```

If the logical expression `form$ = "circle"` is true, then the *first* group of executable statements (the first two indented lines) will be executed, followed by the PRINT statement at the end of the IF - THEN - END block. If the logical expression is false, however, the *second* group of executable statements (the indented lines that follow ELSE) will be executed, followed by the PRINT statement.

Note that the indentation of the executable statements causes the entire IF - THEN - ELSE structure to be readily discernable. Thus, it is easy to identify which group of statements corresponds to IF - THEN and which corresponds to ELSE.

Though IF - THEN - ELSE blocks usually include several executable statements after the IF - THEN and the ELSE statements, the appearance of a single executable statement is also common. The following example illustrates a typical application.

Example 4.7

Consider the following IF - THEN - ELSE block.

```
IF (status$ = "single") THEN
    LET tax = 0.2 * pay
ELSE
    LET tax = 0.14 * pay
END IF
PRINT "Tax ="; tax
```

If the logical expression `status$ = "single"` is true, then the *first* LET statement will be executed, followed by the PRINT statement (the last statement). If the logical expression is false, however, the *second* LET statement will be executed, followed by the PRINT statement.

The inclusion of the ELSE statement is optional in a conditional block. Without the ELSE statement, we have an IF - THEN block that allows a single group of statements to be executed conditionally. This construct is an extension of the IF - THEN statement discussed in the last section.

Example 4.8

The following IF - THEN block permits a single group of statements to be executed conditionally.

```
IF income <= 14000 THEN
    LET tax = 0.2 * pay
    LET net = pay - tax
    PRINT "Gross earnings ="; pay, "Taxes ="; tax, "Net income ="; net
END IF
```

The executable statements (the indented statements) will be executed only if the condition `income <= 14000` is true.

A more general form of the IF - THEN - ELSE block can be written as

```
IF logical expression 1 THEN
    . . . . . . . .
    executable statements
    . . . . . . . .
ELSEIF logical expression 2 THEN
    . . . . . . . .
    executable statements
    . . . . . . . .
repeated ELSEIF clauses
    . . . . . . . .
ELSE
    . . . . . . . .
    executable statements
    . . . . . . . .
END IF
```

In this form, IF - THEN clauses are embedded within prior ELSE clauses. Hence, we can construct conditional execution blocks that involve complex logical conditions.

Example 4.9 Roots of a Quadratic Equation

In Example 3.4 we saw that the roots of the quadratic equation $ax^2 + bx + c = 0$ can be determined using the formulas

$$x_1 = \frac{-b + (b^2 - 4ac)^{1/2}}{2a}$$

$$x_2 = \frac{-b - (b^2 - 4ac)^{1/2}}{2a}$$

provided the quantity $b^2 - 4ac$ is positive. Let us now extend this problem to accommodate all values of $b^2 - 4ac$. If $b^2 - 4ac$ is zero, we have a single (repeated) real root. Hence,

$$x = -b / 2a$$

If $b^2 - 4ac$ is negative, we have two complex roots. In this case,

$$x_1 = \frac{-b + (4ac - b^2)^{1/2} i}{2a}$$

$$x_2 = \frac{-b - (4ac - b^2)^{1/2} i}{2a}$$

where i represents the *imaginary number* $(-1)^{1/2}$.

The computation proceeds in accordance with the following outline.

1. Enter the values for a, b and c interactively, in response to program-generated prompts.

    (a) Generate (PRINT) a prompt for a, then INPUT a value for a.

    (b) Generate (PRINT) a prompt for b, then INPUT a value for b.

    (c) Generate (PRINT) a prompt for c, then INPUT a value for c.

2. Determine the value of $(b^2 - 4ac)$.

3. Calculate values for x_1 and x_2 using the following formulas:

    (a) IF $(b^2 - 4ac) > 0$ THEN

            LET $root = (b^2 - 4ac)^{1/2}$

            LET $x_1 = (-b + root) / 2a$

            LET $x_2 = (-b - root) / 2a$

(b) IF $(b^2 - 4ac) = 0$ THEN

   LET $x = -b/2a$

(c) IF $(b^2 - 4ac) < 0$ THEN

   LET $real = -b/2a$

   LET $imag = (4ac - b^2)^{1/2}/2a$

   LET $x_1 = real + imag\ i$

   LET $x_2 = real - imag\ i$

4. Display (PRINT) the calculated roots, with appropriate labels.

5. END the program execution.

It is now a simple matter to write a BASIC program that corresponds to the above outline. An IF - THEN - ELSE block can be used to execute the different conditions described in step 3. A complete BASIC program is shown below.

```
REM CALCULATE THE ROOTS OF A QUADRATIC EQUATION
PRINT "a = ";
INPUT a
PRINT "b = ";
INPUT b
PRINT "c = ";
INPUT c
LET d = (b ^ 2 - 4 * a * c)
IF d > 0 THEN                              'real roots
   LET x1 = (-b + SQR(d)) / (2 * a)
   LET x2 = (-b - SQR(d)) / (2 * a)
   PRINT "Real roots: x1 ="; x1; "     x2 ="; x2
ELSEIF d = 0 THEN                          'repeated root
   LET x = -b / (2 * a)
   PRINT "Repeated root: x ="; x
ELSE                                       'complex roots
   LET real = -b / (2 * a)
   LET imag = SQR(-d) / (2 * a)
   PRINT "Complex roots: x1 ="; real; "+"; imag; "i";
   PRINT "     x2 ="; real; "-"; imag; "i"
END IF
END
```

The dialog resulting from a typical program execution is shown below. Three sets of data are shown, illustrating the computation of real roots, a repeated real root and complex roots. The user's responses are underlined for clarity.

```
a = ? 2
b = ? 5
c = ? 3
Real roots: x1 =-1      x2 =-1.5
```

```
a = ? 1
b = ? 2
c = ? 1
Repeated root: x =-1

a = ? 1
b = ? 2
c = ? 3
Complex roots: x1 =-1 + 1.414214 i      x2 =-1 - 1.414214 i
```

We will see additional applications of IF - THEN and IF - THEN - ELSE blocks, in conjunction with other BASIC control structures, in the remaining sections of this chapter.

4.5 UNCONDITIONAL LOOPING: FOR - NEXT STRUCTURES

The FOR - NEXT structure is a block of statements that is used to carry out unconditional looping; that is, to execute a sequence of statements some predetermined number of times. The structure begins with a FOR - TO statement and ends with a NEXT statement. In between are the statements to be executed.

In its simplest form, a FOR - NEXT structure is written as

> FOR *index* = *value1* TO *value2*
> . . . .
> *executable statements*
> . . . .
> NEXT *index*

The FOR - TO statement specifies the number of passes through the loop. Within this statement, *index* is a variable whose value begins with *value1*, increases by 1 each time the loop is executed, until it reaches *value2*. Note that the value of *index* will be *value2* during the last pass through the loop.

The NEXT statement identifies the end of the structure. It consists simply of the keyword NEXT, followed by the *index*. The *index* appearing in the FOR - TO and the NEXT statements must be the same. (Some versions of BASIC allow the *index* to be omitted from the NEXT statement in single FOR - NEXT loops, though this is considered poor programming practice.)

The *executable statements* refer to one or more consecutive statements that are executed during each pass through the loop. These statements are usually indented, so that the structure can easily be identified. The indentation is not required, though it is considered good programming practice.

Example 4.10

An unconditional loop structure is shown below.

```
FOR I = 1 TO 10
     PRINT I;
NEXT I
```

This structure will result in 10 passes through the loop. During the first pass, I will be assigned a value of 1. I will then increase by 1 during each successive pass through the loop, until it has reached its final value of 10 during the last pass. Hence, the structure will generate a single line of output containing the integer values 1 through 10; i.e.,

```
1   2   3   4   5   6   7   8   9   10
```

Note the indentation of the PRINT statement.

A more general form of the FOR - NEXT structure can be written as

```
FOR index = value1 TO value2 STEP value3
    . . . . . . . .
    executable statements
    . . . . . . . .
NEXT index
```

Within the FOR - TO statement, *value3* determines the amount by which *value1* changes from one pass to the next. This quantity need not be restricted to an integer, and it can be either positive or negative. If *value3* is negative, then *value1* must be greater than *value2* (because the value assigned to *index* will *decrease* during each successive pass through the loop). Note that *value3* is understood to equal 1 if it is not shown explicitly (i.e., if the STEP clause is omitted).

Example 4.11

The unconditional loop structure

```
FOR count = 2.5 TO -1 STEP -0.5
    PRINT count;
NEXT count
```

will cause count to take on the values 2.5, 2.0, 1.5, . . ., 0.0, -0.5, -1.0. Hence, the output generated by the loop will appear as

```
2.5  2  1.5  1  .5  0 -.5 -1
```

This structure will generate a total of 8 passes through the loop.

Use of the FOR - NEXT structure goes back to the very earliest versions of BASIC. It remains one of the most widely used control structures. The FOR - NEXT structure is generally used when the number of passes through the loop is known in advance.

Example 4.12 Averaging a List of Numbers

Suppose we wish to calculate the average of a list of *n* numbers. We can do this by utilizing a partial sum that is initially set equal to zero and then updated as each new number is read into the computer. Thus, the problem lends itself to the use of a FOR - NEXT structure.

The calculations will be carried out in the following manner.

1. Read in a value for the variable n.

2. Assign an initial value of 0 to the numeric variable sum.

3. Carry out the following steps repeatedly, for I ranging from 1 to n (the variable I is an index for the FOR - NEXT structure).

(a) Enter the ith value within the list. Represent this value by the variable X.

(b) Add the value of X to the current value of sum.

4. After all n passes have been completed, sum will represent the sum of the n values. Hence, divide the value of sum by n to obtain the desired average.

5. Display the calculated value for the average.

A complete BASIC program is shown below. The data input is carried out interactively, using prompts for all numerical values.

```
REM CALCULATE THE AVERAGE OF A LIST OF N NUMBERS
PRINT "How many numbers";          'specify the size of the list
INPUT n
LET sum = 0
FOR I = 1 TO n                     'loop - calculate the sum of the X's
   PRINT "i ="; I; "     X = ";
   INPUT X
   LET sum = sum + X
NEXT I
LET average = sum / n              'calculate the average value
PRINT
PRINT "Average ="; average         'display the results
END
```

The empty PRINT statement near the end of the program generates a blank line separating the interactive data input from the output (see below). Notice the indentation, which allows the FOR - NEXT structure to be readily identified. Also, note the use of comments to identify the major portions of the program.

Now suppose the program is used to process the following six values: 10, 11, 12, 13, 14, 15. Execution of the program results in the following interactive dialog. The user's responses are underlined.

```
How many numbers? 6
i = 1        X = ?  10
i = 2        X = ?  11
i = 3        X = ?  12
i = 4        X = ?  13
i = 5        X = ?  14
i = 6        X = ?  15

Average = 12.5
```

The following rules apply to FOR - NEXT loops.

1. The index variable can appear within a statement inside the loop, but its value cannot be altered.

2. If *value1* and *value2* are equal and *value3* is nonzero, the loop will be executed once.

3. The loop will not be executed at all under any of the following conditions:

   (a) *value1* and *value2* are equal, and *value3* is zero.

(b) *value1* is greater than *value2*, and *value3* is positive.

(c) *value1* is less than *value2*, and *value3* is negative.

4. Control can be transferred out of a loop, but not in (see below).

Most newer versions of BASIC include an EXIT FOR statement. This statement permits a transfer out of a FOR - NEXT loop if some particular condition is satisfied. For example, we may wish to jump out of a loop if an error or a stopping condition is detected during the execution of the loop.

The EXIT FOR statement is generally embedded in an IF - THEN structure. When the EXIT FOR statement is encountered during program execution, control is immediately transferred out of the FOR - NEXT loop, to the first executable statement following NEXT.

Example 4.13 Averaging a List of Positive Numbers using FOR - NEXT

Let us now modify the program shown in Example 4.12 so that it averages only positive numbers. To do so, we will set up a FOR - NEXT loop that will make 10,000 passes, anticipating that this will be much greater than the actual number of passes required. We will include a test for a nonpositive number within the FOR - NEXT loop. If a nonpositive value is detected, control will be transferred out of the loop and the positive numbers entered previously will be averaged.

Here is the complete BASIC program. This program assumes that the first value entered is positive.

```
REM CALCULATE THE AVERAGE OF A LIST OF POSITIVE NUMBERS
PRINT "To STOP, enter zero"        'indicate a stopping condition
LET sum = 0
FOR I = 1 TO 10000                 'loop - calculate the sum of the X's
   PRINT "i ="; I; "      X = ";
   INPUT X
   IF X <= 0 THEN EXIT FOR         'test for loop exit
   LET sum = sum + X
NEXT I
LET average = sum / (I - 1)        'calculate the average value
PRINT
PRINT "Average ="; average         'display the results
END
```

Notice the IF - THEN statement, which includes an embedded EXIT FOR statement. Also, notice that the calculated average (LET average = . . .) is now based upon the *previous* value of the index (I - 1). (Use of the *current* value would include the nonpositive value of X, entered as a stopping condition).

Many older versions of BASIC do not support the EXIT FOR statement. If this is the case the above strategy can still be used, but the IF - THEN statement must be modified to read

```
160    IF X <= 0 THEN GOTO 190       'test for loop exit
```

or simply

```
160    IF X <= 0 THEN 190            'test for loop exit
```

Because these versions of the IF - THEN statement require line numbers, they are less desirable than the use of EXIT FOR. We will discuss the use of line-oriented control statements in Sec. 4.10.

Execution of this program will result in an interactive dialog similar to that shown in Example 4.12. A typical session is presented below.

```
To STOP, enter zero
i = 1       X = ? 10
i = 2       X = ? 11
i = 3       X = ? 12
i = 4       X = ? 13
i = 5       X = ? 14
i = 6       X = ? 15
i = 7       X = ? 0

Average = 12.5
```

Finally, you should understand that the use of a DO - LOOP structure is preferable to *any* form of FOR - NEXT loop for this type of application. We will discuss DO - LOOP structures in the next section.

4.6 CONDITIONAL LOOPING: DO - LOOP STRUCTURES

Newer versions of BASIC that are based upon the 1987 ANSI standard include DO - LOOP structures. Such structures permit both conditional and unconditional looping to be carried out (though unconditional looping is treated as a form of conditional looping).

A DO - LOOP structure always begins with a DO statement and ends with a LOOP statement. However, there are four different ways to write a DO - LOOP structure. Two of the forms require that a logical expression appear in the DO statement (i.e., at the beginning of the block); the other two forms require that the logical expression appear in the LOOP statement (at the end of the block).

The general forms of the DO - LOOP structure are shown below.

First form:

```
DO WHILE logical expression
    . . . . . . . .
    executable statements
    . . . . . . . .
LOOP
```

Second form:

```
DO UNTIL  logical expression
    . . . . . . . .
    executable statements
    . . . . . . . .
LOOP
```

Third form:

```
DO
    . . . . . . . .
    executable statements
    . . . . . . . .
LOOP WHILE logical expression
```

Fourth form:

```
DO
    . . . . . . . .
    executable statements
    . . . . . . . .
LOOP UNTIL logical expression
```

The first form continues to loop as long as the *logical expression* is true, whereas the second form continues to loop as long as the *logical expression* is *not* true (until the *logical expression* becomes true). Similarly, the third form continues to loop as long as the *logical expression* is true, whereas the fourth form continues to loop as long as the *logical expression* is *not* true.

Note that there is a fundamental difference between the first two forms and the last two forms of the DO - LOOP block. In the first two forms, the logical test is made at the *beginning* of each pass through the loop; hence, it is possible that there will not be *any* passes made through the loop, if the indicated logical condition is not satisfied. In the last two forms, however, the logical test is not made until the *end* of each pass; therefore, at least one pass through the loop will always be carried out.

Example 4.14

Consider the following two DO - LOOP structures.

```
    LET flag$ = "False"                    LET flag$ = "False"
    . . . . . . . . .                      . . . . . . . . .
    DO WHILE flag$ = "True"                DO
        . . . . . . . .                        . . . . . . . .
    LOOP                                   LOOP WHILE flag$ = "True"
```

The left loop will not execute at all, because the logical test at the beginning of the loop structure is false. The right loop will execute once, however, because the logical test is not carried out until the end of the first pass through the loop. Moreover, if the string `"True"` is assigned to `flag$` during this first pass through the loop, then the execution will continue indefinitely, until `flag$` is reassigned.

Note that a DO - LOOP structure does not involve a formal index. Thus, the programmer must provide the logic for altering the value of the *logical expression* within the loop. Typically, an initial assignment is made before entering the loop structure. The logical expression is then altered during each pass through the loop.

Example 4.15

Shown below is a conditional loop structure that is comparable to the unconditional loop in Example 4.10.

```
LET count = 1
DO WHILE count <= 10
    PRINT count;
    LET count = count + 1
LOOP
```

This structure will result in 10 passes through the loop. Note that `count` is assigned a value of 1 before entering the loop. The value of `count` is then incremented by 1 during each pass through the loop. Once the value of `count` exceeds 10, the execution will cease.

The resulting output is the same as that shown in Example 4.10:

```
    1  2  3  4  5  6  7  8  9  10
```

Here is another way accomplish the same thing.

```
LET count = 1
DO
    PRINT count;
    LET count = count + 1
LOOP WHILE count <= 10
```

If we choose to use an UNTIL clause rather than a WHILE clause, we can write the control structure in either of the following ways.

```
LET count = 1                           LET count = 1
DO UNTIL count > 10                     DO
    PRINT count;                            PRINT count;
    LET count = count + 1                   LET count = count + 1
LOOP                                    LOOP UNTIL count > 10
```

Notice that the logical expression in these two structures (count > 10) is the opposite of the logical expression in the first two structures (count <= 10).

Control can be transferred out of a DO - LOOP block using the EXIT DO statement. This statement is analogous to EXIT FOR, which is used with FOR - NEXT blocks. Thus, when an EXIT DO statement is encountered during program execution, control is transferred out of the DO - LOOP block, to the first executable statement following LOOP.

Example 4.16 Averaging a List of Positive Numbers using DO - LOOP

Here is another version of the program shown in Example 4.13, for averaging a list of positive numbers. We now use a DO - LOOP structure to carry out the looping action. This is a better approach than the use of a FOR - NEXT block, since this problem requires a conditional looping structure.

A complete BASIC program is shown below. As before, we assume that the first value entered into the computer is positive.

```
REM CALCULATE THE AVERAGE OF A LIST OF POSITIVE NUMBERS
PRINT "To STOP, enter zero"          'indicate a stopping condition
LET sum = 0
LET I = 1
PRINT "i ="; I; "     X = ";
INPUT X
DO UNTIL X <= 0                      'loop - calculate the sum of the X's
    LET sum = sum + X
    LET I = I + 1
    PRINT "i ="; I; "     X = ";
    INPUT X
LOOP
LET average = sum / (I - 1)          'calculate the average value
PRINT
PRINT "Average ="; average           'display the results
END
```

When executed, this program will behave in the same manner as that shown in Example 4.13.

Now let us modify this program so that the looping action will stop once the value of sum equals or exceeds 100. This can be accomplished through the use of an EXIT DO statement, embedded within an IF - THEN statement. A complete program is shown below.

```
REM CALCULATE THE AVERAGE OF A LIST OF POSITIVE NUMBERS
PRINT "To STOP, enter zero"        'indicate a stopping condition
LET sum = 0
LET I = 1
PRINT "i ="; I; "     X = ";
INPUT X
DO UNTIL X = 0                      'loop - calculate the sum of the X's
   LET sum = sum + X
   LET I = I + 1
   IF sum >= 100 THEN EXIT DO       'max value exceeded - end loop
   PRINT "i ="; I; "     X = ";
   INPUT X
LOOP
LET average = sum / (I - 1)         'calculate the average value
PRINT
PRINT "Average ="; average          'display the results
END
```

If the most recent value of sum is equal to or greater than 100, the EXIT DO statement transfers control out of the DO - LOOP block, to the following LET statement.

A sample interactive session is shown below. The user's responses are underlined.

```
To STOP, enter zero
i = 1      X = 30
i = 2      X = 40
i = 3      X = 50
i = 4      X = 0

Average = 40
```

Notice that the program stopped automatically, without the user having entered 0. The reason, of course, is that the value of sum exceeded 100 (sum = 120) during the third pass through the loop. The calculated average is correct, based upon the first three values.

4.7 CONDITIONAL LOOPING: WHILE - WEND STRUCTURES

Some versions of BASIC support WHILE - WEND structures rather than (or in addition to) DO - LOOP structures. This structure permits conditional looping to be carried out, though it is not supported by the 1987 ANSI standard. The structure begins with the WHILE statement (analogous to DO WHILE), and ends with the WEND statement (analogous to LOOP).

The general form of a WHILE - WEND structure is

```
WHILE logical expression
   . . . . . . . .
   executable statements
   . . . . . . . .
WEND
```

The loop created by the WHILE - WEND structure continues to execute as long as the *logical expression* is true. Thus, WHILE - WEND is analogous to a DO WHILE - LOOP structure. Note that the logical expression is tested at the beginning of each pass through the loop.

The WHILE - WEND structure, like the DO - LOOP structure, does not involve a formal index. Therefore the programmer must assign an initial value to the *logical expression* before entering the loop. This value will then be altered within the loop, in accordance with the program logic.

Example 4.17 Averaging a List of Positive Numbers using WHILE - WEND

Here is another version of the first program shown in Example 4.16. This program uses a WHILE - WEND structure rather than the DO - LOOP structure shown earlier. (Note that most versions of BASIC that support WHILE - WEND require line numbers; hence, line numbers are included below.)

```
100 REM CALCULATE THE AVERAGE OF A LIST OF POSITIVE NUMBERS
110 PRINT "To STOP, enter zero"        'indicate a stopping condition
120 LET sum = 0
130 LET I = 1
140 PRINT "i ="; I; "     X = ";
150 INPUT X
160 WHILE X > 0                        'loop - calculate the sum of the X's
170     LET sum = sum + X
180     LET I = I + 1
190     PRINT "i ="; I; "     X = ";
200     INPUT X
210 WEND
220 LET average = sum / (I - 1)        'calculate the average value
230 PRINT
240 PRINT "Average ="; average         'display the results
250 END
```

This program will generate the same interactive dialog and the same output as the program shown in Example 4.13 and the first program in Example 4.16.

Remember that many versions of BASIC do not support WHILE - WEND. Hence, this example may have less generality than the corresponding programs shown earlier.

4.8 NESTED CONTROL STRUCTURES

Control structures can be *nested* (i.e., embedded) one within another. The inner and outer control structures need not be the same. For example, an IF - THEN block can be nesteed within a FOR - NEXT structure (see Example 4.13) or a DO - LOOP structure. Similarly, a FOR - NEXT structure can be nested within a DO - LOOP structure or vice versa. Various other combinations are possible, as required by the program logic.

When nesting one control structure within another, it is essential that there be no overlap; i.e., the inner structure must be contained entirely within the outer structure. Control can be transferred from an inner structure to an outer structure or beyond. However, control cannot be transferred into any structure from a point outside of that structure (except, of course, through a normal entry point; e.g., a FOR - TO statement, in the case of a FOR - NEXT block).

Example 4.18 Solution of an Algebraic Equation

This example illustrates a commonly used technique for solving algebraic equations on a computer. The program makes use of nested IF - THEN - ELSE blocks within a DO - LOOP structure.

To see how the method works, consider the equation

$$x^5 + 3x^2 - 10 = 0$$

This equation cannot be rearranged to yield an exact solution for x. We can, however, determine the solution by a repeated trial-and-error procedure (called an *iterative* procedure) that successively refines an initially crude guess.

We begin by rearranging the equation into the form

$$x = (10 - 3x^2)^{1/5}$$

We will then guess a value for x, substitute this value into the right-hand side of the rearranged equation, and thus calculate a new value for x. If this new value is equal (or very close to) to the guess, we will have obtained a solution to the equation. Otherwise, this new value will be substituted into the right-hand side and still another value obtained for x, and so on. This procedure will continue until either the successive values of x have become sufficiently close (i.e., until the computation has *converged*), or until a specified number of iterations has been exceeded. This last condition prevents the computation from continuing indefinitely if the calculated results do not converge.

Suppose, for example, we choose an initial value of $x = 1.0$. Substituting this value into the right-hand side of the equation, we obtain

$$x = [10 - 3(1.0)^2]^{0.2} = 1.47577$$

We then substitute this new value of x into the equation, resulting in

$$x = [10 - 3(1.47577)^2]^{0.2} = 1.28225$$

Continuing this procedure, we obtain

$$x = [10 - 3(1.28225)^2]^{0.2} = 1.38344$$

$$x = [10 - 3(1.38344)^2]^{0.2} = 1.33613$$

and so on. Notice that the successive values of x appear to be converging to some final answer.

The success of the method depends on the value chosen for the initial guess. If this value is too large in magnitude, the quantity in brackets will be negative; hence, it cannot be raised to a fractional power. We will therefore test for a negative value of $(10 - 3x^2)$ whenever we substitute a new value of x into the right-hand side of the equation.

In order to write a program outline, let us define the following symbols.

count = an iteration counter (count will increase by 1 at each successive iteration)

guess = the value of x substituted into the right-hand side of the equation

x = the newly calculated value of x

test = the quantity $(10 - 3x^2)$

diff = the absolute difference between x and guess

flag$ = a string variable that signifies whether or not to continue the iteration

We will continue the computation until one of the following conditions is satisfied.

1. The variable test takes on a negative value, in which case the computation cannot continue.

2. The value of diff becomes less than or equal to 0.00001, in which case the computation has converged to a satisfactory solution.

3. Fifty iterations have been completed.

We will monitor the progress of the computation by displaying the calculated value of x during each pass through the loop.

We can now write the following detailed outline.

1. Assign initial values to count and flag$ (count = 1 and flag$ = "true").

2. Enter a value for the initial guess.

3. Carry out the following looping action until flag$ becomes false.

    (a) Calculate a new value for test.

    (b) Examine the value of test. If its value is negative, the computation cannot proceed. Hence, display an appropriate error message (e.g., NUMBERS OUT OF RANGE) and assign "false" to flag$ (indicating the last pass through the loop).

    (c) If the current value of test is nonnegative, calculate a new value for x and display the current values of count and x. Then evaluate diff, which is the magnitude of the difference between x and guess.

        (i)   If the value of diff is less than or equal to 0.00001, the computation has converged to a final solution. Hence, display the final values for x and count and assign "false" to flag$ (indicating the last pass through the loop).

        (ii) If the value of diff exceeds 0.00001, then additional passes will be required. Hence, assign the current value of x to guess and increase the value of count by 1.

        (iii) If the current value of count exceeds 50 and diff still exceeds 0.00001, display an error message (e.g., CONVERGENCE NOT OBTAINED) and assign "false" to flag$, indicating the last pass through the loop. Otherwise, proceed with another pass through the loop.

Step 3 will be carried out with a DO - LOOP UNTIL structure. (A WHILE - WEND or a FOR - NEXT structure could also be used.) Within this structure, steps 3(b) and 3(c) will be implemented as an IF - THEN - ELSE block. Within this block, steps (i) and (ii) will be carried out with an embedded IF - THEN - ELSE block. And finally, step (iii) will be implemented as another IF - THEN - ELSE block embedded within the last IF - THEN - ELSE block. Thus, the use of embedded IF - THEN - ELSE blocks enables a complex set of tests to be carried out in a logical, structured manner.

A complete BASIC program is shown on the next page. Beneath the program we see what happens when the program is executed. First, we see the output resulting from an initial guess of x = 1. In this case, the computation converges to a value of x = 1.351955 after 16 iterations. Next, we see what happens when the initial guess (x = 40) is too far from the correct solution. Now the computation terminates with the error message NUMBERS OUT OF RANGE. (Since there are no intermediate results shown, we conclude that the error message was generated at the very onset of the computation, before the first pass through the DO -LOOP structure had been completed).

```
REM ROOTS OF AN ALGEBRAIC EQUATION USING AN ITERATIVE PROCEDURE
LET count = 1
LET flag$ = "true"
PRINT "Initial guess = ";                'prompt for initial guess
INPUT guess
DO                                        'begin iterative loop
    LET test = 10 - 3 * guess ^ 2
    IF (test < 0) THEN                    'test for negative value
        PRINT "NUMBERS OUT OF RANGE"
        LET flag$ = "false"
    ELSE                                  'calculate new value
        LET x = test ^ .2
        PRINT "Iteration number: "; count, "x ="; x
        LET diff = ABS(x - guess)
        IF (diff <= .00001) THEN          'solution has converged
            PRINT
            PRINT "root ="; x, "No. of iterations ="; count
            LET flag$ = "false"
        ELSE                              'solution not converged
            LET count = count + 1
            IF count > 50 THEN            'too many iterations
                PRINT "CONVERGENCE NOT OBTAINED AFTER 50 ITERATIONS"
                LET flag$ = "false"
            ELSE                          'prepare for next iteration
                LET guess = x
            END IF
        END IF
    END IF
LOOP UNTIL (flag$ = "false")              'end iterative loop
END
```

```
Initial guess = ? 1
Iteration number:   1          x = 1.475773
Iteration number:   2          x = 1.28225
Iteration number:   3          x = 1.383435
Iteration number:   4          x = 1.336127
Iteration number:   5          x = 1.359515
Iteration number:   6          x = 1.348257
Iteration number:   7          x = 1.353747
Iteration number:   8          x = 1.351086
Iteration number:   9          x = 1.35238
Iteration number:  10          x = 1.351752
Iteration number:  11          x = 1.352057
Iteration number:  12          x = 1.351909
Iteration number:  13          x = 1.351981
Iteration number:  14          x = 1.351946
Iteration number:  15          x = 1.351963
Iteration number:  16          x = 1.351955

root = 1.351955          No. of iterations = 16
```

```
Initial guess = ? 40
NUMBERS OUT OF RANGE
```

Now suppose the program is changed so that only 10 iterations are permitted. The following changes are required.

```
IF count > 10 THEN
    PRINT "CONVERGENCE NOT OBTAINED AFTER 10 ITERATIONS"
```

Execution of the program will now result in the following output.

```
Initial guess = ? 1
CONVERGENCE NOT OBTAINED AFTER 10 ITERATIONS
```

One FOR - NEXT structure can be nested within another. In such situations, each FOR - NEXT structure must be controlled by a different index. The current values of the indices can be utilized if necessary, as required by the program logic.

Example 4.19 Generation of Fibonacci Numbers and Search for Primes

The Fibonacci numbers are members of an interesting sequence in which each number is equal to the sum of the previous two numbers. In other words,

$$F_i = F_{i-1} + F_{i-2}$$

where F_i refers to the ith Fibonacci number. The first two Fibonacci numbers are defined to equal 1; that is,

$$F_1 = 1$$
$$F_2 = 1$$

Hence,

$$F_3 = F_2 + F_1 = 1 + 1 = 2$$
$$F_4 = F_3 + F_2 = 2 + 1 = 3$$
$$F_5 = F_4 + F_3 = 3 + 2 = 5$$

and so on.

All of the Fibonacci numbers are positive integer quantities and some of them are *primes*. A prime number is a positive integer that is evenly divisible (without a remainder) only by 1 or by itself. For example, 5 is a prime number because it can be divided evenly only by 1 or 5. On the other hand, 8 is not a prime because 8 is divisible by 2 and 4 as well as by 1 and 8.

It is very easy to calculate the first n Fibonacci numbers using the above equations. However, the procedure for determining whether or not a number is prime requires some explanation.

Suppose we want to determine if a given integer whose value is greater than 2 can be divided evenly by a smaller integer. Let us call the given integer F and the divisor D. The procedure is to calculate a quotient, Q, as

```
Q = F / D
```

We then calculate a *truncated* quotient, QINT, as

```
QINT = INT(Q)
```

Recall that INT is a library function that returns the largest integer that does not exceed Q (see Table 2.2 in Sec. 2.14). Thus, if Q has a value of 5.3, then QINT will have a value of 5.

If Q and QINT have the same value, then F is evenly divisible by D. Furthermore, if F is evenly divisible by *any* value of D, from D = 2 to D = INT(SQR(F)), then F cannot be a prime. Hence, F will be a prime number *only if* Q *and* QINT *have different values* for D = 2, 3, . . ., INT(SQR(F)).

We will write a program that will calculate the first *n* Fibonacci numbers, where *n* is assumed to be some integer greater than 5. The first 5 Fibonacci numbers (1, 1, 2, 3 and 5) are all primes. Hence, we need not test these values. We will therefore begin testing for primes with *i* = 6.

Let us refer to F as the given Fibonacci number (i.e., F_i), F1 as the previous Fibonacci number (F_{i-1}) and F2 as the second previous Fibonacci number (F_{i-2}). Also, let us refer to *i* and *n* as I and N, respectively. We can now write a program outline for generating and displaying the first *n* Fibonacci numbers as follows.

1. Enter a value for N.

2. Set F1 and F2 equal to 1.

3. Display the values of F1 and F2, identifying each as a prime.

4. Carry out the following calculations for I = 3, 4, and 5.

    (*a*) Calculate a value for F using the equation

    ```
    F = F1 + F2
    ```

    (*b*) Display the values of I and F, identifying F as a prime.

5. Carry out the following calculations for I = 6, 7, . . ., N.

    (*a*) Calculate a value for F using the equation

    ```
    F = F1 + F2
    ```

    (*b*) Do the following for D = 2, 3, . . ., ROOT, where ROOT is the largest integer that does not exceed SQR(F). (This is the test for a prime number.)

        (*i*) Calculate values for Q and QINT, and test to see if they are equal.

        (*ii*) If Q and QINT are equal for any value of D, then F cannot be a prime number. Hence, jump out of the inner loop and proceed directly to step 5(*c*) below.

    (*c*) Display the values of I and F, identifying F as a prime if Q and QINT are not equal, and continue below.

    (*d*) Update F1 and F2 (i.e., assign the current value of F1 to F2, then assign the current value of F to F1), in preparation for calculating the next Fibonacci number (i.e., a new value for F).

6. Terminate the computation when all N Fibonacci numbers have been determined.

Steps 4 and 5 can be carried out using FOR - NEXT loops. Also, step 5(*b*) can be carried out with an embedded FOR - NEXT loop, with an EXIT FOR statement that transfers control out of the inner loop in the event that a nonprime number has been detected. The inner loop will, of course, require a separate index.

A complete BASIC program corresponding to the above outline is shown below. Note that an IF - THEN - ELSE block is embedded in the outer loop, along with the inner loop. The indentation helps to show where these embedded structures begin and end.

```
REM GENERATION OF FIBONACCI NUMBERS AND SEARCH FOR PRIMES (N > 5)
PRINT "GENERATION OF FIBONACCI NUMBERS AND SEARCH FOR PRIMES"
PRINT
PRINT "N = ";
INPUT N
PRINT
LET F1 = 1                              'first 2 Fibonacci numbers
LET F2 = 1
PRINT "I ="; 1, "F ="; 1; "  (PRIME)"
PRINT "I ="; 2, "F ="; 1; "  (PRIME)"
FOR I = 3 TO 5                          'next 3 Fibonacci numbers
   LET F = F1 + F2
   PRINT "I ="; I, "F ="; F; "  (PRIME)"
   LET F2 = F1
   LET F1 = F
NEXT I
FOR I = 6 TO N                          'remaining Fibonacci numbers
   LET F = F1 + F2
   FOR D = 2 TO INT(SQR(F)) + 2         'test for a prime
      LET Q = F / D
      LET QINT = INT(Q)
      IF Q = QINT THEN EXIT FOR
   NEXT D
   IF Q = QINT THEN
      PRINT "I ="; I, "F ="; F          'print the results
   ELSE
      PRINT "I ="; I, "F ="; F; "  (PRIME)"
   END IF
   LET F2 = F1                          'update for next pass
   LET F1 = F
NEXT I
END
```

If the program is executed for a value of N = 23, we obtain the results shown below. (Note that the value of N entered by the user is underlined for clarity.) From these results we see that the first 23 Fibonacci numbers include 10 primes.

```
GENERATION OF FIBONACCI NUMBERS AND SEARCH FOR PRIMES

N = ? 23

I = 1          F = 1    (PRIME)
I = 2          F = 1    (PRIME)
I = 3          F = 2    (PRIME)
I = 4          F = 3    (PRIME)
I = 5          F = 5    (PRIME)
I = 6          F = 8
I = 7          F = 13   (PRIME)
```

```
I = 8        F = 21
I = 9        F = 34
I = 10       F = 55
I = 11       F = 89      (PRIME)
I = 12       F = 144
I = 13       F = 233     (PRIME)
I = 14       F = 377
I = 15       F = 610
I = 16       F = 987
I = 17       F = 1597    (PRIME)
I = 18       F = 2584
I = 19       F = 4181
I = 20       F = 6765
I = 21       F = 10946
I = 22       F = 17711
I = 23       F = 28657   (PRIME)
```

The program can be executed for larger values of N, though some desktop computers may be restricted to integer values that do not exceed 32,767. In such cases, N cannot exceed 23, because the resulting Fibonacci numbers would be too large.

4.9 SELECTION: SELECT CASE STRUCTURES

The newer versions of BASIC based upon the 1987 ANSI standard include a SELECT - CASE structure, which allows one of several different groups of statements to be executed, depending on the value of an expression.

The most common form of the SELECT - CASE structure is written in general terms as

```
SELECT CASE expression

CASE value1
    executable statements

CASE value2
    executable statements

    . . . . . . .

CASE ELSE
    executable statements

END SELECT
```

The CASE ELSE group is optional; it may omitted if one or more CASE *value* groups are present. Similarly, the CASE *value* groups may be omitted if the CASE ELSE group is present. In practice, however, a CASE ELSE group rarely appears alone, without any preceding CASE *value* groups.

When the SELECT CASE structure is executed, the value of the *expression* is compared successively with *value1*, *value2*, etc., until a match is found. The group of *executable statements* following the matching CASE statement is then executed and control is passed to the first statement following END SELECT. If a match cannot be found among the available values (i.e., *value1*, *value2*, etc.), then the *executable statements* following CASE ELSE are executed.

The SELECT CASE structure is convenient when used in conjunction with a menu entry. In such situations the selection is based upon the menu item that is chosen.

Example 4.20

Shown below is a simple BASIC program that makes use of a SELECT - CASE structure.

```
REM RAISE X TO A SELECTED POWER
PRINT "X = ";
INPUT X
PRINT "N (1, 2 or 3) = ";
INPUT N
SELECT CASE N                    'select a group of statements
CASE 1                           'x ^ 1
   PRINT "X ="; X
CASE 2                           'x ^ 2
   PRINT "X squared ="; X ^ N
CASE 3                           'x ^ 3
   PRINT "X cubed ="; X ^ N
CASE ELSE                        'error
   PRINT "ERROR - Please try again"
END SELECT
END
```

This program will accept values for X and N and then display the value of X, X $^\wedge$ 2 or X $^\wedge$ 3, depending on the value entered for N. An error message will be displayed if N is assigned a value other than 1, 2 or 3.

Two typical interactive sessions are shown below. The user's responses are underlined.

```
X = ? 3
N (1, 2 or 3) = ? 2
X squared = 9

X = ? 3
N (1, 2 or 3) = ? 4
ERROR - Please try again
```

The *expression* in the SELECT CASE statement can be a string rather than a numeric expression. In this case, the *values* in the subsequent CASE statements must also be strings. The original string expression will then be compared with the string values in the subsequent CASE statements until a match is found. As before, CASE ELSE provides a default in the event that a match cannot be found.

Example 4.21

The following program is similar to that shown in Example 4.20, except that the selection is based upon a string rather than the value of a numeric expression. The program asks the user to enter a string that represents the name of a color. (The color may be entered in either uppercase or lowercase.) If the color is RED, WHITE or BLUE, the computer will acknowledge by displaying an appropriate message. If any other color is entered (actually, any other string), an error message will be displayed.

Shown beneath the program listing are several typical interactive sessions, resulting from the program execution. The user's responses are underlined.

```
REM STRING SELECTION (CHOOSE A COLOR)
PRINT "Color = ";
INPUT C$
LET COLOR$ = UCASE$(C$)
SELECT CASE COLOR$                 'select a color
CASE "RED"                         'color is red
   PRINT "Color is RED"
CASE "WHITE"                       'color is white
   PRINT "Color is WHITE"
CASE "BLUE"                        'color is blue
   PRINT "Color is BLUE"
CASE ELSE                          'error
   PRINT "ERROR - Please try again"
END SELECT
END


Color = ? red
Color is RED


Color = ? Blue
Color is BLUE


Color = ? black
ERROR - Please try again
```

Some additional options are available when writing SELECT CASE structures. For example, if the *expression* in the SELECT CASE statement is numeric, then any numeric expression may appear in a succeeding CASE statement. A relational expression may also appear, provided the expression is preceded by the keyword IS. Moreover, multiple values, separated by commas, may appear in a single CASE statement. Also, a range of values, connected by the keyword TO, may appear in a single CASE statement. All of these options are illustrated in the following example.

Example 4.22

The following BASIC program includes a selection based upon the value of a numeric constant.

```
PRINT "X = ";
INPUT X
SELECT CASE X
CASE 1, 3, 5
   PRINT "Odd digit between 1 and 5"
CASE 2, 4, 6
   PRINT "Even digit between 2 and 6"
CASE 7 TO 9
   PRINT "Any digit between 7 and 9"
CASE IS >= 10
   PRINT "Too big"
CASE ELSE
   PRINT "Nonpositive number"
END SELECT
END
```

The first two CASE statements each contain multiple values separated by commas. The third CASE statement contains a range of values connected by the keyword TO (i.e., CASE 7 TO 9). And finally, the fourth CASE statement contains a relational expression preceded by the keyword IS (i.e., CASE IS >= 10).

Similar options are also available if the *expression* in the SELECT CASE statement is a string. A succeeding CASE statement may contain a relational expression, preceded by the keyword IS. A CASE statement may also contain multiple strings, separated by commas. Or, a CASE statement may contain a range of strings, connected by the keyword TO. The following example illustrates these options.

Example 4.23

The following BASIC program includes a selection based upon a single-character string.

```
PRINT "Single character = ";
INPUT C$
LET C$ = UCASE$(C$)
SELECT CASE C$
CASE "A" TO "Z", "a" TO "z"
   PRINT "Character is a LETTER"
CASE "0" TO "9"
   PRINT "Character is a DIGIT"
CASE IS < " ", IS > "~"
   PRINT "Character is NONPRINTING"
CASE ELSE
   PRINT "Character is NOT ALPHANUMERIC"
END SELECT
END
```

The first CASE statement contains two string ranges. Each range includes the keyword TO. The individual ranges are separated by a comma.

The second CASE statement includes a single range of strings. (Note that the digits 0 and 9 are written as strings, not numerical values.) Again, note the use of the keyword TO.

Finally, the third CASE statement includes two relational expressions. Each relational expression is preceded by the keyword IS. The individual expressions are separated by a comma.

The SELECT CASE structure is particularly useful in longer programs, in which each group of executable statements may be lengthy. The following example illustrates a typical application.

Example 4.24 Calculating Depreciation

Let us consider how to calculate the yearly depreciation for some depreciable item, such as a building or a machine. There are three commonly used methods for calculating depreciation; the *straight-line* method, the *double-declining-balance* method, and the *sum-of-the-years'-digits* method. We wish to write a BASIC program that will allow us to select any one of these methods for each set of calculations.

The *straight-line* method is the easiest to use. In this method, the original value of the item is divided by its life (total number of years). The resulting quotient will be the amount by which the item depreciates each year. For example, if an $8000 item is to be depreciated over 10 years, then the annual depreciation would be $8000/10 = $800. Therefore, the value of the item would decrease by $800 each year. Notice that the annual depreciation is the same each year when using straight-line depreciation.

When using the *double-declining-balance* method, the value of the item will decrease by a constant *percentage* each year. Hence the *actual amount* of the depreciation, in dollars, will vary from one year to the next. To obtain the depreciation factor, we divide 2 by the life of the item. This factor is multiplied by the value of the item *at the beginning of each year* (not the original value of the item) to obtain the annual depreciation.

Suppose, for example, that we wish to depreciate an $8000 item over 10 years, using the double-declining-balance method. The depreciation factor will be 2/10 = 0.20. Hence, the depreciation for the first year will be 0.20 x $8000 = $1600. The second year's depreciation will be 0.20 x ($8000 − $1600) = 0.20 x $6400 = $1280; the third year's depreciation will be 0.20 x $5120 = $1024, and so on.

In the *sum-of-the-years'-digits* method, the value of the item will decrease by a percentage that is different each year. The depreciation factor will be a fraction whose denominator is the sum of the digits from 1 to n, where n represents the life of the item. If, for example, we consider a 10-year lifetime, the denominator will be $1 + 2 + 3 + \ldots + 10 = 55$. For the first year, the numerator will be n; for the second year it will be $(n - 1)$; for the third year, $(n - 2)$; and so on. The yearly depreciation is obtained by multiplying the depreciation factor by the *original* value of the item.

To see how the sum-of-the-years'-digits method works, we again depreciate an $8000 item over 10 years. The depreciation for the first year will be (10/55) x $8000 = $1454.55; for the second year, it will be (9/55) x $8000 = $1309.09; and so on.

Now let us define the following symbols, so that we can write the actual program.

> `value` = the current value of the item
>
> `tag` = the original value of the item (i.e., the original value of `value`)
>
> `deprec` = the annual depreciation
>
> `n` = the number of years over which the item will be depreciated.
>
> `i` = a counter ranging from 1 to `n`
>
> `choice` = an integer indicating which method to use

The computation will begin by reading in the original (undepreciated) value of the item, the life of the item (i.e., n) and an integer that indicates which method will be used (`choice`). The yearly depreciation and the remaining (undepreciated) value of the item will then be calculated and written out for each year.

Our BASIC program will follow the outline presented below.

1. Repeat the following steps as long as the value of `choice` is not equal to 4. Use a DO - LOOP WHILE structure for this purpose (though other conditional looping structures could also be used).

   (*a*) Enter a value for `choice`, indicating the type of calculation to be carried out.

   (*b*) If `choice` is assigned a value of 1, 2 or 3, enter numerical values for `value` and n.

   (*c*) Depending on the value assigned to `choice`, select the appropriate part of the program and carry out the indicated operations. In particular,

       (*i*) If `choice` is assigned a value of 1, 2 or 3, calculate the yearly depreciation and the new value of the item on a year-by-year basis. Use the straight-line method if `choice` is equal to 1, the double-declining-balance method if `choice` is equal to 2, and the sum-of-the-years'-digits method if `choice` equals 3.

       (*ii*) If `choice` is assigned any value other than 1, 2, 3 or 4, generate an error message and begin another pass through the loop.

2. If choice is equal to 4, then leave the DO - LOOP structure, display a "goodbye" message and end the computation.

We can now translate the outline into a complete BASIC program, as shown below.

```
REM CALCULATE DEPRECIATION USING ONE OF THREE DIFFERENT METHODS
DO
   PRINT
   PRINT "Method: (1-SL  2-DDB  3-SYD  4-End)";      'enter input data
   INPUT choice
   IF choice > 0 AND choice < 4 THEN
      PRINT "Original value";
      INPUT value
      PRINT "Number of years";
      INPUT n
   END IF
   SELECT CASE choice
   CASE 1                                  'straight-line method
      PRINT
      PRINT "Straight-Line Method"
      PRINT
      LET deprec = value / n
      FOR i = 1 TO n
         LET value = value - deprec
         PRINT "End of Year"; i;
         PRINT TAB(22); "Depreciation:"; deprec;
         PRINT TAB(50); "Current value:"; value
      NEXT i
   CASE 2                                  'double-declining-balance method
      PRINT
      PRINT "Double-Declining-Balance Method"
      PRINT
      FOR i = 1 TO n
         LET deprec = 2 * value / n
         LET value = value - deprec
         PRINT "End of Year"; i;
         PRINT TAB(22); "Depreciation:"; deprec;
         PRINT TAB(50); "Current value:"; value
      NEXT i
   CASE 3                                  'sum-of-the-years'-digits method
      PRINT
      PRINT "Sum-of-the-Years'-Digits Method"
      PRINT
      LET tag = value
      FOR i = 1 TO n
         LET deprec = (n - i + 1) * tag / (n * (n + 1) / 2)
         LET value = value - deprec
         PRINT "End of Year"; i;
         PRINT TAB(22); "Depreciation:"; deprec;
         PRINT TAB(50); "Current value:"; value
      NEXT i
```

```
      CASE IS < 1, IS > 4                        'error message
          PRINT
          PRINT "ERROR - Please try again"
      END SELECT
  LOOP WHILE choice <> 4
  PRINT                                          'end of computation
  PRINT "Goodbye, have a nice day!"
  END
```

The method used for calculating sum-of-the-years'-digits depreciation requires some additional explanation. In particular, the term $(n - i + 1)$ is used to count *backward* (from n down to 1) as i progresses *forward* (from 1 to n). We could, of course, have set up a backward-counting loop instead, i.e.,

```
  FOR i = n TO 1 STEP -1
```

but then we would have required a corresponding forward-counting loop to write out the results of the calculations on a yearly basis.

Also, the term $(n * (n + 1) / 2)$ in the sum-of-the-years'-digits calculation is a formula for the sum of the first n digits; i.e., $1 + 2 + \ldots + n$.

The program is designed to run interactively, with prompts for the required input data. Notice that the program generates a brief menu with four choices, to calculate the depreciation using one of the three methods or to end the computation. The computer will continue to accept new sets of input data and carry out the appropriate calculations for each data set until a value of 4 is selected from the menu. The program automatically generates an error message and returns to the menu if some value other than 1, 2, 3 or 4 is entered in response to the menu request.

Some representative output is shown below. In each case, an $8000 item is depreciated over a 10-year period, using one of the three methods. The error message generated by an incorrect data entry is also illustrated. Finally, the computation is terminated in response to the last menu selection.

```
  Method: (1-SL  2-DDB  3-SYD  4-End)? 1
  Original value? 8000
  Number of years? 10

  Straight-Line Method

  End of Year 1        Depreciation: 800        Current value: 7200
  End of Year 2        Depreciation: 800        Current value: 6400
  End of Year 3        Depreciation: 800        Current value: 5600
  End of Year 4        Depreciation: 800        Current value: 4800
  End of Year 5        Depreciation: 800        Current value: 4000
  End of Year 6        Depreciation: 800        Current value: 3200
  End of Year 7        Depreciation: 800        Current value: 2400
  End of Year 8        Depreciation: 800        Current value: 1600
  End of Year 9        Depreciation: 800        Current value: 800
  End of Year 10       Depreciation: 800        Current value: 0

  Method: (1-SL  2-DDB  3-SYD  4-End)? 2
  Original value? 8000
  Number of years? 10
```

Double-Declining-Balance Method

End of Year 1   Depreciation: 1600   Current value: 6400
End of Year 2   Depreciation: 1280   Current value: 5120
End of Year 3   Depreciation: 1024   Current value: 4096
End of Year 4   Depreciation: 819.2   Current value: 3276.8
End of Year 5   Depreciation: 655.36   Current value: 2621.44
End of Year 6   Depreciation: 524.288   Current value: 2097.152
End of Year 7   Depreciation: 419.4304   Current value: 1677.721
End of Year 8   Depreciation: 335.5443   Current value: 1342.177
End of Year 9   Depreciation: 268.4354   Current value: 1073.742
End of Year 10   Depreciation: 214.7483   Current value: 858.9933

Method: (1-SL 2-DDB 3-SYD 4-End)? 3
Original value? 8000
Number of years? 10

Sum-of-the-Years'-Digits Method

End of Year 1   Depreciation: 1454.545   Current value: 6545.455
End of Year 2   Depreciation: 1309.091   Current value: 5236.364
End of Year 3   Depreciation: 1163.636   Current value: 4072.728
End of Year 4   Depreciation: 1018.182   Current value: 3054.546
End of Year 5   Depreciation: 872.7273   Current value: 2181.818
End of Year 6   Depreciation: 727.2727   Current value: 1454.546
End of Year 7   Depreciation: 581.8182   Current value: 872.7275
End of Year 8   Depreciation: 436.3636   Current value: 436.3638
End of Year 9   Depreciation: 290.9091   Current value: 145.4547
End of Year 10   Depreciation: 145.4545   Current value: 1.983643E-04

Method: (1-SL 2-DDB 3-SYD 4-End)? 0

ERROR - Please try again

Method: (1-SL 2-DDB 3-SYD 4-End)? 4

Goodbye, have a nice day!

Notice that the double-declining-balance method and the sum-of-the-years'-digits method result in a large annual depreciation during the early years but a very small annual depreciation in the last few years of the item's lifetime. Also, we see that the item has a value of zero at the end of its lifetime when using the straight-line method or the sum-of-the-years'-digits method, but a small value remains undepreciated when using the double-declining-balance method. (The value 1.983643E-04, obtained at the end of year 10 using the sum-of-the-years'-digits method, is due to numerical roundoff.)

4.10 LINE-ORIENTED CONTROL STATEMENTS

BASIC also includes a number of line-oriented control statements, such as GOTO, ON - GOTO, GOSUB, ON - GOSUB and IF - THEN. Each of these statements results in a transfer of control to some remote part of the program. In each case the remote entry point is identified by a line number.

For example, the statement

```
100 GO TO 200
```

causes a "jump" (i.e., an unconditional transfer of control) to line number 200.

The ON - GOTO statement is used in a manner similar to the SELECT CASE structure, though it is more primitive. Thus, the statement

```
100 ON flag GOTO 300, 400, 500
```

will result in a conditional transfer of control, depending on the value assigned to flag. In particular, control will be transferred to line number 300 if flag has a value of 1, to line number 400 if flag has a value of 2, and to line number 500 if flag has a value of 3. There is no restriction on the maximum number of line numbers in a single ON - GOTO statement. Remember, however, that each line number represents a jump point that corresponds to a different integer value of flag.

A line number may appear more than once; e.g.,

```
100 ON switch GOTO 150, 220, 310, 220, 400
```

Control will be transferred to line number 220 if switch is assigned a value of either 2 or 4.

Some versions of BASIC permit a target line to be identified by a *line label* rather than a line number. Generally speaking, line labels are written in the same manner as variable names, though they must end with some special character — typically, a colon — wherever they appear as labels in target lines. Thus, the above GOTO statement and its corresponding target statement might be written as

```
GO TO Point1
```

. . . . .

```
Point1:     (followed by a statement equivalent to line 200)
```

The GOSUB and ON - GOSUB statements are similar to the GOTO and ON - GOTO statements, except that they cause transfers to *subroutines* rather than simple executable statements. We will describe these statements in Chap. 6, in conjunction with our discussion of subroutines (see Sec. 6.5).

Finally, a line-oriented version of the IF - THEN statement can be written as

```
100 IF x < 0 THEN GOTO 200
```

or simply

```
100 IF x < 0 THEN 200
```

Each of these statements will transfer control conditionally, depending on the value of the logical expression. Thus, control will be transferred to line number 200 if the value assigned to x is less than 0.

From a perspective of contemporary programming practice, *the use of these line-oriented control statements should be avoided*. The fundamental idea of structured programming is to write the major segments of a program sequentially, so that the program logic is orderly and straightforward. This approach to program development has been illustrated by the programming examples given in this chapter and elsewhere in this book. The use of remote transfers (GOTOs) generally interrupts this orderly, sequential program structure. This is particularly true of programs that employ complex logic, with many remote transfers at different places in the program. Thus, the use of line-oriented control statements is now considered archaic.

Review Questions

4.1   What is meant by conditional execution?

4.2   What is looping? What is the difference between unconditional looping and conditional looping?

4.3   What is meant by selection?

4.4   Name the six relational operators used in BASIC. What is the purpose of each?

4.5   What is a logical expression? What values can a logical expression take on?

4.6   What are operands within a logical expression?

4.7   What is the interpretation of the relational operators <, <=, > and >= when applied to string operands?

4.8   Name the three commonly used logical operators in BASIC. What is the purpose of each? What other logical operators are supported in some versions of BASIC?

4.9   What is the purpose of the IF - THEN statement?

4.10   What is the purpose of an IF - THEN - ELSE block? Compare with the IF - THEN statement.

4.11   How is an IF - THEN - ELSE block ended?

4.12   Describe how one IF - THEN - ELSE block can be embedded within another.

4.13   What is the purpose of the FOR - NEXT structure? What is the purpose of the STEP clause within this structure?

4.14   How is a FOR - NEXT structure ended?

4.15   What is the index in a FOR - NEXT structure? In what way must the index appearing in the FOR - TO statement be related to the index appearing in the NEXT statement?

4.16   Can the index in a FOR - NEXT structure take on fractional values? Can it decrease in value from one pass to another?

4.17   Summarize the rules that apply to FOR - NEXT structures.

4.18   How can control be transferred out of a FOR - NEXT structure?

4.19   What is the purpose of the DO - LOOP structure?

4.20   Describe four different ways to write a DO - LOOP structure.

4.21   What is the principal difference between DO WHILE and DO UNTIL (or LOOP WHILE and LOOP UNTIL)?

4.22   What is the principal difference between DO WHILE - LOOP and DO - LOOP WHILE (or DO UNTIL - LOOP and DO - LOOP UNTIL)?

4.23   How can a conditional loop be written so that at least one pass through the loop will always be executed?

4.24   Write a skeletal outline of a DO - LOOP structure, illustrating the manner in which the logical expression is assigned its initial value and its subsequent values within the loop. Compare with a FOR - NEXT structure.

4.25   How can control be transferred out of a DO - LOOP structure? Compare with a FOR - NEXT structure.

4.26   What is the purpose of the WHILE - WEND structure? Compare with the DO - LOOP structure.

4.27   Is WHILE - WEND supported by the 1987 ANSI standard? Is it commonly available?

4.28   Summarize the restrictions that apply to nested control structures.

4.29   What is the purpose of the SELECT - CASE structure?

4.30   Summarize the principal components of the SELECT - CASE structure. Which are required and which are optional?

4.31   For what type of application is the SELECT - CASE structure well-suited?

4.32   Can the selection in a SELECT - CASE structure be based upon a string rather than a numeric value?

Problems

4.33   Write an appropriate IF - THEN statement or an IF - THEN - ELSE block for each of the following situations.

   (a) Test the value of the variable sum. If sum exceeds 100, then adjust its value so that it equals 100.

   (b) Test the value of the variable sum. If sum exceeds 100, then display its value, adjust its value so that it equals 100 and then display the new value.

   (c) Test the value of the variable sum. If sum is less than or equal to 100, add the value of the variable v to sum and display the value. If sum exceeds 100, then display its value, adjust its value so that it equals 100 and then display the new value.

4.34   Write an appropriate IF - THEN statement or an IF - THEN - ELSE block for each of the following situations.

   (a) Suppose the variable pay has been assigned a value of 4.50. Test the value of the variable hours. If hours exceeds 40, assign the value of 6.25 to pay.

   (b) Test the value of the variable hours. If hours is less than or equal to 40, assign 4.50 to pay and assign "REGULAR" to the variable status$. If pay exceeds 40, assign 6.25 to pay and assign "OVERTIME" to status$.

4.35   Write an appropriate IF -THEN - ELSE block for the following situation.

Test the variable FLAG$. If FLAG$ = "TRUE", set count equal to 0 and display the message "RESETTING THE COUNTER". Then test the value of Z.

If Z exceeds ZMAX, display the message "MAXIMUM VALUE EXCEEDED", and assign the value of ZMIN to Z.

Otherwise, add the value of W to Z and display the new value of Z.

If FLAG$ = "FALSE", increase the value of count by 1 and display its value. Then test the variable TYPE$.

If TYPE$ equals "A", add the value of U to Z.

If TYPE$ equals "B", add the value of V to Z.

Otherwise, add the value of W to Z.

Display the string assigned to TYPE$ and the value of Z. Then assign "TRUE" to FLAG$.

4.36 Write a loop that will calculate the sum of every third integer, beginning with $i = 2$ (i.e., calculate the sum $2 + 5 + 8 + 11 + \ldots$) for all values of i that are less than 100. Write the loop in each of the following ways:

(a)   Using a FOR - NEXT structure

(b)   Using a DO WHILE - LOOP structure

(c)   Using a DO UNTIL - LOOP structure

(d)   Using a DO - LOOP WHILE structure

(e)   Using a DO - LOOP UNTIL structure

4.37 Repeat Problem 4.36, calculating the sum of every n^{th} integer, beginning with nstart (i.e., nstart, nstart + n, nstart + (2 * n), nstart + (3 * n), etc.). Continue the looping process for all values of i that do not exceed nstop.

4.38 Modify Problem 4.37 by transferring out of the loop if sum exceeds some specified value represented by maxsum.

4.39 Generalize Problem 4.36 by generating a *series* of loops, each loop generating the sum of every j^{th} integer, where j ranges from 2 to 13. Begin each loop with a value of $i = 2$ and increase i by j, until i takes on the largest possible value that is less than 100. (In other words, the first loop will calculate the sum $2 + 4 + 6 + \ldots + 98$; the second loop will calculate the sum $2 + 5 + 8 + \ldots + 98$; the third loop will calculate the sum $2 + 6 + 10 + \ldots + 98$; and so on. The last loop will calculate the sum $2 + 15 + 28 + \ldots + 93$.) Display the final value of each sum.
Use a nested loop structure to solve this problem, with one loop embedded within another. Calculate each sum with the inner loop, and let the outer loop control the value of j.

4.40 Write a loop that will generate every third integer, beginning with $i = 2$ and continuing for all integers that are less than 100. Calculate the sum of those integers that are evenly divisible by 5.

4.41   Repeat Problem 4.40, calculating the sum of every n^{th} integer, beginning with `nstart` [i.e., `nstart`, `nstart + n`, `nstart + (2 * n)`, `nstart + (3 * n)`, etc.]. Continue the looping process for all values of `i` that do not exceed `nstop`. Calculate the sum of those integers that are evenly divisible by k, where k represents some positive integer.

4.42   Write a loop that will examine each character in a string called `text$` and determine how many of the characters are letters, how many are digits, how many are blank spaces, and how many are other kinds of characters (e.g., punctuation characters). *Hint*: Use the `LEN` library function to determine the length of the string; then use a library function to extract the individual characters, one at a time.

4.43   Write a loop that will examine each character in a string called `text$` and determine how many of the characters are vowels and how many are consonants. *Hint*: First determine whether or not a character is a letter; if so, determine the type of letter. Also, see the suggestion given at the end of Problem 4.42.

4.44   Write a loop that will display the characters in a string in reverse order (so that the string will appear backwards). *Hint*: See the suggestion at the end of Problem 4.42.

4.45   Write a SELECT CASE structure that will examine the value of a numeric variable called `flag` and display one of the following messages, depending on the value assigned to `flag`.

    (a)   HOT, if `flag` has a value of 1

    (b)   LUKE WARM, if `flag` has a value of 2

    (c)   COLD, if `flag` has a value of 3

    (d)   OUT OF RANGE, if `flag` has any other value

4.46   Write a SELECT CASE structure that will examine the value of a string variable called `color` and display one of the following messages, depending on the value assigned to `color`.

    (a)   RED, if either r or R is assigned to `color`

    (b)   GREEN, if either g or G is assigned to `color`

    (c)   BLUE, if either b or B is assigned to `color`

    (d)   BLACK, if `color` is assigned any other string

4.47   Write an appropriate control structure that will examine the value of a numeric variable called `temp` and display one of the following messages, depending on the value assigned to `temp`.

    (a)   ICE, if the value of `temp` is less than 0

    (b)   WATER, if the value of `temp` lies between 0 and 100

    (c)   STEAM, if the value of `temp` exceeds 100

Can a SELECT CASE structure be used in this instance?

4.48   Describe the output that will be generated by each of the following BASIC programs.

(a)   ```
       LET i = 0
       LET x = 0
       DO WHILE (i < 20)
          IF (i MOD 5 = 0) THEN
             LET x = x + i
             PRINT x;
          END IF
          LET i = i + 1
       LOOP
       END
       ```

(b)   ```
       LET i = 0
       LET x = 0
       DO
          IF (i MOD 5 = 0) THEN
             LET x = x + 1
             PRINT x;
          END IF
          LET i = i + 1
       LOOP WHILE (i < 20)
       END
       ```

(c)   ```
       LET x = 0
       FOR i = 1 TO 10 STEP 2
          LET x = x + 1
          PRINT x;
       NEXT i
       END
       ```

(d)   ```
       LET x = 0
       FOR i = 1 TO 10 STEP 2
          LET x = x + i
          PRINT x;
       NEXT i
       END
       ```

(e)   ```
       LET x = 0
       FOR i = 1 TO 10
          IF (i MOD 2 = 1) THEN
             LET x = x + i
          ELSE
             LET x = x - 1
          END IF
          PRINT x;
       NEXT i
       END
       ```

(f)   ```
       LET x = 0
       FOR i = 1 TO 10
          IF (i MOD 2 = 1) THEN
       ```

```
              LET x = x + i
          ELSE
              LET x = x - 1
          END IF
          PRINT x;
          EXIT FOR
      NEXT i
      END


(g)   LET x = 0
      FOR i = 0 TO 4
          FOR j = 0 TO i - 1
              LET x = x + (i + j - 1)
              PRINT x;
          NEXT j
      NEXT i
      END


(h)   LET x = 0
      FOR i = 0 TO 4
          FOR j = 0 TO i - 1
              LET x = x + (i + j - 1)
              PRINT x;
              EXIT FOR
          NEXT j
      NEXT i
      END


(i)   LET x = 0
      FOR i = 0 TO 4
          FOR j = 0 TO i
              LET x = x + j
              PRINT x;
          NEXT j
          EXIT FOR
      NEXT i
      END


(j)   LET x = 0
      FOR i = 0 TO 4
          FOR j = 0 TO i - 1
              LET k = (i + j - 1)
              IF (k MOD 2 = 0) THEN
                  LET x = x + k
              ELSEIF (k MOD 3 = 0) THEN
                  LET x = x + k - 2
              END IF
              PRINT x;
          NEXT j
      NEXT i
      END
```

```
(k)  LET x = 0
     FOR i = 0 TO 4
        FOR j = 0 TO i - 1
           SELECT CASE (i + j - 1)
           CASE -1, 0
              LET x = x + 1
           CASE 1, 2, 3
              LET x = x + 2
           CASE ELSE
              LET x = x + 3
           END SELECT
           PRINT x;
        NEXT j
     NEXT i
     END
```

Programming Problems

4.49 Modify the program shown in Example 4.9 so that it utilizes a SELECT CASE structure rather than IF - THEN - ELSE.

4.50 Modify the first program given in Example 4.16 so that it makes use of a DO - LOOP WHILE structure rather than a DO UNTIL - LOOP structure. Execute the programs using the following 10 numbers:

27.5	87.0
-13.4	39.9
53.8	-47.7
-29.2	-8.1
74.5	63.2

4.51 Modify the program given in Example 4.18 so that it utilizes a DO WHILE - LOOP structure rather than a DO - LOOP UNTIL structure.

4.52 Modify the program given in Example 4.18 so that it utilizes a DO - LOOP WHILE structure rather than a DO - LOOP UNTIL structure.

4.53 The equation

$$x^5 + 3x^2 - 10 = 0$$

which was presented in Example 4.18 can be rearranged into the form

$$x = [(10 - x^5)/3]^{1/2}$$

Rewrite the program given in Example 4.18 to make use of the above form of the equation. Execute the program and compare the calculated results with those presented in Example 4.18. Why are the results different? (Do computers always generate correct answers?)

4.54 Modify the program for generating Fibonacci numbers given in Example 4.19 so that the outer loops (utilizing the index I) are based upon DO - LOOP structures rather than FOR - NEXT structures.

4.55 Modify the program for generating Fibonacci numbers given in Example 4.19 so that it can properly accommodate input values of N that are less than 6.

4.56 Modify the depreciation program given in Example 4.24 so that it utilizes an IF - THEN - ELSE structure rather than SELECT CASE. Which is better suited for this particular problem?

4.57 Add an error-trapping routine to the depreciation program in Example 4.24. The routine should generate an error message, followed by a request to reenter the data, whenever a nonpositive value is entered for the variable value or for the variable n.

4.58 Write a BASIC program for each of the following problems. Use the most natural type of control statement for each problem. Begin with a detailed outline, then translate the outline into a complete BASIC program. Be sure to use good programming style (comments, indentation, etc.).

(a) Calculate the *weighted average* of a list of n numbers, using the formula

$$x_{avg} = f_1 x_1 + f_2 x_2 + \ldots + f_n x_n$$

where the fs are fractional *weighting factors*, i.e.,

$$0 <= f_i < 1, \text{ and } f_1 + f_2 + \ldots + f_n = 1.$$

Test your program with the following data:

$i=1$	$f=0.06$	$x=27.5$
2	0.08	13.4
3	0.08	53.8
4	0.10	29.2
5	0.10	74.5
6	0.10	87.0
7	0.12	39.9
8	0.12	47.7
9	0.12	8.1
10	0.12	63.2

(b) Calculate the cumulative product of a list of n numbers. Test your program with the following set of data (n = 6): 6.2, 12.3, 5.0, 18.8, 7.1, 12.8.

(c) Calculate the geometric average of a list of n numbers, using the formula

$$x_{avg} = [x_1 x_2 x_3 \ldots x_n]^{1/n}$$

Test your program using the values of x given in part (b) above. Compare the results obtained with the arithmetic average of the same data. Which average is larger?

(d) Write an interactive BASIC program that will read in a positive integer value and determine the following:

(i) if the integer is a prime number.

(ii) if the integer is a Fibonacci number.

(See Example 4.19.)

Write the program in such a manner that it will execute repeatedly, until a zero value is detected for the input quantity. Test the program with several integer values of your choice.

(e) Calculate the sum of the first n odd integers (i.e., $1 + 3 + 5 + \ldots + (2 * n - 1)$). Test the program by calculating the sum of the first 100 odd integers (note that the last integer will be 199).

(f) The sine of x can be calculated approximately by summing the first n terms of the infinite series

$$\sin x = x - x^3/3! + x^5/5! - x^7/7! + \ldots$$

where x is expressed in radians. (*Note*: π radians = 180°.)

Write a BASIC program that will read in a value for x and then calculate its sine. Write the program two different ways:

(i) Sum the first n terms, where n is a positive integer that is read into the computer along with the numerical value for x.

(ii) Continue adding successive terms in the series until the value of the next term becomes smaller (in magnitude) than 10^{-5}.

Test the program for $x = 1$, $x = 2$ and $x = -3$. In each case write out the number of terms used to obtain the final answer.

(g) Suppose that P dollars are borrowed from a bank, with the understanding that A dollars will be repaid each month until the entire loan has been repaid. Part of the monthly payment will be interest, calculated as i percent of the current unpaid balance. The remainder of the monthly payment will be applied toward reducing the unpaid balance.

Write a BASIC program that will determine the following information:

(i) The amount of interest paid each month.

(ii) The amount of money applied toward the unpaid balance each month.

(iii) The cumulative amount of interest that has been paid at the end of each month.

(iv) The amount of the loan that is still unpaid at the end of each month.

(v) The number of monthly payments required to repay the entire loan.

(vi) The amount of the last payment (since it will probably be less than A).

Test your program using the following data: $P = \$40,000$; $A = \$2,000$; $i = 1\%$ per month.

(h) Generate the following "pyramid" of digits, using nested loops.

```
         1
        232
       34543
      4567654
     567898765
    67890109876
   7890123210987
  890123454321098
 90123456765432109
0123456789876543210
```

Do *not* simply write out 10 multidigit strings. Instead, develop a formula to *generate* the appropriate output for each line.

(*i*)   A class of students earned the following scores for the 6 examinations taken in a BASIC programming course.

Name	Exam Scores (percent)					
Adams	45	80	80	95	55	75
Brown	60	50	70	75	55	80
Davis	40	30	10	45	60	55
Fisher	0	5	5	0	10	5
Hamilton	90	85	100	95	90	90
Jones	95	90	80	95	85	80
Ludwig	35	50	55	65	45	70
Osborne	75	60	75	60	70	80
Prince	85	75	60	85	90	100
Richards	50	60	50	35	65	70
Smith	70	60	75	70	55	75
Thomas	10	25	35	20	30	10
Wolfe	25	40	65	75	85	95
Zorba	65	80	70	100	60	95

Write an interactive BASIC program that will accept each student's name and exam scores as input, determine an average score for each student, and then write out the student's name, the individual exam scores and the calculated average.

(*j*)   Modify the program written for part (*i*) above to allow for unequal weighting of the individual exam scores. In particular, assume that each of the first four exams contributes 15 percent to the final score, and each of the last two exams contributes 20 percent.

(*k*)   Extend the program written for part (*j*) above so that an overall class average is determined in addition to the individual student averages.

(*l*)   Write a BASIC program that will allow the computer to be used as an ordinary desk calculator. Consider only the common arithmetic operations (addition, subtraction, multiplication and division). Include a memory that can store one number.

(*m*) Generate a character-oriented plot of the function

$$y = e^{-0.1t} \sin 0.5t$$

on a printer, using an asterisk (*) for each of the points that makes up the plot. Have the plot run vertically down the page, with one point (one asterisk) per line. (*Hint*: Each printed line should be comprised of one asterisk, preceded by an appropriate number of blank spaces. Determine the position of the asterisk by rounding the value of y to the nearest integer, scaled to the maximum number of characters per line.)

(*n*)   Write an interactive BASIC program that will convert a positive integer quantity to a Roman numeral (e.g., 12 will be converted to XII, 14 will be converted to XIV, and so on). Design the program so that it will execute repeatedly, until a value of zero is read in from the keyboard.

(*o*)   Write an interactive BASIC program that will convert a date, entered in the form mm-dd-yy (example: 4-12-69) into an integer that indicates the number of days beyond January 1, 1960. To do so, make use of the following relationships:

(*i*)   The day of the current year can be determined approximately as

        day = INT(30.42 * (mm - 1)) + dd

(*ii*) If mm = 2 (February), increase the value of day by 1

(*iii*) If mm > 2 and mm < 8 (March, April, May, June or July), *decrease* the value of day by 1

(*iv*) If (yy MOD 4) = 0 and mm > 2 (leap year), increase the value of day by 1

(*v*)   Increase the value of day by 1461 for each full 4-year cycle beyond 1-1-60.

(*vi*) Increase day by 365 for each additional full year beyond the completion of the last full 4-year cycle, then add 1 (for the most recent leap year).

Test the program with today's date, or any other date of your choice.

Chapter 5

Arrays

Many applications require the processing of multiple data items that have common characteristics, such as a set of numerical data items represented by $x_1, x_2, \ldots, x_n$. In such situations, it is often convenient to place the data items into an *array*, where they will all share the same name (e.g., x). The data items that make up an array can be either numeric values or strings, though they must all be the same data type. Numeric arrays are named in the same manner as numeric variables, and string arrays are named in the same manner as string variables. Hence, the name of a string array must end with a dollar sign ($).

Each individual array element (i.e., each individual data item) is referred to by specifying the array name followed by one or more *subscripts*, enclosed in parentheses. Each subscript is expressed as an integer quantity. Thus, in the *n*-element array x, the array elements are x(1), x(2),..., x(n).

The number of subscripts determines the *dimensionality* of the array. For example, x(i) refers to the i*th* element in a one-dimensional array x. Similarly, y(i, j) refers to an element in the two-dimensional array y. (Think of a two-dimensional array as a table, where i refers to the row number and j refers to the column number.) Higher dimensional arrays, such as z(i, j, k), are formed by specifying additional subscripts in the same manner.

The layout of the array elements in a one-dimensional array are shown schematically in Fig. 5.1.

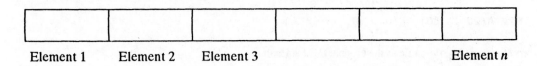

Element 1   Element 2   Element 3   Element *n*

Fig. 5.1

5.1 DEFINING AN ARRAY: THE DIM STATEMENT

An array must be defined before it can appear within an executable statement. The DIM statement (i.e., the DIMENSION statement) is used for this purpose. This statement defines the *dimensionality* (i.e., the number of subscripts) and the *size* (range of each subscript) of an array.

The DIM statement consists of the keyword DIM, followed by one or more array names, separated by commas. Each array name must be followed by one or more integer constants, enclosed in parentheses. If several integer constants are present (indicating a multi-dimensional array), they must be separated by commas. Note that variables *cannot* be used to indicate array sizes.

In some versions of BASIC, the elements of a numeric array are initialized at 0 when the array is defined.

Example 5.1

A BASIC program includes the following DIM statement.

```
DIM sales(50, 100), gross(100), net(100), customers$(200)
```

This statement defines `sales` to be a two-dimensional numeric array having 50 rows and 100 columns, `gross` and `net` are one-dimensional numeric arrays each containing 100 elements, and `customers$` is a one-dimensional string array containing 200 elements.

Some versions of BASIC will automatically assign a value of 0 to each element of `sales`, `gross` and `net`.

In most versions of BASIC, a subscript may range from 1 to a maximum value specified in the DIM statement. Some versions of BASIC allow the subscript to begin at 0 rather than 1. The DIM statement can be modified, however, to specify some lower bound other than 0 or 1. In such cases, the lower bound and the upper bound are both specified in parentheses, separated by the keyword TO. Some versions of BASIC permit the use of a colon (:) in place of the keyword TO.

Example 5.2

A BASIC program contains the statement

```
DIM A(20 TO 100), B(0 TO 10, -10 TO 0)
```

In this example, A is a one-dimensional array whose subscript values can range from 20 to 100. Hence, A contains 81 elements. Similarly, B is a two-dimensional array whose first subscript can range from 0 to 10, and whose second subscript can range from -10 to 0. B will therefore contain 121 elements ($11 \times 11 = 121$).

In some versions of BASIC, the above DIM statement could also have been written as

```
DIM A(20 : 100), B(0 : 10, -10 : 0)
```

The interpretation will be the same as the original DIM statement.

Some versions of BASIC allow an array name to duplicate the name of an ordinary variable. In such situations the array and the variable will be regarded as separate, distinct entities. This is considered to be a poor programming practice, however, and is not recommended.

Example 5.3

A program is to contain a list of names and a table of numbers. The list will be called `names$` and the table will be called `values`. Thus, the program will contain a DIM statement such as

```
DIM names$(100), values(100, 5)
```

The program may also include an ordinary string variable called `names$` and an ordinary numeric variable called `values`. These variables would be separate and distinct from the arrays `names$` and `values`. It would be much better, however, to name these ordinary variables differently (e.g., `xname$`, `xvalue`), thus avoiding any confusion between the array elements and the ordinary variables.

In some versions of BASIC, small arrays can be defined implicitly, without a DIM statement. Generally, this feature is confined to arrays whose subscript values do not exceed 10. The omission of a DIM statement is a poor practice, however, and it is discouraged.

Example 5.4

A program contains the following DIM statement.

```
DIM A(6), B(10), C(5, 15)
```

The inclusion of A and B in the DIM statement may not be necessary in some versions of BASIC, since each subscript value does not exceed 10. On the other hand, C must be defined in a DIM statement, because its second subscript exceeds 10. As a matter of good programming practice, however, the DIM statement should appear as shown above, with A, B and C all dimensioned explicitly.

A DIM statement may appear anywhere within a BASIC program, but an array must be defined before its elements can appear within an executable statement. It is a generally good practice to place the DIM statement at the beginning of a program, where its presence is readily apparent.

5.2 SUBSCRIPTED VARIABLES

The individual elements within an array are known as *subscripted variables*. A subscripted variable can be accessed by writing the array name, followed by the value of the subscript enclosed in parentheses. Multidimensional array elements require the specification of multiple subscripts, separated by commas. The subscripts must be integer valued and they must fall within the range specified by the corresponding DIM statement.

Example 5.5

Consider once again the program described in Example 5.3, which contains the statement

```
DIM names$(100), values(100, 5)
```

The individual names will be referred to as names$(1), names$(2), . . ., names$(100). Note that the single subscript takes on integer values ranging from 1 to 100. Hence, 100 distinct subscript variables can be accessed. (Some versions of BASIC may permit the subscript to range from 0 to 100, thus encompassing 101 separate subscripted variables.)

The numeric values will be arranged in a table having 100 rows and 5 columns. The first subscript will correspond to the row number, and the second subscript will correspond to the column number. Thus, the number in the third row, fourth column will be referred to as value(3, 4), etc. (In some versions of BASIC, the subscripts will range from 0 to 100 and 0 to 5, respectively. Hence there may be as many as 101 rows and 6 columns, though these array elements need not all be utilized.)

A subscript can be written as a constant, a variable or a numeric expression. Noninteger values will automatically be rounded, as required. (Some older versions of BASIC may truncate rather than round noninteger subscript values.) If the value of a subscript is out of range (i.e., too large or too small), execution of the program will be suspended and an error message will be displayed.

Example 5.6

All of the subscripted variables shown below are correctly written.

```
names$(3)                          values(8, 5)
names$(i)                          values(m, n)
names$(k(i))                       values(m - 1, n + 3)
names$(2 * a - b)                  values(a + b, a - b)
names$(sqr(a ^ 2 + b ^ 2))         values(abs(a + b), abs(a - b))
```

Some of the subscripts may not be integer valued as written. In such cases, the noninteger values will automatically be rounded. Suppose, for example, the numeric expression (2 * a - b) has a value of 4.2. Then the subscripted variable names$(2 * a - b) will be interpreted as names$(4). Similarly, if (2 * a - b) has a value of 4.7, then the subscripted variable names$(2 * a - b) will be interpreted as names$(5).

Subscripted variables can be used within a program in the same manner as ordinary variables. This is illustrated in the following examples.

Example 5.7 Deviations About an Average

Suppose we want to read in a list of n numbers and then calculate their average, as in Example 4.12. In addition, we will calculate the deviation of each number about the average, using the formula

$$d = x_i - avg$$

where x_i represents each of the given numbers, $i = 1, 2, \ldots, n$, and avg represents the calculated average.

In order to solve this problem, we must store each of the given numbers in a one-dimensional numeric array. This is an essential part of the program. The reason, which must be clearly understood, is as follows.

In all of the earlier examples in which we calculated the average of a list of numbers, each number was replaced by its successor in the given list (see Examples 4.12, 4.13, 4.16, 4.17). Hence, each individual number was no longer available for subsequent calculations once the next number had been entered. Now, however, each of these individual values must be retained within the computer in order to calculate its corresponding deviation after the average has been determined. We will therefore store them in a one-dimensional array, which we will call list.

Let us define list to be a 100-element array. We need not, however, make use of all 100 elements. Rather, we shall specify the actual number of elements by entering a positive integer quantity (not exceeding 100) for the variable n, as in Example 4.12.

The computation will proceed in accordance with the following outline (an extension of the outline shown in Example 4.12).

1. Define the 100-element numeric array X(100).

2. Read in a value for the variable n.

3. Assign an initial value of 0 to the numeric variable sum.

4. Carry out the following steps repeatedly, for I ranging from 1 to n.

    (a) Enter the ith value within the list. Represent this value by the subscripted variable X(I).

    (b) Add the value of X(I) to the current value of sum.

5. After all n passes have been completed, sum will represent the sum of the n values. Hence, divide the value of sum by n to obtain the desired average.

6. Display the calculated value for the average.

7. Carry out the following steps repeatedly, for I ranging from 1 to n.

    (a) Calculate a current value for the deviation (d) using the formula given above.

    (b) Display the current value of I, the corresponding value of X(I), and the current value of d.

A corresponding BASIC program is shown below. Notice the placement of the DIM statement at the beginning of the program, following the program heading. Also, note the use of the subscripted variable X(I) in place of the ordinary variable X shown in Example 4.12.

```
REM CALCULATE THE DEVIATIONS ABOUT THE AVERAGE FOR A LIST OF N NUMBERS
DIM X(100)
PRINT "How many numbers";          'specify the size of the list
INPUT n
LET sum = 0
FOR I = 1 TO n                     'loop - calculate the sum of the X(I)'s
   PRINT "i ="; I; "    X = ";
   INPUT X(I)
   LET sum = sum + X(I)
NEXT I
LET AVERAGE = sum / n              'calculate the average value
PRINT
PRINT "Average ="; AVERAGE         'display the average
PRINT
FOR I = 1 TO n                     'loop - calculate & display the deviations
   LET d = X(I) - AVERAGE
   PRINT "i ="; I, "x ="; X(I), "d ="; d
NEXT I
END
```

Suppose the program is executed using the following five numerical quantities: $x_1 = 3$, $x_2 = -2$, $x_3 = 12$, $x_4 = 4.4$, $x_5 = 3.5$. The interactive session, including the data entry and the calculated results, is shown below. The user's responses are underlined.

```
How many numbers? 5
i = 1       x = ? 3
i = 2       x = ? -2
i = 3       x = ? 12
i = 4       x = ? 4.4
i = 5       x = ? 3.5

Average = 4.18

i = 1          x = 3       d =-1.18
i = 2          x =-2       d =-6.18
i = 3          x = 12      d = 7.82
i = 4          x = 4.4     d = .22
i = 5          x = 3.5     d =-.68
```

Arrays can be useful in manipulating character data as well as numeric data. We see an illustration of this in the following example.

Example 5.8 Word Unscrambling

An interesting problem involving the manipulation of subscripted variables is that of rearranging a group of letters to form all possible combinations. Suppose, for example, we are given a four letters, such as OPST. We wish to form and then display every possible combination of these four letters. Thus, we can find all possible four-letter words that can be formed from the original four letters (e.g., POST, STOP, etc.).

Our strategy will be to store the individual letters in a one-dimensional string array called L$. Each letter will be represented by a subscripted variable; i.e., L$(1), L$(2), L$(3) or L$(4). Hence, our objective will be to display all possible combinations of the subscripted variables.

Let us display the given four letters in the order designated by the indices I1, I2, I3 and I4, where I1 is the subscript of the first letter to be displayed, I2 refers to the second letter, and so on. For example, if I1 = 3, I2 = 2, I3 = 4 and I4 = 1, we would display the letters in the order

$$L\$(3) \qquad L\$(2) \qquad L\$(4) \qquad L\$(1)$$

We wish to write a BASIC program that will allow I1, I2, I3 and I4 to take on all possible values, with the restriction that each index have a unique numerical value. That is, no two indices will be allowed to represent the same number.

The BASIC program will consist of a nest of three FOR - NEXT loops, with supporting INPUT and PRINT statements. The outermost loop will assign a value to I1. The next loop (i.e., the first embedded loop) will assign a value to I2, with an IF test to prevent I2 from taking on the same value as I1. The innermost loop will assign a value to I3, with an IF test that prevents I3 from taking on the same value as I1 or I2. We can then obtain a value for I4 by noting that the sum of the indices is always 10, regardless of their order. Therefore, once I1, I2 and I3 have each been assigned a unique value, we can calculate the value of I4 from the formula

$$I4 = 10 - I1 - I2 - I3$$

We can outline the entire procedure as follows.

1.   Define the four element string array L$.

2.   Enter a letter for L$(1), L$(2), L$(3) and L$(4).

3.   Do the following for I1 = 1 to 4.

   (a)   Assign a value to I1.

   (b)   For each value of I1, do the following for I2 = 1 to 4.

      (i)   Assign a value to I2.

      (ii)   Test to see if the value of I2 is different than I1. If so, proceed with step (iii) below. Otherwise, increment the value of I2 and make another pass through the middle loop.

      (iii)   For each value of I1 and I2, do the following for I3 = 1 to 4.

         (1)   Assign a value to I3.

         (2)   Test to see if the value of I3 is different than I1 and I2. If so, proceed with step (3) below. Otherwise, increment the value of I3 and make another pass through the innermost loop.

         (3)   Calculate the value of I4 from the above formula.

         (4)   Display the letters represented by L$(I1), L$(I2), L$(I3) and L$(I4).

A complete BASIC program corresponding to the above outline appears below. Following the program is the output generated for the four letters OPST. The user's response has been underlined.

```
REM FOUR-LETTER WORD UNSCRAMBLER
DIM L$(4)
PRINT "Enter any four letters:"                    'enter the four letters
PRINT
INPUT L$(1), L$(2), L$(3), L$(4)
PRINT
FOR I1 = 1 TO 4                                    'assign I1
   FOR I2 = 1 TO 4                                 'assign I2
      IF I2 <> I1 THEN
         FOR I3 = 1 TO 4                           'assign I3
         IF I3 <> I1 AND I3 <> I2 THEN
            LET I4 = 10 - I1 - I2 - I3             'assign I4
            PRINT L$(I1); L$(I2); L$(I3); L$(I4)   'display the results
         END IF
         NEXT I3
      END IF
   NEXT I2
NEXT I1
END

Enter any four letters:

? O,P,S,T

OPST
OPTS
OSPT
OSTP
OTPS
OTSP
POST *
POTS *
PSOT
PSTO
PTOS
PTSO
SOPT
SOTP
SPOT *
SPTO
STOP *
STPO
TOPS *
TOSP
TPOS
TPSO
TSOP
TSPO
```

We see that there are 24 different ways in which the original four letters can be combined. By visual inspection, we can find the five recognizable words POST, POTS, SPOT, STOP and TOPS. For identification purposes, an asterisk has been placed to the right of each recognizable word.

Many applications require that individual characters or groups of characters be extracted from a string and stored individually. This is not difficult, but the procedure for doing so varies from one version of BASIC to another. For example, the 1987 ANSI standard specifies that a substring of the string STRNG$ can be written as STRNG$[i:j], where i refers to the beginning of the substring and j refers to the end of the substring. Thus, if STRNG$ represents "PENNSYLVANIA", then STRNG$[2:5] will represent the group of characters beginning with the second character and ending with the fifth character; i.e., "ENNS". True BASIC follows this convention.

On the other hand, some versions of BASIC include special functions that extract individual characters or groups of characters from a string. For example, the various implementations of Microsoft BASIC include the function MID$(STRNG$, i, j), where i represents the beginning of the substring and j represents its length. Thus, if STRNG$ represents "PENNSYLVANIA", then MID$(STRNG$, 2, 4) will represent the character group "ENNS".

Example 5.9 Writing a String Backwards

Let us write a simple BASIC program that will read in a string of characters and then display the string backwards. To do so, we will extract the individual characters within a string and store them as separate array elements. We will then display the array elements in reverse order.

The general procedure is presented in the following outline.

1. Define an 80-element string array called C$.

2. Enter the string STRNG$

3. Determine the number of characters in STRNG$. Call this value n.

4. Extract each character and assign it to C$(i), for i ranging from 1 to n.

5. Display the characters in reverse order (i.e., display each value of C$(i), for i ranging from n to 1).

Shown below is a corresponding program written in True BASIC. This program extracts the characters from the original string using the method suggested by the 1987 ANSI standard; i.e., C$(i) = STRNG$[i:i]. A typical interactive session is shown beneath the program listing.

```
REM DISPLAY A STRING OF CHARACTERS BACKWARDS
DIM C$(80)
PRINT "Please enter a string below"      !enter the string
INPUT STRNG$
LET n = LEN(STRNG$)                       !determine string length
FOR i = 1 TO n                            !extract the characters
   LET C$(i) = STRNG$[i:i]
NEXT i
FOR i = n TO 1 STEP -1                     !display the characters backwards
   PRINT C$(i);
NEXT i
END

Please enter a string below
? "Now is the time for all good men to come to the aid of their country!"
!yrtnuoc rieht fo dia eht ot emoc ot nem doog lla rof emit eht si woN
```

Another version of the same program is shown below, this one written in QuickBASIC. Note that the library function MID$ is now used to extract the individual characters; i.e., C$(i) = MID$(STRNG$, i, 1). When executed, this program will behave in the same manner as the one shown earlier.

```
REM DISPLAY A STRING OF CHARACTERS BACKWARDS
DIM C$(80)
PRINT "Please enter a string below"      'enter the string
INPUT STRNG$
LET n = LEN(STRNG$)                      'determine the string length
FOR i = 1 TO n
    LET C$(i) = MID$(STRNG$, i, 1)       'extract the characters
NEXT i
FOR i = n TO 1 STEP -1                    'display the characters backwards
    PRINT C$(i);
NEXT i
END
```

5.3 INITIALIZING AN ARRAY: THE DATA AND READ STATEMENTS

Many applications require that an initial data set be assigned to an array at the beginning of the program execution. This can be accomplished with the DATA and READ statements.

The DATA statement is used to store numeric and string data within a program and the READ statement is used to access this data on an item-by-item basis. The use of these statements is not restricted to array initialization, though they are often used for this purpose.

The DATA statement consists of the keyword DATA, followed by a set of numbers and/or strings separated by commas. Similarly, the READ statement consists of the keyword READ, followed by a list of variables separated by commas. The list can contain both ordinary and subscripted variables, representing numeric and/or string values. Each data item in a DATA statement must correspond to a variable of the same type in a READ statement.

Example 5.10

A BASIC program contains the following statements.

```
DIM flavor$(6), value(6)
DATA vanilla, chocolate, strawberry, cherry, butterscotch, pistachio
DATA 12, 15, 9, 7, 8, 4
. . . . .
FOR i = 1 TO 6
    READ flavor$(i)
NEXT i
FOR i = 1 TO 6
    READ value(i)
NEXT i
```

These statements cause the strings vanilla, chocolate,..., pistachio to be assigned to the subscripted variables flavor$(1), flavor$(2),..., flavor$(6), and the numeric values 12, 15,..., 4 to be assigned to the subscripted variables value(1), value(2),..., value(6).

Each DATA statement need not be associated with a particular READ statement on a one-to-one basis, though such correspondence is permitted (as illustrated in the example above) and is often desirable. The important point is that all of the DATA statements in a program collectively form a *block* of data items. Each data item within the block must correspond to a variable within a READ statement. This correspondence must be with respect to both *order* and *data type*.

Example 5.11

Here is a variation on the use of the DATA and READ statements shown in Example 5.10.

```
DIM flavor$(6), value(6)
DATA vanilla, 12, chocolate, 15, strawberry, 9, cherry, 7, butterscotch, 8
DATA pistachio, 4
. . . . .
FOR i = 1 TO 6
    READ flavor$(i), value(i)
NEXT i
```

This form has the advantage of requiring only one loop to read the data items. However, the groups of numeric and string data are intermingled, resulting in a program that is somewhat less clear. Thus, some programmers may prefer the program organization shown in Example 5.10.

Some versions of BASIC (e.g., True BASIC) include the identifiers MORE DATA and END DATA. These identifiers permit the use of conditional looping structures to read data items from a DATA block.

Example 5.12

In some versions of BASIC, the FOR - NEXT loops shown in Example 5.10 can be replaced by conditional loops as follows.

```
DIM flavor$(6), value(6)
DATA vanilla, chocolate, strawberry, cherry, butterscotch, pistachio
DATA 12, 15, 9, 7, 8, 4
. . . . .
DO WHILE MORE DATA
    READ flavor$(i)
LOOP
DO UNTIL END DATA
    READ value(i)
LOOP
```

As a practical matter, most programmers will generally use one identifier or the other in a single programming situation. We have used both forms interchangeably for illustrative purposes only.

Remember that this feature is not available in all versions of BASIC.

The following rules must be observed when placing data items within a DATA block.

1. The individual data items must correspond in order and in type to the variables listed in one or more READ statements. There must be at least as many elements in the data block as there are variables in the READ statements. Extra data items will be ignored.

2. The data items within a DATA statement must be separated by commas. However, the last data item should *not* be followed by a comma.

3. The data items must consist of numeric or string constants. Variables and expressions are not permitted.

4. Strings containing commas or blank spaces *must* be enclosed in double quotes. Other strings *may* be enclosed in double quotes if desired.

Example 5.13

Here is another variation of the READ and DATA statements shown in Example 5.10.

```
DIM flavor$(100), value(100)
DATA 5
DATA vanilla, "chocolate chip", strawberry, butterscotch, "butter pecan"
DATA 12, 15, 9, 7, 8
. . . . .
READ n
FOR i = 1 TO n
   READ flavor$(i)
NEXT i
FOR i = 1 TO n
   READ value(i)
NEXT i
```

In this example, some of the strings contain blank spaces and are therefore enclosed in double quotes. Also, notice that the arrays are dimensioned at 100, and the actual number of data items (5) is read from a DATA statement.

For consistency, we could have enclosed *all* of the strings in double quotes, had we desired to do so. Thus, the second data statement could have been written as

```
DATA "vanilla", "chocolate chip", "strawberry", "butterscotch", "butter pecan"
```

DATA statements may be placed anywhere in a BASIC program. However, it is good programming practice to place all of them in one place, usually at the beginning or the end of the program.

Example 5.14 Reordering a List of Numbers

Consider the well-known problem of rearranging a list of n numbers into a sequence of algebraically increasing values. Let us write a program that will carry out the rearrangement in such a manner that unnecessary storage will not be required. Therefore, the program will contain only one array — a one-dimensional numeric array called v — that will be reordered one element at a time.

The rearrangement will begin by scanning the first n elements of the array for the (algebraically) smallest number. This value will then be interchanged with the first number in the array, thus placing the smallest number at the top of the list. Next the remaining $(n - 1)$ numbers will be scanned for the smallest, which will be exchanged with the second number. Then the remaining $(n - 2)$ numbers will be scanned for the smallest, which will be interchanged with the third number, and so on, until the entire array has been reordered. Note that the entire rearrangement will require a total of $(n - 1)$ passes through the array, though the length of each scan will become progressively smaller with each successive pass.

In order to find the smallest number within each pass (i.e., within the ith pass), we sequentially compare the starting number v(i), with each successive number in the array, v(j). If v(j) is smaller than v(i), we interchange the two numbers; otherwise, we leave the two numbers in their original positions. Once this procedure has been applied to the entire array, the ith number will be smaller than any of the subsequent numbers. This process is carried out $(n - 1)$ times, for $i = 1, 2, \ldots, n - 1$.

The only remaining question is how the two numbers are actually interchanged. To carry out the interchange, we first temporarily save the value of v(i) for future reference. Then we assign the current value of v(j) to v(i). Finally, we assign the original value of v(i), which has temporarily been saved, to v(j). The interchange of the two numbers is now complete.

The most general way to solve this problem is to read the original list of numbers into the computer, carry out the rearrangement, and then display the rearranged list. To illustrate the use of the DATA and READ statements, however, let us place the original list of numbers into a DATA block. The values will then be read from this data block, rearranged, and then displayed.

The following outline describes the overall computational procedure.

1. Define the 100-element array v.

2. Place the original list of numbers in a DATA block. Begin by specifying how many numbers are in the list (n).

3. Read the value of n from the DATA block. Then read the values of v(i) for i ranging from 1 to n.

4. Display the original list of numbers.

5. Interchange the numbers as follows, for i ranging from 1 to n - 1.

    (*a*) Compare v(i) and v(j) for all values of j ranging from i + 1 to n. If v(j) < v(i), then

        (*i*) Assign v(i) to temp.

        (*ii*) Assign v(j) to v(i).

        (*iii*) Assign temp to v(j), thus completing the interchange of v(i) and v(j).

6. Display the reordered list of numbers.

Here is a corresponding program written in Microsoft QuickBASIC. This program includes a 20-element list of numbers within a DATA block. [The data block actually consists of 21 values, including the value of n that precedes the values of v(i).] Note, however, that v can contain as many as 100 numbers, since the DIM statement provides for a 100-element array.

```
'REARRANGE A LIST OF NUMBERS INTO ASCENDING ORDER
DIM v(100)
DATA 20                                          'n = 20 numbers
DATA 595,78,1505,891,29,7,18,191,36,68           '1st 10 numbers
DATA 7051,509,212,46,726,1806,289,401,1488,710   '2nd 10 numbers

'read the data
READ n
FOR i = 1 TO n
   READ v(i)
NEXT i
```

```
'display the original data
PRINT "Original list of numbers:"
PRINT
FOR i = 1 TO n
   PRINT v(i);
NEXT i
PRINT


'carry out the interchange
FOR i = 1 TO n - 1               'repeat the process (n-1) times
   FOR j = i + 1 TO n            'move the smallest number to the top
      IF v(j) < v(i) THEN        'interchange v(j) and v(i)
         LET temp = v(i)
         LET v(i) = v(j)
         LET v(j) = temp
      END IF
   NEXT j
NEXT i


'display the reordered data
PRINT
PRINT "Reordered list of numbers:"
PRINT
FOR i = 1 TO n
   PRINT v(i);
NEXT i
END
```

Execution of the program results in the following output. (Note that this program does not require any user input.)

```
Original list of numbers:

 595   78  1505   891   29   7   18   191   36   68   7051   509   212   46   726   1806   289
 401  1488   710

Reordered list of numbers:

 7   18   29   36   46   68   78   191   212   289   401   509   595   710   726   891   1488
 1505   1806   7051
```

Here is another version of the program, written in True BASIC. This version is preferable to the earlier version because it is not necessary to specify a value for n. (Note the DO UNTIL END DATA loop that is used to read the data from the DATA block.) Remember, however, that this program will not run under all versions of BASIC.

```
!REARRANGE A LIST OF NUMBERS INTO ASCENDING ORDER
DIM v(100)
DATA 595,78,1505,891,29,7,18,191,36,68           !1st 10 numbers
DATA 7051,509,212,46,726,1806,289,401,1488,710    !2nd 10 numbers
```

```
!read the data
LET n = 0
DO UNTIL END DATA
   LET n = n + 1
   READ v(n)
LOOP

!display the original data
PRINT "Original list of numbers:"
PRINT
FOR i = 1 TO n
   PRINT v(i);
NEXT i
PRINT

!carry out the interchange
FOR i = 1 TO n - 1              !repeat the process (n-1) times
   FOR j = i + 1 TO n           !move the smallest number to the top
      IF v(j) < v(i) THEN       !interchange v(j) and v(i)
         LET temp = v(i)
         LET v(i) = v(j)
         LET v(j) = temp
      END IF
   NEXT j
NEXT i

!display the reordered data
print
PRINT "Reordered list of numbers:"
PRINT
FOR i = 1 TO n
   PRINT v(i);
NEXT i
END
```

Execution of this program will result in output that is identical to that shown above.

5.4 REREADING DATA: THE RESTORE STATEMENT

Many applications require that the data within a DATA statement be read more than once. The RESTORE statement is used for this purpose. When the RESTORE statement is executed, an internal "pointer" is reset so that it points to the beginning of the data block. The next READ statement will then begin reading at the start of the data block.

The RESTORE statement consists simply of the keyword RESTORE. (Some versions of BASIC allow a line number or a line label to follow RESTORE.)

Example 5.15

A BASIC program contains the statements

```
DATA 1, 3, 5, 7, 9, 11, 13
. . . . .
READ a, b, c
. . . . .
RESTORE
READ w, x, y, z
```

Execution of this program will result in the following assignments.

$a = 1 \quad b = 3 \quad c = 5$

$w = 1 \quad x = 3 \quad y = 5 \quad z = 7$

If the RESTORE statement were not present, the assigned values would be

$a = 1 \quad b = 3 \quad c = 5$

$w = 7 \quad x = 9 \quad y = 11 \quad z = 13$

Review Questions

5.1   What is an array? In what ways do arrays differ from ordinary variables?

5.2   What condition must be satisfied by all elements within a given array?

5.3   How are numeric arrays distinguished from string arrays?

5.4   How are individual array elements identified?

5.5   What are subscripted variables? How are they written? What restrictions apply to the values that may be assigned to subscripts?

5.6   What is meant by the dimensionality of an array?

5.7   Suggest a practical way to visualize one-dimensional and two-dimensional arrays.

5.8   What is the purpose of the DIM statement? How is a DIM statement written?

5.9   How are the lower and upper bounds of a subscript specified in a DIM statement?

5.10   What rules govern the placement of a DIM statement within a BASIC program? Where are DIM statements usually placed?

5.11   In your particular version of BASIC, how can individual characters or groups of characters be extracted from a string ?

5.12   What is the purpose of the DATA and READ statements?

5.13   Summarize the rules for writing a DATA statement.

5.14   Summarize the rules for writing a READ statement.

5.15   Does each READ statement require a corresponding DATA statement? Explain.

5.16   What is a DATA block? How is a DATA block formed? What rules apply to the placement of data items within a DATA block?

5.17   What rules govern the placement of DATA statements within a BASIC program? Where are DATA statements usually placed?

5.18   Does your particular version of BASIC include special key words that permit conditional looping structures to read data from a DATA block? If so, what are these keywords and how are they used?

5.19   What is the purpose of the RESTORE statement? How is this statement written?

Problems

5.20   The following examples each involve one or more subscripted variables. Describe the array that is referred to in each situation.

(*a*)   `DIM cost(100), items$(100, 3)`

(*b*)   `LET P(I) = P(I) + Q(I, J)`

(*c*)   `IF A$(5) = TARGET$ THEN PRINT "Match Found"`

(*d*)   `PRINT X$(K), Y(K), Z(K, J)`

(*e*)   `LET message$(3) = "ERROR CHECK"`

(*f*)   `PRINT i, k(i), m$(k(i))`

5.21   Write one or more statements for each of the following problem situations.

(*a*)   Sum the first n elements of the one-dimensional array `costs`.

(*b*)   Sum all elements in the third column of the two-dimensional array `values`. Assume `values` has 60 rows and 20 columns.

(*c*)   Sum all elements in the fifth row of the two-dimensional array `values` described in part (*b*).

(*d*)   Sum all elements in the first m rows and the first n columns of the two-dimensional array `values` described in part (*b*).

(*e*)   Display the first 30 even elements in the one-dimensional string array `names$`; i.e., display `names$(2)`, `names$(4)`, . . ., `names$(60)`.

(*f*) Display every other character in the string `"Philadelphia, Pennsylvania"`.

(*g*) Calculate the square root of the sum of the squares of the first 100 odd elements of the one-dimensional array X; i.e., calculate $[X(1)^2 + X(3)^2 + X(5)^2 + \ldots + X(199)^2]^{1/2}$.

(*h*) Generate the elements of the two-dimensional array H, where each element of H is defined by the formula

$$h_{ij} = 1 / (i + j - 1)$$

Assume that H has 8 rows and 12 columns.

(*i*) A one-dimensional array K has N elements. Display the value of each subscript and each corresponding element for those elements whose values do not exceed KMAX. Display the output in two columns, with the value of the subscript in the first column and the corresponding subscripted variable in the second column. Label each column.

(*j*) A two-dimensional array W has K rows and K columns. Calculate the product of the elements on the main diagonal of W, where the main diagonal runs from upper left to lower right. In other words, calculate `W(1, 1) * W(2, 2) * W(3, 3) * . . . * W(K, K)`.

5.22 The following situations involve READ and DATA statements. Write one or more statements for each situation, as required.

(*a*) Assign the values 1, 4, 7, 10, . . ., 34 to the 12-element numeric array C.

(*b*) Assign the strings NORTH, SOUTH, EAST, and WEST to the 4-element string array `directions$`.

(*c*) Assign the strings NORTH, SOUTH, EAST, and WEST to the 4-element string array `player1$`, as in the previous problem. Then reset the pointer in the DATA block and assign the same strings to the 4-element string array `player2$`.

(*d*) Assign the strings New York, St. Louis, San Francisco, and Los Angeles to the 4-element string array `cities$`.

(*e*) Assign the following values to the 3 x 4, two-dimensional array called `consts`.

10	12	14	16
20	22	24	26
30	32	34	36

5.23 The following values are to be assigned to the indicated variables and arrays.

COLOR$(1) = WHITE	P = 2.5E5	T(1, 1) = 1	T(2, 1) = -2
COLOR$(2) = YELLOW	Q = 6.1E-9	T(1, 2) = -3	T(2, 2) = 4
COLOR$(3) = ORANGE	R = 1.3E12	T(1, 3) = 5	T(2, 3) = -6
COLOR$(4) = RED	H$ = RESTART	T(1, 4) = -7	T(2, 4) = 8

(*a*) Write one DATA statement for COLORS$, another DATA statement for the ordinary (nonsubscripted) variables, and a third DATA statement for T. Then write appropriate READ statements.

(b) Repeat part (a) above. At a later point in the program, reset the pointer in the DATA block and assign the listed colors to the variables A1$, A2$, A3$ and A4$.

5.24   Describe the output generated by each of the following programs.

(a)
```
DIM c(10)
DATA 0, 3, 6, 9, 12, 15, 18, 21, 24, 27
LET sum = 0
FOR i = 1 TO 10
    READ c(i)
    IF (c(i) MOD 2 = 0) THEN LET sum = sum + c(i)
NEXT i
PRINT "sum ="; sum
END
```

(b)
```
DIM c(10)
DATA 0, 3, 6, 9, 12, 15, 18, 21, 24, 27
LET sum = 0
FOR i = 1 TO 10
    READ c(i)
    IF (i MOD 2 = 0) THEN LET sum = sum + c(i)
NEXT i
PRINT "sum ="; sum
END
```

(c)
```
DIM c(10)
DATA 0, 3, 6, 9, 12, 15, 18, 21, 24, 27
LET sum = 0
FOR i = 1 TO 10
    READ c(i)
    IF (c(i) MOD 2 = 1) THEN LET sum = sum + c(i)
NEXT i
PRINT "sum ="; sum
END
```

(d)
```
DIM a(3, 4)
DATA 3, 6, 9, 12, 15, 18, 21, 24, 27, 30, 33, 36
LET c = 99
FOR i = 1 TO 3
    FOR j = 1 TO 4
        READ a(i, j)
        IF (a(i, j) < c) THEN LET c = a(i, j)
    NEXT j
NEXT i
PRINT "c ="; c
END
```

```
(e)  DIM a(3, 4)
     DATA 3, 6, 9, 12, 15, 18, 21, 24, 27, 30, 33, 36
     FOR i = 1 TO 3
        LET c = 99
        FOR j = 1 TO 4
           READ a(i, j)
           IF (a(i, j) < c) THEN LET c = a(i, j)
        NEXT j
        PRINT c;
     NEXT i
     END


(f)  DIM a(3, 4)
     DATA 3, 6, 9, 12, 15, 18, 21, 24, 27, 30, 33, 36
     FOR i = 1 TO 3
        LET c = 0
        FOR j = 1 TO 4
           READ a(i, j)
           IF (a(i, j) > c) THEN LET c = a(i, j)
        NEXT j
        PRINT c;
     NEXT i
     END


(g)  DIM a(3, 4)
     DATA 3, 6, 9, 12, 15, 18, 21, 24, 27, 30, 33, 36
     FOR i = 1 TO 3
        FOR j = 1 TO 4
           READ a(i, j)
        NEXT j
     NEXT i
     FOR j = 1 TO 4
        LET c = 0
        FOR i = 1 TO 3
           IF (a(i, j) > c) THEN LET c = a(i, j)
        NEXT i
        PRINT c;
     NEXT j
     END


(h)  LET p$ = "Programming with BASIC can be great fun!"
     LET n = LEN(p$)
     FOR i = 1 TO n
        LET c$ = MID$(p$, i, 1)
        IF (i MOD 2 = 0) THEN
           PRINT UCASE$(c$);
        ELSE
           PRINT LCASE$(c$);
        END IF
     NEXT i
     END
```

```
(i)  LET p$ = "Programming with BASIC can be great fun!"
     LET n = LEN(p$)
     FOR i = 1 TO n
        LET c$ = p$[i:i]
        LET remainder = (i / 2) - INT(i / 2)
        IF (remainder > 0) THEN
           PRINT UCASE$(c$);
        ELSE
           PRINT LCASE$(c$);
        END IF
     NEXT i
     END
```

Programming Problems

5.25 Modify the program shown in Example 5.7 so that it stores m different lists of n numbers each (where the value of n may vary from one list to another). For each list of numbers, calculate the average and the deviations of the individual numbers about the average, as in Example 5.7. Use a two-dimensional array to represent the m lists of numbers.

5.26 Modify the word unscrambler program given in Example 5.8 so that it displays all possible two-letter, three-letter and four-letter combinations of any four letters. Select a group of four letters and execute the program. Identify all valid English words by visual inspection of the displayed lists. (Can you determine, without running the program, how many different combinations of two or more letters will be generated?)

5.27 Modify the program given in Example 5.9 so that it writes a string backwards and inverts the case of each character (i.e., each uppercase letter will be displayed in lowercase, and vice versa).

5.28 Extend the program shown in Example 5.14 so that any one of the following four rearrangements can be carried out:

(a)   Smallest to largest, by magnitude

(b)   Smallest to largest, algebraic (by sign)

(c)   Largest to smallest, by magnitude

(d)   Largest to smallest, algebraic

(Note that the numbers within the list need not necessarily be positive.)
       Generate a menu that will allow the user to select which rearrangement will be used each time the program is executed. Test the program using the following values.

43	−85	−4	65
−83	10	−71	−59
61	−51	−45	−32
14	49	19	23
−94	−34	−50	86

5.29 Write a BASIC program that will rearrange a list of names into alphabetical order. To do so, enter the names into a one-dimensional string array, with each element representing one complete name. The list of names can then be alphabetized in the same manner that a list of numbers is rearranged from smallest to largest, as in Example 5.14.

Use the program to rearrange the following list of names.

Washington	Polk	Arthur	Roosevelt, F. D.
Adams, J.	Taylor	Cleveland	Truman
Jefferson	Fillmore	Harrison, B.	Eisenhower
Madison	Pierce	McKinley	Kennedy
Monroe	Buchanan	Roosevelt, T.	Johnson, L. B.
Adams, J. Q.	Lincoln	Taft	Nixon
Jackson	Johnson, A.	Wilson	Ford
Van Buren	Grant	Harding	Carter
Harrison, W. H.	Hayes	Coolidge	Reagan
Tyler	Garfield	Hoover	Bush

5.30 Write a BASIC program that will generate a table of values of the equation

$$y = 2 e^{-0.1t} \sin 0.5t$$

for integer values of t ranging from 0 to 60. Include a feature that will display the value of the function for any value of t entered by the user. Be sure that the data entry is carried out interactively and the resulting output is adequately labeled.

5.31 Write a BASIC program that will generate a table of $\sin x$, $\cos x$, $\tan x$, $\log_e x$ and e^x. Generate 101 entries for evenly spaced values of x between 0 and π (i.e., let $x = 0$, $\pi/100$, $2\pi/100$, . . ., $99\pi/100$, π). Include a feature that will display the value of all five functions for any value of x entered by the user. Be sure that the data entry is carried out interactively and the resulting output is adequately labeled.

5.32 Write a BASIC program that will sum all of the elements in each row and each column of a table of numbers. Display the sum of each row and the sum of each column. Then calculate the sum of the row sums and the sum of the column sums (they should be equal). Label the sums appropriately.

Test the program using the following table of numbers.

6	0	−12	4	17	21
−8	15	5	5	−18	0
11	3	1	−17	12	7
13	2	13	−9	24	4
−27	−3	0	14	8	−10

5.33 Solve Prob. 5.32 by calculating the *product*, rather than the sum, of each row and each column. Then determine the product of the row products and the product of the column products (they should be equal).

5.34 Write a BASIC program that will generate a table of compound interest factors, F/P, where

$$F/P = (1 + i/100)^n$$

In this formula F represents the future value of a given sum of money, P represents its present value, i represents the annual interest rate expressed as a percentage, and n represents the number of years.

Let each row in the table correspond to a different value of n, with n ranging from 1 to 30 (hence 30 rows). Let each column represent a different interest rate. Include the following interest rates: 4, 4.5, 5, 5.5, 6, 6.5, 7, 7.5, 8, 8.5, 9, 9.5, 10, 11, 12 and 15 percent (hence a total of 16 columns). Be sure to label the rows and columns appropriately.

5.35 Extend the program to calculate student exam scores [Probs. 4.58 (*i*) and 4.58 (*k*)] so that the deviation of each student's average about the overall class average will be determined. Display the class average, followed by each student's name, individual exam scores, final score, and the deviation about the class average. Be sure the output is logically organized and clearly labeled.

5.36 Consider the following foreign currencies and their equivalents to one U. S. dollar.

British pound:	0.6 pounds per U. S. dollar
Canadian dollar:	1.3 dollars per U. S. dollar
Dutch guilder:	2.0 guilders per U. S. dollar
French franc:	6.0 francs per U. S. dollar
Italian lira:	1250 lira per U. S. dollar
Japanese yen:	140 yen per U. S. dollar
Mexican peso:	1600 pesos per U. S. dollar
Swiss franc:	1.4 francs per U. S. dollar
German mark:	1.7 marks per U. S. dollar

Write an interactive, menu-driven program that will accept two different currencies and return the value of the second currency per one unit of the first currency. (For example, if the two currencies are Japanese yen and Mexican pesos, the program will return the number of Mexican pesos equivalent to one Japanese yen.) Use the data given above to carry out the conversions. Design the program so that it executes repetitively, until an ending condition is selected from the menu.

5.37 Consider the following list of countries and their capitals.

Canada	Ottawa
England	London
France	Paris
India	New Delhi
Israel	Jerusalem
Italy	Rome
Japan	Tokyo
Mexico	Mexico City
People's Republic of China	Beijing
Spain	Madrid
United States	Washington
U.S.S.R.	Moscow

Write an interactive, menu-driven program that will accept the name of a country as input and then display the corresponding capital, and vice versa. Design the program so that it executes repetitively, until the word END is entered as input.

5.38   Write a detailed outline and a complete BASIC program for each of the following problems. Include the most appropriate types of arrays for each problem. Be sure to label the output clearly and make use of efficient control structures.

(a)   Suppose we are given a table of integers, A, having *m* rows and *n* columns, and a list of integers, X, having *n* elements. We wish to generate a new list of integers, Y, that is formed by carrying out the following operations.

$$Y(1) = A(1, 1) * X(1) + A(1, 2) * X(2) + \ldots + A(1, n) * X(n)$$

$$Y(2) = A(2, 1) * X(1) + A(2, 2) * X(2) + \ldots + A(2, n) * X(n)$$

$$\cdot \quad \cdot \quad \cdot \quad \cdot \quad \cdot$$

$$Y(m) = A(m, 1) * X(1) + A(m, 2) * X(2) + \ldots + A(m, n) * X(n)$$

Display the input data (i.e., the values of the elements A and X), followed by the values of the elements of Y.
      Use the program to process the following data.

	1	2	3	4	5	6	7	8
	2	3	4	5	6	7	8	9
A =	3	4	5	6	7	8	9	10
	4	5	6	7	8	9	10	11
	5	6	7	8	9	10	11	12
	6	7	8	9	10	11	12	13

	1
	-8
	3
X =	-6
	5
	-4
	7
	-2

(b)   Suppose that A is a matrix (i.e., a two-dimensional numeric array) having k rows and m columns, and B is a matrix having m rows and n columns. We wish to generate the matrix C, where each element of C is determined by

$$C(i, j) = A(i, 1)*B(1, j) + A(i, 2)*B(2, j) + \ldots + A(i, m)*B(m, j)$$

where i = 1, 2,..., k and j = 1, 2,...,n (this is matrix multiplication).
      Use the program to process the following set of data.

	2	-1/3	0	2/3	4
A =	1/2	3/2	4	-2	1
	0	3	-9/7	6/7	4/3

$$B = \begin{vmatrix} 6/5 & 0 & -2 & 1/3 \\ 5 & 7/2 & 3/4 & -3/2 \\ 0 & -1 & 1 & 0 \\ 9/2 & 3/7 & -3 & 3 \\ 4 & -1/2 & 0 & 3/4 \end{vmatrix}$$

Write out the elements of A, B and C. Be sure that everything is clearly labeled.

(c) Consider a sequence of numbers, x_i, where $i = 1, 2, \ldots, m$. The mean is defined as

$$avg = (x_1 + x_2 + \ldots + x_n)/n$$

as in Example 5.7. The deviation about the mean is

$$d_i = (x_i - avg), \quad i = 1, 2, \ldots, n$$

and the *standard deviation* is

$$s = (d_1^2 + d_2^2 + \ldots + d_n^2)^{1/2}/n$$

Read in the first n elements of a one-dimensional array. Calculate the sum of these elements, the mean, the deviations, the standard deviation, the algebraic maximum and the algebraic minimum. Use the program to process the following set of data.

27.5	87.0
13.4	39.9
53.8	47.7
29.2	8.1
74.5	63.2

Repeat the computation for k different lists of numbers. Calculate the overall mean, the overall standard deviation, the absolute (largest) maximum and the absolute (algebraically smallest) minimum.

(d) Write a BASIC program that will calculate the variance, *var*, of a list of numbers two different ways, using the formulas

$$var = [(x_1 - avg)^2 + (x_2 - avg)^2 + \ldots + (x_n - avg)^2]/n$$

and

$$var = (x_1^2 + x_2^2 + \ldots + x_n^2)/n$$

where *avg* is the mean (average) value, calculated as

$$avg = (x_1 + x_2 + \ldots + x_n)/n$$

and n is the number of values in the list.

Mathematically, the two formulas for *var* can be shown to be identical. When the values of the given numbers are very close together, however, then the value obtained for *var* using the second formula can be considerably in error. The reason for this is that we must calculate the difference between two values that are very nearly equal. Such calculated differences can be highly inaccurate. The first formula for the variance yields much more accurate results under these conditions.

Demonstrate that the above statements are true by calculating the variance of the values given below. (The correct answer is $var = 0.00339966$.)

99.944	100.054	100.059	100.061
100.039	100.066	100.029	100.098
99.960	99.936	100.085	100.038
100.093	99.932	100.079	100.024
99.993	99.913	100.095	100.046

(e) Suppose we are given a set of tabulated values for y vs. x, i.e.,

y_0	y_1	y_2	$\ldots$	y_n
x_0	x_1	x_2	$\ldots$	x_n

and we wish to obtain a value of y at some x that lies between two of the tabulated values. This problem is commonly solved by *interpolation*, i.e., by passing a polynomial $y(x)$ through n points such that $y(x_0) = y_0, y(x_1) = y_1, \ldots, y(x_n) = y_n$ and then evaluating y at the desired value of x.

A common way to carry out the interpolation is to use the *Lagrangian form* of the interpolation polynomial. To do this we write

$$y(x) = f_0(x)\,y_0 + f_1(x)\,y_1 + \ldots + f_n(x)\,y_n$$

where $f_i(x)$ is a polynomial such that

$$f_i(x) = \frac{(x - x_0)\,(x - x_1) \ldots (x - x_{i-1})\,(x - x_{i+1}) \ldots (x - x_n)}{(x_i - x_0)\,(x_i - x_1) \ldots (x_i - x_{i-1})\,(x_i - x_{i+1}) \ldots (x_i - x_n)}$$

Notice that $f_i(x_i) = 1$ and $f_i(x_j) = 0$, where x_j is a tabulated value of x different from x_i. Therefore we are assured that $y(x_i) = y_i$.

Write a BASIC program to read in n pairs of data, where n does not exceed 10, and then obtain an interpolated value of y at one or more specified values of x. Use the program to obtain interpolated values of y at $x = 13.7$, $x = 37.2$, $x = 112$ and $x = 147$ from the data listed below. Determine how many tabulated pairs of data are required in each calculation in order to obtain a reasonably accurate interpolated value for y.

$y =$	$x =$
0.21073	0
0.37764	10
0.45482	20
0.49011	30
0.50563	40
0.49245	50
0.47220	60
0.43433	80
0.33824	120
0.19390	180

5.39 Write an interactive BASIC program that will encode or decode a line of text. To encode a line of text, proceed as follows.

1. Convert each character, including blank spaces, to its ASCII equivalent.

2. Enter a positive integer (a *key*). Add this integer to the ASCII equivalent of each character. The same integer will be used for the entire line of text.

3. Suppose that LV represents the lowest permissible value in the ASCII code, and HV represents the highest permissible value. If the number obtained in step 2 above (i.e., the original ASCII equivalent plus the random integer) exceeds HV, then subtract the largest possible multiple of HV from this number, and add the remainder to LV. Hence the encoded number will always fall between LV and HV, and will therefore always represent some ASCII character.

4. Print the characters that correspond to the encoded ASCII values.

The procedure is reversed when decoding a line of text. Be certain, however, that the same integer key is used in decoding as was used in encoding.

Chapter 6

Functions and Subroutines

We have already seen that BASIC includes a number of library functions that are used to carry out many common operations or calculations (see Sect. 2.14). BASIC also allows programmers to define their own functions for carrying out various individual tasks. The use of programmer-defined functions allows specialized operations, such as the evaluation of mathematical formulas or string manipulations, to be represented as individual program components. These components can then be accessed in the same manner as library functions.

A BASIC program can also contain one or more *subroutines*. Subroutines are similar to programmer-defined functions, though they differ in purpose and in syntax. Whereas a function always returns a single numeric or string quantity, a subroutine need not return anything — it is simply an identifiable program segment containing a related group of commands. Subroutines, like functions, can be accessed from multiple points within a BASIC program.

The use of functions and subroutines has several advantages. For example, they eliminate redundancy (that is, repeated programming of the same group of instructions at different places within a program). Also, they enhance the clarity of a program by allowing the program to be broken down into simple, logically concise components. And finally, they allow programmers to develop their own libraries of frequently used routines.

This chapter is concerned with the creation and use of such functions and subroutines. We will consider both *internal* functions and subroutines, which are a part of a single BASIC program, and *external* functions and subroutines, which are self-contained subprograms.

6.1 SINGLE-LINE FUNCTIONS: THE DEF STATEMENT

Normally, a programmer-defined function is *defined* before it is *accessed* (that is, utilized) within an executable statement. A single-line function is defined by means of the DEF (DEFINE) statement. This statement consists of the keyword DEF, followed by the function name, an equal sign and an appropriate constant, variable or expression. Both numeric and string functions can be defined with the DEF statement. (Remember that a numeric function returns a numeric value, whereas a string function returns a string.) String functions are identified by a dollar sign ($) at the end of the function name.

The rules concerning function names vary somewhat from one version of BASIC to another. According to the 1987 ANSI standard, a function name can be any numeric or string identifier. (Hence, the same rules as for variable names.) However, some versions of BASIC adhere to the older function naming convention, which requires the function name to begin with the letters FN.

If the function definition includes arguments, they must appear immediately after the function name, enclosed in parentheses and, if there are more than one, separated by commas. The arguments may be ordinary variables or array names. These arguments that appear in a function definition are often called *formal arguments* or *formal parameters*.

Example 6.1

Several typical single-line function definitions are shown below.

```
DEF f(x) = x ^ 3 + 2 * x ^ 2 - 3 * x + 4
DEF FNROOT(a, b, c) = SQR(b ^ 2 - 4 * a * c)
```

131

```
DEF title$ = "Name and Address:"
DEF FNJ$(A$, B$) = A$ + B$
```

The first function definition (f) returns the value of a numeric expression. It involves one numeric argument (x).

The second function definition (FNROOT) also returns the value of a numeric expression. This function definition involves three numeric arguments (a, b and c). Notice that the numeric expression includes a reference to the SQR library function (hence, a function reference within a function definition).

The third function definition (title$) returns a string constant. It does not not involve any arguments.

Finally, the last function definition (FNJ$) returns the string that is formed by concatenating the two string arguments (A$ and B$).

Notice that the first and third function names resemble ordinary variables, whereas the second and fourth function names begin with FN.

A programmer-defined function is accessed (or *referenced*) in the same manner as a library function, by specifying its name within an expression, as though it were an ordinary variable. The function name must be followed by an appropriate set of arguments, enclosed in parentheses and separated by commas.

Example 6.2

Shown below is the skeletal structure of a BASIC program containing three references to a programmer-defined function.

```
DEF f(x) = x ^ 3 + 2 * x ^ 2 - 3 * x + 4
. . . . .
LET u = f(y)
. . . . .
LET v = f(z)
. . . . .
IF f(w) < 0 THEN fmin = 0
```

In the first LET statement, the function is evaluated using the current value of the variable y as an argument. (Hence, the function will return the value of $y ^ 3 + 2 * y ^ 2 - 3 * y + 4$.) Similarly, the second LET statement causes the function to be evaluated using the current value of the variable z as an argument (thus returning the value of $z ^ 3 + 2 * z ^ 2 - 3 * z + 4$). The last statement involves a test to determine whether or not the value of the expression $w ^ 3 + 2 * w ^ 2 - 3 * w + 4$ is less than zero.

The arguments in a function reference may be constants, variables or expressions, but they must correspond in number and in type to the formal arguments within the function definition. It is the *value* of each argument that is actually passed to the function.

Example 6.3

A BASIC program contains the statements

```
DEF FNROOT(a, b, c) = SQR(b ^ 2 - 4 * a * c)
. . . . .
LET w = FNROOT(3.5, x(i), LOG(z) + 5)
```

The function definition (taken from Example 6.1) contains only ordinary (nonsubscripted) variables as formal arguments. However, the corresponding arguments in the function reference are expressed as a constant, a subscripted variable and a numeric expression, respectively. Notice that the last argument (the numeric expression) includes a reference to the library function LOG.

The variables appearing in a function definition need not be restricted to the formal arguments. Other program variables (including subscripted variables) may also be included in the defining expression. When the function is accessed, the most recently assigned values of these variables will be used in the function evaluation.

Example 6.4

The skeletal structure of a BASIC program is shown below.

```
DEF z(x, y) = (a * x + b * y) / (a + b)
. . . . .
LET a = 10
LET b = 20
. . . . .
LET zstar = z(p, q)
```

Execution of the last function will cause the function

```
(10 * p + 20 * q) / 30
```

to be evaluated. Notice that the values of a and b are not supplied as arguments. Hence, their most recently assigned values (that is, a = 10, b = 20) will be used when the function is evaluated.

The following example presents a more comprehensive illustration of the use of a programmer-defined function.

Example 6.5 Search for a Maximum

Suppose we wish to find the particular value of x that causes the function

$$y = x \cos x$$

to be maximized within the interval bounded by $x = 0$ on the left and $x = \pi$ on the right. We will require that the maximizing value of x be known quite accurately. We will also require that the search scheme be efficient in the sense that the function $y = x \cos x$ should be evaluated as few times as possible.

To solve this problem, we will use the following *elimination scheme*, which is a highly efficient computational procedure for any function that has only one "peak" within the search interval.

Suppose we place two search points at the center of the interval, located a very small distance from each other, as shown in Fig. 6.1. In this figure,

      a = left boundary of the search interval
     xl = left interior search point
     xr = right interior search point
      b = right boundary of the search interval
    sep = distance between xl and xr.

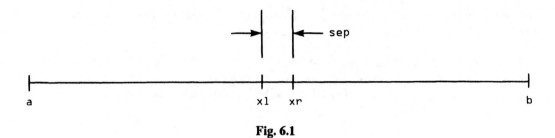

Fig. 6.1

If **a**, **b** and **sep** are known, then the interior points can be calculated as

```
xl = a + 0.5 * (b - a - sep)
xr = a + 0.5 * (b - a + sep) = xl + sep
```

Let us evaluate the function y = x cos(x) at xl and xr. We will call these values yl and yr, respectively. Suppose yl turns out to be greater than yr. Then we know that the maximum that we are seeking will lie somewhere between **a** and xr. Hence, we retain only that portion of the search interval that ranges from $x = xl$ to $x = b$. (We will now refer to the former point xr as b, since it is now the right boundary of the new search interval.) We then generate two *new* search points, xl and xr. These points will be located at the center of the new search interval, a distance sep apart, as shown in Fig. 6.2.

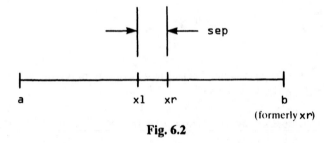

Fig. 6.2

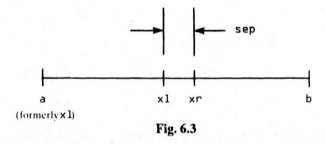

Fig. 6.3

On the other hand, suppose that the value of yr in our *original* search interval turned out to be greater than yl. This would indicate that our new search interval should lie between xl and b. Hence we rename the point that was originally called xl to be **a** and we generate two *new* search points, xl and xr, at the center of the new search interval, as shown in Fig. 6.3.

We continue to generate a new pair of search points at the center of each new interval, compare the respective values of y and eliminate a portion of the search interval until the search interval becomes smaller than 3 * sep. Once this happens, we can no longer distinguish the interior points from the boundaries. Hence, the elimination has gone as far as it can and the search is ended.

Each time we make a comparison between yl and yr we eliminate that portion of the search interval that contains the smaller value of y. If the two interior values should happen to have the same value (which can happen, though it is unusual), then the search procedure stops and the maximum can be assumed to occur at the center of the two search points.

Once the search has ended, either because the search interval has become sufficiently small or because the two interior points yield identical values of y, we can calculate the approximate location of the maximum as

```
xmax = 0.5 * (xl + xr)
```

The corresponding maximum value of the function can then be obtained as `xmax * cos(xmax)`.

A detailed outline of the general computational strategy is given below.

1. Define the function $y = x \cos x$.

2. Read the initial values of a and b and a value for `sep`.

3. Repeat the following steps until either `yl` becomes equal to `yr` (the desired maximum will be at the midpoint), or the most recent value of (b - a) becomes less than or equal to 3 * `sep`:

    (a) Generate the two interior points, `xl` and `xr`.

    (b) Calculate the corresponding values of `yl` and `yr` and determine which is larger.

    (c) Reduce the search interval by eliminating that portion that does not contain the larger value of y.

4. Evaluate `xmax` and `ymax`.

5. Display the values of `xmax` and `ymax`, and stop.

A complete BASIC program, written in True BASIC, is shown below. Notice the function definition at the beginning of the program, the two function references within the loop and the function reference near the end of the program. A different value for the argument (that is, a different value for x) is supplied in each function reference.

```
REM SEARCH FOR A MAXIMUM OF THE FUNCTION y = x * cos(x)

DEF y (x) = x * cos(x)        !function definition

PRINT "Left Boundary = ";
INPUT a
PRINT "Right Boundary = ";
INPUT b
PRINT "Minimum Separation = ";
INPUT sep
DO WHILE (b - a > 3 * sep)
   LET xl = a + .5 * (b - a - sep)
   LET xr = xl + sep
   LET yl = y(xl)
   LET yr = y(xr)
   IF (yl < yr) THEN         !eliminate left half interval
      LET a = xl
   ELSEIF (yl > yr) THEN     !eliminate right half interval
      LET b = xr
   ELSE                      !yl = yr, end loop
      EXIT DO
   END IF
LOOP
```

```
LET xmax = .5 * (xl + xr)
LET ymax = y(xmax)
PRINT
PRINT "xmax = "; xmax, "ymax = "; ymax
END


Left Boundary = ? 0
Right Boundary = ? 3.141593
Minimum Separation = ? 0.0001

  xmax = 0.860394   ymax = 0.561096
```

Beneath the program listing we see the results of executing the program with **a** = 0, **b** = 3.141593 and `sep` = 0.0001. Clearly, the maximum value of y = 0.561096 was obtained at x = 0.860394. Note that the user's responses are again underlined.

6.2 MULTI-LINE FUNCTIONS

Many calculations cannot be carried out using a single statement. This is particularly true of calculations that involve lengthy arithmetic formulas or conditional branching operations. Such calculations are well-suited for inclusion within multi-line functions.

A multi-line function, like a single-line function, can include any number of formal arguments but returns only one value. The first statement must be a DEF statement containing the function name, followed by the (optional) formal arguments, enclosed in parentheses and separated by commas. The last statement must be an END FUNCTION or an END DEF statement. The 1987 ANSI standard specifies the use of END FUNCTION, though some versions of BASIC use END DEF instead.

The rules for naming multi-line functions are the same as those for naming single-line functions. Remember that some versions of BASIC require that the function name begin with the letters FN.

Example 6.6

Shown below is the skeletal structure of a typical multi-line function, written in accordance with the 1987 ANSI standard.

```
DEF wstar(a, b, c)
   . . . . .
   LET wstar = . . .
   . . . . .
END FUNCTION
```

Here are some other ways to write this multi-line function definition.

```
DEF wstar(a, b, c)            DEF fnwstar(a, b, c)
   . . . . .                     . . . . .
   LET wstar = . . .             LET fnwstar = . . .
   . . . . .                     . . . . .
END DEF                       END DEF
```

The choice will depend on your particular version of BASIC. The example on the left is typical of True BASIC, whereas the example on the right is characteristic of QuickBASIC.

Between the DEF and END FUNCTION (or END DEF) statements there can be any number of statements that define the function. At least one of these statements must assign a value to the function name. Typically, this is accomplished with a LET statement.

Example 6.7 Smallest of Three Numbers

Here is a complete program, written in True BASIC, that returns the smallest of three numbers. The program makes use of a multi-line function that finds the smaller of two numbers.

```
DEF min (a, b)              !function definition
   IF a <= b THEN
      LET min = a
   ELSE
      LET min = b
   END IF
END DEF

PRINT "a = ";              !calling portion
INPUT a
PRINT "b = ";
INPUT b
PRINT "c = ";
INPUT c

PRINT "Min value ="; min(min(a, b), min(b, c))
END
```

Notice that the function definition contains two LET statements that assign values to the function name (LET min = a and LET min = b). Also, notice the nested references to min in the PRINT statement, near the end of the program. (The outer reference to min contains two additional references to min as arguments.) This statement causes the smallest of the three quantities a, b and c to be displayed.

A typical program execution is shown below. The user's responses are underlined.

```
a = ? 3
b = ? 7
c = ? 2
Min value = 2
```

If a variable is passed to a multi-line function as an argument, it is the *value* of the variable, rather than the variable itself, that is passed to the function. Hence, if the value of the argument is changed within the function, that change will be recognized *only within the function*. The variable will retain its original value within the calling portion of the program.

Example 6.8

Consider the simple BASIC program shown below.

```
DEF w(x)                   !function definition
   PRINT "x ="; x
   LET x = x + 1
```

```
      PRINT "x ="; x
      LET w = 3 * x ^ 2
END DEF

LET x = 2                    !calling portion
PRINT "x ="; x
LET y = w(x)
PRINT "x ="; x, "y ="; y
END
```

When this program is executed, the following output is obtained.

```
x = 2
x = 2
x = 3
x = 2          y = 27
```

The first line is generated at the beginning of the program (the PRINT statement following LET x = 2). The second line is generated at the start of the multi-line function, whereas the third line is generated later in the multi-line function, after the value of x has been increased by 1. Notice that the value of x has increased from 2 to 3.

The last line is generated by the calling portion of the program, after the function access. Notice that x retains its original value (x = 2). This is expected, since the value of x is not changed within the calling portion of the program. The value of y returned by the function, however, is based upon x = 3; that is, $3 * x ^ 2 = 3 * (3 ^ 2) = 27$.

Variables other than those specified as arguments may appear in a multi-line function definition, just as in a single-line function definition. Both ordinary and subscripted variables may be included. The current values of these variables (which may have been assigned within the calling portion of the program) will be used each time the function is evaluated. Thus, such variables are *global* in nature, since their values are recognized in both the function definition and the calling portion of the program. Moreover, any alterations to such variables within a function definition will be recognized within the calling portion of the program.

Example 6.9

Consider the simple BASIC program shown below.

```
DEF w(x)                     !function definition
    LET w = c * x ^ 2
END DEF

LET x = 2                    !calling portion
LET c = 3
LET y = w(x)
PRINT "c ="; c, "y ="; y

LET c = 1
LET y = w(x)
PRINT "c ="; c, "y ="; y
END
```

When this program is executed, the following output is generated.

```
c = 3        y = 12
c = 1        y = 4
```

The first line of output shows the value returned by the function, based upon the initial value of c (c = 3). The second line shows that the change in c (c = 1) made in the calling portion of the program is recognized within the function during the second function call.

Many versions of BASIC include an EXIT DEF statement, which allows control to be transferred out of a multi-line function. When this statement is encountered during program execution, control is returned to the statement following the function reference in the calling portion of the program.

Example 6.10

Here is a QuickBASIC program that includes a multi-line function containing an EXIT DEF statement.

```
DIM p(10)
DEF fnsum (p, n)                      'function definition
LET sum = 0
FOR i = 1 TO n
   IF (p(i) < 0) THEN
      EXIT DEF
   ELSE
      LET sum = sum + p(i)
   END IF
NEXT i
LET fnsum = sum
END DEF

FOR i = 1 TO 10                       'initialize array
   READ p(i)
NEXT i
DATA 2, 5, 8, 10, 9, 4, 12, 1, 8, 6

LET n = 8                             'calling portion
LET psum = fnsum(p, n)
IF i >= n THEN
   PRINT "Sum ="; psum
ELSE
   PRINT "Negative value encountered - element"; i
END IF
END
```

The multi-line function returns the sum of the first n elements of the one-dimensional numeric array p, providing the first n elements of p are nonnegative. If a negative value is encountered, however, control is returned directly to the calling portion of the program.

The main portion of the program causes the first 8 elements of the 10-element array to be summed. Execution of this program results in the following output.

```
Sum = 51
```

If the sixth data item in the DATA statement is changed from 4 to -4, that is,

```
DATA 2, 5, 8, 10, 9, -4, 12, 1, 8, 6
```

Then the following output will be generated when the program is executed.

```
Negative value encountered - element 6
```

The next example presents a more comprehensive program that contains both a single-line and a multi-line function.

Example 6.11 Simulation of a Game of Chance: Shooting Craps

Craps is a popular dice game in which you throw a pair of dice one or more times, until you either win or lose. The game can be simulated on a computer by substituting the generation of random numbers for the actual throwing of the dice.

There are two ways to win in craps. You can throw the dice once and obtain a score of either 7 or 11; or you can obtain a 4, 5, 6, 8, 9 or 10 on the first throw and then repeat the same score on a subsequent throw before obtaining a 7. Similarly, there are two ways to lose. You can throw the dice once and obtain a 2, 3 or 12; or you can obtain a 4, 5, 6, 8, 9 or 10 on the first throw and then obtain a 7 on a subsequent throw before repeating your original score.

We will develop the game interactively, so that one throw of the dice will be simulated each time you press the RETURN (or ENTER) key on the keyboard. A message will then appear indicating the outcome of each throw. At the end of each game, you will be asked whether or not you want to play again.

Our program will require a random number generator that produces uniformly distributed integers between 1 and 6. (By *uniformly distributed*, we mean that any integer between 1 and 6 is just as likely to occur as any other integer within this range.) To do so, we will make use of the RND library function, which generates *fractional* random numbers that are uniformly distributed between 0 and 1. We will also utilize the RANDOMIZE statement, which is used to initialize the random number generator.

We can generate a random *integer* uniformly distributed between 0 and 5 by writing INT(6 * RND) . Hence, to obtain a random integer that is uniformly distributed between 1 and 6, we simply add 1 to this expression; that is, 1 + INT(6 * RND). This value will represent the result of throwing a single die. To simulate throwing a pair of dice, we repeat the random number generation; that is, 2 + INT(6 * RND) + INT(6 * RND). (In interpreting the meaning of this expression, remember that each reference to RND will return a *different* random value.)

This expression can easily be placed within a single-line programmer-defined function. For example, in Microsoft QuickBASIC, the function can be written as

```
DEF fnroll = 2 + INT(6 * RND) + INT(6 * RND)
```

This function, called fnroll, will return a randomly generated integer quantity whose value varies between 2 and 12. (Note that the final result will *not* be uniformly distributed, even though the individual integers are.)

Now let us define a multi-line function called fngame that can simulate one complete game of craps. This function will return a 1 if the game results in a win and a 0 if the game ends with a loss.

Within fngame, the dice will be thrown as many times as necessary to establish either a win or a loss. To do so, this function will access fnroll as required. It will also include the rules for winning or losing a game. These rules are implemented through a SELECT CASE structure. Several PRINT and INPUT statements are also included, in order to provide an interactive capability.

A Microsoft QuickBASIC version of this function is shown below. Within this function, the INPUT statements require some discussion. First, notice that the value assigned to the input variable dummy$ is not used elsewhere in the program. This variable is present simply to satisfy the syntactic requirements of the INPUT statement. (Typically, the user will respond to the INPUT statements simply by pressing the RETURN/ENTER key.)

In addition, notice that each INPUT statement contains a string followed by a comma. This string is known as a *prompt* string. It generates a prompt message to the user, as would normally be generated by a separate PRINT statement. Thus, an INPUT statement written in this manner replaces a PRINT/INPUT combination. Moreover, the comma that follows the prompt string causes the usual question mark (?) to be suppressed when the INPUT statement is executed.

Many versions of BASIC include provisions for prompt strings and question mark suppression within the INPUT statement. The details for implementing these features vary from one version of BASIC to another.

Finally, it should be pointed out that both function names begin with fn, as is required by Microsoft QuickBASIC. Also, note that neither function requires any arguments.

```
DEF fngame
    PRINT
    INPUT "Roll the dice . . .", dummy$
    LET score1 = fnroll                        'first roll
    PRINT score1;
    SELECT CASE score1
    CASE 7, 11
       LET fngame = 1
       PRINT " - Congratulations!  You WIN on the first throw"
    CASE 2, 3, 12
       LET fngame = 0
       PRINT " - Sorry, You LOSE on the first throw"
    CASE 4, 5, 6, 8, 9, 10
       DO
           INPUT " - Roll the dice again . . .", dummy$
           LET score2 = fnroll                 'later roll
           PRINT score2;
       LOOP UNTIL (score2 = score1 OR score2 = 7)
       IF (score2 = score1) THEN
           LET fngame = 1
           PRINT " - You WIN by matching your first score"
       ELSE
           LET fngame = 0
           PRINT " - You LOSE by failing to match your first score"
       END IF
    END SELECT
END DEF
```

Note that this function includes two references to the single-line function fnroll. The second reference is included within a loop, so that fnroll may be accessed multiple times. Also, notice that the function includes four separate LET statements in which the function name fngame is assigned a value.

A complete BASIC program, including the functions fnroll and fngame (with some comments added), is shown below. The main portion of the program, shown at the bottom, simply provides an opening message, a loop to allow multiple games to be played, and a closing message. The closing message includes a line indicating the number of wins and the total number of games played.

Notice the RANDOMIZE statement that initializes the random number generator, within the main portion of the program. The argument (0) following the keyword RANDOMIZE enables the random number generator to generate a particular sequence of random numbers. A different value for this argument would result in a different sequence of random numbers. The syntactic details for writing the RANDOMIZE statement vary somewhat from one version of BASIC to another.

```
REM SIMULATION OF A GAME OF CRAPS


DEF fnroll = 2 + INT(6 * RND) + INT(6 * RND)        'roll a pair of dice

DEF fngame                                          'play one game
   PRINT
   INPUT "Roll the dice . . .", dummy$
   LET score1 = fnroll                                 'first roll
   PRINT score1;

   SELECT CASE score1
   CASE 7, 11
      LET fngame = 1
      PRINT " - Congratulations!  You WIN on the first throw"
   CASE 2, 3, 12
      LET fngame = 0
      PRINT " - Sorry, You LOSE on the first throw"
   CASE 4, 5, 6, 8, 9, 10
      DO
         INPUT " - Roll the dice again . . .", dummy$
         LET score2 = fnroll                        'later roll
         PRINT score2;
      LOOP UNTIL (score2 = score1 OR score2 = 7)
      IF (score2 = score1) THEN
         LET fngame = 1
         PRINT " - You WIN by matching your first score"
      ELSE
         LET fngame = 0
         PRINT " - You LOSE by failing to match your first score"
      END IF
   END SELECT
END DEF


REM main portion of program


RANDOMIZE (0)                       'initialize the random number generator
LET wins = 0                        'initialize no of wins
LET games = 0                       'initialize total no of games
PRINT "Welcome to the Game of CRAPS"
DO                                  'main loop
   LET wins = wins + fngame         'update no of wins
   LET games = games + 1            'update total no of games
   PRINT
   PRINT "Again (Y/N)";
   INPUT ans$
LOOP UNTIL (ans$ = "N" OR ans$ = "n")
PRINT
PRINT "You've won "; wins; "out of "; games; "games"
PRINT "Bye, have a nice day!"
END
```

Here is a typical interactive session, resulting from the execution of this program. The user's responses are underlined. (The underlined blank spaces indicate user responses generated by pressing the RETURN/ENTER key.)

```
Welcome to the Game of CRAPS

Roll the dice . . ._
  8  - Roll the dice again . . ._
  6  - Roll the dice again . . ._
  5  - Roll the dice again . . ._
  9  - Roll the dice again . . ._
  5  - Roll the dice again . . ._
 11  - Roll the dice again . . ._
  9  - Roll the dice again . . ._
  8  - You WIN by matching your first score

Again (Y/N)? Y

Roll the dice . . ._
  9  - Roll the dice again . . ._
  6  - Roll the dice again . . ._
  3  - Roll the dice again . . ._
  6  - Roll the dice again . . ._
  9  - You WIN by matching your first score

Again (Y/N)? Y

Roll the dice . . ._
  7  - Congratulations!  You WIN on the first throw

Again (Y/N)? Y

Roll the dice . . ._
  5  - Roll the dice again . . ._
  7  - You LOSE by failing to match your first score

Again (Y/N)? Y

Roll the dice . . ._
  3  - Sorry, You LOSE on the first throw

Again (Y/N)? N

You've won  3 out of  5 games
Bye, have a nice day!
```

6.3 EXTERNAL FUNCTIONS

External functions are similar to multi-line functions, with two important differences. First, an external function is defined *after* the END statement in a BASIC program; that is, *after*, rather than *within*, the main portion of the program. Second, any variables defined and utilized within an external function are not recognized outside of that function; that is, they are *local* to that function. Thus, external functions are separate program segments; they communicate with the calling portion of the program only through their arguments and the values that they return.

The 1987 ANSI standard requires that an external function definition begin with EXTERNAL FUNCTION *name*, where *name* is the function name, as described earlier. Formal arguments, if present, must follow the function name, enclosed in parentheses and separated by commas. The function definition must end with END FUNCTION.

Unfortunately, there is considerable variation in the manner in which commercial versions of BASIC implement this feature. True BASIC follows the ANSI standard closely, though not exactly. Microsoft's QuickBASIC involves a somewhat different syntax. We will discuss the principal characteristics of both True BASIC and QuickBASIC within this section.

Example 6.12

Shown below is the skeletal outline of a typical external function that follows the 1987 ANSI standard.

```
EXTERNAL FUNCTION wstar(a, b, c)
   . . . . .
   LET wstar = . . .
   . . . . .
END FUNCTION
```

Here are some other ways to write this multi-line external function definition.

```
EXTERNAL DEF wstar(a, b, c)          FUNCTION wstar(a, b, c)
   . . . .                              . . . . .
   LET wstar = . . .                    LET wstar = . . .
   . . . . .                            . . . . .
END DEF                              END FUNCTION
```

The choice will depend on your particular version of BASIC. The outline on the left applies to True BASIC, while the one on the right is representative of QuickBASIC. (Compare with Example 6.6.)

Before an external function can be referenced within the main portion of a program, it must be *declared* (that is, the function name must be identified as an external function). Otherwise, the function reference may be misinterpreted as a subscripted variable. Function declarations are normally placed at the beginning of the main program, in the same general area as internal function definitions.

According to the 1987 ANSI standard, a function declaration is written as EXTERNAL FUNCTION *name*, where *name* refers to the function name. Multiple function names can be declared within the same statement, provided they are separated by commas.

In True BASIC, a function declaration can be written either as DECLARE FUNCTION *name* or as DECLARE DEF *name*. In Quick BASIC, it is written as DECLARE FUNCTION *name*, with any required arguments shown in parentheses.

Example 6.13

The following program, written in True BASIC, is similar to that shown in Example 6.9. Now, however, the function is written as an external function rather than an internal multi-line function.

```
DECLARE FUNCTION w              !function declaration
LET x = 2                       !calling portion
```

```
    LET c = 3
    PRINT "c ="; c, "y ="; w(x)
    LET c = 1
    PRINT "c ="; c, "y ="; w(x)
    END

    EXTERNAL DEF w(x)              !external function definition
       LET c = 2
       LET w = c * x ^ 2
    END DEF
```

Notice that the first line is a function declaration (not a function definition) within the main portion of the program. The actual function definition comprises the last four lines of the program.

When this program is executed, the following output is generated.

```
    c = 3        y = 8
    c = 1        y = 8
```

Since w is an external function, the variable c in the main portion of the program is not recognized inside the function. Within the function, c is a separate variable whose value will always be 2. Hence, w will always be assigned the value of the expression $2 * x ^ 2$. (Compare with Example 6.9.)

Here is another version of this same program, written in Quick BASIC.

```
    DECLARE FUNCTION w (x)         'function declaration
    LET x = 2                      'calling portion
    LET c = 3
    PRINT "c ="; c, "y ="; w(x)
    LET c = 1
    PRINT "c ="; c, "y ="; w(x)
    END

    FUNCTION w (x)                 'external function definition
       LET c = 2
       LET w = c * x ^ 2
    END FUNCTION
```

Notice that the DECLARE statement is now written somewhat differently, with the argument x shown in parentheses. Also, notice that the first and last statements in the function definition are now written differently, to conform to the required QuickBASIC syntax.

When executed, this program will generate the same output as the earlier version shown above.

Control can be transferred out of an external function, in much the same manner as control is transferred out of an internal multi-line function. To do so, however, you must use the statement EXIT FUNCTION rather than EXIT DEF. This statement causes control to be transferred to the statement following the function reference in the calling portion of the program.

Example 6.14 Craps Revisited

Here is another version of the craps game simulation originally presented in Example 6.11. This version, written in True BASIC, makes use of external functions. The complete BASIC program is shown on the next page.

```
REM SIMULATION OF A GAME OF CRAPS

DECLARE FUNCTION game                        !function declaration

REM main portion of program
RANDOMIZE                          !initialize the random number generator
LET wins = 0                       !initialize no of wins
LET games = 0                      !initialize total no of games
LET ans$ = "Y"

PRINT "Welcome to the Game of CRAPS"          !opening message
DO WHILE (ans$ = "Y" OR ans$ = "y")           !main loop
   LET wins = wins + game                     !update no of wins
   LET games = games + 1                      !update total no of games
   PRINT
   PRINT "Again (Y/N)";
   INPUT ans$
LOOP

PRINT
PRINT "You've won "; wins; "out of "; games; "games"
PRINT "Bye, have a nice day!"
END

EXTERNAL DEF game                             !play one game

   DECLARE FUNCTION throw                     !function declaration

   LET flag = 1
   PRINT
   PRINT "Roll the dice . . .";
   INPUT PROMPT "": dummy$

   LET score1 = throw                         !first throw
   PRINT score1;

   IF (score1 = 7 OR score1 = 11) THEN        !win
      LET game = 1
      PRINT " - Congratulations!  You WIN on the first throw"

   ELSE IF (score1 = 2 OR score1 = 3 OR score1 = 12) THEN    !lose
      LET game = 0
      PRINT " - Sorry, You LOSE on the first throw"

   ELSE                                       !roll again
      DO WHILE (flag = 1)
         PRINT " - Roll the dice again . . .";
         INPUT PROMPT "": dummy$
         LET score2 = throw                   !later throw
         PRINT score2;
         IF (score2 = score1) THEN            !win
            LET game = 1
```

```
               PRINT " - You WIN by matching your first score"
               EXIT FUNCTION
          ELSE IF (score2 = 7) THEN                !lose
               LET game = 0
               PRINT " - You LOSE by failing to match your first score"
               EXIT FUNCTION
          END IF
       LOOP
    END IF
END DEF

    EXTERNAL DEF throw                                !roll a pair of dice
       LET throw = 2 + INT(6 * RND) + INT(6 * RND)
    END DEF
```

This program differs from the earlier version (see Example 6.11) in several respects, since it uses different types of functions and is written in a different version of BASIC. First, it is apparent that the functions throw and game, formerly defined as internal DEF-type functions, are now written as external functions. Note that game is declared in the main portion of the program, since this is where it is accessed. However, throw is declared within game, since it is accessed within game.

The logic within game has been changed to make use of IF - THEN - ELSE structures rather than SELECT CASE. Either structure will work well in this application; we have selected IF - THEN - ELSE to illustrate the EXIT FUNCTION statement, which is used in two different places to escape from an infinite loop.

The INPUT PROMPT statements appearing in game are input statements that include null prompts. The null prompts suppress the question marks that are normally generated by the INPUT statement. This feature differs syntactically from the inclusion of a prompt in a QuickBASIC INPUT statement, though the intent is the same.

Finally, when this program is executed it will be necessary to enter an actual character in response to the prompts, rather than simply pressing the ENTER key, as in Example 6.11. This is a requirement of True BASIC.

If an argument in an external function reference is an array, the argument must be written as an array name, without subscripts (and without accompanying parentheses). Within the function definition, the corresponding formal argument is followed by empty parentheses. If the argument is a multidimensional array, then commas must be placed within the parentheses (a single comma would appear in a two-dimensional array, two commas within a three-dimensional array, and so on).

The formal argument is not dimensioned within the external function definition. Its maximum size will be assumed to be the same as that of the corresponding actual argument (which must be dimensioned within the calling portion of the program). Remember that a formal array argument and a corresponding actual array argument must correspond both in *type* (numeric or string) and in *dimensionality* (number of dimensions). Within the function, the array subscripts cannot exceed the bounds of the actual array, as dimensioned in the calling portion of the program.

These array-transfer rules are defined within the 1987 ANSI standard. True BASIC adheres to these rules.

Example 6.15

Here is a simple program, written in True BASIC, that illustrates passing a one-dimensional array to an external function.

```
    DIM c(4)                             !one-dimensional array definition
    DECLARE FUNCTION sum                 !external function declaration
    FOR i = 1 TO 4
```

```
      READ c(i)
NEXT i
DATA 3, 6, 9, 12

LET n = 3
PRINT "Sum ="; sum(c, n)
END

EXTERNAL DEF sum(c(), n)                !external function definition
   LET s = 0
   FOR i = 1 TO n
      LET s = s + c(i)
   NEXT i
   LET sum = s
END DEF
```

This program first defines and initializes a four-element, one-dimensional numeric array. It then accesses the external function sum that calculates and returns the sum of the first n elements, where n is a positive integer that cannot exceed 4. In the present example, n is assigned a value of 3.

Notice that the function access is written as sum(c, n). Thus, the array argument is expressed as the array name, without accompanying parentheses or subscripts. Within the function definition, the corresponding formal array argument is written as c(). Note the empty parentheses that follow the array name.

Execution of this program results in the following output, which represents the sum of the first three array elements (that is, 3 + 6 + 9).

```
Sum = 18
```

Here is another simple program, written in True BASIC, that is similar to that shown above. Now, however, a *two*-dimensional array is passed to the external function.

```
DIM table(3, 4)                         !two-dimensional array definition
DECLARE FUNCTION sum                    !external function declaration

FOR i = 1 TO 3
   FOR j = 1 TO 4
      READ table(i, j)
   NEXT j
NEXT i
DATA 1, 2, 3, 4, 5, 6, 7, 8, 9, 10, 11, 12

PRINT "Sum ="; sum(table, 3, 3)
END

EXTERNAL DEF sum(table(,), row, n)      !external function definition
   LET s = 0
   FOR i = 1 TO n
      LET s = s + table(row, i)
   NEXT i
   LET sum = s
END DEF
```

The external function sum now calculates the sum of the first n elements within a given row of the two-dimensional array. Notice that the function now has three arguments: the two-dimensional array, followed by two ordinary numeric variables that represent the row number and the number of elements to be summed within that row, respectively.

The function access is written as sum(table, 3, 3). Again, we see that the array argument is expressed as an array name, without accompanying parentheses or subscripts. Within the function definition, however, the corresponding formal array argument is written as table(,). Notice the parentheses containing a single comma that follow the array name.

When this program is executed, the following output is obtained.

```
Sum = 30
```

This value represents the sum of the first three elements in the third row (that is, 9 + 10 + 11).

Microsoft QuickBASIC handles array transfers somewhat differently. In particular, a multi-dimensional array argument consists of the array name followed by an empty pair of parentheses. Commas are not placed within the parentheses, regardless of the dimensionality of the array. In addition, array arguments in external function declarations must be written in the same manner as the actual arguments in the corresponding function calls.

Example 6.16

Here is a QuickBASIC version of the second program shown in the last example.

```
DIM table(3, 4)                              'two-dimensional array definition

DECLARE FUNCTION sum (table(), row, n) 'external function declaration

FOR i = 1 TO 3
    FOR j = 1 TO 4
        READ table(i, j)
    NEXT j
NEXT i
DATA 1, 2, 3, 4, 5, 6, 7, 8, 9, 10, 11, 12

LET n = 3
PRINT "Sum ="; sum(table(), 3, 3)
END

FUNCTION sum (table(), row, n)                'external function definition
    LET s = 0
    FOR i = 1 TO n
        LET s = s + table(row, i)
    NEXT i
    LET sum = s
END FUNCTION
```

Notice that table, when written as an argument, is followed by an empty pair of parentheses, even though table is a two-dimensional array. Also, note that the function declaration at the beginning of the program now includes a list of arguments, enclosed in parentheses. The array argument, table(), is written as though it were an actual argument in a function call. (Compare with the corresponding True BASIC program presented in the last example.)

Most versions of BASIC permit external functions to be defined within separate program segments (called program *modules*) as well as in the same program segment as the main portion. The manner in which this is done varies, however, from one version of BASIC to another. Microsoft QuickBASIC, for example, *requires* that external functions be defined in separate program modules and also requires a nonstandard syntax, relative to the 1987 ANSI standard. A detailed discussion of QuickBASIC program modules is beyond the scope of our present discussion.

6.4 SUBROUTINES

A subroutine (also called a *subprogram*) is an independent program segment that can exchange information with its calling routine through arguments. Every subroutine has its own name. However, subroutine names, unlike function names, do not represent returned quantities. The name simply provides a means of accessing the subroutine. (*Note*: The subroutines discussed in this section do *not* include GOSUB - RETURN transfers, which are referred to as "subroutines" in older versions of BASIC. We briefly mention GOSUB subroutines in Sec. 6.5.)

A subroutine definition may include any number of arguments, including none. The arguments can represent information transferred from the calling routine to the subroutine, or from the subroutine to the calling routine. Thus, a subroutine can accept and return any number of values.

The 1987 ANSI standard permits both internal and external subroutines, though some versions of BASIC, such as Microsoft QuickBASIC, support only external subroutines (in addition to the older GOSUB-type subroutines discussed in the next section). An *internal* subroutine resembles a multi-line function in the sense that its definition is a part of the main program segment; that is, the subroutine definition *precedes* the END statement. Similarly, an *external* subroutine resembles an external function, since its definition appears *after* the END statement. We will consider only internal subroutines in this section; external subroutines will be discussed in Sec. 6.6.

The first statement in a subroutine definition must be a SUB statement containing the function name, followed by the (optional) formal arguments. The formal arguments must be enclosed in parentheses and separated by commas, as in a function definition. The last statement must be an END SUB statement.

Subroutine names generally resemble numeric variable names. However, there is never a need to append a dollar sign to a subroutine name, since a subroutine name does not represent a return quantity.

Example 6.17

Shown below is the skeletal structure of a typical subroutine, written in accordance with the 1987 ANSI standard. True BASIC and QuickBASIC also follow this convention.

```
SUB result(a, b, c)

    . . . . .

END SUB
```

This subroutine is named `result`. It includes three formal arguments, called `a`, `b` and `c` (more about formal arguments later).

Between the SUB and the END SUB statements there can be any number of statements that comprise the subroutine definition. Typically, some of these statements will include expressions involving one or more arguments. The arguments may also be assigned new values. Note, however, that the subroutine name is *not* assigned a value within the subroutine.

Example 6.18

The following subroutine determines the smaller of two numeric values.

```
SUB min (a, b, c)
   IF a <= b THEN
      LET c = a
   ELSE
      LET c = b
   END IF
END SUB
```

This subroutine includes three formal arguments: a, b and c. When accessing the subroutine, it is assumed that specific numeric values will have been assigned to a and b. The subroutine will then assign the smaller of these to c.

The CALL statement is used to access a previously defined subroutine. This statement consists of the keyword CALL, followed by the subroutine name, followed by a list of actual arguments, enclosed in parentheses and separated by commas. The actual arguments can be ordinary variables, subscripted variables, array names, constants or expressions.

If an actual argument is a constant or an expression, its *value* is passed to the subroutine. If this value is altered within the subroutine (by reassigning the corresponding formal argument), the alteration will not be recognized in the calling portion of the program. If an actual argument is a *variable*, however, then any change to the value of the corresponding formal argument will be recognized within the calling portion of the program. This is how subroutines return values to the calling portion of the program. Moreover, this feature applies to arrays and subscripted variables as well as to ordinary variables.

Example 6.19 Smallest of Three Numbers

The following True BASIC program is similar to that shown in Example 6.7 except that it makes use of a subroutine rather than a function.

```
REM DETERMINE THE SMALLEST OF THREE NUMBERS

SUB min (a, b, c)                    !subroutine definition
   IF a <= b THEN
      LET c = a
   ELSE
      LET c = b
   END IF
END SUB

PRINT "a = ";                        !calling portion of program
INPUT a
PRINT "b = ";
INPUT b
PRINT "c = ";
INPUT c
CALL min(a, b, b)                    !b = min(a, b)
CALL min(b, c, c)                    !c = min(b, c)
PRINT "Min value ="; c
END
```

The main portion of the program includes a subroutine declaration and two CALL statements that access the subroutine. The first CALL statement transfers the original values of a and b to the subroutine, and returns the smaller of these. Note that the value returned is assigned to b (hence, the original value of b may change as a result of the first subroutine call). The second subroutine call transfers the current values of b and c to the subroutine and returns the smaller of these. The value returned is assigned to c. Thus, c will represent the smallest value after the second function call.

Execution of this program will result in the same output shown in Example 6.7 (assuming, of course, that the same input quantities are supplied).

Arrays are transferred to a subroutine in much the same manner as arrays are transferred to an external multi-line function. That is, the formal arguments and the actual arguments are written in the same manner as the same array arguments used with an external function. If changes are made to any of the array elements within the subroutine, however, then those changes will be recognized within the corresponding actual array elements (in the calling portion of the program).

Example 6.20 Table Manipulation

Shown below is a complete True BASIC program that multiplies each element of a table (that is, of a two-dimensional array) by a constant factor.

```
REM TABLE MANIPULATION

SUB init(a(,))                  !initialize a 3 x 4 array
FOR i = 1 TO 3
   FOR j = 1 TO 4
      READ a(i, j)
   NEXT j
NEXT i
DATA 1, 2, 3, 4, 5, 6, 7, 8, 9, 10, 11, 12
END SUB


SUB display(a(,))               !display a 3 x 4 array
FOR i = 1 TO 3
   FOR j = 1 TO 4
      PRINT a(i, j);
   NEXT j
   PRINT
NEXT i
END SUB


SUB mult(k, a(,))               !multiply each element in a 3 x 4 array by k
FOR i = 1 TO 3
   FOR j = 1 TO 4
      LET a(i, j) = k * a(i, j)
   NEXT j
NEXT i
END SUB
```

```
DIM a(3, 4)                    !main program portion

CALL init(a)                   !initialize the array elements
PRINT "Initial Array:"
CALL display(a)                !display the initial array

CALL mult(3, a)                !modify the array elements
PRINT
PRINT "Modified Array 1:"
CALL display(a)                !display the first modified array

CALL mult(-1, a)               !modify the array elements
PRINT
PRINT "Modified Array 2:"
CALL display(a)                !display the second modified array
END
```

This program makes use of three separate subroutines. Each subroutine includes an array name as an actual argument. The first subroutine (called init) assigns an initial set of values to the two-dimensional array a. The second subroutine (display) causes the current values of the array elements to be displayed on a row-by-row basis. The third subroutine (mult) causes each array element to be multiplied by the constant k. Be sure that you understand the manner in which the formal array arguments are written.

Notice that the array a is dimensioned only once, in the main portion of the program. Also, notice that mult is called twice and display is called three times, whereas init is called only once. Each call to mult involves a different value for the first argument (that is, the first formal argument in the subroutine definition). The program could have been written in such a manner that display is called from mult rather than from the main portion of the program.

Execution of this program results in the following output:

```
Initial Array:
 1  2  3  4
 5  6  7  8
 9  10  11  12

Modified Array 1:
 3  6  9  12
 15  18  21  24
 27  30  33  36

Modified Array 2:
-3 -6 -9 -12
-15 -18 -21 -24
-27 -30 -33 -36
```

Variables other than formal arguments may appear within a function definition. Such variables will take on whatever values were assigned to them elsewhere (e.g., the calling portion of the program). These variables are global in nature, since their values are recognized both within the subroutine and within the calling portion of the program. Recall that this is true of multi-line functions as well as subroutines (see Sec. 6.2).

Control can be transferred out of a subroutine, just as it can be transferred out of a multi-line function. This is accomplished with an EXIT SUB statement. EXIT SUB has the same characteristics as EXIT DEF, which is used to transfer control out of a multi-line function (see Sec. 6.2).

Example 6.21 Table Manipulation

Here is a variation of the True BASIC program shown in Example 6.20. This program differs from the earlier program in two ways. First, the variable k that multiplies each array element in mult is now a global variable rather than an argument. Its value is assigned in the main portion of the program prior to each call to mult.

The second change concerns the addition of IF - THEN and EXIT SUB statements within mult. The program now transfers control out of mult if the value currently assigned to k is less than or equal to zero, or if it exceeds 100.

```
REM TABLE MANIPULATION

SUB init(a(,))                !initialize a 3 x 4 array
FOR i = 1 TO 3
   FOR j = 1 TO 4
      READ a(i, j)
   NEXT j
NEXT i
DATA 1, 2, 3, 4, 5, 6, 7, 8, 9, 10, 11, 12
END SUB


SUB display(a(,))             !display a 3 x 4 array
FOR i = 1 TO 3
   FOR j = 1 TO 4
      PRINT a(i, j);
   NEXT j
   PRINT
NEXT i
END SUB


SUB mult(a(,))                !multiply each element in a 3 x 4 array by k
IF (k <= 0) OR (k > 100) THEN
   EXIT SUB
END IF
FOR i = 1 TO 3
   FOR j = 1 TO 4
      LET a(i, j) = k * a(i, j)
   NEXT j
NEXT i
END SUB


DIM a(3, 4)                   !main program portion

CALL init(a)                  !initialize the array elements
PRINT "Initial Array:"
CALL display(a)               !display the initial array

LET k = 3
CALL mult(a)                  !modify the array elements
PRINT
PRINT "Modified Array 1:"
```

```
        CALL display(a)                    !display the first modified array

        LET k = -1
        CALL mult(a)                       !modify the array elements
        PRINT
        PRINT "Modified Array 2:"
        CALL display(a)                    !display the second modified array
        END
```

Execution of this program results in the following output. (Compare with Example 6.20.)

```
    Initial Array:
      1   2   3   4
      5   6   7   8
      9  10  11  12

    Modified Array 1:
      3   6   9  12
     15  18  21  24
     27  30  33  36

    Modified Array 2:
      3   6   9  12
     15  18  21  24
     27  30  33  36
```

The 1987 ANSI standard requires that a subroutine *declaration* must *precede* a subroutine access if the subroutine *definition* appears *after* the subroutine access. For an internal subroutine, the declaration is written as SUB *name*, where *name* represents the subroutine name. Multiple subroutine names, separated by commas, may appear in the same declaration. This requirement is not enforced, however, in all implementations of the language. In True BASIC, for example, a subroutine declaration is not required if the subroutine definition appears *anywhere* within the main portion of the program.

Example 6.22 A Pig Latin Generator

Pig Latin is an encoded form of English that is often used by children as a game. A pig Latin word is formed from an English word by transposing the first sound (usually the first letter) to the end of the word, and then adding the letter "*a*." Thus, the word *dog* becomes *ogda, computer* becomes *omputerca, pig Latin* becomes *igpa atinLa*, and so on.

Let us write a program in True BASIC that will accept a line of English text and then display the corresponding pig Latin. We will assume that each textual message can be typed on one 80-character line, with a single blank space between successive words. (Actually, we will require that the pig Latin message not exceed 80 characters. Therefore the original text must be somewhat less than 80 characters, since the corresponding pig Latin message will be lengthened by the addition of an "a" after each word.) For simplicity, we will transpose only the first letter, rather than the first sound, of each word. Also, we will ignore any special consideration that might be given to uppercase letters or punctuation marks.

We will use two subroutines in this program. The first, called scan, will locate the beginning and ending of each of the words comprising the original English text. The logic employed within the subroutine will be based upon a scan for blank spaces, which identify the end of one word and the beginning of another. The second subroutine, called convert, will actually convert the original English text into pig Latin. It does so by extracting individual words from the original text, rearranging each word into pig Latin, and then appending (that is, concatening) the newly converted word to the previously converted words.

The first subroutine will accept the string variable english$, which represents the original line of English text, as an input argument. It will return two numeric arrays and a numeric variable. The first numeric array, beginning, will indicate the beginning of each English word (that is, each element of beginning will point to the first letter of a different word within the line of text). Similarly, the second numeric array, ending, will indicate the end of each English word. The numeric variable, n, will represent the number of words within the original line of text. The second subroutine will accept english$, beginning, ending and n as input arguments and return the string variable piglatin$, which represents the line of pig Latin corresponding to the original English text.

Since most of the detailed program logic is contained in the subroutines, the main program is simply a loop that reads a line of English text, accesses each subroutine, and then displays the resulting line of pig Latin. Each pass through the loop processes a different line of English text. The looping action continues until the word "end" is entered as a separate line of text.

Here is the complete program, written in True BASIC. Notice that the program makes use of two 40-element, one-dimensional arrays. These arrays are larger than they need to be, since each array element will point to either the beginning or the end of a different word. Nevertheless, the array size is not excessive, and is adequate to cover any number of words that we might reasonably expect to find in a single line of text.

```
REM PIG LATIN GENERATOR
DIM beginning(40), ending(40)            !pointers to word beginnings & endings
PRINT "Welcome to Pig Latin"
DO                                       !begin main loop
    PRINT
    PRINT "Enter a line of text below:"
    INPUT english$
    LET beginning(1) = 1

    REM find the beginning and ending of each english word
    CALL scan(english$, beginning, ending, nwords)

    REM convert the english text into a line of pig latin
    CALL convert(english$, piglatin$, beginning, ending, nwords)

    REM display the pig latin
    PRINT piglatin$
LOOP UNTIL UCASE$(english$) = "END"

REM find the beginning and ending of each word
SUB scan(english$, beginning(), ending(), n)
LET length = LEN(english$)
LET n = 1
LET beginning(1) = 1                     !tag start of first word
FOR col = 1 TO length
    LET character$ = english$[col : col] !extract a character
    IF character$ = " " THEN
        LET ending(n) = col - 1          !tag end of word
        LET n = n + 1                    !increment the word count
        LET beginning(n) = col + 1       !tag beginning of next word
    END IF
NEXT col
LET ending(n) = length                   !tag end of last word
END SUB
```

```
REM convert each word into pig latin and add to previous pig Latin text
SUB convert(english$, piglatin$, beginning(), ending(), n)
LET piglatin$ = ""
FOR count = 1 TO n
    REM extract english word
    LET word$ = english$[beginning(count) : ending(count)]
    LET wordlength = LEN(word$)
    LET newword$ = word$[2 : 2 + wordlength] & word$[1 : 1] & "a "
    REM form equivalent pig latin word
    LET piglatin$ = piglatin$ & newword$
NEXT count
END SUB
END
```

Now consider what happens when the program is executed. Here is a typical interactive session, in which the user's entries are underlined.

```
Welcome to Pig Latin

"This is a pig Latin generator"
hisTa sia aa igpa atinLa eneratorga

"What sort of garbled message is this, anyhow?"
hatWa ortsa foa arbledga essagema sia his,ta nyhow?aa

"NOW IS THE TIME FOR ALL GOOD MEN TO COME TO THE AID OF THEIR COUNTRY"
OWNA SIA HETA IMETA ORFA LLAA OODGA ENMA OTA OMECA OTA HETA IDAA FOA HEIRTA OUNTRYCA

END
NDEA
```

6.5 LINE-ORIENTED SUBROUTINE CALLS (GOSUB, ON - GOSUB)

In Sec. 4.10 we mentioned the line-oriented statements GOSUB and ON - GOSUB. These statements are carried over from early (unstructured) versions of BASIC. They cause transfers to primitive "subroutines," which are not really subroutines, in the context of our present discussion, but are simply portions of the main program segment. We will refer to these "subroutines" as GOSUB subroutines, to distinguish them from real subroutines.

A GOSUB subroutine can begin with any numbered statement, but it must end with the RETURN statement. The RETURN statement causes control to be returned to the statement following the GOSUB statement. Control cannot be transferred out of the subroutine except via the RETURN statement. A subroutine may, however, include more than one RETURN statement. Some versions of BASIC permit the RETURN statement to include a line number, indicating the point to where control will be returned.

Many programmers begin a GOSUB subroutine with a REM statement, in order to identify the beginning of the subroutine. Some versions of BASIC permit the first statement in the subroutine to be labeled rather than numbered (see Sec. 4.10).

Example 6.23

A typical GOSUB subroutine usage might appear as

```
100 GOSUB 200

. . . . .

200 REM beginning of GOSUB subroutine

. . . . .

250 RETURN
```

The GOSUB statement causes control to be transferred to line 200, which is the beginning of the GOSUB subroutine. The statements within the subroutine will then be executed, until the RETURN statement (line 200) is encountered. At this time, control will be returned to the statement following the GOSUB statement.

The ON - GOSUB statement permits a transfer of control to one of several different GOSUB subroutines. Its use is directly analogous to the ON - GOTO statement described in Sec. 4.10.

Example 6.24

Here is a typical ON - GOSUB usage.

```
100 ON flag GOSUB 300, 400, 500

. . . . .

300 REM subroutine A            !begin first GOSUB subroutine

. . . . .

350 RETURN

. . . . .

400 REM subroutine B            !begin second GOSUB subroutine

. . . . .

470 RETURN

. . . . .

500 REM subroutine C            !begin third GOSUB subroutine

. . . . .

590 RETURN
```

Thus, control will be transferred to subroutine A (line 300) if `flag` has a value of 1, to subroutine B (line 400) if `flag` has a value of 2, and to subroutine C (line 500) if `flag` has a value of 3.

It should be understood that GOSUB subroutines are very primitive constructs. They do not permit the transfer of arguments and they cannot be placed in separate program modules. All internal variables are recognized globally throughout the program. And finally, their use interrupts the orderly, sequential structure that is characteristic of structured programs. For these reasons, *the use of the GOSUB and ON - GOSUB statements, together with GOSUB subroutines, should be avoided.*

On the other hand, it should also be recognized that GOSUB subroutines may be the only subroutines available in many earlier (nonstructured) versions of BASIC. Moreover, their use may be required, even in newer versions of BASIC, in order to make use of certain special features. (We will encounter such uses of GOSUB subroutines in Chaps. 10 and 11.) It should be understood, however, that this practice runs contrary to the style and spirit of structured BASIC programming, and should be adopted only if absolutely necessary.

6.6 EXTERNAL SUBROUTINES

External subroutines, like external functions, are defined after the END statement in a BASIC program. The rules that apply to transferring arguments to or from an external subroutine are the same as those for transferring arguments to or from an internal subroutine. However, any variables that are defined within an external subroutine are recognized only within that subroutine; that is, they are local to that subroutine.

The 1987 ANSI standard requires that external subroutines be *declared* within those program segments that access external subroutines. An external subroutine declaration is written as EXTERNAL SUB *name*, where *name* refers to the external subroutine name. Multiple names, separated by commas, are permitted in a single subroutine declaration.

Some implementations of BASIC do not require a subroutine declaration for external subroutines provided the external subroutines appear within the same program module as the calling portion of the program. True BASIC, for example, waives the subroutine declarations under these conditions. An illustration is shown below.

Example 6.25

Here is a simple True BASIC program that includes two subroutines, one internal and the other external. The program illustrates the difference between internal and external subroutines in the interpretation of variables defined within the subroutines.

```
LET a = 3
PRINT "a ="; a; "(original value)"
CALL sub1
PRINT "a ="; a; "(after calling sub1)"
PRINT
CALL sub2
PRINT "a ="; a; "(after calling sub2)"

SUB sub1                    !internal subroutine definition
   LET a = 2
   PRINT "a ="; a; "(redefined within sub1)"
END sub
END
```

```
SUB sub2                   !external subroutine definition
   LET a = 1
   PRINT "a ="; a; "(redefined within sub2)"
END sub
```

Notice that there are no subroutine declarations within the main portion of the program, since True BASIC does not require them.

When the program is executed, the following output is generated.

```
a = 3 (original value)
a = 2 (redefined within sub1)
a = 2 (after calling sub1)

a = 1 (redefined within sub2)
a = 2 (after calling sub2)
```

The output shows that the value assigned to a within the internal subroutine (sub1) is recognized within the main portion of the program. However, the value assigned to a within the external subroutine (sub2) is *not* recognized within the main portion of the program.

Some versions of BASIC require that subroutines (other than GOSUB subroutines) be written as external subroutines, within separate program modules. Microsoft QuickBASIC, for example, imposes such a requirement.

Example 6.26

The following QuickBASIC program generates the same output as the True BASIC program shown in the last example.

```
DECLARE SUB sub1 (a)
DECLARE SUB sub2 ()

LET a = 3
PRINT "a ="; a; "(original value)"
CALL sub1(a)
PRINT "a ="; a; "(after calling sub1)"
PRINT
CALL sub2
PRINT "a ="; a; "(after calling sub2)"
END

SUB sub1 (a)               'external subroutine definition
   LET a = 2
   PRINT "a ="; a; "(redefined within sub1)"
END SUB

SUB sub2                   'external subroutine definition
   LET a = 1
   PRINT "a ="; a; "(redefined within sub2)"
END SUB
```

In this program both subroutines are external, since QuickBASIC does not support internal subroutines. Hence, the variable a will be a *local* variable within each subroutine. In order to transfer the new value of a from the first subroutine to the calling portion of the program, we therefore include a as an argument in sub1. This was not required in the earlier program because sub1 was an *internal* subroutine, and therefore a was recognized globally throughout sub1 and the calling portion of the program.

6.7 RECURSION

Recursion is a process in which a function or subroutine calls itself repeatedly, until some specified condition has been satisfied. The process is used for repetitive computations in which a given computation is stated in terms of a previous result. Many iterative (that is, repetitive) problems can be formulated in this manner.

In order to solve a problem recursively, two conditions must be satisfied. First, the problem must be written in a recursive form, and second, the problem statement must include a stopping condition. Suppose, for example, we wish to calculate the factorial of a positive integer quantity. We would normally express this problem as $n! = 1 \times 2 \times 3 \times \ldots \times n$, where n is the specified positive integer. However, we can also express this problem in another way, as $n! = n \times (n - 1)!$. This is a recursive form of the problem statement, in which the desired calculation (the evaluation of $n!$) is expressed in terms of a previous result (the evaluation of $(n - 1)!$, which is assumed to be known). Also, we know that $1! = 1$, by definition. This last expression provides a stopping condition for the recursion.

The 1987 ANSI standard allows recursion to be utilized in multi-line internal functions, external functions, and all subroutines (other than GOSUB subroutines). True BASIC follows this convention. However, some versions of BASIC, such as Microsoft QuickBASIC, permit recursion only with external functions and subroutines. Consult your programmer's reference manual to determine the manner in which recursion can be implemented with your particular version of BASIC.

Example 6.27 Calculating Factorials

The following True BASIC program utilizes a recursive function to calculate the factorial of a positive integer. The function, called `factorial`, is an internal multi-line DEF function. This function calls itself recursively, with an argument (n − 1) that decreases with each successive call. The recursive calls terminate when the value of the argument becomes less than 2.

The main portion of the program begins by displaying a message indicating how to end the program execution. This is followed by a loop, where each pass reads a positive integer value for n and then displays the corresponding value of n!. Note that the initial function reference, which initiates the recursion, is placed in the PRINT statement. The looping action continues until a zero value (actually, a nonpositive value) is entered for n.

```
REM RECURSIVE FACTORIAL CALCULATIONS
DEF factorial(n)                            !recursive function definition
   IF (n < 2) THEN
      LET factorial = 1
   ELSE
      LET factorial = n * factorial(n - 1)  !recursive function call
   END IF
END DEF
```

```
REM MAIN PROGRAM SEGMENT
PRINT "Factorial Calculations (To STOP, enter 0)"
DO
    PRINT
    PRINT "n = ";
    INPUT n
    PRINT "n! ="; factorial(n)              !initial function call
LOOP UNTIL (n <= 0)
PRINT
PRINT "Bye, Have a Nice Day"
END
```

When the program is executed, the user is prompted for successive values of n. The corresponding value of n! is returned for each n that is entered. A typical session is shown below. The user's responses are underlined.

```
Factorial Calculations (To STOP, enter 0)

n = ? 3
n! = 6

n = ? 5
n! = 120

n = ? 0
n! = 1

Bye, Have a Nice Day
```

Here is another version, using a recursive subroutine rather than a recursive function.

```
REM RECURSIVE FACTORIAL CALCULATIONS
SUB factorial(n, nfac)                    !recursive subroutine definition
    IF (n < 2) THEN
        LET nfac = 1
    ELSE
        CALL factorial(n - 1, nfac)        !recursive subroutine call
        LET nfac = n * nfac
    END IF
END SUB

REM MAIN PROGRAM SEGMENT
PRINT "Factorial Calculations (To STOP, enter 0)"
DO
    PRINT
    PRINT "n = ";
    INPUT n
    CALL factorial(n, nfac)                !initial subroutine call
    PRINT "n! ="; nfac
LOOP UNTIL (n <= 0)
PRINT
PRINT "Bye, Have a Nice Day"
END
```

Notice the call to `factorial` within the subroutine definition. This call transfers the value of $(n - 1)$ to the subroutine and returns the value of `nfac` = $(n - 1)!$. Following the subroutine call is a LET statement that multiplies the value of `nfac` by the current value of n. (Compare with the `factorial` function , defined in the earlier version of the program.)

Execution of this program will result in output that is identical to the output produced by the earlier version of the program.

When a recursive program is executed, the recursive function or subroutine calls are not executed immediately. Rather, they are placed on a *stack* until the condition that terminates the recursion is encountered.* The function or subroutine calls are then executed in reverse order, as they are "popped" off the stack. Thus, when evaluating a factorial recursively, the function/subroutine calls will proceed in the following order:

$$n! = n \times (n - 1)!$$
$$(n - 1)! = (n - 1) \times (n - 2)!$$
$$(n - 2)! = (n - 2) \times (n - 3)!$$
$$. . . . .$$
$$2! = 2 \times 1!$$

The actual values will then be returned in the following reverse order:

$$1! = 1$$
$$2! = 2 \times 1! = 2 \times 1 = 2$$
$$3! = 3 \times 2! = 3 \times 2 = 6$$
$$4! = 4 \times 3! = 4 \times 6 = 24$$
$$. . . . .$$
$$n! = n \times (n - 1)! = . . .$$

This reversal in the order of execution is a characteristic of all functions that are executed recursively.

Example 6.28 The Towers of Hanoi

This is a well-known problem that illustrates how recursion can be used to simplify a complicated repetitive process.

The Towers of Hanoi is a game that is played with three poles and a number of different-sized disks. Each disk has a hole in the center, allowing it to be stacked around any of the poles. Initially, the disks are stacked on the leftmost pole in the order of decreasing size, with the largest on the bottom and the smallest on the top (see Fig. 6.4).

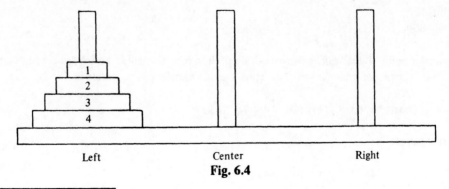

Left   Center   Right

Fig. 6.4

---

* A *stack* is a *last-in, first-out* data structure in which successive data items are "pushed down" upon preceding data items. The data items are later removed (that is, they are "popped") from the stack in reverse order, as indicated by the last-in, first-out designation.

The object of the game is to transfer the disks from the left-most pole to the right-most pole without ever placing a larger disk on top of a smaller disk. Only one disk can be moved at a time. Each disk must always be placed around one of the poles.

Consider one of the poles to be the origin and another to be the destination. The remaining pole will be used for temporary storage, thus allowing the disks to be moved without placing a larger disk over a smaller one. Assume there are n disks, numbered from smallest to largest, as in Fig. 6.4. If the disks are initially stacked on the left pole, the problem of moving all n disks to the right pole can be stated recursively as follows:

1. Move the top $n - 1$ disks from the left pole to the center pole.

2. Move the nth disk (the largest disk) to the right pole.

3. Move the $n - 1$ disks from the center pole to the right pole.

The problem can be solved in this manner for any value of n greater than 0. The value $n = 0$ can therefore be used as a stopping condition.

In order to program this problem we first label the poles so that the left pole is represented as L, the center pole as C and the right pole as R. We then construct a recursive subroutine called transfer that will transfer n disks from one pole to another. Let us refer to the individual poles with the string variables from$, to$ and temp$. These variables will represent the origin, destination and temporary storage, respectively. Therefore, if we assign the character L to from$, R to to$ and C to temp$, we will, in effect, be specifying the movement of n disks from the leftmost pole to the rightmost pole.

With this notation, the subroutine will have the following skeletal structure.

```
SUB transfer(n, from$, to$, temp$)
IF (n > 0) THEN
    REM move n-1 disks from their origin to the temporary pole


    . . . . .


    REM move the nth disk from its origin to its destination


    . . . . .


    REM move the n-1 disks from the temporary pole to their destination


    . . . . .


    END IF
END SUB
```

Each transfer of $n - 1$ disks can be carried out simply by a recursive call to transfer, though some care must be used in specifying the proper calling arguments. Thus, the first transfer can be written as

```
CALL transfer(n-1, from$, temp$, to$)
```

and the second transfer is

```
CALL transfer(n-1, temp$, to$, from$)
```

The movement of the nth disk from the origin to the destination requires nothing more than displaying the current values of from$ and to$.

The complete subroutine, written in QuickBASIC, will therefore appear as follows.

```
SUB transfer(n, from$, to$, temp$)
REM transfer n disks from one pole to another
IF (n > 0) THEN
    REM move n-1 disks from origin to temporary
    CALL transfer(n-1, from$, temp$, to$)

    REM move nth disk from origin to destination
    PRINT "Move disk"; n; " from "; from$; " to "; to$

    REM move n-1 disks from temporary to destination
    CALL transfer(n-1, temp$, to$, from$)
END IF
END SUB
```

It is now a simple matter to add the main portion of the program, which merely reads in a value for *n* and then initiates the computation by calling `transfer`. In this first subroutine call, the actual parameters will be specified as single-character strings; that is,

```
CALL transfer(n, "L", "R", "C")
```

This subroutine call specifies the transfer of all *n* disks from the left-most pole (the origin) to the right-most pole (the destination), using the center pole for temporary storage.

The complete QuickBASIC program is shown below.

```
REM TOWERS OF HANOI - SOLVED USING RECURSIVE SUBROUTINE CALLS

DECLARE SUB transfer(n, from$, to$, temp$)

REM MAIN PROGRAM SEGMENT
PRINT "Welcome to the TOWERS OF HANOI"
PRINT
PRINT "How many disks";
INPUT n
PRINT
CALL transfer(n, "L", "R", "C")
END

SUB transfer(n, from$, to$, temp$)
REM transfer n disks from one pole to another
IF (n > 0) THEN
    REM move n-1 disks from origin to temporary
    CALL transfer(n-1, from$, temp$, to$)

    REM move nth disk from origin to destination
    PRINT "Move disk"; n; " from "; from$; " to "; to$

    REM move n-1 disks from temporary to destination
    CALL transfer(n-1, temp$, to$, from$)
END IF
END SUB
```

It should be understood that the subroutine `transfer` receives a different set of values for its arguments each time the subroutine is called. Each set of values will be pushed onto the stack separately, so that it will be independent of the others. Each set is then popped from the stack at the proper time during the execution of the program. It is this ability to store and retrieve these values independently that allows the recursion to work.

When the program is executed for the case where $n = 3$, the following output is obtained:

```
Welcome to the TOWERS OF HANOI

How many disks? 3

Move disk 1   from L to R
Move disk 2   from L to C
Move disk 1   from R to C
Move disk 3   from L to R
Move disk 1   from C to L
Move disk 2   from C to R
Move disk 1   from L to R
```

Study this example carefully. The logic is very tricky, despite the apparent simplicity of the program. Think through each move to verify that the solution is indeed correct.

The use of recursion is not necessarily the best way to approach a problem, even though the problem definition may be recursive in nature. A nonrecursive implementation may be more efficient in terms of memory utilization and execution speed. As a result, the use of recursion may involve a tradeoff between simplicity and performance. Each individual problem should therefore be judged on its own individual merits. You should be comfortable with either type of problem formulation.

Review Questions

6.1   How do subroutines differ from functions in BASIC?

6.2   Name three significant advantages to the use of functions and subroutines.

6.3   Summarize the rules for defining a single-line function.

6.4   How are single-line string functions distinguished from single-line numeric functions?

6.5   What types of formal arguments are permitted in a single-line function?

6.6   How is a single-line function accessed?

6.7   What types of arguments are permitted in a single-line function reference? Compare with Question 6.5.

6.8   What is meant by passing an argument to a function by value?

6.9   What values will be assigned to non-argument variables that appear within a function definition? Will these variables be recognized outside of the function definition? What values will they have?

6.10   How does a multi-line function definition begin? How does it end?

6.11   What requirement must be satisfied by at least one statement within a multi-line function?

6.12   Suppose the value of an argument is changed within a multi-line function. Will this new value be recognized outside of the function definition?

6.13   Suppose the value of a non-argument variable is changed within a multi-line function. Will this new value be recognized outside of the function definition? Compare with Question 6.12.

6.14   How is control transferred out of a multi-line function? When this type of transfer occurs, to where will control be transferred?

6.15   How are random numbers generated in BASIC? How is the random number generation process initialized?

6.16   How do external functions differ from multi-line functions?

6.17   How does an external function definition begin? How does it end? Compare with Question 6.10.

6.18   What is the purpose of an external function declaration? How is it written?

6.19   Within a BASIC program, where must a function declaration appear, relative to the corresponding function definition?

6.20   How is control transferred out of an external function? Compare with Question 6.14.

6.21   Suppose an entire one-dimensional array is transferred to an external function. Within the function reference, how is the array argument written? Within the function definition, how is the corresponding formal argument written?

6.22   Suppose a multi-dimensional array is transferred to an external function. Within the function reference, how is the array argument written? Within the function definition, how is the corresponding formal argument written? Compare with Question 6.21.

6.23   Summarize the principal differences between a subprogram-type subroutine and a multi-line function. What is the significance of a subroutine name, compared with a function name?

6.24   What is the difference between an internal subroutine and an external subroutine?

6.25   How does an internal subroutine definition begin? How does it end? Is the subroutine name assigned a value within the subroutine definition? Compare with Question 6.10.

6.26   How is a subroutine accessed? How does a subroutine return values to the calling portion of the program?

6.27   Suppose a constant or an expression is passed to an internal subprogram-type subroutine and the value of the corresponding formal argument is altered within the subroutine. Will this change be recognized outside the subroutine definition?

6.28   Suppose a variable is passed to an internal subprogram-type subroutine and the value of the corresponding formal argument is altered within the subroutine. Will this change be recognized outside the subroutine definition? Does your answer also apply to subscripted variables? Compare with Question 6.27.

6.29   Suppose an entire array is passed to an internal subprogram-type subroutine and the values of the array elements are altered within the subroutine. Will these changes be recognized outside the subroutine definition? Compare with Questions 6.27 and 6.28.

6.30   Suppose the value of a non-argument variable is changed within an internal subprogram-type subroutine. Will this new value be recognized outside of the function definition? Compare with Question 6.13.

6.31   How is control transferred out of a subroutine? When this type of transfer occurs, to where will control be transferred? Compare with Question 6.20.

6.32   What is the purpose of an internal subroutine declaration? How is it written? Are internal subroutine declarations always required (explain)? Compare with Question 6.18.

6.33   Within a BASIC program, where must an internal subroutine declaration appear, relative to the corresponding subroutine definition? Compare with Question 6.19.

6.34   What is a GOSUB subroutine? How is a GOSUB subroutine accessed? How is control transferred back to the calling portion of the program?

6.35   How is information transferred between a GOSUB subroutine and the calling portion of the program? Are arguments permitted?

6.36   Describe the role of GOSUB subroutines in contemporary structured BASIC programs.

6.37   What are external subroutines? How do they differ from internal subprogram-type subroutines?

6.38   What is the purpose of an external subroutine declaration? How is it written? Are external subroutine declarations always required (explain)? Compare with Question 6.32.

6.39   Within a BASIC program, where must an external subroutine declaration appear, relative to the corresponding subroutine definition? Compare with Question 6.33.

6.40   What is meant by recursion? What kinds of functions and subroutines can be accessed recursively in BASIC?

6.41   What two conditions must be satisfied in order to solve a problem recursively in BASIC?

6.42   What is a stack? In what order is information added to and removed from a stack?

6.43   Explain what happens when a program containing recursive function or subroutine calls is executed (in terms of information being added to and removed from the stack).

6.44   If a repetitive process is programmed recursively, will the resulting program necessarily be more efficient than a nonrecursive version?

Problems

6.45   Answer the following questions for your particular version of BASIC.

    (*a*) Are external functions supported? If so, determine the exact syntactical rules associated with their use.

(b) How are entire arrays transferred as arguments?

(c) Are subprogram-type subroutines supported? If so, summarize the exact syntactical rules associated with their use. Are subroutine declarations required? If so, how are they written? Do any restrictions apply to the kinds of subroutines that can be defined (such as external subroutines only)?

(d) Can external functions and subroutines be placed in separate program modules? If so, how are these program modules written, edited and saved?

(e) Is recursion supported? If so, summarize the exact syntactical rules associated with its use. Are there any restrictions (such as recursive functions but no recursive subroutines)?

6.46 Write a single-line BASIC function for each of the situations described below.

(a) Evaluate the algebraic formula

$$z = [(u/v) + (x/y)]/2$$

(b) If X represents a positive fractional quantity, obtain a rounded value for X with two digits to the right of the decimal point.

(c) Evaluate the algebraic formula

$$y = ax^b$$

(d) Evaluate the algebraic formula

$$q = c_0 + c_1 r + c_2 r^2 + c_3 r^3 + c_4 r^4$$

(e) Evaluate the algebraic formula

$$i = (j + k)^{j + k}$$

6.47 Each of the following situations requires a reference to one of the functions defined in Prob. 6.46. Write an appropriate BASIC statement, or a sequence of statements, in each case.

(a) Display a value for f, where

$$f = [(a/b) + (c/d)]/2 \quad \text{[see Prob. 6.46(a)]}$$

(b) Suppose t represents some positive quantity whose value may exceed 1. Calculate a value for v, where v has the same value as t except that the decimal portion of v has been rounded to two digits [see Prob. 6.46(b)].

(c) Display a value of t, where

$$t = (c_1 + c_2)(x + y)^3 \quad \text{[see Prob. 6.46(c)]}$$

(d) Display a value of q, where

$$q = c_0 + c_1 \log (x) + c_2 [\log (x)]^2 + c_3 [\log (x)]^3 + c_4 [\log (x)]^4 \quad \text{[see Prob. 6.46(d)]}$$

(e) Display a value of f, where

$$f = (a - b + c)^{a - b + c} \quad \text{[see Prob. 6.46(e)]}$$

6.48 Write a multi-line BASIC function for each of the situations described below.

(a) Evaluate the algebraic formula

$$p = \log(t^2 - a) \quad \text{if } t^2 > a$$

$$p = \log(t^2) \qquad \text{if } t^2 \leq a$$

(b) Calculate the sum of the first n elements of the one-dimensional array a; that is, compute the sum

```
a(1) + a(2) + . . . + a(n).
```

(c) Suppose that M$ and N$ each represent a single letter. Construct a single string containing the two letters, arranged in alphabetical order.

(d) Calculate the average of two random numbers, each having a value between a and b.

(e) Examine the sign of the number represented by the variable X. If the value of X is negative, return the string NEGATIVE; if the value of X is positive, return the string POSITIVE; and if the value of X is zero, return the string ZERO.

(f) Suppose word$ represents a multi-letter word. Examine each of the letters and return the letter that comes first in the alphabet.

6.49 Write an external function for each of the problem situations described in Prob. 6.48.

6.50 Each of the situations described below requires a reference to one of the functions defined in Prob. 6.48. Write an appropriate BASIC statement, or a sequence of statements, in each case.

(a) Display a value for q, where q is evaluated as

$$\log[(a + b)^2 - c] \quad \text{if } (a + b)^2 > c,$$
and
$$\log[(a + b)^2] \qquad \text{if } (a + b)^2 \leq c \quad \text{[see Prob. 6.48(a)]}.$$

(b) Determine the difference between the sum of the first m elements and the sum of the first n elements of a one-dimensional numeric array [see Prob. 6.48(b)].

(c) Suppose c$ and d$ each represent a lowercase letter. Form an uppercase string consisting of the two letters, arranged in alphabetical order [see Prob. 6.48(c)].

(d) Determine the average of two random numbers, each having a value between 1 and 10 [see Prob. 6.48(d)].

(e) The one-dimensional numeric array list contains 100 elements. Beginning with list(1), determine whether the value of each element is positive, negative or zero. Display an appropriate message for each element [see Prob. 6.48(e)].

6.51 Write a subprogram-type subroutine for each of the situations described below.

   (*a*) Determine which element of a one-dimensional array has the largest value. Return the value of the array element and the value of the corresponding subscript.

   (*b*) Examine the sign of the number represented by the variable X. If the value of X is negative, display the message NEGATIVE VALUE; if the value is positive, display the message POSITIVE VALUE; and if the value is zero, display the message ZERO VALUE [compare with Prob. 6.48(*e*)].

   (*c*) Examine the individual characters within a string. Return the number of vowels, the number of consonants, the number of digits, and the number of other-type characters (punctuation marks, etc.).

   (*d*) Modify the subroutine written for part (*c*) above so that it displays a message and returns control to the calling portion of the program if a character is encountered that is not a letter or a digit.

   (*e*) Return the *transpose* of a two-dimensional numeric array; that is, if the given array has *m* rows and *n* columns, return another array having *n* rows and *m* columns. The element in row *m*, column *n* of the original array will become the element in row *n*, column *m* of the new array.

6.52 Write appropriate declarations and CALL statements for each of the subroutines described in Prob. 6.51.

6.53 Determine the output generated by each of the following programs.

   (*a*)
```
DEF fnq$ (message$) = "'" + message$ + "'"
LET message$ = "Hello, There!"
PRINT fnq$(message$)
END
```

   (*b*)
```
DEF fnz (y) = y ^ 2 + 2 * y + 3
LET x = 2
PRINT "z ="; fnz(x)
END
```

   (*c*)
```
DEF fnz (y) = y ^ 2 + 2 * y + 3
LET x = 2
PRINT "z ="; fnz(fnz(x))
END
```

   (*d*)
```
DEF fnz (y) = a * y ^ 2 + b * y + c
LET a = 3
LET b = 4
LET c = 5
LET x = 2
PRINT "z ="; fnz(x)
END
```

(e)
```
DEF fnscramble$ (message$)
    LET new$ = ""
    LET n = LEN(message$)
    FOR i = 1 TO n
        LET c$ = MID$(message$, i, 1)
        LET new$ = new$ + CHR$(ASC(c$) + 1)
    NEXT i
    LET fnscramble$ = new$
END DEF

LET message$ = "Hello, There!"
PRINT fnscramble$(message$)
END
```

(f)
```
DIM a(10)

DEF fnsum (n, max)
    IF n > 10 THEN EXIT DEF
    LET sum = 0
    FOR i = 1 TO n
        IF (a(i) <= max) THEN LET sum = sum + a(i)
    NEXT i
    LET fnsum = sum
END DEF

FOR i = 1 TO 10
    LET a(i) = i ^ 2
NEXT i

PRINT fnsum(8, 30)
END
```

(g)
```
DIM a(10)

DEF fnsum (a, n, max)
    IF n > 10 THEN EXIT DEF
    LET sum = 0
    FOR i = 1 TO n
        IF (a(i) <= max) THEN LET sum = sum + a(i)
    NEXT i
    LET fnsum = sum
END DEF

FOR i = 1 TO 10
    LET a(i) = i ^ 2
NEXT i

PRINT fnsum(a, 8, 30)
END
```

```
(h)  DIM a(10)

     DEF fnsum (a, n, max)
        IF n > 10 THEN EXIT DEF
        LET sum = 0
        FOR i = 1 TO n
           IF (a(i) <= max) THEN LET sum = sum + a(i)
        NEXT i
        LET fnsum = sum
     END DEF

     FOR i = 1 TO 10
        LET a(i) = i ^ 2
     NEXT i

     PRINT fnsum(a, 12, 300)
     END


(i)  DIM table(3, 3)
     DECLARE FUNCTION sum (table(), n)
     FOR i = 1 TO 3
        FOR j = 1 TO 3
           READ table(i, j)
        NEXT j
     NEXT i
     DATA 1, 2, 3, 4, 5, 6, 7, 8, 9

     PRINT "Sum ="; sum(table(), 3)
     END

     FUNCTION sum (table(), n)
        LET s = 0
        FOR i = 1 TO n
           LET s = s + table(i, i)
        NEXT i
        LET sum = s
     END FUNCTION


(j)  DIM table(3, 3)
     DECLARE FUNCTION sum (table())
     FOR i = 1 TO 3
        FOR j = 1 TO 3
           READ table(i, j)
        NEXT j
     NEXT i
     DATA 1, 2, 3, 4, 5, 6, 7, 8, 9

     LET n = 3
     PRINT "Sum ="; sum(table())
     END
```

```
FUNCTION sum (table())
   LET s = 0
   FOR i = 1 TO n
      LET s = s + table(i, i)
   NEXT i
   LET sum = s
END FUNCTION
```

(k)
```
DIM c(10)
DECLARE FUNCTION sum (c(), n, k)
FOR i = 1 TO 10
   READ c(i)
NEXT i
DATA 3, 6, 9, 12, 15, 18, 21, 24, 27, 30

PRINT "Sum ="; sum(c(), 7, 3)
END


FUNCTION sum (c(), n, k)
   IF n > 10 THEN EXIT FUNCTION
   LET s = 0
   FOR i = 1 TO n STEP k
      LET s = s + c(i)
   NEXT i
   LET sum = s
END FUNCTION
```

(l)
```
DIM c(10)
DECLARE FUNCTION sum (c(), n, k)
FOR i = 1 TO 10
   READ c(i)
NEXT i
DATA 3, 6, 9, 12, 15, 18, 21, 24, 27, 30

PRINT "Sum ="; sum(c(), 12, 2)
END


FUNCTION sum (c(), n, k)
   IF n > 10 THEN EXIT FUNCTION
   LET s = 0
   FOR i = 1 TO n STEP k
      LET s = s + c(i)
   NEXT i
   LET sum = s
END FUNCTION
```

```
(m) DECLARE SUB change (m$)
    LET m$ = "1600 Pennsylvania Avenue NW, Washington, DC 20500"
    PRINT m$
    CALL change(m$)
    PRINT m$
    CALL change(m$)
    PRINT m$
    END

    SUB change (a$)
       LET n = LEN(a$)
       LET b$ = ""
       FOR i = 1 TO n
          LET c$ = MID$(a$, i, 1)
          IF (c$ >= "A" AND c$ <= "Z") THEN
             LET b$ = b$ + LCASE$(c$)
          ELSEIF (c$ >= "a" AND c$ <= "z") THEN
             LET b$ = b$ + UCASE$(c$)
          ELSE
             LET b$ = b$ + c$
          END IF
       NEXT i
       LET a$ = b$
    END SUB


(n) DIM a(3, 3), b(3, 3)

    DECLARE SUB init (b())
    DECLARE SUB decomp (a(), b(), c$)
    DECLARE SUB display (a())

    FOR i = 1 TO 3
       FOR j = 1 TO 3
          READ a(i, j)
       NEXT j
    NEXT i
    DATA 1, 2, 3, 4, 5, 6, 7, 8, 9

    CALL display(a())

    CALL init(b())
    CALL decomp(a(), b(), "L")
    CALL display(b())

    CALL init(b())
    CALL decomp(a(), b(), "D")
    CALL display(b())

    CALL init(b())
    CALL decomp(a(), b(), "U")
    CALL display(b())
```

```
CALL init(b())
CALL decomp(a(), b(), "A")
CALL display(b())
END


SUB init (a())
   FOR i = 1 TO 3
      FOR j = 1 TO 3
         LET a(i, j) = 0
      NEXT j
   NEXT i
END SUB


SUB decomp (a(), b(), c$)
   LET p$ = UCASE$(c$)
   IF (p$ = "U") THEN
      FOR i = 1 TO 3
         FOR j = i TO 3
            LET b(i, j) = a(i, j)
         NEXT j
      NEXT i
   ELSEIF (p$ = "L") THEN
      FOR i = 1 TO 3
         FOR j = 1 TO i
            LET b(i, j) = a(i, j)
         NEXT j
      NEXT i
   ELSEIF (p$ = "D") THEN
      FOR i = 1 TO 3
         LET b(i, i) = a(i, i)
      NEXT i
   ELSE
      FOR i = 1 TO 3
         FOR j = 1 TO 3
            LET b(i, j) = a(i, j)
         NEXT j
      NEXT i
   END IF
END SUB


SUB display (a())
   FOR i = 1 TO 3
      FOR j = 1 TO 3
         PRINT a(i, j);
      NEXT j
      PRINT
   NEXT i
   PRINT
END SUB
```

```
(o)  DECLARE SUB change (m$, n)
     LET m$ = "1600 Pennsylvania Avenue NW, Washington, DC 20500"
     PRINT m$
     LET n = LEN(m$)
     CALL change(m$, n)
     END

     SUB change (a$, n)
        LET c$ = MID$(a$, n, 1)
        PRINT c$;
        IF (n = 1) THEN
           EXIT SUB
        ELSE
           CALL change(a$, n - 1)
        END IF
     END SUB
```

6.54 Express each of the following algebraic formulas in a recursive form.

(a) $y = (x_1 + x_2 + \ldots + x_n)$

(b) $y = 1 - x + x^2/2 - x^3/6 + x^4/24 + \ldots + (-1)^n x^n / n!$

(c) $p = (f_1 f_2 \ldots f_i)$

Programming Problems

6.55 Modify the program shown in Example 6.5 (search for a maximum) so that the following values are displayed for each subinterval during the elimination process: a, xl, xr, b, yl and yr. For each subinterval, display the first four quantities on one line, and the last two on another line, directly below the corresponding xs (that is, display yl directly below xl and yr directly below xr). Place a blank line after each pair, so that the history of the computation, showing successive subintervals, will be clearly visible.

6.56 Modify the program shown in Example 6.5 so that it will *minimize* a function of x. Use this minimization routine to calculate the roots of a nonlinear algebraic equation by minimizing the quantity $y(x) = f(x)^2$. Note that $y(x)$ will always be positive, except for those values of x that are roots of the given equation (that is, for which $f(x)$, and hence $y(x)$, will be zero). Therefore, any value of x that causes $y(x)$ to be minimized will also be a root of the equation $f(x) = 0$.

Use the program to obtain the roots of the following equations:

(a) $x + \cos(x) = 1 + \sin(x), \quad \pi/2 < x < \pi$

(b) $x^5 + 3x^2 = 10, \quad 0 \le x \le 3$

6.57 Modify the program shown in Example 6.8 so that it uses an external function rather than a multi-line DEF function.

6.58   Modify the program shown in Example 6.11 (shooting craps) so that it utilizes subprogram-type subroutines rather than functions.

6.59   Modify the program shown in Example 6.11 so that a sequence of craps games will be simulated automatically and noninteractively. Enter the total number of games as an input quantity. Add a counter to the program that will determine the total number of wins. Execute the program to simulate 1000 successive craps games. Use the results to estimate the probability of coming out ahead when playing multiple games of craps. (This value, expressed as a decimal, is the total number of wins divided by the total number of games played. If the probability exceeds 0.5, it favors the player; otherwise, it favors the house.)

6.60   Rewrite the pig Latin generator shown in Example 6.22 so that it utilizes multi-line functions rather than subroutines. Which approach is better, and why?

6.61   Rewrite the pig Latin generator shown in Example 6.22 so that it utilizes external functions rather than subroutines. Compare with the program written for the previous problem. Which type of function is better suited for this problem, and why?

6.62   Rewrite the depreciation program in Example 4.24 so that it utilizes subprogram-subroutines. Use a separate subroutine for each type of depreciation calculation. Also, place all common output (PRINT) statements into a single subroutine.

6.63   Rewrite the recursive program shown in Example 6.28 (the Towers of Hanoi) so that it utilizes a recursive function rather than a recursive subroutine. Which approach is better, and why?

6.64   Write a complete BASIC program for each of the following problems. Include one or more functions and/or subroutines in each program. Also, utilize arrays wherever appropriate.

   (*a*)   Calculate the weighted average of a list of *n* numbers [see Prob. 4.58(*a*)].

   (*b*)   Calculate the geometric average of a list of *n* numbers [see Prob. 4.58(*c*)].

   (*c*)   Calculate the sine of *x* by summing the first *n* terms of an infinite series [see Prob. 4.58(*f*)].

   (*d*)   Calculate the status of a bank loan on a month-by-month basis, as described in Prob. 4.58(*g*).

   (*e*)   Calculate a set of averages for student exam scores, as described in Prob. 4.58(*i*). Include a provision for unequal weighting of the individual exam grades [see Prob. 4.58(*j*)]. Also, determine the overall class average in addition to the individual student averages [see Prob. 4.58(*k*)].

   (*f*)   Extend the student grade average problem so that the deviation of each student's average about the overall class average will be determined (see Prob. 5.35).

   (*g*)   Simulate a simple calculator with a one-word memory [see Prob. 4.58(*l*)]. Use a separate function or subroutine for each operation, including the memory storage/retrieval operations.

   (*h*)   Convert a date into the number of days beyond January 1, 1960 [see Prob. 4.58(*o*)].

   (*i*)   Reorder a list of numbers any one of four different ways (see Prob. 5.28 and Example 5.14).

(j)   Sum the elements in each row and each column of a table of numbers (see Prob. 5.32).

(k)   Convert a sum of money from one currency to another (see Prob. 5.36).

(l)   Match a country with its capital (see Prob. 5.37).

(m)   Carry out the table manipulations described in Prob. 5.38(a).

(n)   Carry out the matrix multiplication operations described in Prob. 5.38(b).

(o)   Determine the characteristics of a list of numbers, as described in Prob. 5.38(c).

(p)   Calculate the variance of a list of numbers two different ways, as described in Prob. 5.38(d).

(q)   Carry out Lagrangian interpolation [see Prob. 5.38(e)].

(r)   Encode and decode a line of text, as described in Prob. 5.39.

6.65   Write a BASIC program that will generate a picture of the American flag. Use an asterisk to denote each star. Represent each stripe by several lines of repeated Rs or Ws, depending on the color of the stripe. Use a different subroutine to generate each type of output (that is, the block of stars, the short stripes and the long stripes).

6.66   Write a BASIC program that will allow a person to play a game of tic-tac-toe against the computer. Write the program in such a manner that the computer can be either the first or the second player. If the computer is to be the first player, let the first move be generated randomly. Display the complete status of the game after each move. Have the computer acknowledge a win by either player when it occurs. Include functions and subroutines within the program, as appropriate.

6.67   Write a BASIC program that will simulate a game of blackjack between two players. Note that the computer will not be a participant in this game but will simply deal the cards to each player and provide each player with one or more "hits" (additional cards) when requested.

The cards are dealt in order, first one card to each player, then a second card to each player. Additional hits may then be requested by the first player and then by the second player.

The object of the game is to obtain 21 points, or as many points as possible without exceeding 21 points. A player is automatically disqualified if his or her hand exceeds 21 points. Face cards count 10 points and an ace can count either 1 point or 11 points. Thus a player can obtain 21 points with the first two cards (blackjack!) if dealt an ace and either a 10 or a face card. If a player has a relatively low score with the first two cards, he or she may request one or more hits.

Use a random number generator to simulate the dealing of the cards. Be sure to include a provision that the same card is not dealt more than once. Include functions and subroutines wherever appropriate.

6.68   Roulette is played with a wheel containing 38 different squares along its circumference. Two of these squares, numbered 0 and 00, are green; 18 squares are red, and 18 are black. The red and black squares alternate in color and are numbered 1 through 36 in random order. Each number appears once and only once.

A small marble is spun within the wheel. Eventually, the marble comes to rest in a groove beneath one of the squares. The game is played by betting on the outcome of each spin in any one of the following ways:

1.   By selecting a single red or black square, at 35-to-1 odds. (Thus, if a player were to bet $1.00 and win, he or she would receive a total of $36.00 — the original $1.00 plus an additional $35.00.)

2.   By selecting a color (either red or black) at 1-to-1 odds. (Thus, if a player chose red on a $1.00 bet, he or she would receive $2.00 if the marble came to rest beneath any red square.)

3.   By selecting either the odd or the even numbers (excluding 0 and 00) at 1-to-1 odds.

4.   By selecting either the low 18 or the high 18 numbers at 1-to-1 odds (again, 0 and 00 are excluded).

The player will automatically lose if the marble comes to rest beneath one of the green squares (0 or 00).

Write an interactive BASIC program that will simulate a roulette game. Allow the players to bet any way they wish. Then display the outcome of each game, followed by a message indicating whether each player has won or lost. Include functions and subroutines as appropriate.

6.69   Write a BASIC program that will simulate a game of BINGO. Display each letter-number combination as it is drawn. Be sure that no combination is drawn more than once. Remember that each of the letters B-I-N-G-O corresponds to a certain range of numbers, as indicated below.

```
B :  1 - 15
I :  16 - 30
N :  31 - 45
G :  46 - 60
O :  61 - 75
```

Include functions and subroutines within the program, as appropriate.

Chapter 7

Some Additional Features of BASIC

In this chapter we discuss some additional features of BASIC that are commonly used in many elementary programming situations. Some of these features are included in the ANSI standard and some are not. However, all of these features are available in recent versions of either True BASIC or QuickBASIC (though relatively few of these features are supported by both versions of the language).

It should be understood that the list of features presented in this chapter is not meant to be exhaustive. Most commercial implementations of BASIC provide many additional features, some of which are hardware-dependent (i.e., they are intended to be used on a particular computer system). Only the more common features are discussed in this chapter. You should consult the reference manual that accompanies your particular version of BASIC for a complete description of all available features.

7.1 ADDITIONAL DATA TYPES

Many newer versions of BASIC recognize several different types of numeric quantities. Microsoft's QuickBASIC, for example, recognizes *integer, long-integer, real* and *double-precision* numeric quantities.

Integer quantities are either positive or negative whole numbers that typically fall within the range of $-32,768$ to $32,767$. They are not subject to roundoff errors. Hence, integer quantities are useful as counters, as subscripts for array elements or as indices in FOR - NEXT or DO - LOOP structures. Integer quantities may also be desirable when carrying out certain logical tests within IF - THEN or IF - THEN - ELSE structures.

Long integers are integer quantities whose permissible range extends beyond the limits of ordinary integers. In QuickBASIC, for example, a long integer can fall within the range of $-2,147,483,648$ to $2,147,483,647$. Because of their extended range, long integers require more bits than ordinary integers, and therefore occupy more space within the computer's memory.

Real quantities are ordinary fixed or floating-point numeric quantities, as discussed in Chapter 2. A real quantity may or may not include a fractional (decimal) component and/or an exponent. Typically, real quantities range (in magnitude) from approximately 10^{-38} (a very small number) to 10^{+38} (a very large number). The value 0.0 is also an acceptable real quantity. A number that looks like an integer (i.e., no decimal point and no exponent) can be forced to be a real by placing an exclamation point at the end (e.g., 5!).

Double-precision quantities are essentially real (single-precision) quantities with a greater range and a greater number of significant figures. Typically, double-precision quantities range (in magnitude) from approximately 10^{-308} (an extremely small number) to 10^{+308} (an extremely large number). The letter D, rather than the letter E, is used to represent the exponent (e.g., the value 10^{215} would be written as 10D215). The value 0.0 is also permissible. Furthermore, double-precision quantities can include as many as 15 digits (excluding the exponent), whereas single-precision quantities are restricted to seven or fewer digits. A number that looks like an integer (no decimal point and no exponent) or a fixed-point real (no exponent) can be forced to be double-precision by placing a pound sign at the end (e.g., 5#, 0.2#).

It should be understood that real and double-precision quantities are represented differently than integer and long-integer quantities within the computer's memory. Real and double-precision quantities are imprecise (they are subject to roundoff errors), whereas integer and long-integer quantities are exact. The details of the various internal representations is beyond the scope of our present discussion.

Some newer versions of BASIC (e.g., QuickBASIC) recognize other numeric data types, such as *octal* (base 8) and *hexadecimal* (base 16) integers. The use of these data types is beyond the scope of our present discussion.

Example 7.1

Several different types of numeric quantities are shown below.

Number	Type
16458	integer
16458!	real (fixed-point)
16458#	double-precision
2074816458	long-integer
36.55	real (fixed-point)
36.55#	double-precision
12E6	real (floating-point)
12D6	double-precision
0.2D-256	double-precision
-0.666667E-3	real (floating-point)
-0.666666666666667D-3	double-precision

When a numeric quantity is represented by a variable, the number and the variable must be of the same type. Thus, integer, long-integer, real and double-precision quantities must be represented by integer, long-integer, real and double-precision variables, respectively. The different variable types are often identified by the last character of the variable name, called *suffixes*. In QuickBASIC, for example, an integer variable will end with a percent sign (%), a long-integer variable will end with an ampersand (&), a real variable will end with an exclamation point (!) and a double-precision variable will end with a pound sign (#). Remember also that a *string* variable always ends with a dollar sign ($).

If a variable name does not end with one of these special characters, it will be interpreted as a real variable. The same name with different suffixes will be interpreted as different variables.

Example 7.2

Several BASIC variables and their corresponding data types are shown below.

Variable	Type
Count%	integer
Index&	long-integer
PAY	real
TAX!	real
ERROR#	double-precision
Name$	string

Remember that the memory requirements for the different data types are not the same. Integer quantities require the least amount of memory (typically 2 bytes), whereas double-precision quantities require the most (8 bytes). Moreover, the choice of data types may affect program execution times. As a rule, programs that make use of integer variables run faster than programs containing real or double-precision variables. Thus, programs that involve a great deal of numerical computation should utilize integer quantities wherever practicable.

Example 7.3

The QuickBASIC memory requirements for various data types are shown below.

Data Type	Memory Requirements (Bytes)
integer	2
long-integer	4
real	4
double-precision	8
string	4 + 1 byte / character

Microsoft's QuickBASIC includes several DEF-type statements that permit the type of several different variables to be specified at once. These statements are DEFINT, DEFLNG, DEFSNG, DEFDBL and DEFSTR. Their use requires that all variable names of a given type begin with the same first letter or fall within a specified range. An individual variable name that includes a suffix takes precedence over any DEF type specifications.

Example 7.4

A BASIC program contains the following statements.

```
DEFINT I
DEFLNG J, K
DEFSNG a, b, c
DEFDBL u, v, x-z
DEFSTR s, t
```

The DEFINT statement specifies that all variable names beginning with the letter I will be integer variables. The DEFLNG statement specifies that all variable names beginning with either J or K will be long-integer variables. The DEFSNG statement specifies that all variable names beginning with a, b or c will be real (single-precision) variables.

According to the DEFDBL statement, all variables beginning with u, v, x, y or z will be double-precision variables. Note that the variable names beginning with x, y and z are specified as a range. Finally, the DEFSTR statement specifies that all variable names beginning with s or t will be string variables.

Suppose the program includes the variable tag&. This will be a long-integer variable rather than a string variable, even though the variable name begins with t. The reason is that the suffix (&) takes precedence over the DEFSTR specification.

7.2 MORE ABOUT EXPRESSIONS

We have already discussed the fact that some versions of BASIC include the arithmetic operators \ and MOD for carrying out integer division and for determining an integer remainder (see Sec. 2.5). Moreover, the logical operations XOR, EQV and IMP are available in some versions of BASIC (see Sec. 4.2). Microsoft QuickBASIC, for example, supports the use of these additional operators. Thus, many versions of BASIC permit expressions that involve a variety of different operators and data types.

When arithmetic operations are carried out between different types of numeric data, the result will always be expressed at the highest possible level of precision. Thus, arithmetic operations involving both integer and real data will produce a real result. Similarly, arithmetic operations involving both integer and double-precision data, or both real and double-precision data, will produce a double-precision result. Arithmetic operations involving both integer and long-integer data will produce a long-integer result. And finally, arithmetic operations involving both long-integer and real (or double-precision) data will produce a real (or double-precision) result.

Example 7.5

In each of the following expressions, assume I% = 4, J& = 987654321, R! = −0.2 and D# = 0.16666666D−4.

Expression	Value
I% * R!	−0.8 (real)
3 * I% * D#	0.000199999992 (double-precision)
(1 + R!) * D#	0.1333333275032946D−05 (double-precision)
J& / 3	329218107 (long-integer)
D# + J&	987654321.0000167 (double-precision)

When a numeric value is assigned to a variable of a different type, the number will automatically be converted to the same data type as the variable to which it is assigned. Usually, this will cause a fractional quantity on the right to be *rounded* if assigned to an integer variable on the left (as in Microsoft BASIC), though some versions of BASIC will *truncate* rather than round the fractional quantity.

Example 7.6

In each of the following assignment statements, assume that I% = 4, R! = −0.2 and D# = 0.16666666D−4.

Assignment Statement	Result
LET N% = 3 * R!	N% = -1
LET FRACT = 1 / 3	FRACT = 0.3333333
LET FRACT# = 1 / 3	FRACT = 0.3333333333333333
LET ANS% = I% ^ 2 / 3	ANS% = 5
LET RATIO = (I% - R!) / D#	RATIO = 252000

Notice the rounding that results from the first statement. Truncation would have resulted in N% = 0 rather than N% = -1.

7.3 MORE ABOUT STATEMENTS

Some versions of BASIC allow the keyword LET to be omitted from assignment statements. Also, some versions of BASIC allow two or more statements to appear on the same line. Typically, a colon (:) will be used to separate one such statement from another. The various dialects of Microsoft BASIC support both of these features.

Example 7.7

The following program segments are written in Microsoft QuickBASIC. Each line contains at least two different BASIC statements.

```
LET a = 0.25 : LET b = 0.5 : LET c = -0.125
PRINT "x ="; : INPUT x
FOR i = 1 to n : READ A(i) : NEXT i
```

Note that the keyword LET could have been omitted from the first line; i.e.,

```
a = 0.25 : b = 0.5 : c = -0.125
```

Remember that these special features are not supported by all versions of BASIC.

Placing two or more statements on the same line is sometimes convenient, since it allows related statements to be grouped together. However, we recommend that this feature be used sparingly, if at all, since programs that contain multiple statements per line can be difficult to read and to edit. Moreover, the use of this feature is in conflict with the structured program philosophy, which encourages a clear, sequential program structure.

Example 7.8 Generation of Fibonacci Numbers and Search for Primes

In Example 4.19 we saw a complete BASIC program that generates a sequence of Fibonacci numbers and determines which of them are prime numbers. Here is another such program, written in QuickBASIC.

```
REM GENERATION OF FIBONACCI NUMBERS AND SEARCH FOR PRIMES (N > 5)
PRINT "GENERATION OF FIBONACCI NUMBERS AND SEARCH FOR PRIMES": PRINT
PRINT "N = "; : INPUT N%: PRINT
F1& = 1: F2& = 1                          'first 2 Fibonacci numbers
PRINT "I ="; 1, "F ="; 1; "  (PRIME)"
PRINT "I ="; 2, "F ="; 1; "  (PRIME)"
FOR I% = 3 TO 5                           'next 3 Fibonacci numbers
   F& = F1& + F2&
   PRINT "I ="; I%, "F ="; F&; "  (PRIME)"
   F2& = F1&: F1& = F&
NEXT I%
FOR I% = 6 TO N%                          'remaining Fibonacci numbers
   F& = F1& + F2&
   FOR D& = 2 TO INT(SQR(F&)) + 2         'test for a prime
      R& = F& MOD D&
      IF R& = 0 THEN EXIT FOR
   NEXT D&
   IF R& = 0 THEN
      PRINT "I ="; I%, "F ="; F&          'print the results
   ELSE
      PRINT "I ="; I%, "F ="; F&; "  (PRIME)"
   END IF
   F2& = F1&: F1& = F&                    'update for next pass
NEXT I%
END
```

This program utilizes several of the language extensions presented earlier in this chapter. In particular, we see the use of integer-type variables (I% and N%), long-integer variables (F&, F1&, F2&, D& and R&) and multiple statements on several of the lines. Also, the logic used to identify prime numbers is now somewhat more straightforward, since we now make use of the integer remainder (MOD) operation. Note, however, that the present version of the program lacks the clarity of the original version shown in Example 4.19.

Execution of this program results in output similar to that shown in Example 4.19. Note that the value assigned to N% can now exceed 23, even on a desktop computer, since the Fibonacci numbers are now represented as long integers.

7.4 CLEARING THE SCREEN: THE CLEAR AND CLS STATEMENTS

Practically all computers now use TV monitors as primary output devices. Most monitors can display at least 25 lines of text, with 80 or more characters per line. Some higher resolution monitors are capable of displaying a greater number of lines and lines containing a greater number of characters. Both monochrome and color monitors are now commonly available.

Most newer versions of BASIC include a statement that will clear the monitor screen. The 1987 ANSI standard includes such a statement, consisting simply of the keyword CLEAR. True BASIC also includes a CLEAR statement. In Microsoft BASIC, the corresponding statement is CLS (CLear Screen). Each is a complete statement, requiring no additional information.

Example 7.9

The following statement is used to clear the screen within a True BASIC program.

    CLEAR

In QuickBASIC, the screen is cleared simply by writing

    CLS

Execution of either statement will clear the screen and position the *cursor* in the upper left-hand corner (see below).

7.5 POSITIONING THE CURSOR: THE SET CURSOR AND LOCATE STATEMENTS

On a TV monitor, the active location (where, for example, new text may be entered, or old text deleted) is indicated by a *cursor*. This is generally a blinking square that is superimposed over a character, a blinking underscore beneath a character, or a blinking vertical line next to a character. Most newer versions of BASIC include a statement to specify the location of the cursor (though the 1987 ANSI standard does *not* include such a statement in text mode). In True BASIC, for example, the cursor is positioned with the SET CURSOR statement. This statement consists of the key words SET CURSOR, followed by a row number and a column number, separated by a comma. (The upper left-hand corner of the screen corresponds to row 0, column 0. Hence, the cursor is positioned relative to the upper left-hand corner).

Example 7.10

Here is a simple BASIC program that clears the screen and then displays the message "Good Morning" at the center of the screen. The program assumes a 25-line screen, with 80 characters per line.

Two different versions are shown, one in True BASIC, the other in QuickBASIC.

True BASIC	*QuickBASIC*

```
CLEAR                        CLS
SET CURSOR 12, 34            LOCATE 12, 34
PRINT "Good Morning"        PRINT "Good Morning"
END                          END
```

In each case the message is written on line number 12, which is actually the 13*th* line on the screen (the top line is line number 0). The 12-character string begins in column 34 (actually, the 35*th* character) and extends to column 45.

Here is a more sophisticated version of the True BASIC program. This version will center a string of *any* length (not exceeding 80 characters) on line number 12.

```
CLEAR
LET message$ = "Good Morning"
LET n = LEN(message$) / 2
SET CURSOR 12, (40 - n)
PRINT message$
END
```

When a new line of text is generated at the bottom of the monitor screen, the text that was previously at the bottom will be pushed up one line to make room for the new text. If the entire screen is full and a new line is generated at the bottom, then all of the previous text will be pushed up one line, thus causing the line that was previously at the top of the screen to be lost. This is known as *vertical scrolling*.

Vertical scrolling can be an annoyance, since it may cause a text display to disappear before it can be read. Occasionally, however, it can be used to obtain desired special effects, as illustrated in the following example.

Example 7.11 Programming a Screen Display (Nothing Can Go Wrong, Go Wrong, Go Wrong . . .)

Here is a short program, written in QuickBASIC, that manipulates the screen in an entertaining manner. The program is designed to cause the message

```
GO WRONG! GO WRONG! GO WRONG! GO WRONG! GO WRONG! GO WRONG! GO WRONG! GO WRONG!
```

to fill an 80-character screen and scroll vertically, creating the obviously false impression that the trustworthy computer, which presumably never goes awry, has indeed done so. The net effect is a dynamic, animated display with high visual impact.

The program contains a number of CLS and LOCATE statements. These statements control the appearance of the screen, particularly the location of the various messages. The scrolling effect is created by repeating the string "Go Wrong!" to fill an entire line, and then regenerating the line within a FOR - NEXT loop. An empty PRINT statement is also placed within this loop, in order to double space the text.

The program also includes several empty FOR - NEXT loops, which create time delays. The number of passes through each loop, presently 32,767, may need to be altered to accommodate the speed of your computer. (Notice that the second empty loop is repeated five times, in order to lengthen the time delay. This could also have been accomplished using a long-integer constant.)

```
REM NOTHING CAN GO WRONG

CLS
LOCATE 10, 28                                              'first message
PRINT "Welcome to the Wonderful"
LOCATE 12, 27
PRINT "World of Personal Computing"
FOR i = 1 TO 32767: NEXT i                                 'time delay

LOCATE 16, 18                                              'second message
PRINT "Just relax, enjoy yourself and remember that"
LOCATE 18, 25
PRINT "NOTHING CAN POSSIBLY GO WRONG!"
FOR m = 1 TO 5                                             'time delay
   FOR i = 1 TO 32767: NEXT i
NEXT m

CLS
LOCATE 24                                                  'repeated message
FOR j = 1 TO 12
   FOR k = 1 TO 7
      PRINT "GO WRONG! ";
   NEXT k
   PRINT "GO WRONG"
   PRINT
   FOR i = 1 TO 32767: NEXT i                              'time delay
NEXT j

CLS
LOCATE 12, 37                                              'final message
PRINT "DARN!"
LOCATE 15, 30
PRINT "Something went wrong!"
END
```

You are urged to execute this program yourself, in order to observe the actual effect. This will greatly enhance your appreciation for what happens.

7.6 MORE ABOUT INPUT

We have already seen that a prompt can be generated within an INPUT statement (see Examples 6.11 and 6.14 in Sec. 6.2). The manner in which this is accomplished varies from one version of BASIC to another, as shown in the following example. Note that the method used in True BASIC follows the recommendation in the 1987 ANSI standard.

Example 7.12

Several INPUT statements with imbedded prompt strings are shown below.

```
INPUT PROMPT "Enter a value for x: ": x          (True BASIC)

INPUT "Enter a value for x: ", x                 (QuickBASIC, no question mark)

INPUT "x = "; x                                  (QuickBASIC, with question mark)
```

In QuickBASIC, the prompt will be followed by a question mark if the prompt string is followed by a semicolon, as in the last example. The question mark will be suppressed, however, if the prompt string is followed by a comma, as in the last example. In True BASIC (and in the 1987 ANSI standard), the question mark will always be suppressed by the prompt string. In each case, a typical user's response is shown underlined.

The prompt generated by each of the preceding INPUT statements is shown below.

```
Enter a value for x: 3             (True BASIC)

Enter a value for x: 3             (QuickBASIC)

x = ? 3                            (QuickBASIC)
```

The INKEY$ Function

Microsoft BASIC (e.g., QuickBASIC, QBASIC) includes the INKEY$ function, which is used to enter a single character from the keyboard. A question mark prompting for input data is not generated by this function. (Note that INKEY$ is a *function*, not a *statement*).

When utilizing this function, the user does *not* press the ENTER key after the character has been entered. Moreover, the character will *not* appear on the screen

Example 7.13

The following two QuickBASIC statements illustrate the use of the INKEY$ function.

```
PRINT "Press any key to continue"
LET A$ = INKEY$
```

These two statements will cause the string

```
Press any key to continue
```

to appear on the screen, followed by a pause in the program execution. The program will resume execution once the user enters a single character from the keyboard. The character entered will not appear on the screen.

Here is another QuickBASIC construct that illustrates the use of the INKEY$ function.

```
DO

       . . . . .

LOOP WHILE INKEY$ = ""
```

In this example, the executable statements within the loop will continue to execute repeatedly until a single character is entered from the keyboard.

The KEY INPUT Expression

In True BASIC, the same thing can be accomplished through the use of KEY INPUT, which is a special logical expression that is included in the language. KEY INPUT is *true* if a character has been entered from the keyboard and *false* otherwise.

Example 7.14

The following True BASIC construct is analogous to the second QuickBASIC construct shown in the preceding example.

```
DO

    . . . . .

LOOP UNTIL (KEY INPUT)
```

The value of KEY INPUT will be false until a character is entered from the keyboard. Thus, the executable statements within the loop will continue to execute repeatedly until the character has been entered.

The INPUT$ Function

The dialects of Microsoft BASIC include an INPUT$ function, which allows a string of a specified length to be entered from the keyboard. The use of this function is sometimes convenient in applications that involve menu choices. Like the INKEY$ function, the INPUT$ function does not generate a prompt symbol. The ENTER key need not be pressed after the string has been entered.

Example 7.15

Here is a short QuickBASIC program that generates and responds to a simple menu.

```
DO
    PRINT "Selections: 1 - Red   2 - White   3 - Blue   4 - End"
    LET a$ = INPUT$(1)
    SELECT CASE a$
    CASE "1"
        PRINT "Red"
    CASE "2"
        PRINT "White"
    CASE "3"
        PRINT "Blue"
    CASE "4"
        PRINT "Have a Nice Day"
    CASE ELSE
    END SELECT
LOOP WHILE a$ <> "4"
END
```

This program prompts the user for a single character, which must be a digit whose value is 1, 2, 3 or 4. The character entered from the keyboard will not appear on the screen. The user need not press the ENTER key after typing the single character.

After the character has been entered, the message Red, White, Blue or Have a Nice Day will appear on the screen. The particular message will, of course, depend upon the character entered from the keyboard.

The GET KEY Statement

True BASIC includes the GET KEY statement, which assigns the ASCII equivalent of a character entered from the keyboard to a numeric variable. The use of this statement is similar to the use of INPUT$(1) in Microsoft BASIC.

Example 7.16

Here is a True BASIC program that does essentially the same thing as the QuickBASIC program shown in Example 7.15.

```
DO
    PRINT "Selections: 1 - Red    2 - White    3 - Blue    4 - End"
    GET KEY v
    LET a$ = CHR$(v)
    SELECT CASE a$
    CASE "1"
        PRINT "Red"
    CASE "2"
        PRINT "White"
    CASE "3"
        PRINT "Blue"
    CASE "4"
        PRINT "Have a Nice Day"
    CASE ELSE
    END SELECT
LOOP WHILE a$ <> "4"
END
```

Note the use of the CHR$ function, which converts the ASCII equivalent of the input character into an ASCII character.

The LINE INPUT Statement

The LINE INPUT statement is included in the 1987 ANSI standard and is supported by most versions of BASIC. This statement allows an entire line of input to be assigned to a single string variable. The input line need not be enclosed in quotation marks, regardless of its content.

Example 7.17

Suppose the string PITTSBURGH, PENNSYLVANIA is to be assigned to the string variable city$. If the INPUT statement is used to enter the data, the string must be enclosed in quotation marks because of the comma separating PITTSBURGH and PENNSYLVANIA (see Sec. 2.10). Thus, in response to the statement

```
INPUT city$
```

the user would enter the string

```
"PITTSBURGH, PENNSYLVANIA"
```

If the LINE INPUT statement is used, however, i.e.

```
LINE INPUT city$
```

the user would simply type

```
PITTSBURGH, PENNSYLVANIA
```

Prompt strings can be included in the LINE INPUT statement in the same manner as in the INPUT statement, as discussed earlier in this section. Remember that the syntax for including a prompt string varies from one version of BASIC to another.

The LINE INPUT statement is particularly useful when reading string input from a data file, as discussed in Chap. 8.

7.7 FORMATTED OUTPUT: THE PRINT USING STATEMENT

Most versions of BASIC support the PRINT USING statement, which is included in the 1987 ANSI standard. This statement allows output data to be *formatted*, thus specifying the appearance, precision and location of each data item. Both numerical and string data can be formatted.

The general form of the PRINT USING statement, as defined by the 1987 ANSI standard, is

```
PRINT USING format string: data list
```

where *format string* is a string comprised of one or more special format characters and *data list* contains the data items to be displayed. The format string determines the appearance, precision and location of each item in the data list.

True BASIC utilizes the same syntax as the 1987 ANSI standard.

Example 7.18

Here is the most common form of the PRINT USING statement, as defined by the 1987 ANSI standard and implemented in True BASIC.

```
PRINT USING "##.##": const
```

The format string is "##.##". It specifies a numeric field containing a decimal point, with not more than two digits on each side. Decimals extending beyond two digits will be rounded.

Suppose the variable const has been assigned the value 17.66698. Then the above PRINT USING statement will cause the value

```
17.67
```

to be displayed.

If the data list contains multiple data items, the format string *may* contain multiple format groups (note that this is not an absolute requirement, since a single format group can apply to multiple data items). If multiple format groups do appear, they must be separated by one or more blank spaces. Each format group will define a *field*.

Example 7.19

Suppose that a, b and c are numeric variables that have been assigned the values −2, 0.00017 and 12345, respectively. Then the True BASIC statement

```
PRINT USING "##   #.####   ##,###": a, b, c
```

will cause the following values to be displayed.

```
   -2   0.0002   12,345
```

Notice the decimal point in the second value (which has been rounded) and the comma within the third value. These characters are placed within the formatted values by the corresponding characters within the format string.

If the size of a numerical value exceeds the size of the corresponding field, the value is said to *overflow* the field. When this occurs, a series of asterisks is displayed rather than the desired numerical value. The number of asterisks displayed is equal to the number of characters within the field.

Example 7.20

Now suppose that the variables a, b and c are assigned the values −25, −1.00017 and 300, respectively. Then the True BASIC statement

```
PRINT USING "##   #.####   ##,###": a, b, c
```

will cause the following values to be displayed.

```
   **   ******        300
```

The first two values overflow their respective fields. Hence, the first value is replaced by two asterisks and the second value is replaced by six asterisks. (Note that these particular overflows occur because of the minus signs.) Finally, the last value is preceded by six blank spaces — three spaces because of the spacing between the fields and three additional spaces because the actual value is smaller than its corresponding field.

Floating-point values can be displayed with an exponent if desired. To do so, attach several carets (^) at the end of the field. The carets define the location of the characters comprising the exponent, as shown in the following example.

Example 7.21

Suppose the variable v has been assigned the value 856.077. Each of the following PRINT USING statements, written in True BASIC, displays the value of v somewhat differently.

Statement	_Display_
`PRINT USING "v = ##.###^^^^": v`	`v = 85.608e+01`
`PRINT USING "v = #.###^^^": v`	`v = 8.561e+2`
`PRINT USING "v = #.###^^^^^": v`	`v = 8.561e+002`
`PRINT USING "v = .###^^^": v`	`v = .856e+3`
`PRINT USING "v = #.######^^^": v`	`v = 8.560770e+2`

Note that the label `v =` is included within the format string in each of the preceding examples.

The value of a string variable can also be displayed in a formatted form using PRINT USING. The field is defined using pound signs (#), as with an integer variable. The field must be large enough to accommodate all of the characters in the string; otherwise, a sequence of asterisks will appear in place of the actual string. If the size of the field exceeds the size of the string, the string will be centered within the field. The string can be _left justified_ (positioned at the left end of the field) or _right justified_ (positioned at the right end of the field) by including the format character < or >, respectively, in place of the first pound sign.

Example 7.22

Now suppose the string variable v$ represents the string `"BASIC"`. Each of the following True BASIC statements displays this string somewhat differently.

Statement	_Display_
`PRINT USING "#####": v$`	`BASIC`
`PRINT USING "#########": v$`	`  BASIC`
`PRINT USING "<########": v$`	`BASIC`
`PRINT USING ">########": v$`	`   BASIC`
`PRINT USING "####": v$`	`****`

Notice that the string is centered within the nine-character field in the second example. In the third example, the string is left justified because of the substitution of the < character in place of the first #. Similarly, the string is right justified in the fourth example because of the > in place of the first #. The last example illustrates an overflow condition, since a five-character string cannot be displayed within a four-character field.

The 1987 ANSI standard defines a number of additional format characters. Their use is illustrated in the following example.

Example 7.23

Suppose the variable x has been assigned the value 12345.678. Each of the following True BASIC statements displays the value of x somewhat differently.

Statement	_Display_
`PRINT USING "$##,###.##": x`	`$12,345.68`
`PRINT USING "$#,###,###.##": x`	`$   12,345.68`
`PRINT USING "$$$$##,###.##": x`	`   $12,345.68`
`PRINT USING "$%,%%%,%%%.%%": x`	`$0,012,345.68`
`PRINT USING "$*,***,***.**": x`	`$*,*12,345.68`

The dollar sign ($) in the first statement causes the numerical quantity to be preceded by a dollar sign. In the second statement we see that the field is wider than the numerical quantity, so that some blank spaces precede the numerical quantity. A dollar sign appears to the extreme left of the field.

The third statement is similar to the second statement, but the blank space within the field is now designated by repeated dollar signs. This causes the numerical quantity to be *immediately* preceded by a single dollar sign, with the blank spaces at the extreme left of the field.

The last two statements illustrate the use of percent signs (%) and asterisks (*) in place of pound signs (#). Percent signs in the format string cause zeros to appear in place of blank spaces. Similarly, asterisks in the format string cause asterisks to appear in place of blank spaces.

The syntax associated with the PRINT USING statement may differ from one version of BASIC to another. QuickBASIC, for example, requires a semicolon rather than a colon following the format string. In addition, QuickBASIC defines some of the format characters differently.

Example 7.24

Suppose the numeric variable x and the string variable v$ have been assigned the values 12345.678 and BASIC, respectively. Each of the following QuickBASIC statements displays the value of x or v$ somewhat differently.

Statement	*Display*
PRINT USING "$##,###.##"; x	$12,345.68
PRINT USING "$#,###,###.##"; x	$ 12,345.68
PRINT USING "$$,###,###.##"; x	$12,345.68
PRINT USING "**,###,###.##"; x	****12,345.68
PRINT USING "**$###,###.##"; x	***$12,345.68
PRINT USING "&"; v$	BASIC

The first two statements behave in the same manner as in the 1987 ANSI standard (note the semicolon, rather than a colon, at the end of each format string). In the third statement, the double dollar sign in the format string causes the numerical quantity to be *immediately* preceded by a single dollar sign, with the blank spaces at the extreme left of the field. The last statement results in a display that is similar to that resulting from the previous statement, except that the blank spaces are replaced by asterisks.

Consult the programmer's reference manual that accompanies your particular version of BASIC for further information on the use of PRINT USING.

Example 7.25 Personal Finance (Compound Interest Calculations)

Many problems in consumer economics are concerned with compound interest calculations. For example, we may wish to know how much money will accumulate in a savings account over a given period of time, or how much it will cost to repay a loan for a given interest rate and a given frequency of compounding.

In this example we consider three calculations of this type. They are

1. Future value of a given amount of money
2. Future value of a series of monthly deposits
3. Monthly loan repayments

We will develop a single, menu-driven program that will allow all of these calculations to be carried out. The program will be written in QuickBASIC and will make use of the following symbols.

    $P =$ present sum of money, either deposited or borrowed
    $F =$ future accumulation of money
    $A =$ uniform monthly deposit or uniform monthly payment
    $i \ =$ annual interest rate (expressed as a decimal)
    $m =$ number of interest periods per year
    $n =$ number of years

The formulas required for each type of calculation are presented below.

1.   Future value (F) of a given amount of money (P)

    (a) Annual, semiannual, quarterly, monthly or daily compounding ($m = 1, 2, 4, 12$, or 365, respectively)

$$F = P \left(1 + i/m\right)^{mn}$$

    (b) Continuous compounding

$$F = P e^{in}$$

2.   Future value (F) of a series of monthly deposits (A)

    (a) Annual, semiannual, quarterly or monthly compounding ($m = 1, 2, 4$ or 12, respectively)

$$F = 12A \left(1 + i/m\right)^{mn} - 1)/i$$

    (b) Daily compounding ($m = 365$)

$$F = A \left[(1 + i/m)^{mn} - 1\right]/\left[(1 + i/m)^{m/12} - 1\right]$$

    (c) Continuous compounding

$$F = A \left(e^{in} - 1\right)/\left(e^{i/12} - 1\right)$$

3.   Monthly repayments (A) of a loan (P)

    (a) Annual, semiannual, quarterly or monthly compounding ($m = 1, 2, 4$ or 12, respectively)

$$A = i P \left(1 + i/m\right)^{mn}/\left[12 \left(1 + i/m\right)^{mn} - 1\right]$$

    (b) Daily compounding ($m = 365$)

$$A = P \left(1 + i/m\right)^{mn} \left[(1 + i/m)^{m/12} - 1\right]/\left[(1 + i/m)^{mn} - 1\right]$$

    (c) Continuous compounding

$$A = P e^{in} \left(e^{i/12} - 1\right)/\left(e^{in} - 1\right)$$

    Let us design a program that is conversational in nature and as general as possible, within practical limits. The program will begin by displaying a main menu which allows the user to select one of the three different types of calculations or to end the computation. The screen will then clear and the program will prompt for the required input data. A submenu will be used to assist the user in specifying the frequency of compounding.

Once the data have been supplied, the appropriate calculations will be carried out and the answer displayed at the bottom of the screen. The screen will remain unchanged until the user presses any key, which will then return the user to the main menu.

Let us begin by defining the following program variables.

P = present sum of money
F = future accumulation of money
A = uniform monthly deposit (or payment)
rate = annual interest rate, expressed as a *percentage*
i = annual interest rate, expressed as a *fraction* (note that i = 0.01 * rate)
m% = number of interest periods per year (e.g., m% = 12 for monthly compounding)
n% = number of years
choice% = a variable that determines which type of calculation will be carried out (choice% will be assigned a value of 1, 2 or 3)
F$ = a variable that determines the frequency of compounding (F$ will be assigned A, S, Q, M, D or C for annual, semiannual, quarterly, monthly, daily or continuous compounding)

The program will then proceed as follows:

Carry out the following steps repeatedly, until a stopping condition is detected (i.e., until choice% is assigned a value of 4).

1. Display the main menu.

2. Read a value for choice%.

3. Select an appropriate type of calculation, as determined by the value assigned to choice%.

    (*a*) choice% = 1 (future value of a given amount of money)

        (*i*) Read a value for P.

        (*ii*) Call subroutine DataIn, which will read values for n% and rate, calculate a value for i using the formula i = .01 * rate, read a value of F$ from a submenu and then assign an appropriate value to m%.

        (*iii*) Calculate a value for F, using the appropriate formula.

        (*iv*) Display the calculated value for F.

        (*v*) Call subroutine Message, which will display the message "Press any key to continue."

        (*vi*) Return to the main menu.

    (*b*) choice% = 2 (future value of a series of monthly payments)

        (*i*) Read a value for A.

        (*ii*) Call subroutine DataIn, which will read values for n% and rate, calculate a value for i using the formula i = .01 * rate, read a value of F$ from a submenu and then assign an appropriate value to m%.

(*iii*) Calculate a value for F, using the appropriate formula.

(*iv*) Display the calculated value for F.

(*v*) Call subroutine `Message`, which will display the message "Press any key to continue."

(*vi*) Return to the main menu.

(*c*) `choice%` = 3 (monthly loan repayments)

(*i*) Read a value for P

(*ii*) Call subroutine `DataIn`, which will read values for `n%` and `rate`, calculate a value for `i` using the formula `i = .01 * rate`, read a value of `F$` from a submenu and then assign an appropriate value to `m%`.

(*iii*) Calculate a value for A, using the appropriate formula.

(*iv*) Display the calculated value for A.

(*v*) Call subroutine `Message`, which will display the message "Press any key to continue."

(*vi*) Return to the main menu.

4.   When `choice%` has been assigned a value of 4, display a sign-off message and end the computation.

The complete QuickBASIC program is shown below.

```
REM COMPOUND INTEREST CALCULATIONS

DECLARE SUB Message ()
DECLARE SUB DataIn (n%, m%, i, F$)
DO
    REM GENERATE MAIN MENU
    DO
        CLS
        LOCATE 1, 1: PRINT "COMPOUND INTEREST CALCULATIONS"
        LOCATE 3, 1: PRINT " 1 - Future Value of a Given Amount of Money"
        LOCATE 5, 1: PRINT " 2 - Future Value of a Series of Monthly Deposits"
        LOCATE 7, 1: PRINT " 3 - Monthly Loan Repayments"
        LOCATE 9, 1: PRINT " 4 - End"
        LOCATE 11, 1: INPUT "Please enter your selection: ", choice%
    LOOP WHILE (choice% < 1 OR choice% > 4)

    SELECT CASE choice%
    CASE 1              'FUTURE VALUE OF A GIVEN AMOUNT OF MONEY (F/P)
        DO
            CLS
            LOCATE 1, 1: PRINT "FUTURE VALUE OF A GIVEN AMOUNT OF MONEY"
            LOCATE 3, 1: INPUT "Original Amount of Money: $", P
        LOOP WHILE (P <= 0)
        CALL DataIn(n%, m%, i, F$)
```

```
          IF F$ = "C" THEN
             LET F = P * EXP(i * n%)                        'continuous compounding
          ELSE
             LET F = P * (1 + i / m%) ^ (m% * n%)           'discrete compounding
          END IF
          LOCATE 18, 1: PRINT "FINAL AMOUNT =";
          PRINT USING "$$#,###,###.##"; F
          CALL Message
       CASE 2            'FUTURE VALUE OF A SERIES OF MONTHLY DEPOSITS        (F/A)
          DO
             CLS
             LOCATE 1, 1: PRINT "FUTURE VALUE OF A SERIES OF MONTHLY DEPOSITS"
             LOCATE 3, 1: INPUT "Amount of Each Payment: $", A
          LOOP WHILE (A <= 0)
          CALL DataIn(n%, m%, i, F$)
          IF F$ = "C" THEN
             LET F = A * (EXP(i * n%) - 1) / (EXP(i / 12) - 1)        'continuous
          ELSE
             LET factor = (1 + i / m%) ^ (m% * n%) - 1
             IF F$ = "D" THEN
                LET F = A * factor / ((1 + i / m%) ^ (m% / 12) - 1)  'daily
             ELSE
                LET F = 12 * A * factor / i
             END IF                                                   'other
          END IF
          LOCATE 18, 1: PRINT "FINAL AMOUNT =";
          PRINT USING "$$#,###,###.##"; F
          CALL Message
       CASE 3              'MONTHLY LOAN REPAYMENTS (A/P)
          DO
             CLS
             LOCATE 1, 1: PRINT "MONTHLY LOAN REPAYMENTS"
             LOCATE 3, 1: INPUT "Amount of Money Borrowed: $", P
          LOOP WHILE (P <= 0)
          CALL DataIn(n%, m%, i, F$)
          IF F$ = "C" THEN
             LET A = P * (EXP(i * n%) * (EXP(i / 12) - 1)) / (EXP(i * n%) - 1)
          ELSE
             LET factor = (1 + i / m%) ^ (m% * n%) - 1
             IF F$ = "D" THEN
                LET A = P * (factor + 1) * ((1 + i / m%) ^ (m% / 12) - 1) / factor
             ELSE
                LET A = i * P * (factor + 1) / (12 * factor)
             END IF
          END IF
          LOCATE 18, 1: PRINT "MONTHLY PAYMENT =";
          PRINT USING "$$###,###.##"; A
          CALL Message
    END SELECT
LOOP UNTIL choice% = 4
LOCATE 14, 1: PRINT "GOODBYE, HAVE A NICE DAY"
END
```

```
SUB DataIn (n%, m%, i, F$)
   DO
      LOCATE 4, 1: INPUT "Number of Years: ", n%
   LOOP WHILE (n% <= 0)

   DO
      LOCATE 5, 1: INPUT "Annual Interest Rate (Percent): ", rate
      LET i = .01 * rate
   LOOP WHILE (i <= 0)

   LOCATE 7, 1:  PRINT "Frequency of Compounding:"
   LOCATE 9, 1:  PRINT "  A - Annual"
   LOCATE 10, 1: PRINT "  S - Semiannual"
   LOCATE 11, 1: PRINT "  Q - Quarterly"
   LOCATE 12, 1: PRINT "  M - Monthly"
   LOCATE 13, 1: PRINT "  D - Daily"
   LOCATE 14, 1: PRINT "  C - Continuous"
   LOCATE 16, 1: INPUT "Please enter your selection: ", ans$

   LET F$ = UCASE$(ans$)

   SELECT CASE F$
   CASE "A"
      LET m% = 1
   CASE "S"
      LET m% = 2
   CASE "Q"
      LET m% = 4
   CASE "M"
      LET m% = 12
   CASE "D"
      LET m% = 365
   END SELECT
END SUB


SUB Message
   LOCATE 21, 1: PRINT "(Press any key to continue)";
   LET ans$ = INPUT$(1)
END SUB
```

The program is relatively long, due to the use of prompts, error checks and menus. These "user-friendly" features simplify the use of the program, though they require additional work on the part of the programmer. Notice that the program includes a number of the programming features discussed in this chapter, such as explicit integer variables, multiple statements per line (though used sparingly, in accordance with good programming practice), periodic use of CLS to clear the screen, INPUT statements with prompts, use of the INPUT$ function (in the last subroutine) and the PRINT USING statement.

A typical interactive session resulting from the execution of this program is shown on the next page. Three different cases are shown, illustrating the three major categories of calculations. Various compounding frequencies are also illustrated. Remember that the appearance of the output is altered somewhat, since the effects of the CLS commands are not shown. The user's responses are underlined.

Here is the actual dialog.

```
COMPOUND INTEREST CALCULATIONS

    1 - Future Value of a Given Amount of Money

    2 - Future Value of a Series of Monthly Deposits

    3 - Monthly Loan Repayments

    4 - End

Please enter your selection: 1



FUTURE VALUE OF A GIVEN AMOUNT OF MONEY

Original Amount of Money: $1000
Number of Years: 10
Annual Interest Rate (Percent): 12

Frequency of Compounding:

    A - Annual
    S - Semiannual
    Q - Quarterly
    M - Monthly
    D - Daily
    C - Continuous

Please enter your selection: Q

FINAL AMOUNT =      $3,262.04


(Press any key to continue)



COMPOUND INTEREST CALCULATIONS

    1 - Future Value of a Given Amount of Money

    2 - Future Value of a Series of Monthly Deposits

    3 - Monthly Loan Repayments

    4 - End

Please enter your selection: 2
```

FUTURE VALUE OF A SERIES OF MONTHLY DEPOSITS

Amount of Each Payment: $100
Number of Years: 7
Annual Interest Rate (Percent): 8.5

Frequency of Compounding:

    A - Annual
    S - Semiannual
    Q - Quarterly
    M - Monthly
    D - Daily
    C - Continuous

Please enter your selection: M

FINAL AMOUNT = $11,424.46

(Press any key to continue)

COMPOUND INTEREST CALCULATIONS

    1 - Future Value of a Given Amount of Money

    2 - Future Value of a Series of Monthly Deposits

    3 - Monthly Loan Repayments

    4 - End

Please enter your selection: 3

MONTHLY LOAN REPAYMENTS

Amount of Money Borrowed: $5000
Number of Years: 5
Annual Interest Rate (Percent): 12.5

Frequency of Compounding:

    A - Annual
    S - Semiannual
    Q - Quarterly
    M - Monthly
    D - Daily
    C - Continuous

```
Please enter your selection: C

MONTHLY PAYMENT =        $112.66


(Press any key to continue)



COMPOUND INTEREST CALCULATIONS

    1 - Future Value of a Given Amount of Money

    2 - Future Value of a Series of Monthly Deposits

    3 - Monthly Loan Repayments

    4 - End

Please enter your selection: 4


    GOODBYE, HAVE A NICE DAY
```

7.8 SOME ADDITIONAL MISCELLANEOUS COMMANDS

Most versions of BASIC contain a number of additional commands, a few of which are mentioned briefly below.

LPRINT and LPRINT USING

Some versions of BASIC (e.g., Microsoft QuickBASIC) include the LPRINT statement, which is used specifically to print output data on a printer. The statement is identical to the PRINT statement except for the use of the keyword LPRINT rather than PRINT. Moreover, the USING clause (i.e., LPRINT USING) is also supported if both LPRINT and PRINT USING are available.

Example 7.26

A QuickBASIC program contains the following two print statements.

```
PRINT "a ="; a; "b ="; b; "c ="; c
LPRINT "a ="; a; "b ="; b; "c ="; c
```

The first statement will cause the values of a, b and c to be displayed on a monitor, whereas the second statement will generate a hard copy of these values on a printer.

Those versions of BASIC that do not support the LPRINT statement are generally able to divert output to a printer through the use of file management statements. This topic will be discussed in the next chapter.

ASK and SET

The 1987 ANSI standard defines families of ASK and SET statements. Within each family are individual statements that are generally complementary to statements in the other family (e.g., ASK MARGIN and SET MARGIN). Some of these statements are used for file management purposes, as discussed in Chap. 8. Others are used to determine a system characteristic or to reset a system characteristic, as illustrated below.

Example 7.27

Shown below are several representative ASK and SET statements, written in True BASIC. An explanation accompanies each statement.

Statement	*Purpose*
ASK MARGIN mval	Determines the margin (i.e., the number of characters that comprise the maximum screen width) and assigns this value to mval.
SET MARGIN 55	Sets the current margin to 55 characters.
ASK COLOR fcolor	Determines the numerical value of the foreground color and assigns this value to fcolor.
SET COLOR 15	Sets the current foreground color to color number 15.
ASK BACKGROUND COLOR bcolor	Determines the numerical value of the background color and assigns this value to bcolor.
SET BACKGROUND COLOR newbackcolor	Sets the current background color to the value represented by newbackcolor.
ASK PIXELS xval, yval	Determines the number of pixels in the horizontal and vertical directions and assigns these values to xval and yval, respectively.
ASK WINDOW left, right, bottom, top	Determines the coordinates of the left, right, bottom and top window coordinates, and assigns these values to left, right, bottom and top, respectively.
SET WINDOW 0.25, 0.75, 0.2, 0.8	Sets the current left, right, bottom and top window coordinates to 0.25, 0.75, 0.2 and 0.8, respectively.

Note that the window coordinates are normalized in True BASIC. That is, they range from 0 to 1 in each direction (left to right and bottom to top).

ASK and SET statements are sometimes used together, as illustrated in the following example.

Example 7.28

The following True BASIC statements establish foreground and background colors that are compatible with each other.

```
ASK BACKGROUND COLOR background
IF (background = 7) THEN             !white background
    SET COLOR 0                      !black foreground
ELSE
    SET COLOR 15                     !bright white foreground
END IF
```

Notice the manner in which the ASK and SET statements complement one another. In particular, the current background color returned from the ASK statement is used to set the foreground color to an appropriate value.

Consult your user's reference manual for more detailed information on the use of ASK and SET. Remember that these statements are not supported by all versions of BASIC.

PAUSE

The PAUSE statement causes program execution to be suspended for a specified number of seconds. This feature may be convenient in a highly interactive application, such as a computer game. The PAUSE statement is not supported, however, by all versions of BASIC.

Example 7.29

The following True BASIC statement will cause a 3-second time delay when it is encountered during program execution.

```
PAUSE 3
```

Similarly, the following True BASIC statement will cause a time delay whose duration will be determined by the value assigned to delay.

```
PAUSE delay
```


PEEK, POKE and DEF SEG

Some versions of BASIC (particularly the variations of Microsoft BASIC) support the PEEK function and the POKE statement. PEEK is used to examine the content of a memory location, whereas POKE is used to change the content of a memory location. These features are useful for certain types of advanced programming applications.

Closely associated with PEEK and POKE is the DEF SEG statement, which is used to select the beginning of a memory segment for certain types of computers (in particular, desktop computers utilizing Intel microprocessors). The use of PEEK, POKE and DEF SEG is illustrated in the following example.

Example 7.30

Shown below are representative PEEK, POKE and DEF SEG statements, all written in QuickBASIC. An explanation accompanies each statement.

Statement	*Purpose*
DEF SEG = 32768	Selects a memory segment beginning with (decimal) location 32768.
LET z = PEEK(768)	Determines the content of (decimal) memory location 768 and assigns the content to z.
POKE 200, 65	Places the (decimal) value 65 in (decimal) memory location 200.

IF PEEK(768) > 127 THEN
    POKE 768, 127
END IF
	Determines the content of (decimal) memory location 768 and replaces the value with 127 if the original value exceeds 127.

The addresses (i.e., the memory locations) in PEEK and POKE are located relative to the beginning of the memory segment defined by DEF SEG. These addresses can be stated in decimal notation, as shown above, or in *hexadecimal* (base 16). Thus, the above statements can be written in hexadecimal notation as

```
DEF SEG = &H8000

LET z = PEEK(&H300)

POKE &HC8, &H41

IF PEEK(&H300) > &H7F THEN
    POKE &H300, &H7F
END IF
```

A further discussion of the hexadecimal number system and its uses is beyond the scope of this book.

Review Questions

7.1   Describe the different data types that are available with your particular version of BASIC. How are the corresponding variable types distinguished from one another?

7.2   What is the largest integer constant available with your particular version of BASIC? What is the largest long integer?

7.3   What is the largest real constant available with your particular version of BASIC? What is the largest double-precision constant? How many significant figures are permitted in each type of constant?

7.4   Does your particular version of BASIC support the DEFINT, DEFLNG, DEFSNG, DEFDBL and DEFSTR statements? If so, what is their purpose? How does the use of these statements compare with the use of suffixes on variable names?

7.5   What type of result is obtained from an arithmetic operation involving

   (*a*)   Integer and real data?

   (*b*)   Integer and double-precision data?

   (*c*)   Real and double-precision data?

   (*d*)   Integer and long-integer data?

   (*e*)   Long-integer and real data?

   (*f*)   Long-integer and double-precision data?

7.6   What happens when numeric data of one type is assigned to a numeric variable of a different type?

7.7   In your particular version of BASIC, what happens when a real or double-precision quantity is assigned to an integer or long-integer quantity?

7.8   In your particular version of BASIC, can multiple statements be placed on one line? If so, how are the statements separated from one another?

7.9   Does your particular version of BASIC include screen clearing and cursor positioning statements? If so, what are they? How are they used?

7.10   What is meant by vertical scrolling? How can undesired vertical scrolling be prevented?

7.11   Does your particular version of BASIC allow you to include a prompt string within an INPUT statement? If so, summarize the syntax associated with this feature.

7.12   Does your particular version of BASIC support either the INKEY$ function or the KEY INPUT expression? If so, what is its purpose? Describe its syntax.

7.13   Does your particular version of BASIC support either the INPUT$ function or the GET KEY statement? If so, what is its purpose? Describe its syntax.

7.14   Does your particular version of BASIC support the LINE INPUT statement? If so, what is its purpose? How does it differ from an ordinary INPUT statement?

7.15   Summarize the more common features provided by the PRINT USING statement. Which of these features are available in your particular version of BASIC? How are they implemented?

7.16   Does your particular version of BASIC support the LPRINT and LPRINT USING statements? If so, what is the purpose of each? How do they differ from the ordinary PRINT and PRINT USING statements?

7.17   Does your particular version of BASIC support the families of ASK and SET statements? If so, which particular ASK and SET statements are available? What is the purpose of each?

7.18   Does your particular version of BASIC support DEF SEG, PEEK and POKE? If so, what is the purpose of each? How is each feature implemented?

Problems

7.19   Describe the data type associated with each of the following numeric constants or expressions.

(a) 8027   (h) 0.5037e3

(b) 8027#   (i) 0.5037d3

(c) 8027!   (j) 1.21212E-5

(d) 8027133   (k) 1.21212D-5

(e) 503.7   (l) 1.2121212121212D-5

(f) 503.7#   (m) 3! * 0.5037d3

(g) 503.7!   (n) 503.7# / 1.21212D-5

7.20   Add an appropriate suffix to the variable name X for each of the following data types.

(a)   integer

(b)   long-integer

(c)   real

(d)   double-precision

(e)   string

7.21   Write an appropriate DEF-type statement for each of the following situations.

(a)   Declare all variables beginning with r, t and u through z to be double precision.

(b)   Declare all variables beginning with i through n to be integer.

(c)   Declare all variables beginning with c, e and g to be real.

(d)   Declare all variables beginning with p through r to be long integers.

(e)   Declare all variables beginning with s to be strings.

7.22   In each of the following expressions, assume that i% = 5, j& = 123456789, r! = 0.15 and d# = 0.333333333d+2. Determine the value of each expression.

(a)   i% * r! / 3

    (b)   i% * d# / 3

    (c)   (j& * r!) / i%

    (d)   r! + d#

    (e)   (i% * j& * r!) / d#

    (f)   i% + j&

    (g)   i% + j& + d#

7.23   In each of the following assignment statements, assume that i% = 7, j& = 50000, r! = 508.75 and d# = 0.4d−3. Determine the value assigned to each left-hand variable. Be sure to convert data types wherever appropriate.

    (a)   LET a% = 3 * r!

    (b)   LET c! = 3 * r!

    (c)   LET n# = 3 * r!

    (d)   LET a% = 3 * j&

    (e)   LET b& = 3 * j&

    (f)   LET c! = 3 * j&

    (g)   LET n# = 3 * j&

    (h)   LET a% = 3 * d#

    (i)   LET c! = 3 * d#

    (j)   LET n# = 3 * d#

    (k)   LET b& = 3 * i%

    (l)   LET c! = 3 * i%

    (m)   LET n# = 3 * i%

7.24   Write an INPUT statement to accommodate each of the following situations.

    (a)   Generate the prompt Name: , then enter a string representing a person's name.

    (b)   Generate the prompt What is your name? , then enter a string representing a person's name.

7.25   Describe the output produced by each of the following PRINT USING statements, written in True BASIC. In each case, assume that a = 1.5555555, i = 30287 and city$ = "BOSTON".

(a)   PRINT USING "##.##   ##,###": a, i

(b)   PRINT USING "####   ####": a, i

(c)   PRINT USING ".#####^^^^": a

(d)   PRINT USING "$##,###": i

(e)   PRINT USING "$#,###,###": i

(f)   PRINT USING "$$$$#,###,###": i

(g)   PRINT USING "$%,%%%,%%%": i

(h)   PRINT USING "####": city$

(i)   PRINT USING "##########": city$

(j)   PRINT USING ">#########": city$

(k)   PRINT USING "<#########": city$

(l)   PRINT USING "$#.#### $###,###   ######": a, i, city$

7.26 Describe the output produced by each of the following PRINT USING statements, written in QuickBASIC. In each case, assume that a = 1.5555555, i = 30287 and city$ = "BOSTON".

(a)   PRINT USING "##.##   ##,###"; a; i

(b)   PRINT USING "####   ####"; a; i

(c)   PRINT USING ".#####^^^^"; a

(d)   PRINT USING "$##,###"; i

(e)   PRINT USING "$#,###,###"; i

(f)   PRINT USING "$$#,###,###"; i

(g)   PRINT USING "**#,###,###"; i

(h)   PRINT USING "&" city$

(i)   PRINT USING "$#.#### $###,###   &"; a; i; city$

7.27 Suppose x and y are numeric variables whose assigned values are −1.29E+05 and 4.87E−03, respectively. Write a PRINT USING statement so that the values will be displayed in each of the following ways.

(a) $-129,000   .00487

(b)   -.12900E+06   .48700E-02

    (c)   -129E+03   48.7E-04

    (d)   -1.3E+05   4.9E-03

7.28 Suppose c is a numeric variable whose assigned value is 2408513. Write a PRINT USING statement so that this value will be displayed in each of the following ways.

    (a) $2,408,513

    (b)   .241E+07

    (c)   .2408513E+07

    (d) $ 2,408,513

Programming Problems

7.29 The program shown in Example 7.11 contains several empty loops that are intended to create time delays. The duration of these time delays will be dependent on the speed of each computer. Modify these loops so that the program executes smoothly on your particular computer (i.e., so that the timing loops are not too short and not too long). Also, modify the program if necessary, so that the repeated line

        GO WRONG! GO WRONG! . . .

fills the screen properly and the scrolling executes smoothly.

7.30 Modify the program shown in Example 7.25 so that the menus make use of the INPUT$ function or the GET KEY statement, depending on your particular version of BASIC (see Examples 7.15 and 7.16).

7.31 Modify the program shown in Example 7.25 so that a printed copy of the calculated results is generated for each case. Use the LPRINT statement to generate the printed copy. Print out the input values as well as the calculated values, so that each case can be identified.

7.32 Rewrite each of the following programs so that it fully utilizes the enhanced features available in your particular version of BASIC.

    (a)   Roots of a quadratic equation (Example 4.9)

    (b)   Roots of an algebraic equation (Example 4.18)

    (c)   Generation of Fibonacci numbers and search for primes (Example 4.19)

    (d)   Calculating depreciation (Example 4.24)

    (e)   Reordering a list of numbers (Example 5.14)

    (f)   Search for a maximum (Example 6.4)

(g)   Simulation of a game of chance: shooting craps (Examples 6.11 and 6.14))

(h)   Table manipulation (Example 6.20)

7.33   Extend the word unscrambler (Example 5.8) so that it will rearrange the letters in *any* word (having any number of letters) into all possible combinations. Make full use of the string library functions that are available in your particular version of BASIC. (*Hint:* Consider the use of recursion.)

7.34   Rewrite the pig Latin generator given in Example 6.22 so that it includes the following additional features.

(a)   Accepts multiple lines of English text

(b)   Processes punctuation marks

(c)   Distinguishes between uppercase and lowercase letters amd makes appropriate corrections (e.g., Washington to Ashingtonwa)

(d)   Accommodates double-letter sounds (e.g., converts Philadelphia to Iladelphiapha)

7.35   Solve each of the following programming problems making full use of the enhanced features available in your particular version of BASIC.

(a)   Calculating a weighted average [Prob. 4.58(a)]

(b)   Calculating the sine of x [Prob. 4.58(f)]

(c)   Loan repayments [Prob. 4.58(g)]

(d)   Generating a pyramid of digits [Prob. 4.58(h)]

(e)   Simulating a four-function desk calculator [Prob. 4.58(l)]

(f)   Generating a character-oriented plot [Prob. 4.58(m)]

(g)   Converting a positive integer quantity to a Roman numeral [Prob. 4.58(n)]

(h)   Converting dates [Prob. 4.58(o)]

(i)   Alphabetizing a list of names [Prob. 5.29]

(j)   Generating a table of compound interest factors [Prob. 5.34]

(k)   Converting currencies [Prob. 5.36]

(l)   Matching countries with their capitals [Prob. 5.37]

(m)   Matrix multiplication [Prob. 5.38(b)]

(n)   Statistical calculations [Prob. 5.38(c)]

    (*o*)   Lagrangian interpolation [Prob. 5.38(*e*)]

    (*p*)   Simulating a game of blackjack [Prob. 6.67]

    (*q*)   Simulating a game of roulette [Prob. 6.68]

    (*r*)   Simulating a game of BINGO [Prob. 6.69]

7.36 Solve Problem 5.35 (computation of student exam scores, including the class average and the deviation of each student's average about the class average) using the enhanced features available in your particular version of BASIC. In particular, be sure to use the PRINT USING statement.

7.37 Solve Problem 5.38(*d*) (calculating the variance of a list of numbers using two different formulas) using real (single-precision) numbers. Then repeat the calculations using double-precision numbers. Compare the results obtained from the two sets of calculations.

Chapter 8

Data Files

A *file* is an orderly, self-contained collection of information. Any type of information can be stored within a file. Thus, a file may contain the instructions that comprise a BASIC program, or it may consist of data values (i.e., numeric constants and strings). The latter type of file is commonly known as a *data file*.

Data files offer a convenient means of storing information, since they can be stored on auxiliary storage devices and read into the computer as needed. Moreover, individual data items within a data file can easily be read into the computer, updated and written back out to the data file under the control of a BASIC program. This chapter is concerned with BASIC programs that create and use the more common types of data files.

8.1 DATA FILE FUNDAMENTALS

There are many different types of data files. Some contain recognizable data items, such as numeric constants and strings. Files of this type are generally referred to as *text* files or *formatted* files. Text files can be displayed on a computer screen, printed, loaded into an editor or word processor, etc.

Other data files contain continuous sequences of bytes. The information contained in such files can be interpreted only by specially written programs. Files of this type are referred to as *binary* files, *stream* files or *unformatted* files. Binary files appear unintelligible when printed or displayed on a computer screen, but their contents can be read into or written out of a computer much faster than text files.

Some data files contain unrelated data items, whereas others are organized into *records*. (A *record* is a set of related data items, such as a name, an address and a telephone number. Each data item within a record fills a *field*). Sometimes these distinctions become blurred, as when each record within a file contains only one data item.

Data files can also be characterized as being *sequential* or *direct* (direct data files are also referred to as *random access* data files). In a sequential data file, a particular record can be reached only from the beginning of the file, by reading the first record, then the second record, etc., until the desired record has been found. Thus, the processing of information in such files will be relatively slow, unless all of the records are processed sequentially (in the same order in which they are stored.)

The records within a sequential data file need not all be the same — they can vary in size and composition (*composition* refers to the number and type of fields within each record). This can be an advantage in certain kinds of applications. Moreover, applications involving sequential data files are relatively easy to program.

Sequential data files were originally developed for use with sequential auxiliary storage devices, such as magnetic tapes. Today, they are commonly used with both sequential storage devices and direct storage devices (e.g., diskettes, fixed disks, etc.)

In a direct data file, any record can be accessed directly by specifying the corresponding record number or record location. Thus, it is not necessary to read through the entire file in order to access a particular record. Applications that require direct access to individual records without regard to their order (as, for example, the daily updating of customer accounts as they are received) will therefore execute much faster with direct rather than sequential data files.

Some versions of BASIC support several different types of direct data files. One type might allow variable record composition, whereas another might require the records to have the same composition or even the same length. In such situations the various file types have different names, as, for example, *random files* and *record files*, to cite the designations used in True BASIC.

Clearly, this situation can be confusing to a beginning programmer. To make matters worse, file designations vary considerably from one version of BASIC to another. In this chapter we will therefore restrict our attention to formatted sequential files (i.e., text files) and to formatted direct files. These file types are supported by virtually all versions of BASIC and they are used in many different programming applications. Examples are presented in both True BASIC (which closely parallels the 1987 ANSI standard) and QuickBASIC. To keep things simple, our emphasis will be on concepts rather than the syntactic details required by each language.

8.2 PROCESSING A DATA FILE

All applications involving the use of data files are based upon the same general sequence of events. Specifically, the following three tasks must be carried out.

1. Open the data file.

2. Process the records, as required by the application.

3. Close the file.

Opening the data file associates a *channel number* (also called a *file number*) with a named data file. It also specifies certain information about the data file, such as the *mode* (e.g., sequential or random), the *access type* (e.g., read or write) and the *status* (e.g., new or old). Some versions of BASIC assign default values for certain of these items. The details differ from one version of BASIC to another.

Processing the records generally involves reading the records, modifying the records and then writing out the modified records. There are many variations of this theme, depending upon the particular application.

Closing the data file is a formality that simply deactivates the conditions that were specified when the file was opened. Some versions of BASIC will automatically close all data files at the end of program execution if explicit CLOSE statements are not included within the program. Good programming practice suggests, however, that all open data files be closed explicitly.

A file can no longer be accessed after it is closed, unless it is later reopened. Note, however, that a file can be reopened in another mode, with another access type, etc. after it has been closed. Some applications require that a file be reopened after it has been closed, as, for example, to read a set of records after the records have been created or modified by the same program.

Example 8.1

The skeletal outline of a QuickBASIC program is shown below.

```
OPEN "SCORES.DAT" FOR INPUT AS #1
OPEN "UPDATE.DAT" FOR OUTPUT AS #2
. . . . .
FOR i = 1 to n
   INPUT #1, AcctNo, OldBalance
   . . . . .
   PRINT #2, AcctNo, NewBalance
NEXT i

CLOSE
END
```

The OPEN statements specify that the file called `"SCORES.DAT"` will be a sequential input file associated with data channel number 1 and the file called `"UPDATE.DAT"` will be a sequential output file associated with data channel number 2. The FOR - NEXT loop then reads each record from the input file, updates the record (the details of which are not shown) and writes the updated record to the output file. (Note that the INPUT and PRINT statements refer to their respective files by channel number, not by file name.) Finally, the CLOSE statement closes both files.

If the program were written in True BASIC rather than QuickBASIC, the program outline might appear as

```
OPEN #1: NAME "SCORES.DAT", ACCESS INPUT, CREATE OLD
OPEN #2: NAME "UPDATE.DAT", ACCESS OUTPUT, CREATE NEW
. . . . .
FOR i = 1 TO n
    INPUT #1: AcctNo, OldBalance
    . . . . .
    PRINT #2: AcctNo, NewBalance
NEXT i

CLOSE #1
CLOSE #2
END
```

8.3 SEQUENTIAL DATA FILES

A sequential data file is characterized by the fact that the records are arranged sequentially, one after the other. In most versions of BASIC, the records within a sequential data file correspond to individual lines of text. Each record (each line) can contain both numeric constants and strings, in any combination, separated by commas. Some versions of BASIC (e.g., QuickBASIC) also allow the data items to be separated by blank spaces. (Remember that a string must be enclosed in quotation marks if it contains commas or blank spaces as a part of the string.)

Example 8.2

A sequential data file contains the name and exam scores of each student in a computer science programming class. The file appears as follows.

```
"Comp Sci 100 - Programming with BASIC"
5
"Adams, B F", 45, 80, 80, 95, 55
"Brown, P", 60, 50, 70, 75, 55
"Davis, R A", 50, 30, 10, 45, 60
"Fisher, E K", 0, 5, 5, 0, 10
"Hamilton, S P", 90, 85, 100, 95, 90
"Jones, J J", 95, 90, 80, 95, 85
"Ludwig, C W", 35, 50, 55, 65, 45
"Osborne, T", 75, 60, 75, 60, 70
"Prince, W F", 85, 75, 60, 85, 90
"Richards, E N", 50, 60, 50, 35, 65
"Smith, M C", 70, 60, 75, 70, 55
"Thomas, B A", 10, 25, 35, 20, 30
"Wolfe, H", 25, 40, 65, 75, 85
"Zorba, D R", 65, 80, 70, 100, 60
```

The first line contains a string representing the course title, and the second line contains an integer indicating the number of exam scores for each student. Each successive line contains the name of a student (a string) followed by five examination scores. Notice that the strings are enclosed in quotation marks because of the commas and blank spaces included within the strings.

A sequential data file can easily be created with a text editor or a word processor. (Remember, however, to save the data file *without formatting characters* if a word processor is used to create the file.) Sequential data files can also be created directly by a BASIC program. We will see how to do this in the next example.

Example 8.3 Creating a Sequential Data File in QuickBASIC: Student Exam Scores

Here is a QuickBASIC program that creates a sequential data file containing the student names and examination scores shown in the last example. (Note that the sequential data file is now being created by a BASIC program rather than a text editor.) The program is written in such a manner that as many as 10 exam scores can be entered for each student. The number of exams must be the same, however, for all of the students when the program is executed.

```
'CREATE A SEQUENTIAL DATA FILE CONTAINING STUDENT EXAMINATION SCORES

DIM score(10)
OPEN "SCORES.DAT" FOR OUTPUT AS #1

LINE INPUT "Course Title: "; title$
PRINT #1, title$
INPUT "Number of Exams: ", n              'enter number of exams per student
PRINT #1, n

'main loop - enter name and exam scores for each student

PRINT
LINE INPUT "Name: "; name$                'enter first student's name
DO UNTIL UCASE$(name$) = "END"
   PRINT #1, name$;
   PRINT "Exam Scores: ";
   FOR i = 1 TO n
      INPUT ; " ", score(i)                'enter student's exam scores
      PRINT #1, ","; STR$(score(i));
   NEXT i
   PRINT
   PRINT #1, ""
   LINE INPUT "Name: "; name$              'enter next student's name
LOOP

CLOSE #1
END
```

The purpose of the first two statements is to dimension the array scores, which contains the exam scores for each student, and open the sequential data file "SCORES.DAT" as an output file. The course title and the number of exams per student are then entered from the keyboard and written out to the data file. Note that the course title is a string which is entered from the keyboard via the LINE INPUT statement. The number of exams per student is an integer quantity whose value must be between 1 and 10.

The next block of statements forms a loop. During each pass through the loop, the name of one student is entered, followed by the exam scores for that student. The set of exam scores for each student is entered via an inner FOR - NEXT loop. Each exam score is converted to a string with the STR$ function before being written to the data file. This assures that the data items will be spaced correctly.

The outer looping action continues until the string "END" is entered for a student name. The last two statements close the data file and end the program.

Notice the repeated INPUT statement within the innermost loop. The semicolon following INPUT causes the cursor to remain on the same line after each data item is entered from the keyboard. The empty prompt string forms a separator between data items and the comma following the empty string suppresses the question mark each time the INPUT statement is executed.

Execution of this program results in the generation of a data file identical to that shown in the previous example. A portion of the interactive data entry is shown below. The user's responses are underlined.

```
Course Title: "Comp Sci 100 - Programming with BASIC"
Number of Exams: 5

Name: "Adams, B F"
Exam Scores:  45 80 80 95 55
Name: "Brown, P"
Exam Scores:  60 50 70 75 55


. . . . .


Name: end
```

Note that the user must press the ENTER key after each exam score is entered. Also, note that the course title and each student name must be enclosed in quotation marks when it is entered from the keyboard. However, the last string (end) must *not* be enclosed in quotation marks.

Try running this program and comparing the resulting data file with that shown in Example 8.2.

Example 8.4 Creating a Sequential Data File in True BASIC: Student Exam Scores

Here is a True BASIC program that parallels the QuickBASIC program shown in the previous example. This program executes somewhat differently than the QuickBASIC program in that each exam score is entered on a different line.

```
!CREATE A SEQUENTIAL DATA FILE CONTAINING STUDENT EXAMINATION SCORES

DIM score(10)
OPEN #1: NAME "SCORES.DAT", CREATE NEW, ORGANIZATION TEXT

LINE INPUT PROMPT "Course Title: ": title$
PRINT #1: title$
INPUT PROMPT "Number of Exams: ": n    !enter number of exams per student
PRINT #1: n
```

```
!main loop - enter name and exam scores for each student

PRINT
LINE INPUT PROMPT "Name: ": name$          !enter first student's name
DO UNTIL UCASE$(name$) = "END"
   PRINT #1: name$;
   PRINT "Exam Scores: ";
   FOR i = 1 TO n
      INPUT PROMPT " ": score(i)            !enter student's exam scores
      PRINT #1: ", "; STR$(score(i));
   NEXT i
   PRINT
   PRINT #1: ""
   LINE INPUT PROMPT "Name: ": name$     !enter next student's name
LOOP

CLOSE #1
END
```

When executed, this program will produce a sequential data file identical with that produced by the QuickBASIC program in the previous example. A portion of the interactive session is shown below.

```
Course Title: "Comp Sci 100 - Programming with BASIC"
Number of Exams: 5

Name: "Adams, B F"
Exam Scores: 45
   80
   80
   95
   55

Name: "Brown, P"
Exam Scores: 60
   50
   70
   75
   55

. . . . .

Name: end
```

Try running this program and comparing the resulting data file with those shown in the last two examples.

In many applications, the information stored in a data file will be read and then processed by a BASIC program. The data items in a sequential data file must be read in the same order they are stored, starting at the beginning of the file. All of the information that is read is preserved within the data file for subsequent use.

When reading a sequential data file, it is generally not known in advance how many records are included in the file. Hence, we will want to enter a conditional loop that reads records sequentially until an end-of-file condition is detected.

Example 8.5 Reading a Sequential Data File in QuickBASIC: Student Exam Scores

Let us return to the sequential data file containing student names and exam scores shown in Example 8.2. Suppose we want to carry out the following operations for each student in the class.

1. Read the student's name from the data file and display it on the screen.

2. Read the student's exam scores from the data file and prompt for an additional exam score.

3. Enter an additional exam score from the keyboard.

4. Calculate an average of all exam scores.

5. Display the student's average on the screen.

The computation will continue until all of the student records have been processed (i.e., until the end of the data file has been reached).

Here is a complete QuickBASIC program that carries out these operations.

```
'READ A SEQUENTIAL DATA FILE CONTAINING STUDENT EXAM SCORES,
'THEN PROCESS THE DATA (ADD A NEW SCORE AND CALCULATE AN AVERAGE)

DIM score(10)
OPEN "SCORES.DAT" FOR INPUT AS #1

INPUT #1, title$
PRINT title$
INPUT #1, n                       'enter the number of exams per student

'main loop - enter scores and display average for each student

PRINT
DO UNTIL EOF(1)
   INPUT #1, name$                'enter student's name
   PRINT name$;

   LET sum = 0
   FOR i = 1 TO n
      INPUT #1, score(i)          'enter student's exam scores
      LET sum = sum + score(i)
   NEXT i

   INPUT "   Score: ", newscore   'enter the new exam score
   LET sum = sum + newscore
   LET average = sum / (n + 1)    'calculate the average score
   PRINT "Average =";             'display the calculated average
   PRINT USING "###"; average
   PRINT
LOOP

CLOSE #1
END
```

The organization of this program is generally similar to the program shown in Example 8.3. Now, however, the data file is opened as an input file rather than an output file. Note that the course title and the name of each student are entered via an INPUT statement rather than a LINE INPUT statement. (In the case of the course title, we want the title itself, but not the quotation marks surrounding it. In the case of the student names, we want to read each student name separately from the exam scores, which are on the same line.)

The most significant difference between this program and the one presented in Example 8.3 is the outer loop, which now executes until an end-of-file condition is found on data channel 1. The EOF function is used for this purpose. Thus, the main loop begins with the statement DO UNTIL EOF(1). Within the loop, each student's name and exam scores are read from the data file, a new exam score is entered from the keyboard, and the student's overall average is displayed on the screen. Note the use of the PRINT USING statement to display the average.

Here is a typical interactive session resulting from the execution of this program with data read from data file SCORES.DAT. The user's responses are again underlined.

```
Comp Sci 100 - Programming with BASIC

Adams, B F    Score: 75
Average = 72

Brown, P    Score: 80
Average = 65

Davis, R A    Score: 55
Average = 42

Fisher, E K    Score: 5
Average =  4

Hamilton, S P    Score: 90
Average = 92

Jones, J J    Score: 80
Average = 88

Ludwig, C W    Score: 70
Average = 53

Osborne, T    Score: 80
Average = 70

Prince, W F    Score: 100
Average = 83

Richards, E N    Score: 70
Average = 55

Smith, M C    Score: 75
Average = 68

Thomas, B A    Score: 10
Average = 22
```

```
Wolfe, H   Score: 95
Average = 64


Zorba, D R   Score: 95
Average = 78
```

Example 8.6 Reading a Sequential Data File in True BASIC: Student Exam Scores

Here is a True BASIC program that has the same purpose as the QuickBASIC program shown in the last example.

```
!READ A SEQUENTIAL DATA FILE CONTAINING STUDENT EXAM SCORES,
!THEN PROCESS THE DATA (ADD A NEW SCORE AND CALCULATE AN AVERAGE)

DIM score(10)
OPEN #1: NAME "SCORES.DAT", CREATE OLD, ORGANIZATION TEXT

INPUT #1: title$
PRINT title$
INPUT #1: n                              !number of exams per student

!main loop - enter scores and display average for each student

PRINT
DO UNTIL END #1
   INPUT #1: name$,                      !enter student's name
   PRINT name$;

   LET sum = 0
   FOR i = 1 TO n - 1
      INPUT #1: score(i),                !enter student's exam scores
      LET sum = sum + score(i)
   NEXT i
   INPUT #1: score(n)
   LET sum = sum + score(n)

   INPUT PROMPT "   Score: ": newscore   !enter the new exam score
   LET sum = sum + newscore
   LET average = sum / (n + 1)           !calculate the average score
   PRINT "Average =";                    !display the calculated average
   PRINT USING "###": average
   PRINT
LOOP

CLOSE #1
END
```

Notice that the end-of-file condition is written somewhat differently in True BASIC; namely, DO UNTIL END #1. Also, notice that within the DO UNTIL loop, there are two INPUT #1 statements that end with commas; i.e.,

```
INPUT #1: names$,
```

and

```
INPUT #1: score(i),
```

True BASIC requires these commas so that the next input item will be read from the same record (i.e., the same line).

When executed, this program behaves in exactly the same manner as the QuickBASIC program presented in the last example.

Many applications require that the information in a data file be upgraded by modifying the information in the data file or by adding new information. The general procedure for updating a sequential data file is to copy the contents of the old data file to a new data file, incorporating any additions or changes to the data during the copy procedure. After the updating has been completed, the old data file is deleted and the new (updated) data file is given the name of the old file. The procedure is illustrated in the following examples.

Example 8.7 Updating a Sequential Data File in QuickBASIC: Student Exam Scores

In this example we will continue with the problem situation described in Examples 8.3 and 8.5 — namely, creating and processing a set of exam scores for a class of students. Let us now develop a more comprehensive program that will enter an additional exam score for each student and add it to the data file. In addition, users will have the option of calculating an overall average for each student if they wish. (Presumably, the average would be calculated at the end of each term, after the last exam score has been entered.) The computation will be based upon the general update procedure discussed above; i.e., read the old data from an existing data file and write the updated data to a new data file.

The program will proceed in accordance with the following outline.

1. Read the course title from an existing data file (e.g., SCORES.DAT) and display it on the screen.

2. Ask the user whether or not to calculate averages.

3. Do the following for each student:

    (a) Read the student's name from the data file and display it on the screen.

    (b) Read the student's exam scores from the data file and prompt for an additional data file.

    (c) Enter an additional exam score from the keyboard.

    (d) Calculate an optional average of all exam scores.

    (e) Display the student's average on the screen.

    (f) Write the new record (i.e., the student's name, the old exam scores, the new exam score and the calculated average) onto a new data file (e.g., UPDATE.DAT).

4. After all of the student records have been processed, delete the old data file and rename the new data file so that it has the same name as the old file.

Here is a QuickBASIC program that carries out all of these operations.

```
'UPDATE A SEQUENTIAL DATA FILE CONTAINING STUDENT EXAM SCORES
'(READ THE OLD DATA, ADD NEW INFORMATION AND WRITE TO A NEW DATA FILE)

DIM score(10)
LET quote$ = CHR$(34)                    'double quotation mark
OPEN "SCORES.DAT" FOR INPUT AS #1
OPEN "UPDATE.DAT" FOR OUTPUT AS #2

INPUT #1, title$
PRINT #2, quote$; title$; quote$
PRINT title$
PRINT

INPUT #1, n                              'enter the no. of exams per student
PRINT #2, n + 1

INPUT "Calculate averages (Y/N)"; ans$

'main loop - enter scores and update information for each student

DO UNTIL EOF(1)
   PRINT
   INPUT #1, name$                       'enter name from data file
   PRINT #2, quote$; name$; quote$;
   PRINT name$;
                                         'enter exam scores from data file
   LET sum = 0
   FOR i = 1 TO n
      INPUT #1, score(i)
      PRINT #2, ","; STR$(score(i));
      LET sum = sum + score(i)
   NEXT i

   INPUT "   Score: ", newscore          'enter the new exam score
   LET sum = sum + newscore

   IF UCASE$(ans$) = "Y" THEN
      LET average = sum / (n + 1)         'calculate the average score
      PRINT #2, ","; STR$(newscore);
      PRINT #2, ","; STR$(CINT(average))
      PRINT "Average =";                  'display the calculated average
      PRINT USING "###"; average
   ELSE
      PRINT #2, ","; STR$(newscore)
   END IF
LOOP

CLOSE
KILL "SCORES.DAT"                         'delete the original data file
NAME "UPDATE.DAT" AS "SCORES.DAT"         'rename the new data file
END
```

The program is generally straightforward, though there are a few statements that require some explanation. Notice the first LET statement, which assigns the double quote character (whose ASCII code is 34) to the string variable `quote$`. This variable is used in two PRINT statements; namely,

```
PRINT #2, quote$; title$; quote$

PRINT #2, quote$; name$; quote$;
```

Here we engage in some mild trickery, so that the course title and each student's name will be enclosed by quotation marks when written to the new data file. Without the quotation marks we would not be able to read these strings correctly.

Within the IF - ELSE block, we see the statement

```
PRINT #2, ","; STR$(CINT(average))
```

This statement utilizes the CINT function, which rounds the numerical value of `average` to the nearest integer. Note that we cannot use PRINT USING to round the number because we are treating the data item as a string rather than a numerical quantity. (We convert to a string in order to control the spacing of the data items within the file.)

At the end of the program we see the statements

```
KILL "SCORES.DAT"                          'delete the original data file
NAME "UPDATE.DAT" AS "SCORES.DAT"          'rename the new data file
```

The first statement deletes the old data file SCORES.DAT. The second statement causes the new data file, called UPDATE.DAT, to be renamed as SCORES.DAT, thus replacing the deleted file.

Execution of this program results in an interactive session identical to that shown in Example 8.5. Now, however, the original data file will be updated as well. The updated data file resulting from the execution of this program with SCORES.DAT, as originally listed in Example 8.2, is shown below.

```
"Comp Sci 100 - Programming with BASIC"
 6
"Adams, B F", 45, 80, 80, 95, 55, 75, 72
"Brown, P", 60, 50, 70, 75, 55, 80, 65
"Davis, R A", 50, 30, 10, 45, 60, 55, 42
"Fisher, E K", 0, 5, 5, 0, 10, 5, 4
"Hamilton, S P", 90, 85, 100, 95, 90, 90, 92
"Jones, J J", 95, 90, 80, 95, 85, 80, 88
"Ludwig, C W", 35, 50, 55, 65, 45, 70, 53
"Osborne, T", 75, 60, 75, 60, 70, 80, 70
"Prince, W F", 85, 75, 60, 85, 90, 100, 82
"Richards, E N", 50, 60, 50, 35, 65, 70, 55
"Smith, M C", 70, 60, 75, 70, 55, 75, 68
"Thomas, B A", 10, 25, 35, 20, 30, 10, 22
"Wolfe, H", 25, 40, 65, 75, 85, 95, 64
"Zorba, D R", 65, 80, 70, 100, 60, 95, 78
```

Notice that each student record now contains six exam scores plus the calculated average. (Compare with the listing shown in Example 8.2).

Example 8.8 Updating a Sequential Data File in True BASIC: Student Exam Scores

Once again, we show the True BASIC equivalent of the last QuickBASIC program.

```
!UPDATE A SEQUENTIAL DATA FILE CONTAINING STUDENT EXAM SCORES
!(READ THE OLD DATA, ADD NEW INFORMATION AND WRITE TO A NEW DATA FILE)

DIM score(10)
LET quote$ = CHR$(34)                        !double quotation mark
OPEN #1: NAME "SCORES.DAT", CREATE OLD, ORG TEXT
OPEN #2: NAME "UPDATE.DAT", CREATE NEW, ORG TEXT

INPUT #1: title$
PRINT #2: quote$; title$; quote$
PRINT title$
PRINT
INPUT #1: n                                  !enter the number of exams per student
PRINT #2: n + 1

INPUT PROMPT "Calculate averages (Y/N)": ans$

!main loop - enter scores and update information for each student

DO UNTIL END #1
   PRINT
   INPUT #1: name$,                          !enter name from data file
   PRINT #2: quote$; name$; quote$;
   PRINT name$;

   LET sum = 0
   FOR i = 1 TO n - 1
      INPUT #1: score(i),                    !enter student's exam scores
      PRINT #2: ", "; STR$(score(i));
      LET sum = sum + score(i)
   NEXT i
   INPUT #1: score(n)
   PRINT #2: ", "; STR$(score(n));
   LET sum = sum + score(n)

   INPUT PROMPT "   Score: ": newscore !enter the new exam score
   LET sum = sum + newscore

   IF UCASE$(ans$) = "Y" THEN
      LET average = sum / (n + 1)            !calculate the average score
      PRINT #2: ", "; STR$(newscore);
      PRINT #2: ", "; STR$(ROUND(average))
      PRINT "Average =";                     !display the calculated average
      PRINT USING "###": average
   ELSE
      PRINT #2: ", "; STR$(newscore)
   END IF
LOOP
```

```
CLOSE #1
CLOSE #2
UNSAVE "SCORES.DAT"                        !delete the original data file
PRINT
PRINT "Remember to rename UPDATE.DAT as SCORES.DAT after program execution"
END
```

Notice that the original data file, SCORES.DAT, is deleted using True BASIC's UNSAVE command. However, True BASIC does not have a command that permits us to rename the new data file within the program. Hence, we generate a message reminding the user to rename the data file after the program execution.

Note once again the commas following two of the INPUT #1 statements. We originally saw this in Example 8.6. Recall that these commas allow the next data item to be read from the current line (i.e., the same line of input data).

When executed, this program generates an interactive dialog that is largely the same as that shown in Example 8.7. The only difference is the message

```
Remember to rename UPDATE.DAT as SCORES.DAT after program execution
```

which appears at the end of the interactive dialog, after all of the required exam scores have been entered. The resulting data file is identical to that shown in Example 8.7.

8.4 FILE-DIRECTED DEVICE OUTPUT (PRINT FILES)

In Sec. 7.8 we saw that some versions of BASIC include the LPRINT and LPRINT USING statements, which permit output data to be directed to a printer. Alternatively, many versions of BASIC permit output data to be printed by associating the printer with a sequential data file, and then writing to that data file. This association is carried out by opening a file, with a channel number, as a printer file. Output is then directed to that file as though it were an ordinary sequential data file.

Example 8.9

Shown below is a portion of a True BASIC program in which output is directed to the printer.

```
OPEN #1: PRINTER
. . . . .
PRINT "a ="; a; "b ="; b; "c ="; c
PRINT #1: "a ="; a; "b ="; b; "c ="; c
. . . . .
CLOSE #1
```

The first PRINT statement causes the values of a, b and c to be displayed on the screen, whereas the second PRINT statement causes these values to be printed on a printer. (Compare with the QuickBASIC statements shown in Example 7.26.)

8.5 DIRECT DATA FILES

Direct (random access) data files generally consist of a collection of records, each of which is assigned a unique record number. Once a direct file has been opened, an individual record can be accessed by referencing its record number. Information can then be read from the record or written to the record, as required by the individual application.

The characteristics of direct data files differ markedly, however, from one version of BASIC to another. In True BASIC, for example, the records in a direct file can vary in length and composition, though the contents of the file will be encoded and must therefore be read via a BASIC program. QuickBASIC, on the other hand, requires that all of the records within a direct file be of the same length. Thus, it should come as no surprise that the syntactic details associated with direct data files vary significantly from one version of BASIC to another. You should consult your programmer's reference manual before beginning a program that utilizes direct data files.

In the following examples we illustrate the use of direct access data files in True BASIC and in QuickBASIC. We begin with True BASIC, since it closely follows the 1987 ANSI standard.

Example 8.10 Creating a Direct Data File in True BASIC: States and their Capitals

The following True BASIC program creates a direct access data file containing the names of the 50 states and their capitals. Each record will contain the name of one state and the corresponding state capital. The records will be stored sequentially, in the same order they are created, though the individual records need not be accessed in this order once the file has been created (see Example 8.12).

```
!CREATE A RANDOM DATA FILE CONTAINING A LIST OF STATES AND THEIR CAPITALS

CLEAR
INPUT PROMPT "File Name: ": FileName$ !enter the data file name

OPEN #1: NAME FileName$, CREATE NEW, ORG RANDOM, RECSIZE 30

PRINT
INPUT PROMPT "State:    ": State$        !enter the first state

DO UNTIL UCASE$(State$) = "END"
   INPUT PROMPT "Capital: ": Capital$ !enter the state capital
   WRITE #1: State$, Capital$             !write the record to the data file

   PRINT
   INPUT PROMPT "State:    ": State$      !enter the next state
LOOP

CLOSE #1
END
```

The program begins by prompting the user for the name of the data file that is about to be created. Note that this feature differs from the programs presented in Sec. 8.3, which included the required file names within each program. We could, of course, have entered those file names as input parameters, as we do here.

We then open the new data file as a random (direct) data file with a maximum record size of 30 bytes. We can then place as many data items as we wish in any record, as long as the total size of the combined data items does not exceed 30 bytes. Note that the name of the new data file will be determined by the string assigned to FileName$. Also, note that the file will be associated with data channel number 1.

Following the OPEN statement is a loop that prompts the user for the name of a state and its capital and then writes these two data items to the data file. The WRITE statement is used to transfer the data items to the data file. A new record will be created each time the WRITE statement is encountered; hence, each pair of data items will comprise a new record. The looping action will continue until END is entered (either upper- or lowercase) as the name of a state.

5454545

A portion of a typical interactive session is shown below. The user's responses are underlined.

```
File Name: STATES.DAT

State:   ALABAMA
Capital: MONTGOMERY

State:   ALASKA
Capital: JUNEAU

. . . . .

State:   WYOMING
Capital: CHEYENNE

State:   END
```

Example 8.11 Creating a Direct Data File in QuickBASIC: States and their Capitals

Shown below is a QuickBASIC program that parallels the True BASIC program shown in the previous example.

```
'CREATE A RANDOM DATA FILE CONTAINING A LIST OF STATES AND THEIR CAPITALS

CLS
INPUT "File Name: ", FileName$          'enter the data file name

TYPE RecordDef                          'define the record type
   State AS STRING * 15
   Capital AS STRING * 15
END TYPE

DIM Record AS RecordDef                 'declare a record variable

OPEN FileName$ FOR RANDOM AS #1 LEN = LEN(Record)

LET RecNo = 1                           'first record
PRINT
INPUT "State:   ", Record.State         'enter the first state

DO UNTIL UCASE$(LEFT$(Record.State, 3)) = "END"
   INPUT "Capital: ", Record.Capital    'enter the state capital
   PUT #1, RecNo, Record                'write the record to the data file

   LET RecNo = RecNo + 1                'next record
   PRINT
   INPUT "State:   ", Record.State      'enter the next state
LOOP
CLOSE #1
END
```

This program begins by prompting for a file name, as in the last example. Following the prompt we see a *record definition*, beginning with the TYPE statement and ending with the END TYPE statement. This block of statements defines `State` as the first item in each record and `Capital` as the second item. Each data item will be a string, consisting of exactly 15 bytes. Note that `RecordDef` represents the *record type*.

The DIM statement following the record definition defines `Record` to be a *record variable* of type `RecordDef`. This variable has two components: `Record.State` and `Record.Capital`. Each component will be a 15-character string, in accordance with the record definition.

The remainder of the program is similar to that shown in Example 8.10. A random (direct) data file is opened on data channel number 1. Each record will have the same length, as defined by record type `RecordDef`. (Hence, each record will consist of exactly 30 bytes. Note that this differs from the True BASIC record definition, in which each record can be any arbitrary size *not exceeding* 30 bytes.)

The program then enters a loop in which the user is prompted for a state and its capital. When these two items are entered they are written to the data file as a new record. The looping action will continue until the user enters END when prompted for the name of a state.

Note that QuickBASIC uses a PUT statement to write to the data file. This statement is similar to the WRITE statement used in True BASIC. With the PUT statement, however, the entire record is written simply by specifying the record variable — in this case, `Record`. (The WRITE statement used in True BASIC requires that each data item within a record be written separately.) Note also that the PUT statement requires that a record number be specified in order to write out each record (more about this later).

When executed, this program results in an interactive dialog that is identical to that shown in Example 8.10.

Although the records within a direct data file are not arranged in any special order, the *locations* of the records are numbered sequentially from the start of the file, beginning with record number 1 and increasing by one unit for each consecutive data item. A *pointer* is used to to indicate the location of any particular record. The pointer must be positioned properly before a record can be read from or written to a direct data file.

We have already encountered some use of pointer control, in the previous two examples. The True BASIC program shown in Example 8.10 did not require explicit pointer assignments because the pointer always begins with a value of 1 and automatically advances by one unit when reading or writing records sequentially (as when creating a new file). The QuickBASIC program shown in Example 8.11 controls the pointer location by assigning values to the variable `RecNo`.

Most versions of BASIC include several statements and functions that indicate the size of a file and the location of the pointer, and allow the pointer to be repositioned. In True BASIC, several ASK and SET statements are available for this purpose. QuickBASIC uses the functions LOF (Length Of File) to determine the file size and LOC to determine the pointer location. In addition, QuickBASIC uses the SEEK statement to set the pointer for the next file I/O operation. We will utilize several of these statements and functions in the next few programming examples.

Example 8.12 Reading a Direct Data File in True BASIC: Locating State Capitals via Binary Search

In this example we present a True BASIC program that will allow the user to specify a state and have the computer return the name of the state capital. In fact, the user will not have to enter the entire name of the state, but only those first few letters that uniquely identify each state (e.g., ALAS for Alaska, CA for California, TEX for Texas, etc.). To do so, we will read the direct data file STATES.DAT, created in each of the last two examples.

The basic idea will be to search the data file until the record containing the desired state has been found and then display the corresponding state capital. We will make use of an efficient search technique known as *binary search* to locate the desired record as quickly as possible. The method is based upon the assumption that the the records are stored in alphabetical order with respect to the names of the states. Thus, the method is intended for a direct access data file in which the records are arranged sequentially with respect to the search parameter.

To see how the binary search technique works, consider a search interval consisting of several consecutive records within the file. Our overall strategy will be to compare the desired state with the state within the middle record. One of three possible conditions will be obtained.

1. The desired record will be the middle record, in which case we display the corresponding state capital and end the search.

2. The desired record will be in the first half of the search interval. Hence we eliminate the second half of the search interval and compare the desired state with the state within the middle record of the remaining subinterval.

3. The desired record will be in the second half of the search interval. In this case we eliminate the first half of the search interval and compare the desired state with the state within the middle record of the remaining subinterval.

This procedure is repeated until either the desired record has been found or it has been determined that the desired state cannot be found.

The relationship between a given search interval and its two possible subintervals is illustrated in Fig. 8.1.

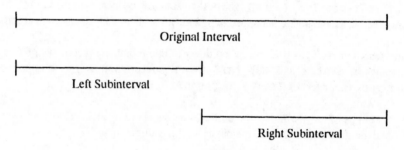

Fig. 8.1

We will place this entire search procedure into an outer loop so that the state capitals of many different states can be located, one after the other. This overall looping action will continue until the string END has been entered for the desired state.

Because the computational strategy is somewhat complicated, we present a detailed program outline. First, however, let us define the following variables.

FileName$ = the name of the direct data file (STATES.DAT)
         n = the number of characters used to identify the desired state
  target$ = the uppercase equivalent of the desired state (or the first n letters of the state)
   found$ = the uppercase equivalent of the state in the current record (or the first n letters of the state)
    RecNo = the current record number
    First = pointer to the first record in the current search interval
     Last = pointer to the last record in the current search interval

The computation will proceed as follows.

1. Prompt the user for the name of the data file.

2. Prompt the user for the name of the desired state. The number of characters entered is then assigned to n, and the uppercase equivalent of the state name is assigned to target$.

3.   End the computation if the user enters END (either upper- or lowercase). Otherwise, continue with step 4
     below.

4.   Assign the values 1 and FILESIZE to the pointers `First` and `Last`, respectively. These assignments
     define the initial search interval. (Note that FILESIZE represents the number of *records* contained within
     the data file.)

5.   Carry out the binary search as follows.

     (*a*) Determine the record at the middle of the search interval and assign its record number to `RecNo`.

     (*b*) Locate the middle record and read the values of `State$` and `Capital$`, respectively. Then assign
            uppercase equivalent of the left-most `n` characters of `State$` to `found$`.

     (*c*) If `target$ = found$`, the desired state has been located. Hence, display the record number and
            the state capital and exit the binary search routine (proceed to step 6 below).

     (*d*) If `target$ < found$`, the desired state will be located in the first half of the search interval. Hence,
            define a new subinterval by assigning `RecNo - 1` to `Last` and repeat this step.

     (*e*) Otherwise (`target$ > found$`), the desired state will be located in the last half of the search interval.
            Hence, define a new subinterval by assigning `RecNo + 1` to `First` and repeat this step.

     (*f*) If the search interval has been narrowed down to one remaining record (`First = Last`), then read
            the values of `State$` and `Capital$` from this record and assign the uppercase equivalent of the
            left-most `n` characters of `State$` to `found$`.

            (*i*) If `target$ = found$`, the desired state has been located. Hence, display the record number
                   and the state capital and end the binary search routine.

            (*ii*) Otherwise, display a message indicating that the desired state cannot be found and end the binary
                    search routine.

6.   Continue the entire procedure (steps 2 through 5) until END has been entered for the desired state, as
     explained in step 3 above.

The following True BASIC program is based upon the above outline.

```
!LOCATE STATE CAPITALS WITHIN A RANDOM DATA FILE VIA BINARY SEARCH

CLEAR
INPUT PROMPT "File Name: ": FileName$        !enter the data file name

OPEN #1: NAME FileName$, ORG RANDOM
ASK #1:  RECSIZE RecordSize                  !determine the record size

PRINT
INPUT PROMPT "State: ": State$               !enter the target state
LET n = LEN(State$)                          !string length
LET target$ = UCASE$(State$)
```

```
DO UNTIL UCASE$(target$) = "END"
    LET First = 1                              !beginning of search interval
    ASK #1: FILESIZE Last                      !end of search interval

    !binary search routine

DO
    LET RecNo = INT((First + Last) / 2)
    SET #1: RECORD RecNo               !locate a state
    READ #1: State$, Capital$
    LET found$ = UCASE$(State$[1:n])
    IF (target$ = found$) THEN                          !found the target state
        PRINT "Record "; RecNo; TAB(16); Capital$
        EXIT DO
    ELSEIF (target$ < found$) THEN
        LET Last = RecNo - 1           !retain first half of search interval
        IF (Last < First) THEN Last = First
    ELSE
        LET First = RecNo + 1          !retain last half of search interval
    END IF

    IF (First = Last) THEN             !try remaining end point
        SET #1: RECORD First
        READ #1: State$, Capital$
        LET found$ = UCASE$(State$[1:n])
        IF (target$ = found$) THEN                      !found the target state
            PRINT "Record "; First; TAB(16); Capital$
        ELSE
            PRINT "Cannot find this state - Please try again"
        END IF
    END IF
LOOP UNTIL (First = Last)

    PRINT
    INPUT PROMPT "State: ": State$               !enter the next target state
    LET n = LEN(State$)
    LET target$ = UCASE$(State$)
LOOP

CLOSE #1
END
```

The program consists primarily of two loops. The outer loop is required to process multiple target states. Locating the capital of a particular state requires one pass through this loop. The inner loop implements the binary search procedure, as described in the above outline. A new binary search is initiated for each target state.

Notice the two ASK statements early in the program. The first determines the number of records within the file and assigns this value to `RecordSize` (note that `RecordSize` is not used elsewhere in the program). The second determines the number of the last record in the file.

Within the inner loop, we see that the SET statement is used to access a particular record and the READ statement is used to read the contents of that record. Note that the READ statement is analogous to the WRITE statement shown in Example 8.10.

Finally, the uppercase equivalent of the left-most n characters in the state name is determined by the expression UCASE$(State$[1:N]), as described in Chap. 5 (see Sec. 5.2).

Execution of the program results in an interactive session such as the one shown below. The user's responses are underlined.

```
File Name: STATES.DAT

State: OHIO
Record  35      COLUMBUS


State: CA
Record  5       SACRAMENTO


State: CO
Record  6       DENVER


State: TE
Record  42      NASHVILLE


State: TEX
Record  43      AUSTIN


State: FLA
Cannot find this state - Please try again


State: FLO
Record  9       TALLAHASSEE


State: NEW H
Record  29      CONCORD


State: NEW M
Record  31      SANTA FE


State: WEST
Record  48      CHARLESTON


State: END
```

Notice that the user must enter only enough characters to identify each state. If the identification is not unique (as, for example, TE, which can represent Tennessee or Texas), the first match located by the binary search is displayed. Abbreviations that are not a part of the state name (for example, FLA for Florida) are not recognized.

Example 8.13 Reading a Direct Data File in QuickBASIC: Locating State Capitals via Binary Search

Here is QuickBASIC version of the program shown in the previous example.

```
'LOCATE STATE CAPITALS WITHIN A RANDOM DATA FILE VIA BINARY SEARCH

CLS
INPUT "File Name: ", FileName$       'enter the data file name
```

```
    TYPE RecordDef                          'define the record type
       State AS STRING * 15
       Capital AS STRING * 15
    END TYPE

    DIM Record AS RecordDef                 'declare a record variable
    OPEN FileName$ FOR RANDOM AS #1 LEN = LEN(Record)

    PRINT
    INPUT "State: ", State$                 'enter the target state
    LET n = LEN(State$)                      'no of characters in target
    LET target$ = UCASE$(State$)

    DO UNTIL UCASE$(target$) = "END"
       LET First = 1                        'beginning of search interval
       LET Last = LOF(1) / LEN(Record)      'end of search interval

       'binary search routine

       DO
          LET RecNo = INT((First + Last) / 2)
          GET #1, RecNo, Record             'locate a state
          LET found$ = UCASE$(LEFT$(Record.State, n))
          IF (target$ = found$) THEN                    'found the target state
             PRINT "Record "; RecNo; TAB(16); Record.Capital
             EXIT DO
          ELSEIF (target$ < found$) THEN
             LET Last = RecNo - 1           'retain first half of search interval
             IF (Last < First) THEN Last = First
          ELSE
             LET First = RecNo + 1          'retain last half of search interval
          END IF

          IF (First = Last) THEN            'try remaining end point
             LET RecNo = First
             GET #1, RecNo, Record
             LET found$ = UCASE$(LEFT$(Record.State, n))
             IF (target$ = found$) THEN                 'found the target state
                PRINT "Record "; RecNo; TAB(16); Record.Capital
             ELSE
                PRINT "Cannot find this state - Please try again"
             END IF
          END IF
       LOOP UNTIL (First = Last)

       PRINT
       INPUT "State: ", State$              'enter the next target state
       LET n = LEN(State$)                  'no of characters in target
       LET target$ = UCASE$(State$)
    LOOP
    CLOSE #1
    END
```

This program utilizes the same logic as the TrueBASIC program shown in Example 8.12, though there are some notable syntactic differences. In particular, notice the definition of the record type RecordDef and the record variable Record, as in Example 8.11. Also, notice that the location of the last record in the file is given by the expression LOF(1) / LEN(Record), where LOF and LEN are QuickBASIC library functions. The numerator returns the length of the entire file (in bytes), whereas the denominator returns the length of one record (in bytes); hence, the quotient represents the number of records in the file.

Within the inner loop, we see that the GET statement is used to read the current record from the file. This statement is analogous to the PUT statement shown in Example 8.11. Also, note that the uppercase equivalent of the left-most n characters in the state name is now determined by the expression UCASE$(LEFT$(Record.State, n)). The inner expression (LEFT$(Record.State, n)) determines the left-most n characters, which are then converted to uppercase by the UCASE$ function.

This program executes in exactly the same manner as the True BASIC program shown in the previous example. The resulting interactive dialog is identical to that shown earlier.

Direct data files are well-suited for applications that require periodic record updates, because information can be read from and written to the same data file. (Recall that a *sequential* data file can be opened in an input mode or an output mode, but not both). Thus, for any given record, old information can be read from a direct data file and displayed on the screen. Updated information can then be entered from the keyboard and written to the data file. This procedure can be repeated for all of the records in the file, or for a selective number of records that specifically require updating. The procedure is illustrated in the following example.

Example 8.14 Updating a Direct Data File in True BASIC: Baseball Team Records

A Little League manager keeps records of all teams within the league on a computer. The records are maintained in a direct data file. Each record contains the team name, the number of wins and the number of losses.

After each round of new games, the manager updates the records, indicating whether each team won or lost its most recent game. The updated number of wins and losses is then written to the data file. In addition, the current team status (team name, number of wins, number of losses and percentage of games won) is displayed on the screen as the new information is entered into the computer.

Suppose, for example, this program will be used to update a file called TEAMS.DAT, containing the following information. (Presumably, the file containing this information will have been created with another BASIC program.)

Team Name	Wins	Losses
GIANTS	3	4
JETS	1	6
NERDS	3	4
ROCKETS	5	2
SLUGGERS	4	3
TECHIES	5	2

Here is the True BASIC program that is used to update the student records.

```
!UPDATE A RANDOM DATA FILE CONTAINING A LIST OF BASEBALL TEAM RECORDS


CLEAR
INPUT PROMPT "File Name: ": FileName$              !enter the data file name

OPEN #1: NAME FileName$, ORG RANDOM
```

```
ASK #1: RECSIZE RecordSize              !determine the record size
ASK #1: FILESIZE Last                   !determine the last record number

PRINT
PRINT "UPDATING TEAM STANDINGS"

LET Count = 1
DO
   READ #1: Team$, Wins, Losses         !read the record from the data file
   PRINT
   PRINT Team$; ": W/L";
   INPUT Game$                          !update win/loss record
   IF (UCASE$(Game$)) = "W" THEN
      LET Wins = Wins + 1
   ELSEIF (UCASE$(Game$)) = "L" THEN
      LET Losses = Losses + 1
   END IF

   LET Percent = 100 * Wins / (Wins + Losses)
   SET #1: POINTER SAME
   WRITE #1: Team$, Wins, Losses        !write updated record to data file
   PRINT "Wins: "; Wins, "Losses: "; Losses, "Percentage: ";
   PRINT USING "###.#": Percent

   LET Count = Count + 1
LOOP UNTIL Count > Last

CLOSE #1
END
```

The program is mostly straightforward, though a few features require some discussion. In particular, notice that the size of each record and the number of records are determined with two ASK statements immediately after opening the file. The program then enters a loop that reads information from each record, prompts the user for new information and writes the updated information back to the file.

Notice the SET #1: POINTER SAME statement, which resets the pointer to the previous record before each WRITE statement. This statement negates the normal advancement of the pointer caused by the READ statement. Hence, the WRITE statement applies to the same record as the preceding READ statement.

Execution of this program to process the file TEAMS.DAT will result in the following interactive dialog.

```
File Name: TEAMS.DAT

UPDATING TEAM STANDINGS

Giants: W/L? L
Wins:  3        Losses:  5       Percentage:  37.5

Jets: W/L? L
Wins:  1        Losses:  7       Percentage:  12.5

Nerds: W/L? W
Wins:  4        Losses:  4       Percentage:  50.0
```

```
Rockets: W/L? W
Wins:  6         Losses:  2      Percentage:  75.0

Sluggers: W/L? W
Wins:  5         Losses:  3      Percentage:  62.5

Techies: W/L? L
Wins:  5         Losses:  3      Percentage:  62.5
```

Example 8.15 Updating a Direct Data File in QuickBASIC: Baseball Team Records

Here is a QuickBASIC program that parallels the True BASIC program shown in the previous example.

```
'UPDATE A RANDOM DATA FILE CONTAINING A LIST OF BASEBALL TEAM RECORDS

CLS
INPUT "File Name: ", FileName$              'enter the data file name

TYPE RecordType                             'define the record type
   Team AS STRING * 8
   Wins AS INTEGER
   Losses AS INTEGER
END TYPE
DIM TeamRec AS RecordType                   'declare a record variable

OPEN FileName$ FOR RANDOM AS #1 LEN = LEN(TeamRec)
LET Last = LOF(1) / LEN(TeamRec)
LET RecNo = 1                               'first record

PRINT
PRINT "UPDATING TEAM STANDINGS"
DO
   GET #1, RecNo, TeamRec                    'read the record from the data file
   PRINT
   PRINT TeamRec.Team; ": W/L";
   INPUT Game$                               'update win/loss record

   IF (UCASE$(Game$)) = "W" THEN
      LET TeamRec.Wins = TeamRec.Wins + 1
   ELSEIF (UCASE$(Game$)) = "L" THEN
      LET TeamRec.Losses = TeamRec.Losses + 1
   END IF
   LET Percent = 100 * TeamRec.Wins / (TeamRec.Wins + TeamRec.Losses)
   PUT #1, RecNo, TeamRec                    'write updated record to data file
   PRINT "Wins: "; TeamRec.Wins, "Losses: "; TeamRec.Losses, "Percentage: ";
   PRINT USING "###.#"; Percent

   LET RecNo = RecNo + 1                      'next record
LOOP UNTIL RecNo > Last
CLOSE #1
END
```

In this program we again see the use of a record type definition (RecordType), followed by the declaration of a record variable (TeamRec) of this type. Also, we see that the record size is determined by the expression LEN(TeamRec) in the OPEN statement, and the number of records (i.e., the number of the last record) by the expression LOF(1) / LEN(TeamRec), as in Example 8.13.

Entire records are read from the data file and written to the data file using the GET and PUT statements, respectively. Each statement requires the specification of a record number. Note that the execution of these statements does not automatically reset the pointer to the next record number. Thus, the pointer is reset at the end of the loop (LET RecNo = RecNo + 1) after updating each record.

When executed, this program results in an interactive dialog that is identical to that shown in the preceding example.

Remember that the material in this chapter is intended to be illustrative rather than exhaustive. Most versions of BASIC support several different types of data files, with their own unique syntax for each file type. Even with the most common types of data files, such as sequential and direct data files, the instruction set may vary significantly from one version of BASIC to another. You should consult your programmer's reference manual before embarking on any significant programming project involving the use of data files.

Review Questions

8.1 What is a file? What kinds of information can be contained within a file?

8.2 What is the difference between formatted data files and unformatted data files? What are the advantages and disadvantages of each?

8.3 What other terms are used to describe formatted data files? What other terms are used to describe unformatted data files?

8.4 What is a record? What is a field? What is the relationship between records and fields?

8.5 What is the difference between a sequential and a direct data file? What are the advantages and disadvantages of each?

8.6 What other term is commonly used to describe direct data files?

8.7 Describe the three major steps involved in processing the information within a multi-record data file.

8.8 What happens when a data file is opened? What happens when it is closed?

8.9 Describe each of the following file-related terms: channel number, mode, access type, status.

8.10 How are the records ordered in a sequential data file?

8.11 Can a sequential data file contain both numeric constants and strings?

8.12 Must the records in a sequential data file be read in any particular order? Explain.

8.13 Can a text editor or word processor be used to edit a sequential data file?

8.14 Describe a two-file procedure that is often used when updating the information in a sequential data file.

8.15   How can sequential data file procedures be used to direct output to a printer?

8.16   How are the records ordered in a direct data file? How can an individual record be accessed?

8.17   Can a direct data file contain both numeric constants and string? (Compare with Question 8.11.)

8.18   What is a pointer? How can the location of a pointer be determined? How can a pointer be repositioned?

8.19   How are records read from a direct data file? Can the records be read sequentially? Explain.

8.20   How are records written to a direct data file? Can the records be written sequentially? Explain.

8.21   Can a text editor or word processor be used to edit a direct data file? (Compare with Question 8.13.)

8.22   Describe a procedure for updating the information in a direct data file. Compare with the procedure used with a sequential data file (see Question 8.14).

Problems

8.23   Answer the following questions for your particular version of BASIC.

   (*a*)   How is a file opened? What information is specified in the OPEN statement?

   (*b*)   How is a file closed? Can two or more files be closed with a single CLOSE statement?

   (*c*)   How is an end-of-file detected?

   (*d*)   How is the current pointer location determined?

   (*e*)   How is the pointer repositioned?

   (*f*)   How is the number of records in the file determined?

   (*g*)   How is the record size determined?

   (*h*)   Can a file be deleted from within a BASIC program? If so, how?

   (*i*)   Can a file be renamed from within a BASIC program? If so, how?

   (*j*)   How are records read from and written to a direct data file?

8.24   Describe the data file associated with each of the following True BASIC OPEN statements.

   (*a*)   `OPEN #1: NAME "SAMPLE.001", ACCESS OUTPUT, CREATE NEW, ORG TEXT`

   (*b*)   `OPEN #2: NAME filename$, CREATE OLD, ORG RANDOM, RECSIZE 48`

   (*c*)   `OPEN #3: NAME newfile$, CREATE NEW, ORG RANDOM, RECSIZE nchars`

   (*d*)   `OPEN #4: NAME "BACKUP.DAT", ACCESS INPUT, CREATE OLD, ORG TEXT` (*e*)   `OPEN #5: PRINTER`

8.25 Describe the data file associated with each of the following QuickBASIC statements.

    (*a*)   `OPEN "DEMO.DAT" FOR INPUT AS #3`

    (*b*)   `OPEN datafile$ FOR OUTPUT AS #5`

    (*c*)   `OPEN datafile$ FOR RANDOM AS #2 LEN = LEN(recname)`

    (*d*)   `OPEN "customers.dat" FOR APPEND AS #1`

8.26 Write an OPEN statement in True BASIC for each of the following situations.

    (*a*)   Open an existing text file called `"students.dat"` as an input file on data channel number 3.

    (*b*)   Open a new text file called `"grades.dat"` as an output file on data channel number 5.

    (*c*)   Open a new direct data file called `"orders.dat"` with a maximum record size of 72 characters on data channel number 2.

    (*d*)   Open an existing direct data file whose name is given by `filename$` and whose maximum record size is given by `recsize` on data channel number 4.

    (*e*)   Open a printer file associated with data channel number 9.

8.27 Write an OPEN statement in QuickBASIC for each of the following situations.

    (*a*)   Open an existing sequential file called `"students.dat"` as an input file on data channel number 3.

    (*b*)   Open a new sequential file called `"grades.dat"` as an output file on data channel number 5.

    (*c*)   Open an existing sequential file whose name is given by `filename$` as an append file on data channel number 2.

    (*d*)   Open a new direct data file called `"orders.dat"` with a record size of 72 characters on data channel number 1.

    (*e*)   Open an existing direct data file whose name is given by `filename$` and whose record size is given by `recsize` on data channel number 2.

8.28 Outline a BASIC program that will read the values of the variables `name$`, `salary`, `taxes` and `netpay` from a record in the sequential (text) file `oldrecs.dat`, update the values as required and write them to the sequential file `newrecs.dat`. Include a loop that causes the process to be repeated for every record in the file. Show the OPEN and CLOSE statements and the skeletal structure of the loop. Do not show the details of the updates.

8.29 Outline a BASIC program that will read the values of the variables `name$`, `salary`, `taxes` and `netpay` from a record in the direct data file `salaries.dat`, update the values as required and write them back to the data file. Include a loop that causes the process to be repeated for every record in the file. Show the OPEN and CLOSE statements and the skeletal structure of the loop, including the pointer positioning statements. Do not show the details of the updates. Compare with the solution to Prob. 8.28.

8.30 Outline a BASIC program that will read the values of the variables name$, salary, taxes and netpay from a record in the sequential (text) file oldrecs.dat, display the values on the screen and write them out on a printer. Include a loop so that the process is repeated for every record in the file. Show the OPEN and CLOSE statements and the main features of the loop.

8.31 Outline a BASIC program that will read the values of the variables name$, salary, taxes and netpay from a record in the sequential (text) file oldrecs.dat, display the values on the screen and write them to a new direct data file called newrecs.dat. Include a loop so that the process is repeated for every record in the file. Show the OPEN and CLOSE statements and the main features of the loop, including the conversion of data items from one type of data file format to the other.

8.32 Outline a BASIC program that will read the values of the variables name$, salary, taxes and netpay from a record in the direct data file oldrecs.dat, display the values on the screen and write them to a new sequential (text) file called newrecs.dat. Include a loop so that the process is repeated for every record in the file. Show the OPEN and CLOSE statements and the main features of the loop, including the conversion of data items from one type of data file format to the other.

8.33 Outline a BASIC program that will ask the user for a record number (i.e., a pointer value) and locate that record from the direct data file oldrecs.dat. Then read the values of the variables name$, salary, taxes and netpay from the record and display them on the screen. Include a loop so that the process continues until the user enters record number 0. Show the OPEN and CLOSE statements and the main features of the loop, including the statements used to locate the record.

Programming Problems

8.34 Modify one of the programs shown in Examples 8.3 and 8.4 so that the student exam scores are entered into a direct (random) access file rather than a sequential file. Include a provision for entering the name of the data file from the keyboard when the program execution begins.

8.35 Modify one of the programs shown in Examples 8.5 and 8.6 so that the direct access data file created in Prob. 8.34 will be read and processed. Include a provision for entering the name of the data file from the keyboard when the program execution begins.

8.36 Modify one of the programs shown in Examples 8.5 and 8.6 so that it will do one of two different things.

(a) Enter individual exam scores interactively, as described in Example 8.5.

(b) Print a summary report of all students in the class. The report should include each student's name, exam scores and average score, based upon the exam scores that are currently in the data file.

Display a menu at the beginning of the program execution so that the user can select which of the above options will be carried out.

8.37   Modify the program written for Prob. 8.36 so that the summary report includes the overall class average and the difference between each student's average and the overall class average.

8.38   Modify one of the programs shown in Examples 8.7 and 8.8 so that the student records are maintained on a single direct data file rather than two sequential data files. (This problem should be viewed as an extension of Prob. 8.35.) Include a provision for generating a printed summary report, as described in Prob. 8.36.

8.39   Modify one of the programs shown in Examples 8.10 and 8.11 so that each record includes the name of a state, its population and its capital.

8.40   Modify one of the programs shown in Examples 8.12 and 8.13 so that it will read the data file created in Prob. 8.39 and do any one of the following.

   (*a*)   Locate and display both the population and the capital of each state requested.

   (*b*)   Prompt for the name of the state capital. Then locate and display the name and population of the corresponding state. (Note that a binary search cannot be carried out for this option, since the state capitals are not arranged alphabetically.)

Display a menu at the beginning of the program execution so that the user can select which of the above options will be carried out.

8.41   Modify one of the programs shown in Examples 8.12 and 8.13 so that it will read the data file created in Prob. 8.39 and do any one of the following.

   (*a*)   Sort the data file so that the states are listed in the order of decreasing populations (largest to smallest).

   (*b*)   Sort the data file so that the state capitals rather than the state names are arranged alphabetically.

Use a sort strategy similar to that described in Example 5.14 to carry out the sorts. Display a menu at the beginning of the program execution so that the user can select which of the above options will be carried out.

8.42   Write one program that combines all of the features described in Probs. 8.40 and 8.41. Display a menu at the beginning of the program execution so that the user can select any of the above options.

8.43   Write a program that will allow the state populations in the data file created for Prob. 8.39 to be updated periodically.

8.44   Write a program that will create the direct data file required by either Example 8.14 or 8.15. Test the program by executing either Example 8.14 or 8.15 with the data file.

8.45   Write a program that will read a direct data file containing baseball team records, as described in either Example 8.14 or 8.15, and do any one of the following.

   (*a*)   Update the team standings, as described in Examples 8.14 and 8.15.

(b)   Sort the teams with respect to the percentage of games won (highest to lowest) and display the sorted list on the screen. Include complete information (i.e., name, games won, games lost and percentage of games won) for each team.

(c)   Provide the same features as in part (b) and, in addition, generate a printed report showing the sorted list of teams with all of the information described above.

Use a sort strategy similar to that described in Example 5.14. Display a menu at the beginning of the program execution so that the user can select which of the above options will be carried out.

8.46   Write a program that will create a *sequential* data file containing baseball team records. Include the information described in Example 8.14 within each record.

8.47   Write a program that will read the sequential data file containing baseball team records created in Prob. 8.46 and do any one of the following.

(a)   Update the team standings, as described in Examples 8.14 and 8.15.

(b)   Sort the teams with respect to the percentage of games won (highest to lowest) and display the sorted list on the screen. Include complete information (i.e., name, games won, games lost and percentage of games won) for each team.

(c)   Provide the same features as in part (b) and, in addition, generate a printed report showing the sorted list of teams with all of the information described above.

Use a two-file update procedure, as described in Example 8.7. Also, use a sort strategy similar to that described in Example 5.14. Display a menu at the beginning of the program execution so that the user can select which of the above options will be carried out. Test the program with the sequential data file created in Prob. 8.46.

8.48   Expand the program described in Prob. 8.45 so that new records (new baseball teams) can be added, old records can be deleted and existing records can be modified. Be sure to maintain the records in alphabetical order. Allow the user to choose which option will be executed before each record is processed.

8.49   Modify one of the craps game simulators given in Examples 6.11 and 6.14 so that it simulates a specified number of games and saves the outcome of each game in a data file. At the end of the simulation, read the data file to determine the percentage of wins and losses that the player has experienced.

Test the program by simulating 1000 consecutive games. Based upon these results, estimate the odds of winning when playing craps.

8.50   Modify the pig Latin generator presented in Example 6.22 so that multiple lines of text can be entered from the keyboard. Save the entire English text in a data file, and save the corresponding pig Latin in another data file.

Include a menu so that the user can select any one of the following features:

(a)   Enter the new text, convert to pig Latin and save. (Save both the original text and the pig Latin, as described above.)

(b)   Read previously entered English text from a data file and display.

(c)   Read the pig Latin equivalent of previously entered English text and display.

Test the program using several arbitrary lines of text.

8.51   Expand the program shown in Example 4.19 (generation of Fibonacci numbers and search for primes) so that each Fibonacci number and its status (prime or nonprime) is written out to a direct access data file. Include the following features in the program.

(a)   Generate the list of Fibonacci numbers and write it out to the data file, as described above.

(b)   Read the contents of a specified record number and display it on the screen.

(c)   Read the entire data file and display it on the screen.

(d)   Generate a printed report containing the entire data file.

Include a menu so that the user can decide which options to execute.

8.52   Extend the program in Prob. 5.28 (reordering a list of numbers four different ways) so that the original set of numbers are written to a direct access data file, which is later updated by replacing the original set of numbers with the sorted numbers. Generate a menu that allows the user to select any of the following features.

(a)   Enter a set of numbers from the keyboard and write it out to the data file.

(b)   Read the numbers from the data file, sort the numbers in one of the four ways indicated in Prob. 5.28 and write the sorted numbers out to the data file.

(c)   Read the numbers (either sorted or unsorted) from the data file and display them on the screen.

(d)   Generate a printed report containing the entire data set read from the data file (either sorted or unsorted).

8.53   Extend the program in Prob. 5.34 (generating a table of compound interest factors) so that the table is written to a sequential data file. Display a menu that allows the user to select any of the following features.

(a)   Generate the table and write it to the data file, with each row occupying a separate line in the data file.

(b)   Read a particular compound interest factor from the table (i.e., from the data file), corresponding to specified values of i and n, and display it on the screen. Include appropriate prompts for i and n, and label the interest factor clearly.

(c)   Read the entire table from the data file and print it in a well-labeled, orderly manner.

8.54   Extend the program in Prob. 5.36 (foreign currencies and their U.S. equivalents) so that the list of currencies is stored alphabetically in a direct access data file. Place each currency and its U.S. equivalent in a separate record. Display a menu that allows the user to select any of the following features.

(a) Enter the list from the keyboard and write it to the data file, with the names of the countries stored alphabetically.

(b) Convert a particular amount of money from one currency to another. Include appropriate prompts for the amount of money, the original currency and the final currency.

(c) Read the entire data file and display its contents on the screen in a well-labeled manner.

Use a binary search routine to locate each record, as required.

8.55 Expand the program in Prob. 8.54 so that it is able to do any of the following, in addition to the features described in Prob. 8.54.

(a) Enter a new record (a new currency).

(b) Delete an existing record.

(c) Modify the U.S. dollar equivalent for any existing record.

Remember to maintain the records in alphabetical order so that the binary search procedure can be used for the conversions.

8.56 Write an interactive BASIC program that will encode or decode multiple lines of text, using the encoding/decoding procedure described in Prob. 5.39. Store the encoded text within a sequential data file, so that it can be retrieved and decoded at any time. The program should include the following features.

(a) Enter text from the keyboard, encode the text and store the encoded text in a data file.

(b) Retrieve the encoded text and display it in its encoded form.

(c) Retrieve the encoded text, decode it and then display the decoded text.

Include a menu so that the user can decide which options to execute. Test the program using several lines of text of your choice.

8.57 Extend the program described in Prob. 8.56 so that multiple keys can be entered, where each successive key is used to encode each consecutive line of text. Thus, the first key will be used to encode the first line of text, the second key will be used to encode the second line of text, and so on. Test the program using several lines of text of your choice.

8.58 Write an interactive BASIC program that will create and utilize a sequential data file containing names, addresses and telephone numbers. Include a provision for each of the following features.

(a) Add a new record (i.e., a new name, address and telephone number) to the file.

(b) Delete an existing record.

(c) Find and display the contents of a particular record corresponding to a particular name.

(d) Modify the contents of an existing record.

(e) Display a complete list of all names, addresses and telephone numbers.

(f) Print a complete list of all names, addresses and telephone numbers.

Be sure to rearrange the records whenever a new record is added or an existing record is deleted, so that the records are always maintained in alphabetical order.

8.59 Repeat Prob. 8.58 utilizing a direct access data file. Compare with the sequential data file version from a standpoint of programming ease and execution speed.

8.60 Write a program that can be used as a simple line-oriented text editor. This program must include the following capabilities.

(a) Enter several lines of text and store in a data file.

(b) Display the contents of the data file.

(c) Print the contents of the data file.

(d) Retrieve and display a particular line, determined by line number.

(e) Insert n lines.

(f) Delete n lines.

(g) Save the newly edited text.

Carry out each of these tasks in response to a one-letter command, preceded by a dollar sign ($). The find (retrieve) command should be followed by an unsigned integer to indicate which line should be retrieved. Also, the insert and delete commands can be followed by an optional positive integer if several consecutive lines are to be inserted or deleted.

Each command should appear on a line by itself, thus providing a means of distinguishing commands from lines of text. Note that a command line will always begin with a dollar sign, followed by a single-letter command and an optional integer.

The following commands are recommended:

$E	enter new text
$L	display (list) the entire block of text
$P	print the entire block of text
Fk$	find (retrieve) line number k
In$	insert n lines after line number k
Dn$	delete n lines after line number k
$S	save the edited block of text
$X	save the edited block of text and exit from the editor

Chapter 9

Vectors and Matrices

In Chap. 5 we learned that all of the elements in an array can be referred to collectively by specifying a common array name. When manipulating arrays, however, we processed each array element (i.e., each subscripted variable) individually, using FOR - NEXT or DO - LOOP structures.

The 1987 ANSI standard includes a collection of special statements, known as *matrix statements*, for carrying out most common array operations. These statements permit us to manipulate all of the elements in an array at once, without making use of FOR - NEXT or DO - LOOP structures. Generally, each of the common matrix operations can be carried out with a special matrix statement. Some of the matrix statements are restricted to one- and two-dimensional arrays (vectors and matrices), whereas others can be used with arrays of any dimensionality.

It should be understood, however, that *some versions of BASIC do not support matrix statements*. In particular, the various implementations of Microsoft BASIC, including QuickBASIC, *do not* include matrix statements. True BASIC, on the other hand, follows the ANSI standard very closely and therefore includes all of the matrix statements defined in the standard. Hence, all of the material in this chapter will be based upon the use of True BASIC. Consult the programmer's reference manual for your particular version of BASIC before attempting to use matrix statements.

9.1 VECTOR AND MATRIX OPERATIONS

Vector and *matrix* are mathematical terms that refer to one-dimensional and two-dimensional arrays, respectively. Thus, a vector can be thought of as a list of numbers (or a list of strings) and a matrix as a table of numbers (or strings). Since a vector is actually a special kind of matrix, most of the rules that apply to matrices are also valid for vectors.

As before, we will use subscripted variables to represent the individual array elements. In the case of a matrix, the first subscript will represent the row and the second subscript will represent the column. Thus, A(3, 2) will represent the element in the third row, second column of the matrix A. Moreover, we will refer to a matrix having m rows and n columns as an m x n matrix. (Remember that the size and dimensionality of an array must be specified in a DIM statement. As described in Chap. 5, the DIM statement must precede any reference to the array or any of the array elements).

The most common matrix operations are assignment, addition, subtraction and multiplication by a constant. Special matrix statements are available to carry out each of these operations. These statements apply to arrays of any dimensionality. There is also a matrix multiplication statement, which is much more restricted in how it can be used. Each of these matrix statements is discussed below.

Assignment

The matrix assignment statement takes on two different forms, permitting scalar assignment (assigning a single value to every element in an array) or matrix assignment (assigning one array to another). In its first form, the matrix assignment statement appears as

MAT C = *expression*

where C is an array of any dimensionality and *expression* is a numeric or string expression. (Remember that a numeric array can only be assigned numeric values and a string array can only be assigned strings.) This statement causes *expression* to be assigned to each element of C.

Example 9.1

Several True BASIC statements are shown below.

```
DIM names$(20), values(3, 4)

MAT names$ = "Santa Claus"
MAT values = 5
```

The DIM statement defines `names$` as a 20-element, one-dimensional string array and `values` as a two-dimensional numeric array having 3 rows and 4 columns. The first MAT statement assigns the string `"Santa Claus"` to each element of `names$` and the second MAT statement assigns the constant 5 to each element of `values`.

In its second form, the matrix assignment statement is written as

$$\text{MAT } C = A$$

where A and C are arrays of the same dimensionality. This statement causes each element of A to be assigned to the corresponding element of C. If the sizes of the two arrays are different (but the number of dimensions is the same), then the size of C will automatically be adjusted to match that of A.

Example 9.2

Suppose that A represents the following 2 x 3 matrix:

$$A = \begin{vmatrix} 3 & 5 & -9 \\ 2 & -6 & 7 \end{vmatrix}$$

The matrix statement

```
MAT C = A
```

will cause C to be a 2 x 3 matrix whose elements are the same as those of A; i.e.,

$$C = \begin{vmatrix} 3 & 5 & -9 \\ 2 & -6 & 7 \end{vmatrix}$$

The matrix assignment statement can also be used to assign the elements of one string array to another. Thus, the matrix assignment statement can be written as

$$\text{MAT } C\$ = A\$$$

where A$ and C$ are string arrays of the same dimensionality. The string represented by each element of A$ will be assigned to the corresponding element of C$.

Addition

Matrix addition is carried out by a statement of the form

MAT C = A + B

This statement causes each element of C to be assigned the sum of the corresponding elements of A and B; e.g., $C(I, J) = A(I, J) + B(I, J)$. All of the arrays must be of the same dimensionality. Moreover, the arrays A and B must have the same number of elements in each direction (for two-dimensional arrays, the same number of rows and columns). The number of elements of C will adjust to that of A and B if necessary.

Example 9.3

Suppose that A and B are 2 x 3 matrices whose elements have the following values:

$$A = \begin{vmatrix} 3 & 5 & -9 \\ 2 & -6 & 7 \end{vmatrix} \qquad\qquad B = \begin{vmatrix} 2 & 2 & 0 \\ -4 & 5 & 1 \end{vmatrix}$$

The matrix statement

MAT C = A + B

will cause C to be a 2 x 3 matrix whose elements are as follows:

$$C = \begin{vmatrix} (3 + 2) & (5 + 2) & (-9 + 0) \\ (2 - 4) & (-6 + 5) & (7 + 1) \end{vmatrix} = \begin{vmatrix} 5 & 7 & -9 \\ -2 & -1 & 8 \end{vmatrix}$$

An array can be updated with a matrix addition statement; e.g., a statement of the form

MAT A = A + B

However, multiple sums, such as

MAT D = A + B + C

are not allowed.

Subtraction

The matrix subtraction statement is identical to the matrix addition statement except that the plus sign is replaced by a minus sign. Thus the statement

MAT C = A − B

causes each element of C to be assigned the difference $C(I, J) = A(I, J) − B(I, J)$. The arrays A and B must have the same number of rows and the same number of columns.

Example 9.4

Suppose A and B are 2 x 3 matrices having the same elements as in Example 9.3. The matrix statement

```
MAT C = A - B
```

will cause the following values to be assigned to C:

$$C = \begin{vmatrix} (3-2) & (5-2) & (-9-0) \\ (2+4) & (-6-5) & (7-1) \end{vmatrix} = \begin{vmatrix} 1 & 3 & -9 \\ 6 & -11 & 6 \end{vmatrix}$$

An array can be updated via matrix subtraction in the same manner as matrix addition. Thus a statement such as

$$MAT\ A = A - B$$

is permissible. On the other hand, statements involving multiple sums and differences, such as

$$MAT\ D = A - B - C \quad or \quad MAT\ D = A + B - C$$

are not allowed.

Multiplication by a Constant

All of the elements in an array can be multiplied by a constant numeric value. This is accomplished with a statement of the form

$$MAT\ C = value * A$$

where A and C are arrays of the same dimensionality and *value* represents a constant, a variable or a numeric expression. Each element of C will then be assigned the value $C(I, J) = value * A(I, J)$. If *value* represents a numeric expression involving operators, the expression must be enclosed in parentheses.

Example 9.5

Suppose that A is the same 2 x 3 matrix given in Example 9.2 and k is a numeric variable whose value is 3. The statement

```
MAT C = k * A
```

will cause the elements of C to have the following values.

$$C = 3 * \begin{vmatrix} 3 & 5 & -9 \\ 2 & -6 & 7 \end{vmatrix} = \begin{vmatrix} 9 & 15 & -27 \\ 6 & -18 & 21 \end{vmatrix}$$

The numeric value that multiplies the matrix can be a complex expression involving subscripted variables and function references as well as constants and ordinary variables. Remember that the expression must be enclosed in parentheses.

Example 9.6

Several additional examples of arrays multiplied by numeric constants are shown below.

```
MAT C = 100 * A
MAT C = (2 * X + Y) * A
MAT C = (SQR(P ^ 2 + Q ^ 2)) * A
```

In these examples A and C are arrays of the same dimensionality, X, Y, P and Q are ordinary numeric variables, and SQR represents the square root library function. Note that the numeric expressions are enclosed in parentheses.

An array can be updated by multiplying itself by a constant. Thus the statement

$$\text{MAT } A = 10 * A$$

is permissible. As with matrix addition and subtraction, however, statements with multiple operators, such as

$$\text{MAT } C = 10 * A + B$$

are not allowed.

Remember that the above expressions can be applied to arrays of any dimensionality, but the dimensionality of the array on the left must be the same as the dimensionality of the arrays on the right. Moreover, if two arrays appear on the right (as in the case of matrix addition or matrix subtraction), the sizes of the right-hand arrays (i.e., the number of elements in each dimension) must be the same.

Example 9.7

Suppose that C is a three-dimensional, 4 x 4 x 6 array, and A and B are three-dimensional, 10 x 10 x 12 arrays. Then the matrix addition statement

```
MAT C = A + B
```

will cause each elemental sum A(I, J, K) + B(I, J, K) to be assigned to C(I, J, K).

For this statement to be valid, all of the arrays must be of the same dimensionality (in this case, 3 dimensions) and the right-hand arrays (A and B) must be the same size (10 x 10 x 12). C need not be the same size as A and B. When the statement is executed C will become a 10 x 10 x 12 array, thus conforming in size to A and B.

Matrix Multiplication

Two matrices can be multiplied if the number of columns in the first matrix is the same as the number of rows in the second matrix. Thus, if A is a $k \times m$ matrix and B is an $m \times n$ matrix, then the matrix operation C = A * B will generate a new matrix, C, having k rows and n columns. Each element of C will be determined as

$$C(I, J) = A(I, 1) * B(1, J) + A(I, 2) * B(2, J) + \ldots + A(I, M) * B(M, J)$$

Note that C will be a scalar (i.e., a single numeric quantity) if A and B are both *n*-element vectors (i.e., one-dimensional arrays). In this case, the product is determined as

$$C = A(1) * B(1) + A(2) * B(2) + \ldots + A(N) * B(N)$$

The BASIC matrix multiplication statement is written as

MAT C = A * B

where A and B are vectors or matrices that conform to the rules of matrix multiplication (A must have the same number of columns as B has rows).

Example 9.8

Suppose we are given the following two matrices:

$$A = \begin{vmatrix} 1 & 3 & 5 & 7 & 9 \\ 11 & 13 & 15 & 17 & 19 \\ 21 & 23 & 25 & 27 & 29 \end{vmatrix} \qquad B = \begin{vmatrix} 2 & 4 & 6 \\ 8 & 10 & 12 \\ 14 & 16 & 18 \\ 20 & 22 & 24 \\ 26 & 28 & 30 \end{vmatrix}$$

The matrix statement

MAT C = A * B

will result in the 3 x 3 matrix

$$C = \begin{vmatrix} 470 & 520 & 570 \\ 1170 & 1320 & 1470 \\ 1870 & 2120 & 2370 \end{vmatrix}$$

where the individual elements were obtained as follows:

```
C(1, 1) = (1 x 2) + (3 x 8) + (5 x 14) + (7 x 20) + (9 x 26) = 470
C(1, 2) = (1 x 4) + (3 x 10) + (5 x 16) + (7 x 22) + (9 x 28) = 520
     . . . . .
C(2, 1) = (11 x 2) + (13 x 8) + (15 x 14) + (17 x 20) + (19 x 26) = 1170
     . . . . .
C(3, 3) = (21 x 6) + (23 x 12) + (25 x 18) + (27 x 24) + (29 x 30) = 2370
```

Unlike the matrix statements presented earlier, *the matrix multiplication statement cannot be applied to higher-dimensional arrays.* Moreover, a matrix cannot be updated by means of the matrix multiplication statement. Nor can more than two matrices appear in a matrix product. Thus statements of the form

MAT A = A * C　and　MAT D = A * B * C

are not allowed. It is possible, however, to multiply a matrix by itself, i.e., to write

MAT C = A * A

provided A is a square matrix (i.e., A must have the same number of rows and columns).

The DOT Function

The *dot product* is a special case of matrix multiplication between two vectors (i.e., two one-dimensional arrays). In order to comply with the rules of matrix multiplication, each vector must have the same number of elements. The resulting product is a single numeric value (called a *scalar* in matrix notation), which is determined as

$$C = A(1) * B(1) + A(2) * B(2) + \ldots + A(N) * B(N)$$

where A and B are each one-dimensional numeric arrays containing n elements.

BASIC contains a special function called DOT that returns the dot product of two vectors. A statement utilizing this function might appear as

LET C = DOT(A, B)

where A, B and C are defined above.

Example 9.9

Here is a simple True BASIC program that illustrates the use of the DOT function.

```
DIM A(4), B(4)
MAT READ A, B
DATA 2, 4, 6, 8, 10, 12, 14, 16
PRINT "A Vector:";
MAT PRINT A;
PRINT "B Vector:";
MAT PRINT B;
LET C = DOT(A, B)
PRINT "C ="; C
END
```

Execution of this program results in the following output.

```
A Vector:
 2   4   6   8

B Vector:
 10  12  14  16

C = 280
```

Thus, we see that the dot product of A and B is 280. This value was determined as follows.

$$(2 \times 10) + (4 \times 12) + (6 \times 14) + (8 \times 16) = 280$$

9.2 MATRIX INPUT/OUTPUT

BASIC includes several matrix input/output statements that permit entire arrays to be keyed into the computer, read from a data file, displayed on the screen or written out to a data file. The actual operations are carried out in much the same manner as ordinary input/output operations. Each statement is discussed individually below.

MAT READ

The MAT READ statement assigns values to the elements of a numeric or a string array. This statement is used in conjunction with one or more DATA statements (see Sec. 5.3).

The MAT READ statement is written as

MAT READ A

where A represents an array of any dimensionality. This statement assigns a set of values within a data block to the appropriate elements of the array. In the case of a multi-dimensional array, the array elements are assigned in such a manner that the last subscript increases most rapidly and the first subscript least rapidly. Thus, if A is a two-dimensional array, the data will be assigned on a row-by-row basis (all of the columns will be assigned for each row).

Example 9.10

A portion of a True BASIC program is shown below.

```
DIM A(3, 5)
. . . . .
MAT READ A
. . . . .
DATA 1, 3, 5, 7, 9, 11, 13, 15, 17, 19, 21, 23, 25, 27, 29
```

Execution of this program will cause the following values to be assigned to the elements of A.

```
A(1, 1) = 1   A(1, 2) = 3   A(1, 3) = 5   A(1, 4) = 7   A(1, 5) = 9
A(2, 1) = 11  A(2, 2) = 13  A(2, 3) = 15  A(2, 4) = 17  A(2, 5) = 19
A(3, 1) = 21  A(3, 2) = 23  A(3, 3) = 25  A(3, 4) = 27  A(3, 5) = 29
```

Notice that the numeric values are read from the DATA statement and assigned to the matrix A on a row-by-row basis.

A single MAT READ statement can contain more than one array; e.g.,

MAT READ A, B, C

The successive arrays must be separated by commas. All elements of the first array will be assigned before any elements of the second array, and so on. As before, the elements of each multi-dimensional array will be assigned with the last subscript increasing most rapidly and the first subscript least rapidly.

Example 9.11

A portion of a True BASIC program is shown below.

```
DIM X(2, 2), Y(5), Z(2, 3)
.  .  .  .  .
MAT READ X, Y, Z
.  .  .  .  .
DATA 1, 2, 3, 4, 5, 6, 7, 8, 9, 10, 11, 12, 13, 14, 15
```

When the program is executed, the following values will be assigned to the elements of X, Y and Z.

```
X(1, 1) = 1    Y(1) = 5    Z(1, 1) = 10
X(1, 2) = 2    Y(2) = 6    Z(1, 2) = 11
X(2, 1) = 3    Y(3) = 7    Z(1, 3) = 12
X(2, 2) = 4    Y(4) = 8    Z(2, 1) = 13
               Y(5) = 9    Z(2, 2) = 14
                           Z(2, 3) = 15
```

Notice that the first four values in the data block are assigned to X, the next five values are assigned to Y and the last six values to Z. Each matrix is assigned its values on a row-by-row basis.

MAT PRINT

The MAT PRINT statement is used to display the elements of an array. It is written as

MAT PRINT A

where A represents an array of any dimensionality. The array elements will be displayed in the same order as they are read from a DATA statement; i.e., the last subscript increasing most rapidly, and the first subscript least rapidly. Multiple arrays can appear in a single MAT PRINT statement; e.g.,

MAT PRINT A, B, C

The MAT PRINT statement is particularly convenient when displaying vectors and matrices because of the way the elements are arranged on the screen. If A is a vector, all of its elements will be displayed as a single row (though several lines may be required on the screen if the vector is long). If A is a matrix, all of its elements will be displayed as a table, by rows, with a blank line following the last row.

Example 9.12

A simple True BASIC program is shown below.

```
DIM X(3, 8), Y(6)
MAT READ X, Y
MAT PRINT X, Y
DATA 1, 2, 3, 4, 5, 6, 7, 8, 9, 10, 11, 12, 13, 14, 15
DATA 16, 17, 18, 19, 20, 21, 22, 23, 24, 25, 26, 27, 28, 29, 30
END
```

Execution of this program will produce the following output.

1	2	3	4	5
6	7	8		
9	10	11	12	13
14	15	16		
17	18	19	20	21
22	23	24		
25	26	27	28	29
30				

Notice that each row requires two lines, since only five elements are printed on each line. Each row of X begins with a new line. A blank line follows the last row of X, thus distinguishing it from the next array (Y).

The spacing between successive array elements can be decreased by placing semicolons after the array names in the MAT PRINT statement. This will result in minimum spacing between the elements (typically, two spaces between positive numbers).

Example 9.13

Here is a True BASIC program similar to that shown in Example 9.12. The only difference is the semicolon that follows each array name in the MAT PRINT statement.

```
DIM X(3, 8), Y(6)
MAT READ X, Y
MAT PRINT X; Y;
DATA 1, 2, 3, 4, 5, 6, 7, 8, 9, 10, 11, 12, 13, 14, 15
DATA 16, 17, 18, 19, 20, 21, 22, 23, 24, 25, 26, 27, 28, 29, 30
END
```

Execution of this program will produce the following output.

```
1   2   3   4   5   6   7   8
9  10  11  12  13  14  15  16
17  18  19  20  21  22  23  24

25  26  27  28  29  30
```

Each row can now be displayed on a single line, since the spacing of the elements is much closer.

The MAT PRINT statement can be used in conjunction with PRINT USING (see Sec. 7.7). To do so, a *format string* must be included in the MAT PRINT statement. The format string specifies the number of fields per line and the appearance of each field.

Example 9.14

The following True BASIC statement illustrates the use of the MAT PRINT USING statement. The program displays a formatted string array and two formatted numeric arrays.

```
DIM colors$(4), X(3, 8), Y(6)
MAT READ colors$, X, Y
LET text$ = REPEAT$("<##### ", 4)          !format string
LET line$ = REPEAT$("##.## ", 8)           !format string
MAT PRINT USING text$: colors$
MAT PRINT USING line$: X, Y
DATA red, white, blue, green
DATA 1, 2, 3, 4, 5, 6, 7, 8, 9, 10, 11, 12, 13, 14, 15
DATA 16, 17, 18, 19, 20, 21, 22, 23, 24, 25, 26, 27, 28, 29, 30
END
```

Note the use of the REPEAT$ function to define the two format strings text$ and line$. The first format string (text$) specifies that each field will contain up to five characters, left justified within the field (if there are fewer than five characters), with a single blank space following each string. Up to four strings can appear on each line.

The second string (line$) specifies that each numeric quantity will consist of 5 characters, including a decimal point and two digits to the right of the decimal point. Up to eight numeric quantities can appear on each line.

Execution of this program results in the following output.

```
red    white blue  green
 1.00   2.00   3.00   4.00   5.00   6.00   7.00   8.00
 9.00  10.00  11.00  12.00  13.00  14.00  15.00  16.00
17.00  18.00  19.00  20.00  21.00  22.00  23.00  24.00
25.00  26.00  27.00  28.00  29.00  30.00
```

The MAT PRINT statement can contain only array names. Expressions, function references, etc., are not permitted. Thus, we cannot not write statements such as

MAT PRINT A + B, C * D, p * X

MAT INPUT

The MAT INPUT statement is used to enter array elements directly from the keyboard. This statement is written as

MAT INPUT A

where A represents either a numeric or a string array of any dimensionality.

When the MAT INPUT statement is executed the customary question mark appears at the beginning of a new line, indicating a request for data. Further execution of the program will be halted temporarily while the user enters the required values, separated by commas. The values will be assigned to the appropriate array elements after they have all been entered and the user has pressed the RETURN (or ENTER) key. In the case of a multi-dimensional array, the data items will be assigned in the same order as with a MAT READ statement; i.e., last subscript increasing most rapidly, first subscript least rapidly.

Normally, the MAT INPUT statement will require as many input values as there are array elements in A. However, if A is a vector (i.e., a one-dimensional array), a variable number of values can be entered provided the MAT INPUT statement is written as

MAT INPUT A(?)

This feature allows us to enter only a partial set of array elements. The size of the vector will automatically be lowered to correspond to the number of values entered.

Example 9.15

A BASIC program contains the following two statements.

```
DIM A(100)

MAT INPUT A(?)
```

When the MAT INPUT statement is encountered during program execution, a question mark will appear at the beginning of a new line. Further execution of the program will temporarily be suspended.

Suppose that the following line of data is entered in response to the question mark. The user's responses are underlined.

```
?12,-3,17,10,62,-87,49,5,39,9,-7,-22
```

Once the RETURN (or ENTER) key is pressed, the data will be transmitted to the computer and assigned to the first 12 elements of A as follows.

```
A(1) = 12    A(2) = -3    A(3) = 17    A(4) = 10
A(5) = 62    A(6) = -87   A(7) = 49    A(8) = 5
A(9) = 39    A(10) = 9    A(11) = -7   A(12) = -22
```

The size of the array will then be adjusted to a total of 12 elements.

Sometimes there are too many data items to be entered on a single line on the screen. When this happens, the remaining data items may be entered on subsequent lines. A comma must be placed at the end of a line of data to indicate that a subsequent line will be entered. The comma must appear at the end of every line except the final line. The RETURN key is then pressed at the end of each line of data. A new question mark will appear at the beginning of each new line.

Example 9.16

Suppose that the following two lines of input data have been typed in response to the MAT INPUT statement shown in Example 9.15.

```
?3,6,9,12,15,18,21,24,27,30,
?33,36,39,42,45,48,51,54,57,60
```

Notice the comma at the end of the first line. The question mark at the beginning of the second line indicates a request for more data. It was generated by the comma at the end of the first line. This procedure could have been continued as long as necessary (i.e., a comma could have been typed at the end of the second line, generating a request for a third line of data, and so on).

The program will resume execution after the second line of data has been entered (by pressing the RETURN key at the end of the line). The one-dimensional array A will then have the following values assigned to its first 20 elements:

```
A(1) = 3    A(2) = 6    A(3) = 9    . . .    A(19) = 57    A(20) = 60.
```

The size of A will then be lowered, so that A consists of only 20 elements.

An INPUT PROMPT option can be included in the MAT INPUT statement (see Sec. 7.6). When this feature is included, the MAT INPUT statement is written as

MAT INPUT PROMPT *"prompt string"*: A

where *prompt string* is the prompt message that is generated when the MAT INPUT statement is executed. Recall that the prompt message appears in place of the question mark.

Example 9.17

A simple True BASIC program is shown below.

```
DIM A(2, 3)
MAT INPUT PROMPT "Enter 6 values: ": A
MAT PRINT A;
END
```

Notice the INPUT PROMPT feature that is included in the MAT INPUT statement. This will generate a prompt for input data when the program is executed.

A typical interactive dialog, resulting from execution of this program, is shown below. The user's responses are underlined for clarity.

```
Enter 6 values: 10,20,30,40,50,60
  10   20   30
  40   50   60
```

There is also a MAT LINE INPUT statement (see Sec. 7.6), which permits multiple lines of text to be entered and assigned to the elements of a string array. This statement is written as

MAT LINE INPUT A$

where A$ represents a string array of any dimensionality.

An INPUT PROMPT feature can also be included; i.e.,

MAT LINE INPUT PROMPT *"prompt string"*: A$

This statement causes the input prompt to appear once, requesting the first input line. The customary question mark will appear for each subsequent line.

Example 9.18

The following True BASIC program illustrates the use of the MAT LINE INPUT PROMPT statement.

```
DIM text$(4)
MAT LINE INPUT PROMPT "Please enter 4 lines of text: ": text$
MAT PRINT text$;
END
```

This program will accept four lines of text from the keyboard and store each line as an element of the string array text$. The array elements will then be displayed as one consecutive string, because of the semicolon at the end of the MAT PRINT statement.

Execution of this program results in an interactive dialog such as that shown below. The user's responses are again underlined for clarity.

```
Please enter 4 lines of text: Now is the time
? for all good men
? to come to the aid
? of their country!
Now is the time for all good men to come to the aid of their country!
```

Matrix File I/O

BASIC includes a statement for reading array elements from a sequential data file (i.e., a text file). This statement is written as

MAT INPUT #*n*: A

where *n* represents the data channel number and A is either a numeric array or a string array of any dimensionality. This statement behaves the same as MAT INPUT, except that the array elements are read from the indicated data file rather than the keyboard. Thus, if A is a multi-dimensional array, the last subscript will increase most rapidly and the first subscript least rapidly when assigning data items to the array elements.

Example 9.19

Shown below is the skeletal structure of a True BASIC program that reads numeric data from a sequential data file and assigns the data items to an array.

```
DIM exams(60, 8)
OPEN #1: NAME "SCORES.DAT", CREATE OLD, ORGANIZATION TEXT
. . . . .
MAT INPUT #1: exams
. . . . .
CLOSE #1
END
```

When the program is executed, the data items will be read from the sequential data file SCORES.DAT and assigned to the array exams in the following order: exams(1, 1) exams(1, 2) . . . exams(1, 8) exams(2, 1) exams(2, 2) . . . exams(2, 8) . . . exams(60, 1) exams(60, 2) . . . exams(60, 8). Thus, all 8 columns of the first row must be assigned before any data is assigned to the second row, and so on.

Note that a FOR - NEXT structure or a DO - LOOP structure would be required if we wanted to read the first six columns of the first row, then the first six columns of the second row, etc. This restriction limits the practicality of the MAT INPUT #*n* statement for reading multidimensional arrays.

BASIC also includes a statement for writing array elements to a sequential data file. This statement is written as

MAT PRINT #*n*: A

where *n* represents the data channel number and A is either a numeric array or a string array of any dimensionality. This statement follows the same rules as MAT PRINT, except that the array elements are written to the indicated data file rather than displayed on the screen. The order in which the array elements are written, if A is multidimensional, is the same as with MAT INPUT #*n*; i.e., the last subscript will increase most rapidly and the first subscript least rapidly.

Example 9.20

Here is a skeletal outline of a True BASIC program that writes the elements of a string array to a sequential data file.

```
DIM customers$(100)
OPEN #1: NAME "ACCOUNTS.DAT", CREATE NEW, ORG TEXT
. . . . .
MAT PRINT #1: customers$
. . . . .
CLOSE #1
END
```

When this program is executed, the array elements will be written sequentially to the data file ACCOUNTS.DAT. There should be no problem with respect to the order in which the array elements are written, since customers$ is a one-dimensional array.

There is also a MAT LINE INPUT #n statement, for reading entire lines of text from a sequential data file and assigning them to the elements of a string array.

On the surface, it might appear that the MAT INPUT #n and MAT PRINT #n statements would be used frequently in many programming applications. There are, however, some factors that tend to restrict their use. First, all of the data items must be of the same type (either numeric or string), since they will all be elements of the same array. This prevents the use of these statements in applications such as those in Chap. 8, where numeric and string data items appear together in each line of text.

Moreover, the MAT INPUT #n and MAT PRINT #n statements do not work well together in the same application, because the MAT INPUT #n statement requires that the data items read from a data file be separated by commas but the MAT PRINT #n statement does not include commas between data items written to a data file. Hence, it is not possible to write data with MAT PRINT #n and then read the same data with MAT INPUT #n.

Entire arrays can also be read from and written to direct (random access) data files, using the MAT READ #n and MAT WRITE #n statements. These statements are written as

MAT READ #n: A

MAT WRITE #n: A

where n represents the data channel number and A is either a numeric array or a string array of any dimensionality. The MAT WRITE #n statement places all of the array elements in one record, and the MAT READ #n statement reads them back from one record. Obviously, some care is required in defining a sufficiently large record size. Otherwise, the rules governing the use of these statements is the same as for MAT INPUT #n and MAT PRINT #n, except that these statements apply to direct rather than sequential data files.

Example 9.21

Here is a complete True BASIC program that generates a two-dimensional array, writes it to a direct-access data file, reads it back and then displays it.

```
DIM A(3, 4)
OPEN #3: NAME "SAMPLE.DAT", CREATE NEW, ORG RANDOM, RECSIZE 120
FOR I = 1 TO 3              !generate the array elements
   FOR J = 1 TO 4
      LET A(I, J) = 10 * (I + J - 1)
   NEXT J
NEXT I
MAT WRITE #3: A            !write the array to the data file
SET #3: POINTER BEGIN     !reset the pointer
MAT READ #3: A            !read the array from the data file
MAT PRINT A               !display the array
CLOSE #3
END
```

The program includes a MAT WRITE #3 statement to write the array to the data file and a MAT READ #3 statement to read the array from the data file.

When this program is executed, the following output is generated. This output represents the array that was read in from the data file. The validity of the output verifies the proper functioning of the entire program.

10	20	30	40
20	30	40	50
30	40	50	60

9.3 SPECIAL MATRICES

When carrying out matrix operations, we sometimes require certain special matrices, such as the identity matrix, the transpose of a matrix or the inverse of a matrix. BASIC contains a number of matrix functions that allow these and other special matrices to be formed. Some of these functions can be used only with vectors or matrices (i.e., one- or two-dimensional arrays). Moreover, certain of these functions impose additional restrictions on the dimensionality or the matrix size.

MAT ZER

The MAT ZER function is used to assign 0 to each element of an array. A typical statement utilizing the MAT ZER function is written as

MAT A = ZER

where A represents a numeric array of any dimensionality.

MAT CON

The MAT CON function assigns the constant 1 to each element of an array. A typical MAT CON statement is written as

MAT B = CON

where B represents a numeric array of any dimensionality.

MAT IDN

The MAT IDN function assigns 0s to all of the elements of a square matrix except those on the *principal diagonal* (i.e., the diagonal running from upper left to lower right), where 1s are assigned. A matrix whose elements are assigned these values is known as an *identity matrix*.

A typical MAT IDN statement is written as

MAT I = IDN

where I represents a square numeric matrix (i.e., a matrix with the same number of rows and columns).

The identity matrix has the following important characteristic: If a square matrix A is multiplied by the identity matrix I, then the product will simply be the original matrix A (provided A and I conform to the rules of matrix multiplication). In other words,

I * A = A * I = A

Hence, multiplication of a matrix by the identity matrix is analogous to multiplication of an ordinary numeric constant by 1.

Example 9.22

A simple True BASIC program is shown below.

```
DIM A(3, 3), B(3, 3), C(3, 3), V(3)
MAT A = ZER
MAT B = CON
MAT C = IDN
MAT V = 5 * CON
MAT PRINT A; B; C; V;
END
```

Execution of this program results in the following output.

```
0   0   0
0   0   0
0   0   0

1   1   1
1   1   1
1   1   1

1   0   0
0   1   0
0   0   1

5   5   5
```

Thus, A is a 3 x 3 matrix consisting entirely of 0s, B is a 3 x 3 matrix consisting entirely of 1s, C is a 3 x 3 identity matrix and V is a 3-element vector consisting entirely of 5s.

MAT TRN

The MAT TRN function causes the rows and columns of a given matrix to be transposed (i.e., interchanged). A typical statement utilizing this function is written as

MAT B = TRN(A)

Thus, if A is an $m \times n$ matrix, then B will be an $n \times m$ matrix whose elements are determined as

B(I, J) = A(J, I)

The matrix B is called the *transpose* of A.

Example 9.23

Here is a simple True BASIC program that illustrates the use of the MAT TRN function.

```
DIM A(2, 3), B(3, 2)
MAT READ A
DATA 1, 3, 5, 7, 9, 11
MAT B = TRN(A)
MAT PRINT A; B;
END
```

When this program is executed, the following output is obtained.

```
1   3   5
7   9   11

1   7
3   9
5   11
```

Notice that the rows and columns of A are interchanged in B. Thus, we see that B is the transpose A.

MAT INV

The *inverse* of a square matrix is itself a square matrix having the following important property: The product of a matrix and its inverse is equal to the identity matrix. In other words, if A is a square matrix and B is its inverse, then

A * B = B * A = I

where I is the identity matrix.

Not every square matrix has an inverse. If an inverse does exist, it can be calculated by means of the MAT INV function. A typical MAT INV statement can be written as

MAT B = INV(A)

where A and B are square matrices of the same size.

If a matrix does not have an inverse, then an attempt to calculate its inverse with the INV function will result in an error message.

The DET Function

BASIC includes a library function called DET, which returns the *determinant* of a square matrix — a single value whose significance is discussed in textbooks on matrix algebra. The DET function accepts a square matrix as an optional argument. If an argument is provided, the function returns the determinant of the argument; e.g.,

      LET D = DET(A)

where A is a square matrix and D is its determinant.

If the DET function is utilized without an argument, it returns the determinant of the matrix whose inverse was most recently calculated. For example,

      MAT B = INV(A)
      LET D = DET

will return the determinant of A.

A word of caution: The computation of both the inverse and the determinant of a matrix may be inaccurate under certain conditions, e.g., if the original matrix is large (many rows and columns) or if it is nearly *singular* (i.e., the true value of its determinant is close to zero). Some authors advise against the use of the INV and DET functions for this reason. In fact, this is one reason why some versions of BASIC do not support matrix statements.

Example 9.24 Matrix Inversion

The following True BASIC program determines the inverse and the determinant of a matrix.

```
DIM A(2, 2), B(2, 2), C(2, 2)
MAT READ A
DATA 2, 4, 1, 8
PRINT "A Matrix:"
MAT PRINT A
LET D = DET(A)
PRINT "Determinant of A ="; D
PRINT
IF (D <> 0) THEN
   MAT B = INV(A)
   PRINT "Inverse of A:"
   MAT PRINT B
   MAT C = A * B
   PRINT "Product of A and its Inverse:"
   MAT PRINT C
END IF
END
```

Note that this program first determines the determinant of a matrix and then calculates the inverse of the matrix if the value of the determinant is nonzero.

Execution of this program results in the following output.

```
A Matrix:
 2              4
 1              8

Determinant of A = 12

Inverse of A:
 .66666667      -.33333333
-3.3333333e-2    .16666667

Product of A and its Inverse:
 1              0
 1.110223e-16   1
```

Notice that the first value in the second line, $1.110223e-16$, in principle should be zero. The nonzero value shown is the result of numerical roundoff.

It is interesting to change the DATA statement in the above program to

```
DATA 2, 8, 1, 4
```

When executed, this program will result in the following output.

```
A Matrix:
 2              8
 1              4

Determinant of A = 0
```

(Students of matrix algebra will recognize that the determinant of A is now $(2 \times 4) - (1 \times 8) = 0$.) If we were to attempt to calculate the inverse of A with the MAT INV function, we would obtain the following message.

```
Can't invert singular matrix
```

Solution of Simultaneous Equations

The MAT INV function allows us to solve a system of simultaneous, linear algebraic equations very easily. To understand how the method works we must utilize the properties of both the inverse and the identity matrices. Suppose, for example, that we are given the system of n equations

$$c_{1,1} x_1 + c_{1,2} x_2 + \ldots + c_{1,n} x_n = d_1$$
$$c_{2,1} x_1 + c_{2,2} x_2 + \ldots + c_{2,n} x_n = d_2$$
$$c_{3,1} x_1 + c_{3,2} x_2 + \ldots + c_{3,n} x_n = d_3$$
$$\ldots\ldots$$
$$c_{n,1} x_1 + c_{n,2} x_2 + \ldots + c_{n,n} x_n = d_n$$

where $c_{i,j}$ and d_i represent known values and x_i are the unknown quantities.

We can write the given equations in matrix form as follows.

$$C * X = D$$

where C is a matrix containing the values of the coefficients, D is a vector containing the values on the right-hand side and X is a vector containing the unknown quantities. Thus,

$$C = \begin{vmatrix} c_{1,1} & c_{1,2} & \cdots & c_{1,n} \\ c_{2,1} & c_{2,2} & \cdots & c_{2,n} \\ c_{3,1} & c_{3,2} & \cdots & c_{3,n} \\ \cdots & \cdots & & \cdots \\ c_{n,1} & c_{n,2} & \cdots & c_{n,n} \end{vmatrix} \qquad D = \begin{vmatrix} d_1 \\ d_2 \\ d_3 \\ \cdots \\ d_n \end{vmatrix} \qquad X = \begin{vmatrix} x_1 \\ x_2 \\ x_3 \\ \cdots \\ x_n \end{vmatrix}$$

Let us multiply our given matrix equation by E, where E represents the inverse of C. Then we have

$$E * C * X = E * D$$

But the matrix product E * C is simply the identity matrix, which we will call I. Therefore we can write

$$I * X = E * D$$

Since I * X = X, our matrix equation simplifies to

$$X = E * D$$

which is the desired result.

The significance of this result is the following. *The solution to a system of simultaneous, linear algebraic equations is equal to the product of the inverse of the coefficient matrix and the right-hand side vector.* Example 9.25 illustrates how easily this idea can be incorporated into a BASIC program.

Example 9.25 Simultaneous Equations

Suppose we are given the following system of five equations and five unknowns.

$$
\begin{array}{rrrrrrr}
11x_1 & + 3x_2 & & + x_4 & + 2x_5 & = & 51 \\
& 4x_2 & + 2x_3 & & + x_5 & = & 15 \\
3x_1 & + 2x_2 & + 7x_3 & + x_4 & & = & 15 \\
4x_1 & & + 4x_3 & + 10x_4 & + x_5 & = & 20 \\
2x_1 & + 5x_2 & + x_3 & + 3x_4 & + 13x_5 & = & 92
\end{array}
$$

We wish to determine the values of the unknowns x_1, x_2, x_3, x_4 and x_5. To do so, let us rewrite the equations in matrix form as

$$C * X = D$$

where

$$C = \begin{vmatrix} 11 & 3 & 0 & 1 & 2 \\ 0 & 4 & 2 & 0 & 1 \\ 3 & 2 & 7 & 1 & 0 \\ 4 & 0 & 4 & 10 & 1 \\ 2 & 5 & 1 & 3 & 13 \end{vmatrix} \qquad D = \begin{vmatrix} 51 \\ 15 \\ 15 \\ 20 \\ 92 \end{vmatrix}$$

and X will contain the values for x_1, x_2, x_3, x_4 and x_5. We can obtain these values simply by calculating the matrix product

$$X = E * D$$

where E is the inverse of C.

Once we have determined the values of x_1 through x_5, we can check the accuracy of the solution by calculating the product

$$F = C * X$$

If the elements of X have been determined correctly, then the vector F will be the same as the original vector D. Any differences in magnitude between the elements of F and the corresponding elements of D therefore provide a measure of the errors involved in calculating X. Such differences can be seen by computing the vector G, where

$$G = D - F$$

A complete True BASIC program is shown below. The structure of the program is very straightforward, since branches and loops are not required. This simplicity results from the use of the matrix statements, which free the programmer from considering the logical details of matrix manipulation.

```
!SOLUTION OF SIMULTANEOUS, LINEAR ALGEBRAIC EQUATIONS

DIM C(5, 5), D(5), E(5, 5), F(5), G(5), X(5)
MAT READ C                   !coefficient matrix
DATA 11, 3, 0, 1, 2, 0, 4, 2, 0, 1, 3, 2, 7, 1, 0
MAT READ D                   !right-hand side
DATA 4, 0, 4, 10, 1, 2, 5, 1, 3, 13, 51, 15, 15, 20, 92

PRINT "Coefficient Matrix:"
MAT PRINT C;
PRINT "Right-Hand Side:"
MAT PRINT D;

MAT E = INV(C)               !inverse of C
MAT X = E * D                !desired solution
PRINT "Solution Vector:"
MAT PRINT X;

MAT F = C * X                !calculated right-hand side (check)
MAT G = D - F                !error vector (right-hand side values)
PRINT "Error Vector:"
MAT PRINT G;
END
```

When this program is executed the following output is generated.

```
Coefficient Matrix:
 11  3  0  1  2
  0  4  2  0  1
  3  2  7  1  0
  4  0  4 10  1
  2  5  1  3 13

Right-Hand Side:
 51  15  15  20  92

Solution Vector:
 2.9791652  2.2155996  .21128405  .15231694  5.7150336

Error Vector:
 0  0 -1.7763568e-15 -3.5527137e-15  1.4210855e-14
```

From this output we see that the solution is (approximately) $x_1 = 3.0$, $x_2 = 2.2$, $x_3 = 0.21$, $x_4 = 0.15$ and $x_5 = 5.7$. Moreover, we see that the components of the error vector G are very small (two are identically zero, two are approximately 10^{-15} and the remaining one is approximately 10^{-14} in magnitude). These values assure us that the solution is accurate.

MAT NUL$

The MAT NUL$ function is used to assign a null string (i.e., the empty string "") to each element of a string array. This function permits the elements of the array to be "cleared" with minimum effort.

A typical statement utilizing the MAT NUL$ function is written as

    MAT A$ = NUL$

where A$ represents a string array of any dimensionality.

Example 9.26

A BASIC statement includes the statements

```
DIM message$(20)

MAT message$ = NUL$
```

When the second statement is executed, each element of message$ will be assigned a null string ("").

9.4 CHANGING DIMENSIONS

We have already seen that the MAT INPUT statement allows us to enter an unspecified number of vector elements from the keyboard, thus providing us with a variable dimension feature. In addition, several of the matrix statements allow us to alter the dimensions of an array during program execution. In fact we can, if we wish, change the effective size of an array at different places within a program. This capability can be used to extend the generality of many BASIC programs that involve vectors and matrices.

The matrix statements that permit an array to be redimensioned are MAT INPUT, MAT READ, MAT ZER, MAT CON, MAT IDN and MAT NUL$. (Note that the MAT PRINT and MAT WRITE statements are not included.) This feature is implemented by enclosing the effective dimensions in parentheses, following the array name. In the case of a multi-dimensional array, the dimensions must be separated by a comma.

Example 9.27

A BASIC program includes the statements

```
DIM A(24, 24), B(24, 24), C(24, 24), T$(20)
. . . . .
MAT A = IDN(20, 20)
MAT B = CON(8, 12)
. . . . .
INPUT PROMPT "Size:": n
MAT C = 3 * CON(n, n)
. . . . .
MAT T$ = NUL$(10)
```

When the program is executed, A will become a 20 x 20 identity matrix and B will become an 8 x 12 matrix whose elements are all 1s. C will become a square matrix having n elements, where n is entered from the keyboard. Each element of C will be assigned the value 3. Finally, T$ will become a 10-element string vector whose elements all represent the null vector.

The SIZE function returns the current size (i.e., the number of elements) in an array. For example, SIZE(A) returns the total number of elements currently in the array A. Similarly, SIZE(A, 2) returns the number of elements associated with the second dimension of A.

The SIZE function is often used to determine the size of a variable-size array, as illustrated in the following example.

Example 9.28

A BASIC program includes the statements

```
DIM X(200)
. . . . .
MAT INPUT X(?)
PRINT SIZE(X); " elements have been entered"
```

Recall that the number of elements entered into X will not be known when the MAT INPUT statement is written in this manner. The PRINT statement, which utilizes the SIZE function, will provide this information.

The MAT REDIM statement allows the size of a dimensioned array to be changed at a later point in a program. This statement can appear anywhere after the original DIM statement. It follows the same syntactic rules as the DIM statement.

Note that the *number of elements, not the dimensionality* (i.e., the number of dimensions), is changed with the MAT REDIM statement. Thus, a three-dimensional array will remain a three-dimensional array, though the number of elements associated with each dimension may change. Some care is required if the array elements have been assigned individual values and the number of elements then changes.

Example 9.29

A BASIC program contains the statements

```
DIM A(100), B(80), C(0 TO 10, -10 TO 0)
.  .  .  .  .
MAT REDIM A(40), B(20 TO 100), C(8, 8)
```

The MAT REDIM statement changes A from a 100-element array to a 40-element array. Similarly, B is changed from an ordinary 80-element array to an 81-element array in which the subscript ranges from 20 to 100. Also, C is decreased in size, from 121 elements (11 x 11) to 64 elements (8 x 8). Note that the dimensionality of the arrays does not change.

For the more mathematically inclined reader, the following example illustrates the use of a number of special matrix features.

Example 9.30 Least Squares Curve Fitting

The method of least squares is a common technique for fitting a curve

$$y = f(x)$$

to a set of data points $(x_1, y_1), (x_2, y_2), \ldots, (x_n, y_n)$. The method is based upon the idea of minimizing the sum of the square errors,

$$e_1^2 + e_2^2 + \ldots + e_n^2$$

where e_i is the ith error. That is, for a given x_i, e_i is the difference between the data point y_i and the value $y = f(x_i)$, which is determined from the fitted curve (see Fig. 9.1). The *square* of the error is used because it is a nonnegative quantity. Hence, for a given x_i, minimizing the square error forces the point on the curve, $f(x_i)$, to be as close as possible to the actual data point, y_i. This assures the closest possible fit.

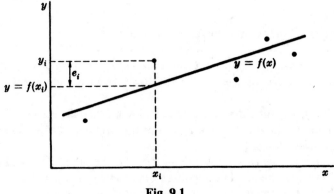

Fig. 9.1

The method is commonly applied to the following kinds of mathematical functions.

(a)   Power function: $y = a x^b$

(b)   Exponential function: $y = a e^{bx}$

(c)   Polynomial: $y = c_1 + c_2 x + c_3 x^2 + \ldots + c_{m+1} x^m$

Each mathematical function represents a different type of curve.

In each case, the method requires solving a set of simultaneous, linear algebraic equations. The unknown quantities are the *constants* in the equation for the curve. For example, to fit a power function to a set of n data points, we must solve the following two equations for a and b.

$$n \log a + b \{\Sigma \log x_i\} = \Sigma \log y_i$$

$$\log a \{\Sigma \log x_i\} + b \{\Sigma (\log x_i)^2\} = \Sigma (\log x_i)(\log y_i)$$

where i ranges from 1 to n and Σ indicates summation over all n sets of data values; e.g.,

$$\Sigma \log x_i = \log x_1 + \log x_2 + \ldots + \log x_n$$

Note that these are linear algebraic equations in terms of u and b, where $u = \log a$. Once u has been determined, then a can be obtained as

$$a = e^u$$

(This assumes that natural logarithms are used in the calculations.)

Now suppose we wish to pass the exponential curve

$$y = a e^{bx}$$

through the set of n data points. The equations to be solved are

$$n \log a + b \{\Sigma x_i\} = \Sigma \log y_i$$

$$\log a \{\Sigma x_i\} + b \{\Sigma x_i^2\} = \Sigma x_i \log y_i$$

Again we solve two simultaneous, linear algebraic equations for $\log a$ and b.

If the curve is the polynomial

$$y = c_1 + c_2 x + c_3 x^2 + \ldots + c_{m+1} x^m$$

then we must determine the coefficients $c_1, c_2, \ldots c_{m+1}$ by solving the system of equations

$$n c_1 + c_2 \{\Sigma x_i\} + c_3 \{\Sigma x_i^2\} + \ldots + c_{m+1} \{\Sigma x_i^m\} = \Sigma y_i$$

$$c_1 \{\Sigma x_i\} + c_2 \{\Sigma x_i^2\} + c_3 \{\Sigma x_i^3\} + \ldots + c_{m+1} \{\Sigma x_i^{m+1}\} = \Sigma x_i y_i$$

$$\ldots\ldots\ldots\ldots\ldots\ldots\ldots\ldots\ldots\ldots\ldots\ldots\ldots\ldots\ldots\ldots\ldots\ldots\ldots\ldots\ldots$$

$$c_1 \{\Sigma x_i^m\} + c_2 \{\Sigma x_i^{m+1}\} + c_3 \{\Sigma x_i^{m+2}\} + \ldots + c_{m+1} \{\Sigma x_i^{2n}\} = \Sigma x_i^m y_i$$

Since each of the above cases involves the solution of simultaneous, linear algebraic equations, we will incorporate several matrix statements in our program, in a manner similar to Example 9.25. We will also include a number of features which will extend the generality of the program. For example, we will include a provision for fitting any of the mathematical functions discussed above. Moreover, any size polynomial will be allowed provided it does not have more than 10 terms (i.e., x is not raised to a power higher than 9). We will allow for as many as 100 data points, and we will convert the values of x_i and y_i to $\log x_i$ and $\log y_i$ internally if necessary. We will include variable dimensioning within the program, since the type of curve fit will vary from one problem to another. The data will be entered from an existing sequential data file (i.e., a text file).

The complexity of the program suggests that it be preceded by a general outline. First, however, let us define the following arrays and variables.

> X = a 100-element vector containing the input values x_i
> Y = a 100-element vector containing the input values y_i
> A = a square matrix containing the coefficients of the unknown constants in the linear equations (these
>   are the terms with the many summation signs that we encountered earlier)
> AINV = the inverse of A
> C = a 10-element vector containing the unknown constants in the system of linear equations
> RHS = a 10-element vector containing the right-hand terms in the system of linear equations
> curve = an integer indicating the type of curve to be fitted
>   curve = 1 indicates a power function
>   curve = 2 indicates an exponential function
>   curve = 3 indicates a polynomial
> m = the highest power in the polynomial expression (an integer ranging from 1 to 9)
> ns = the number of unknowns in the system of simultaneous linear algebraic equations (an integer that ranges
>   from 2 to 10)
> ndata = the number of data points
> f = the mathematical function $f(x_i)$ for a given x_i
> sumsq = the sum of the square errors

The computation will be carried out in accordance with the following outline.

1. Define the arrays.

2. Open an existing text file called "leastsq.dat."

3. Generate a brief menu that prompts the user for the type of curve to be fitted and, in the case of a polynomial, for the highest power within the polynomial.

4. After the user has entered the responses to the menu prompts, redimension the arrays so that they correspond to the requested curve and assign initial zeros to A and RHS.

5. Read the data from the data file. Continue until all of the data in the file have been read. Then tag the number of data points entered (assign the most recent value of the counter to ndata).

6. Transform the data points into logarithmic form if necessary. (Transform both x_i and y_i for the power function, and just y_i for the exponential function.)

7. Calculate and display the coefficients in the system of simultaneous linear algebraic equations using the equations presented on the previous page.

8. Solve the simultaneous equations by calculating AINV and then forming the product AINV * RHS. Then display the results.

9. In the case of a power function or an exponential function, restore the original data from their logarithms, thus reversing the transformation in step 6.

10. Enter a loop that will display the original data and the corresponding calculated *y*-values from the fitted function. Also, calculate the sum of the square errors within this loop.

11. Display the sum of the square errors, thus enabling the user to assess the quality of the fit and compare this fit with others.

12. Close the data file and end the computation.

A complete True BASIC program, based upon the above outline, is shown below.

```
!CURVE FITTING VIA THE METHOD OF LEAST SQUARES

DIM A(2, 2), AINV(2, 2), C(2), RHS(2), X(100), Y(100)
OPEN #1: NAME "leastsq.dat", CREATE OLD, ORG TEXT

!input menu

PRINT "Least Squares Curve Fitting"
PRINT "  1 - Power Function"
PRINT "  2 - Exponential Function"
PRINT "  3 - Polynomial"
INPUT PROMPT "Please enter 1, 2 or 3: ": curve
IF (curve = 3) THEN
    INPUT PROMPT "Highest power of polynomial: ": m
END IF

!adjust the array sizes

LET ns = 2
IF (curve = 3 AND m > 1) THEN
    LET ns = m + 1
    MAT REDIM A(ns, ns), C(ns), RHS(ns)
END IF
MAT A = ZER(ns, ns)
MAT RHS = ZER(ns)

!enter data points

LET i = 0
DO UNTIL END #1
    LET i = i + 1
    INPUT #1: X(i), Y(i)
LOOP
LET ndata = i

!calculate logarithms if necessary

IF (curve < 3) THEN
    FOR i = 1 TO ndata
```

```
            LET Y(i) = LOG(Y(i))
            IF (curve = 1) THEN LET X(i) = LOG(X(i))
      NEXT i
END IF

!calculate the array elements

FOR i = 1 TO ns
   FOR j = 1 TO ns
      IF (i + j = 2) THEN
         LET A(i, j) = ndata
      ELSE
        FOR k = 1 TO ndata
           LET A(i, j) = A(i, j) + X(k) ^ (i + j - 2)
        NEXT k
      END IF
   NEXT j
   FOR k = 1 to ndata
      LET RHS(i) = RHS(i) + Y(k) * X(k) ^ (i - 1)
   NEXT k
NEXT i

PRINT
PRINT "Coefficient Matrix:"
MAT PRINT A;
PRINT "Right-Hand Side:"
MAT PRINT RHS;

!solve simultaneous equations and display the results

MAT AINV = INV(A)
MAT C = AINV * RHS
PRINT "Unknown Coefficients for ";
IF (curve = 1) THEN
   LET C(1) = EXP(C(1))
   PRINT "Power Function"
ELSEIF (curve = 2) THEN
   LET C(1) = EXP(C(1))
   PRINT "Exponential Function"
ELSEIF (curve = 3) THEN
   PRINT "Polynomial"
END IF
MAT PRINT C;

!restore the original data from logarithms if required

IF (curve < 3) THEN
   FOR i = 1 TO ndata
      LET Y(i) = EXP(Y(i))
      IF (curve = 1) THEN LET X(i) = EXP(X(i))
   NEXT i
END IF
```

```
!display input data and calculated y-values

PRINT TAB(2); "X";TAB(19);"Y";TAB(37);"F(X)"
LET sumsq = 0
FOR i = 1 TO ndata
   IF (curve = 1) THEN
      LET f = C(1) * X(i) ^ C(2)                !power function
   ELSE IF (curve = 2) THEN
      LET f = C(1) * EXP(C(2) * X(i))           !exponential function
   ELSE IF (curve = 3) THEN
      LET f = C(1)
      FOR j = 1 TO m
         LET f = f + C(j + 1) * X(i) ^ j        !polynomial
      NEXT j
   END IF

   LET sumsq = sumsq + (Y(i) - f) ^ 2           !square error
   PRINT X(i), Y(i), f
NEXT i
PRINT
PRINT "Sum of Square Errors = ";
PRINT USING "#.###^^^^": sumsq

CLOSE #1
END
```

Notice the use of several matrix statements, including a matrix redimension statement, within this program. The use of MAT INPUT was avoided when reading from the data file, however, so that the data could be entered into the data file in a more natural manner (i.e., successive values of x_i and y_i). If the MAT INPUT statement had been used, it would have been necessary to read all of the x-values first, followed by all of the y-values.

The interactive dialogs generated by four different program executions are shown below. Each execution is based upon the same set of input data. Multiple program executions are presented so that you may compare the results obtained when several different curves are fit to the same set of data.

(*a*) *Power function*

```
Least Squares Curve Fitting
   1 - Power Function
   2 - Exponential Function
   3 - Polynomial
Please enter 1, 2 or 3: 1

Coefficient Matrix:
 19  51.424354
 51.424354  141.87102

Right-Hand Side:
-26.033356 -56.621305

Unknown Coefficients for Power Function
```

2.2635163e-7 5.1471525

X	Y	F(X)
7.	.01	5.0656139e-3
8.	.02	1.0072226e-2
9.	.02	1.8467806e-2
10.	.03	3.1764066e-2
11.	.03	5.1878876e-2
12	.04	8.1188411e-2
13	.04	.12258008
14.	.09	.17950617
15	.24	.25603814
16.	.38	.35692155
17	.63	.48763159
18.	.93	.6544291
19.	1.24	.86441717
20.	1.48	1.1255982
21	1.73	1.4469314
22.	2.07	1.8383908
23	2.5	2.3110238
24.	3.12	2.8770097
25.	3.48	3.5497192

Sum of Square Errors = 6.142e-01

(b) *Exponential function*

Least Squares Curve Fitting
    1 - Power Function
    2 - Exponential Function
    3 - Polynomial
Please enter 1, 2 or 3: 2

Coefficient Matrix:
 19   304
304   5434

Right-Hand Side:
-26.033356 -213.60733

Unknown Coefficients for Exponential Function
 8.5333757e-4   .35601117

X	Y	F(X)
7	.01	1.0313752e-2
8	.02	1.4724154e-2
9	.02	2.1020548e-2
10	.03	3.0009429e-2
11	.03	4.2842165e-2
12	.04	6.1162482e-2
13	.04	8.7316996e-2
14	.09	.12465579

15	.24	.17796154
16	.38	.25406208
17	.63	.36270499
18	.93	.51780616
19	1.24	.73923224
20	1.48	1.0553453
21	1.73	1.5066358
22	2.07	2.1509086
23	2.5	3.0706877
24	3.12	4.3837859
25	3.48	6.2583957

Sum of Square Errors = 1.040e+01

(c) *Second-degree polynomial (quadratic)*

```
Least Squares Curve Fitting
  1 - Power Function
  2 - Exponential Function
  3 - Polynomial
Please enter 1, 2 or 3: 3
Highest power of polynomial: 2

Coefficient Matrix:
 19   304   5434
 304   5434   105184
 5434   105184   2151370

Right-Hand Side:
 18.08   394.84   8773.92

Unknown Coefficients for Polynomial
 1.7388318  -.34582869   1.6594427e-2
```

X	Y	F(X)
7	.01	.13115789
8	.02	3.4245614e-2
9	.02	-2.9477812e-2
10	.03	-6.0012384e-2
11	.03	-5.7358101e-2
12	.04	-2.1514964e-2
13	.04	4.7517028e-2
14	.09	.14973787
15	.24	.28514757
16	.38	.45374613
17	.63	.65553354
18	.93	.8905098
19	1.24	1.1586749
20	1.48	1.4600289
21	1.73	1.7945717
22	2.07	2.1623034
23	2.5	2.5632239

```
24              3.12              2.9973333
25              3.48              3.4646316
```

Sum of Square Errors = 8.914e-02

(d) *Fourth-degree polynomial*

```
Least Squares Curve Fitting
   1 - Power Function
   2 - Exponential Function
   3 - Polynomial
Please enter 1, 2 or 3: 3
Highest power of polynomial: 4

Coefficient Matrix:
 19   304   5434   105184   2151370
 304   5434   105184   2151370   45723424
 5434   105184   2151370   45723424   9.9881415e+8
 105184   2151370   45723424   9.9881415e+8   2.2267169e+10
 2151370   45723424   9.9881415e+8   2.2267169e+10   5.0421151e+11

Right-Hand Side:
 18.08   394.84   8773.92   197719   4507584

Unknown Coefficients for Polynomial
 -.73370762  .33278413 -4.8084034e-2  2.5728003e-3 -3.6476625e-5
```

```
X               Y                 F(X)
7              .01              3.4553776e-2
8              .02              .01905277
9              .02              2.7911094e-3
10             .03              -6.2356368e-3
11             .03              -9.0733694e-4
12             .04              2.5020701e-2
13             .04              .07691773
14             .09              .15927756
15             .24              .27571858
16             .38              .42898371
17             .63              .62094046
18             .93              .85258088
19             1.24             1.1240216
20             1.48             1.4345038
21             1.73             1.7823932
22             2.07             2.1651801
23             2.5              2.5794794
24             3.12             3.0210304
25             3.48             3.4846973
```

Sum of Square Errors = 6.277e-02

Summarizing the calculated values of the square errors, we obtain the following results.

Curve Fit	Square Error
Power function	0.614
Exponential function	10.4
Second-degree polynomial (quadratic)	0.0891
Fourth-degree polynomial	0.0628

These results suggest that the fourth-degree polynomial provides the best fit, while the exponential function results in the worst fit.

The user is again reminded that some versions of BASIC *do not* include matrix statements. Check the programmer's reference manual that accompanies your particular version of BASIC before attempting to use these statements in your own programs.

Review Questions

9.1   What is a vector? What is a matrix?

9.2   Is it necessary to use matrix statements to carry out vector and matrix operations? What advantage is there in the use of matrix statements?

9.3   Describe the two different forms of a matrix assignment statement.

9.4   Summarize the rules for writing each of the following matrix statements: addition, subtraction, multiplication by a constant and matrix multiplication.

9.5   What is the difference between multiplication by a constant and matrix multiplication? What conditions must be satisfied in order to multiply one matrix by another?

9.6   What is the purpose of the DOT function? Explain in terms of matrix multiplication. Describe the product that is obtained from this function.

9.7   What is the purpose of the MAT READ statement? What other statement must be used in conjunction with MAT READ?

9.8   Summarize the rules for writing a MAT READ statement.

9.9   Suppose a single MAT READ statement contains several array names. In what order will the values in the data block be assigned to the matrix elements?

9.10 What is the purpose of the MAT PRINT statement? Summarize the rules for writing this statement.

9.11 Suppose a MAT PRINT statement contains the name of a single matrix. In what order will the matrix elements be displayed? How can we distinguish one row of the matrix from another? How can the spacing of the elements be altered?

9.12 Suppose a MAT PRINT statement contains several array names. In what order will the array elements be printed? How can the elements of one array be distinguished from the elements of another array?

9.13 What is the purpose of the REPEAT$ function? Describe its use in conjunction with the MAT PRINT USING statement.

9.14   Can expressions be included in a MAT PRINT statement?

9.15   What is the purpose of the MAT INPUT statement? How does it differ from the MAT READ statement?

9.16   Describe how a MAT INPUT statement can be used to enter an unspecified number of vector elements. How can the number of vector elements entered be determined?

9.17   How can multiple lines of input data be read with a single MAT INPUT statement?

9.18   Summarize the rules for writing a MAT INPUT PROMPT statement.

9.19   Summarize the rules for writing a MAT LINE INPUT statement. Can MAT LINE INPUT be combined with MAT INPUT PROMPT?

9.20   What is the purpose of the MAT INPUT #n and the MAT PRINT #n statements? How does their use differ from the ordinary MAT INPUT and MAT PRINT statements?

9.21   What is the purpose of the MAT LINE INPUT #n statement?

9.22   Describe the factors that tend to restrict the use of the MAT INPUT #n and MAT PRINT #n statements in many practical applications.

9.23   What is the purpose of the MAT READ #n and the MAT WRITE #n statements? How do they differ from the MAT INPUT #n and the MAT PRINT #n statements?

9.24   How many records are associated with an array that is read from a data file or written to a data file using the MAT READ #n and MAT WRITE #n statements?

9.25   What is an identity matrix?

9.26   What is meant by the transpose of a matrix?

9.27   What is meant by the inverse of a matrix? Does an inverse always exist? Explain.

9.28   What relationship must exist between the number of rows and the number of columns of an identity matrix? An inverse matrix?

9.29   What relationship must exist between the number of rows and columns of a given matrix and its transpose? Can a vector have a transpose?

9.30   What is the result of multiplying a matrix by an identity matrix?

9.31   What is the result of multiplying a matrix by its inverse?

9.32   State the purpose and summarize the rules for utilizing each of the following matrix functions: MAT ZER, MAT CON, MAT IDN, MAT TRN, MAT INV.

9.33   What is the purpose of the DET function? For what kinds of matrices can the DET function be used? How is the DET function written?

9.34   If the DET function is used without an argument, what does it return?

9.35   What can be said about the accuracy of the values returned by the INV and DET functions?

9.36   Explain how a system of simultaneous, linear algebraic equations can be solved using matrix statements. How can the accuracy of the solution be checked?

9.37   What is the purpose of the MAT NUL$ function? What restrictions are there on its use?

9.38   Can the size of an array be changed through array redimensioning? Can the dimensionality of the array be changed? Explain.

9.39   Which matrix statements allow an array to be redimensioned at a later point in a program, after it has originally been dimensioned? How is the redimensioning accomplished?

9.40   Compare the concept of array redimensioning discussed in Sec. 9.4 with the variable dimension feature included in the MAT INPUT statement.

9.41   What operations can be performed on string arrays? Which matrix statements can be used for the manipulation of string arrays?

9.42   Which matrix statements apply only to matrices (i.e., two-dimensional arrays)? Which can be applied to either vectors or matrices? Which can be applied to higher dimensional arrays?

9.43   Are matrix statements commonly available in most versions of BASIC?

Problems

9.44   Determine the purpose of each of the following groups of BASIC statements.

(a)
```
DIM A$(10, 10), B$(10, 10), C(3, 4), D(3, 4)

MAT C = 0.3
MAT D = C

MAT A$ = "Hello, there!"
MAT B$ = A$
```

(b)
```
DIM A(2, 4), B(2, 4), C(2, 4), D(2, 4), E(2, 4)

MAT READ A, B
DATA 10, 12, 14, 16, 18, 20, 22, 24, 26, 28, 30, 32, 34, 36, 38, 40

MAT C = A + B
MAT D = B - A
MAT E = 2 * D

MAT PRINT A, B
MAT PRINT C; D; E;
```

(c) DIM A(2, 4), B(4, 2), C(2, 2)

```
MAT READ A, B
DATA 10, 12, 14, 16, 18, 20, 22, 24, 26, 28, 30, 32, 34, 36, 38, 40

MAT C = A * B
MAT PRINT C
```

(d) DIM U(3), V(3)

```
MAT READ U, V
DATA 5, 10, 15, 20, 25, 30

LET C = DOT(U, V)
PRINT "C ="; C
```

(e) DIM fract(3, 3)

```
FOR i = 1 TO 3
   FOR j =1 TO 3
      LET fract(i, j) = (i + j - 1) / 9
   NEXT j
NEXT i

LET fst$ = REPEAT$("#.###^^^^  ", 3)
MAT PRINT USING fst$: fract
```

9.45 The following values are to be entered into the 100-element vector X, using the MAT INPUT statement with an unspecified number of data items.

5, 10, 15, 20, 25, 30, 35, 40, 45, 50, 55, 60

Show how the DIM and MAT INPUT statements are written. Then show how the data values are entered, assuming the the first six values are entered on one line and the next six values on the next line.

9.46 Modify the MAT INPUT statement written for the last problem so that the prompt "Please enter six values per line: " appears at the start of the data entry process.

9.47 A list of cities and their states is to be entered into the 8-element vector cities$, using the MAT LINE INPUT statement. Show how the MAT LINE INPUT statement should appear. In addition, show how the data values are entered, assuming the data consists of the following list of cities.

Boston, MA   New York, NY
Chicago, IL   Pittsburgh, PA
Denver, CO   San Diego, CA
Honolulu, HI   Seattle, WA

9.48 Modify the MAT LINE INPUT statement written for the last problem so that the prompt "Please enter each city on a new line: " appears at the start of the data entry process.

9.49 Show the skeletal structure of a BASIC program that will read the values of the 100-element vector X from a sequential data file and then display them on the screen. Assume the sequential data file is called "VALUES.DAT."

9.50 Show the skeletal structure of a BASIC program that will enter the values of the 100-element vector X from the keyboard and then write them to a sequential data file called "VALUES.DAT."

9.51 Show the skeletal structure of a BASIC program that will read the values of the 100-element vector cities$ from a sequential data file and then display them on the screen. Assume the sequential data file is called "CITIES.DAT." Assume also that each value is a string consisting of a city and a state, as in Prob. 9.47.

9.52 Show the skeletal structure of a BASIC program that will enter the values of the 100-element vector cities$ from the keyboard and then write them to a sequential data file called "CITIES.DAT."

9.53 Show the skeletal structure of a BASIC program that will read the values of the 20 x 30 matrix A from a direct data file and then display them on the screen. Assume the direct data file is called "MATRIX.DAT."

9.54 Show the skeletal structure of a BASIC program that will enter the values of the 20 x 30 matrix A from the keyboard and then write them to a direct data file called "MATRIX.DAT."

9.55 Write one or more BASIC statements for each of the situations described below.

(a) Evaluate the formula

$$Y = X^T * A * X$$

where A is a 10 x 10 matrix, X is a 10-element vector, and X^T is the transpose of X. What will be the dimensionality of Y?

(b) Evaluate the formula

$$T = V * F^{-1} * G + H$$

where F, G and H are 50 x 50 matrices, V is an ordinary variable and F^{-1} represents the inverse of F. What will be the dimensionality of T?

(c) Calculate the difference between I and $A^{-1} * A$, where A is a 10 x 10 matrix, A^{-1} represents the inverse of A and I is a 10 x 10 identity matrix. (Note that this difference should, in principle, be a matrix whose elements are zero. In reality, the matrix elements may be different from zero because of numerical errors.)

(d) Display the answer obtained for part (c) above in matrix form, with elements spaced as closely as possible.

(e) Suppose that A and B are 10 x 10 matrices whose elements are given in a data block. Read the elements of A, one row at a time, followed by the elements of B, one column at a time.

(f) Suppose that P is a 5 x 12 matrix, T is a 6 x 6 matrix and X is a 10-element vector. Display the values of P, T and X.

(g) Repeat part (f) above, with the array elements spaced as closely as possible.

(h) Suppose that A, B, C and D are 10 x 10 matrices. Calculate the determinant of G, where

    G = A * C - B * D

and display its value.

(i) Modify part (h) above to display the elements of G, followed by the inverse of G and the determinant of G. Space the matrix elements as closely as possible.

(j) Suppose that A is a 20 x 30 matrix. Resize the array, assigning zeros to the elements in the first 8 columns of the first 12 rows.

(k) Suppose that SYMBOLS$ is a 20 x 20 string matrix. Resize the array, assigning null strings to the elements in the first 12 columns of the first 12 rows.

(l) Suppose that A and B are 20 x 30 matrices. Read the elements in the first 12 columns of the first 8 rows of A, followed by the elements in the first 15 columns of the first 6 rows of B. How must the data be arranged in the data block?

(m) Suppose that A and B are 20 x 30 matrices. Display the elements in the first 12 columns of the first 8 rows of A, followed by the elements in the first 15 columns of the first 6 rows of B. Compare with the solution to part (l) above.

Programming Problems

9.56 Modify the program given in Example 9.25 so that any system of n equations in n unknowns can be solved. Use the variable dimension feature described in Sec. 9.4. Add a provision for calculating and displaying the determinant of the coefficient matrix.

9.57 When numerical errors are generated in solving the system of simultaneous equations C * X = D, it is often helpful to proceed as follows.

(a) Calculate the vector F = C * X.

(b) Calculate the error vector ERR = D - F. (If numerical errors are not present, then F will be the same as the given vector D, and the elements of ERR will be zeros.)

(c) If the elements of ERR are not all equal to zero, then solve the system of simultaneous equations

    A * Y = ERR

for the values of Y(1), Y(2), . . ., Y(N).

(d) Add the elements of Y to the corresponding elements of X to obtain an improved solution.

Modify the program given in Example 9.25 to include this error-correction feature. Include a provision for calculating the determinant of the coefficient matrix. Use the program to solve the following system of simultaneous equations.

$$x_1 + x_2/2 + x_3/3 + x_4/4 + x_5/5 = 1/6$$
$$x_1/2 + x_2/3 + x_3/4 + x_4/5 + x_5/6 = 1/7$$
$$x_1/3 + x_2/4 + x_3/5 + x_4/6 + x_5/7 = 1/8$$
$$x_1/4 + x_2/5 + x_3/6 + x_4/7 + x_5/8 = 1/9$$
$$x_1/5 + x_2/6 + x_3/7 + x_4/8 + x_5/9 = 1/10$$

Compare the answers obtained with and without the error-correction feature.

9.58   Modify the program given in Example 9.30 so that several different curves can be fit to the same set of data (i.e., the program can be executed several times consecutively) without rereading the data each time a different curve is selected.

9.59   Write a BASIC program for each of the problems described below.

(a)   Starting with the following matrix,

$$A = \begin{vmatrix} 5 & 3 & 1 \\ 3 & 7 & 4 \\ 1 & 4 & 9 \end{vmatrix}$$

calculate a new matrix D, where each element of D is the reciprocal of the corresponding element of A, i.e., D(I, J) = 1 / A(I, J). Compare each element of D with the corresponding element B, where B is the inverse of A. Are they the same?

(b)   Calculate the inverse of the matrix B described in the last problem (i.e., calculate the inverse of the inverse of A). Compare the elements of this matrix with the elements of the original A matrix. Are they the same? If not, why?

(c)   For the matrices A and B given in Example 9.3, show that A * B does not equal B * A.

(d)   Repeat the previous problem for the nonsquare matrices given in Example 9.8.

(e)   For the matrices A and B given in Example 9.8, show that $(A * B)^T = B^T * A^T$, where A^T represents the transpose of A, B^T represents the transpose of B, etc.

(f)   Evaluate the matrix formula

$$Y = D^T * C^T * C * D$$

using the matrix C and the vector D given in Example 9.25. What will be the dimensionality of Y?

(g)   Evaluate the matrix formula

$$P = I + A + A^2 + A^3 + A^4$$

using the matrix A in Example 9.24. (Note that I represents the identity matrix, $A^2 = A * A$, $A^3 = A * A * A$, etc.) What will be the dimensionality of P?

Chapter 10

Programming a Personal Computer

Most BASIC programming is now carried out on personal computers (PCs), since PCs are now very inexpensive and widely available. Accordingly, many versions of BASIC that are intended for use on PCs include special instructions that allow the programmer to interact with the PC's hardware. For example, statements that allow the programmer to control the keyboard function keys, various pointing devices (such as light pens, joysticks and mice) and the appearance of the screen are now quite common. We will examine some of these hardware-oriented statements in this chapter.

Our emphasis will be on Microsoft's QuickBASIC and QBASIC, since they are widely used and are very rich in these special features. We will consider the use of QuickBASIC/QBASIC on MS-DOS (i.e., IBM-compatible) PCs.

10.1 THE KEYBOARD FUNCTION KEYS

Most PC keyboards contain various groups of keys in addition to the standard "typewriter-style" keys. Typically, a PC keyboard will include a group of *function keys*, a group of *cursor-* and *screen-movement keys* and a *numeric keypad* (i.e., a set of numeric keys that duplicates the numeric typewriter keys but has a calculator-type arrangement). Certain of these keys can be programmed to perform special tasks during the execution of a BASIC program.

A typical PC keyboard is shown in Fig. 10.1. Notice that the typewriter keys are located in the center of the keyboard. A group of 12 programmable function keys, labeled F1 through F12, runs across the top. (On some keyboards the function keys are grouped to the left of the typewriter keys.) To the right of the typewriter keys are two small clusters of keys — a screen-movement group on top, and a cursor-movement group on the bottom. At the extreme right is the numeric keypad. The numeric keypad can be converted into screen-movement and cursor-movement keys by depressing the NumLock key at the top of this group.

Fig. 10.1

QuickBASIC contains several special commands that allow the computer to determine if any of the function keys or certain of the cursor-movement keys have been pressed. The computer can then carry out any action the programmer may wish, through a special form of the ON - GOSUB statement. This type of activity is known as *event trapping*. We will see how event trapping is carried out in the next example.

It should be understood that QuickBASIC *requires* the use of the ON - GOSUB statement, and its associated "subroutines," in order to initiate event trapping. These features are remnants of early versions of BASIC and are generally no longer used. Their use in the present context is, however, unavoidable.

Example 10.1 Programming the Function Keys

Here is a simple QuickBASIC program that displays consecutive line numbers on the screen, one integer constant per line. Since the screen can display only a few lines (typically 25) at any one time, the numbers scroll vertically upward once the screen becomes filled.

Within this program, the screen colors can be "reversed" (that is, changed from white characters on a black background to black characters on a white background, and vice versa) at any time by pressing function key F1 while the program is executing. In addition, the program can be terminated at any time simply by pressing function key F2.

```
'*** PROGRAMMABLE FUNCTION KEY DEMO ***

ON KEY(1) GOSUB Reverse
KEY(1) ON

ON KEY(2) GOSUB Terminate
KEY(2) ON

'initial instructions

CLS
LET flag = 1
PRINT "FUNCTION KEY DEMONSTRATION": PRINT
PRINT "Press F1 to REVERSE the screen, F2 to STOP": PRINT
PRINT "Press any other key to begin"
LET dummy$ = INPUT$(1)

'main loop

LET count = 1
DO WHILE flag >= 0
   PRINT "Line number"; count
   LET count = count + 1
LOOP

Reverse:        'routine to reverse the screen
   IF flag = 1 THEN
      COLOR 0, 7
      LET flag = 0
   ELSE
      COLOR 7, 0
      LET flag = 1
   END IF
RETURN

Terminate:      'routine to end the computation
END
```

The first statement (ON KEY(1) GOSUB Reverse) associates function key F1 with the subroutine labelled Reverse. This subroutine, which is located near the bottom of the program, begins with the label Reverse: (note the colon at the end of the label) and ends with the RETURN statement. It specifies the action to be taken when this function key is pressed. The following statement (KEY(1) ON) activates the event trapping associated with this function key.

The next two statements have the same purpose for function key F2. Following these statements is a block of initialization statements. The first of these (CLS) clears the screen and the second (LET flag = 1) assigns a value to the variable flag, thus selecting an initial set of screen colors (white characters on a black background). These statements are followed by several PRINT statements, which provide instructions in the use of the program.

The next group of statements make up the main program loop. The first of these simply assigns 1 to the variable count. The program then enters a DO - LOOP structure that simply displays the value of count and then increases its value by 1. This loop will run indefinitely. Thus, the only way to terminate the execution is to press function key F2.

The next group of statements comprise the first subroutine (associated with F1), which reverses the colors. The principal part of the subroutine is the IF - THEN - ELSE structure. The color reversals are carried out with the COLOR statement. Thus if flag = 1, indicating white on black, the colors are reversed by specifying COLOR 0,7 (the 0 indicates black characters, and the 7 indicates a white background) and flag is set equal to 0. Similarly, if flag is not equal to 1, the colors are reversed by specifying COLOR 7,0 (white characters, black background) and flag is reset to 1. The RETURN statement at the end of the subroutine causes control to be returned to the statement following the point where the function key was depressed.

The second subroutine consists simply of a label and an END statement. A RETURN statement is not required here since the purpose of this subroutine is to terminate the computation.

We will say more about the COLOR statement later in this chapter (see Sec. 10.3). It should be apparent, however, that this statement is used to produce colored text against a different colored background. It can also be used to generate color graphics, as we shall see in Chap. 11.

When the program is executed, the messages

```
Line number 1
Line number 2
Line number 3
Line number 4
Line number 5

.  .  .  .  .
```

will scroll vertically across the screen, with either white characters against a black background or black characters against a white background. The colors can be reversed at any time during the scrolling by pressing F1. The scrolling will continue until the user presses F2. You should see this program in operation to appreciate what it does and how it works.

10.2 OTIIER PROGRAMMABLE INPUT DEVICES

Personal computers are able to make use of several different types of programmable input devices in addition to the keyboard. Three commonly used devices are the *light pen*, the *mouse* and the *joystick*. The light pen is a pointing device that can be programmed to sense a location on the screen and then activate some function. The mouse is a widely used pointing device that can, among other things, position the cursor by dragging the mouse along a flat surface. It can then determine the screen location and activate some function by depressing a button. The joystick is a similar though simpler positioning device that can position the cursor and then activate a function by depressing a button. QuickBASIC allows these devices to be programmed in much the same manner as the keyboard function keys, as described above.

The Light Pen

The light pen is a light-sensitive device with a switch built into its tip. The switch is actuated by pressing the light pen against a light source on the TV monitor. The location of the light source (row and column) can then be determined by the computer. The use of a typical light pen is illustrated in Fig. 10.2.

Fig. 10.2

QuickBASIC contains several special statements and functions that are designed to be used with a light pen. Use of these special features is illustrated in the next example.

Example 10.2 Programming a Light Pen

In this example we see a QuickBASIC program that allows the user to select a menu item using a light pen. Once the light pen is pointed at an item, an action is taken which is specific to that selection. In particular, the program generates a menu containing the names of eight different languages, each preceded by a square block of light. The user then presses the point of the light pen against the block corresponding to the language of his or her choice. An appropriate greeting, in the chosen language, will then appear adjacent to the language name. The greeting will remain on the screen for a second or two (long enough for it to be read comfortably) and then erased. The user may then choose another language, and the process will be repeated. This process continues until the user selects the last menu time (END), which causes the program to stop.

Here is the actual QuickBASIC program.

```
'*** LIGHT PEN DEMO ***

LET tmax = 100000

ON PEN GOSUB Greetings
PEN ON
LET square$ = CHR$(219) + CHR$(219)
LET flag = 1
```

```
'generate menu

CLS
PRINT "Multi-Lingual Greetings"
LOCATE 4, 1: PRINT "Please Select a Language"
LOCATE 6, 4: PRINT square$; SPC(4); "English"
LOCATE 8, 4: PRINT square$; SPC(4); "French"
LOCATE 10, 4: PRINT square$; SPC(4); "German"
LOCATE 12, 4: PRINT square$; SPC(4); "Hawaiian"
LOCATE 14, 4: PRINT square$; SPC(4); "Hebrew"
LOCATE 16, 4: PRINT square$; SPC(4); "Italian"
LOCATE 18, 4: PRINT square$; SPC(4); "Japanese"
LOCATE 20, 4: PRINT square$; SPC(4); "Spanish"
LOCATE 22, 4: PRINT square$; SPC(4); "END"

'main loop

DO WHILE flag = 1
LOOP

Greetings:              'light pen response routine
   LET row = PEN(6)    'return row number where light pen was depressed

   IF row = 6 THEN LOCATE row, 20: PRINT "Hello"
   IF row = 8 THEN LOCATE row, 20: PRINT "Bonjour"
   IF row = 10 THEN LOCATE row, 20: PRINT "Guten Tag"
   IF row = 12 THEN LOCATE row, 20: PRINT "Aloha"
   IF row = 14 THEN LOCATE row, 20: PRINT "Shalom"
   IF row = 16 THEN LOCATE row, 20: PRINT "Bon Giorno"
   IF row = 18 THEN LOCATE row, 20: PRINT "Konichihua"
   IF row = 20 THEN LOCATE row, 20: PRINT "Buenos Dias"
   IF row = 22 THEN LOCATE 23, 1: STOP

   FOR count = 1 TO tmax: NEXT count   'time delay

   LOCATE row, 20: PRINT SPACE$(15)
RETURN

END
```

The first statement assigns a value to `tmax`, which is used to create a time delay. The second statement (ON PEN GOSUB Greetings) associates the light pen activation with the subroutine labeled Greetings. This subroutine occupies the lower portion of the program.

The third statement (PEN ON) activates the event trapping associated with the light pen. It is followed by two assignment statements for variables that are used later in the program.

The main menu is generated by the following block of statements. The individual statements are straightforward. Note that each line within the menu will consist of a square block (which provides a light source for activating the light pen) and the name of a language. The user will select a language by pressing the light pen against the corresponding square block.

Beneath the main menu are two statements that create an infinite loop. This loop will allow the user to activate the light pen functions successively, until the last menu item (END) is selected.

Within the function labeled `Greetings`, the first statement (`LET row = PEN(6)`) assigns the row number corresponding to the most recent light pen activation to the variable `row`. The following block of `IF` statements cause the appropriate message to be displayed in column 20 of the same row, thus providing the response to the light pen selection. The `FOR - NEXT` loop at the bottom causes a time delay, so that the user may read the message. (Note that the value assigned to `tmax` may have to be altered to accommodate the speed of the particular computer on which this program is executed.)

When the program is executed, the following screen display is generated. (Note that the dark blocks will appear as blocks of light on the TV monitor.)

```
Multi-Lingual Greetings


Please Select a Language

   ■    English
   ■    French
   ■    German
   ■    Hawaiian
   ■    Hebrew
   ■    Italian
   ■    Japanese
   ■    Spanish
   ■    END
```

If the user presses the light pen against one of the blocks, the appropriate greeting will occur to the right of the line selected. For example, if the light pen is pressed against the second block, the greeting `Bonjour` will appear to the right of the word `French`, as shown below. The greeting will disappear after a short time delay. The user may then make other selections, as desired. The program can be ended at any time simply by selecting the last block (END).

```
Multi-Lingual Greetings


Please Select a Language

   ■    English
   ■    French    Bonjour
   ■    German
   ■    Hawaiian
   ■    Hebrew
   ■    Italian
   ■    Japanese
   ■    Spanish
   ■    END
```

The Mouse

Currently, the mouse is the most versatile and the most widely used PC pointing device. It is commonly used with many commercial programming applications, such as word processors, spreadsheets and database managers. Graphical applications are heavily dependent upon the availability and use of the mouse, both as a pointing device and a drawing device.

The mouse is designed to be used on a flat desktop surface. It consists of two buttons (some have three buttons) placed on a housing that fits comfortably within the palm of the user's hand. Beneath the mouse housing is a ball that rolls as the mouse is moved along the surface of the desk. By sensing relative motions of the ball, the mouse is able to relate its position on the desktop to the position of an associated *mouse cursor* on the screen. Once the mouse is positioned where the user wants it, one or both buttons can be depressed, causing various functions to become activated. A typical mouse is shown in Fig. 10.3.

Fig. 10.3

The mouse is a more recent development than other pointing devices, such as the light pen or the joystick. Moreover, it is more complicated to program than other pointing devices. For these reasons, QuickBASIC does not contain simple event-trapping statements for the mouse. However, it is possible to use the mouse as a *light pen emulator*. Thus, clicking both mouse buttons on a particular line within a menu will have the same effect as pressing a light pen against a light block. This permits us to write QuickBASIC programs that incorporate the use of a mouse, in much the same manner as we would write QuickBASIC programs that utilize a light pen. The programming details are illustrated in the following example.

Example 10.3 Programming a Mouse

In this example we consider another version of the menu-driven, pointer-activated "Greetings" program shown in Example 10.2. Now, however, we make use of a mouse rather than a light pen to select an item from the main menu. We will program the mouse by utilizing its *light-pen emulation mode*. Thus, the program will be very similar to that shown in Example 10.2.

Here is the complete QuickBASIC program.

```
'*** MOUSE DEMO (USES LIGHT PEN EMULATION) ***

'mouse setup

DEFINT M
DECLARE SUB MOUSE (M1, M2, M3, M4)

LET tmax = 100000

LET M1 = 0
```

```
CALL MOUSE(M1, M2, M3, M4)              'initialize the mouse

LET M1 = 1
CALL MOUSE(M1, M2, M3, M4)              'show the mouse cursor

LET M1 = 13
CALL MOUSE(M1, M2, M3, M4)              'activate light pen emulation

ON PEN GOSUB Greetings
PEN ON

LET square$ = CHR$(219) + CHR$(219)
LET flag = 1

'generate menu

CLS
PRINT "Multi-Lingual Greetings"
LOCATE 4, 1: PRINT "Please Select a Language"
LOCATE 6, 4: PRINT square$; SPC(4); "English"
LOCATE 8, 4: PRINT square$; SPC(4); "French"
LOCATE 10, 4: PRINT square$; SPC(4); "German"
LOCATE 12, 4: PRINT square$; SPC(4); "Hawaiian"
LOCATE 14, 4: PRINT square$; SPC(4); "Hebrew"
LOCATE 16, 4: PRINT square$; SPC(4); "Italian"
LOCATE 18, 4: PRINT square$; SPC(4); "Japanese"
LOCATE 20, 4: PRINT square$; SPC(4); "Spanish"
LOCATE 22, 4: PRINT square$; SPC(4); "END"

'main loop

DO WHILE flag = 1
LOOP

Greetings:                  'light pen response routine
    LET row = PEN(6)    'return row number where mouse was double clicked

    IF row = 6 THEN LOCATE row, 20: PRINT "Hello"
    IF row = 8 THEN LOCATE row, 20: PRINT "Bonjour"
    IF row = 10 THEN LOCATE row, 20: PRINT "Guten Tag"
    IF row = 12 THEN LOCATE row, 20: PRINT "Aloha"
    IF row = 14 THEN LOCATE row, 20: PRINT "Shalom"
    IF row = 16 THEN LOCATE row, 20: PRINT "Bon Giorno"
    IF row = 18 THEN LOCATE row, 20: PRINT "Konichihua"
    IF row = 20 THEN LOCATE row, 20: PRINT "Buenos Dias"
    IF row = 22 THEN LOCATE 23, 1: STOP

    FOR count = 1 TO tmax: NEXT count   'time delay

    LOCATE row, 20: PRINT SPACE$(15)
RETURN
END
```

The program begins with a DEFINT statement, which defines all variable names beginning with M as integer variables. This is intended for the four variables M1, M2, M3 and M4, which are required for the external mouse subroutine calls described below.

Following the DEFINT statement is a declaration for an external subroutine called MOUSE. Note that this subroutine is not defined within the present program. Rather, it is included in a *mouse library* called MOUSE.LIB. This library must be linked to QuickBASIC when QuickBASIC is first activated. The detailed procedure for linking a library to QuickBASIC is beyond the scope of our present discussion, though the procedure is simple and is well-documented within the QuickBASIC manuals.

Next is an assignment statement that assigns a value to the time-delay variable tmax. This is followed by three calls to the external subroutine MOUSE. Each call passes a different value of M1 to the subroutine, and returns values for M2, M3 and M4. (The returned values are not used in the present application.) In particular, the first call, with M1 = 0, initializes the mouse. The second call (M1 = 1) displays the mouse cursor, and the third call (M1 = 13) activates light pen emulation; i.e., it allows the mouse to be programmed as though it were a light pen. The remainder of the program is identical to the light pen program presented in Example 10.2.

When the program is executed, it behaves in the same manner as the light pen program shown earlier. Now, however, the user makes a selection by clicking both mouse buttons on the desired line. The program will then respond in the customary manner, by displaying the appropriate greeting on the selected line. Note that the mouse can be clicked anywhere on a line, not just on the lighted square.

The Joystick

Now consider a joystick, such as that illustrated in Fig. 10.4. This device has a handle (i.e., a "stick") that can be moved in two different directions — up/down and left/right. The position of the handle is described by a pair of integer values representing x and y coordinates. These values are continuously transmitted to the computer, where they can be transformed into a cursor position (i.e., row and column numbers). If the joystick handle is moved, the cursor position will change correspondingly. Hence, the computer can be programmed to move the cursor to a desired location by moving the joystick handle and then activate some function by pressing one of the buttons. Each button can be programmed separately to activate its own unique function.

Fig 10.4

QuickBASIC includes several special statements that can be used to program a joystick. The manner in which this is accomplished is illustrated in the following example.

Example 10.4 Calibrating a Joystick

In order to utilize a joystick in a BASIC program, we must know the range of values that represent the joystick coordinates. Presented below is a QuickBASIC program that returns these values. The user first moves the joystick handle to one corner and then presses button 1 (the top button, closest to the handle in Fig. 10.4). The joystick coordinates for that position will then be displayed on the screen. By repeating this procedure for the three remaining corners, the complete range of joystick coordinates can be determined.

```
' *** JOYSTICK CALIBRATION PROGRAM ***

ON STRIG(0) GOSUB Display
STRIG(0) ON

ON STRIG(4) GOSUB Terminate
STRIG(4) ON

PRINT "MOVE THE JOYSTICK TO EACH CORNER AND PRESS THE TOP BUTTON"
LET flag = 1

'main loop

DO WHILE flag = 1
   LET x = STICK(0)
   LET y = STICK(1)
LOOP

Display:                    'display the joystick coordinates
   PRINT "x ="; x; "y ="; y
RETURN

Terminate:                  'end the computation
END
```

This program utilizes event trapping in a manner that resembles the programs presented earlier in this chapter. The first statement (ON STRIG(0) GOSUB Display) associates joystick button 0 (the top button) with the subroutine labeled Display. The second statement (STRIG(0) ON) activates the actual event trapping. The next two statements provide a similar capability for button 4 (the lower button), associating it with the subroutine labeled Terminate.

The corresponding subroutines are listed at the end of the program. The first subroutine displays the x- and y-coordinates of the joystick handle when button 0 is pressed. The second subroutine simply ends the computation.

The remainder of the program generates an opening message and then enters an infinite loop which awaits the event trapping. Subroutine Display will be activated whenever button 0 is pressed, displaying the joystick coordinates on the screen.

Now suppose the program is executed and the top joystick button is pressed when the joystick handle is positioned in the upper-left, the lower-left, the upper-right and the lower-right corners, resulting in the following output.

```
x = 40 y = 40
x = 40 y = 194
x = 213 y = 40
x = 213 y = 194
```

This information tells us that the x-coordinates range from 40 to 213 and the y-coordinates range from 40 to 194.

Once the joystick has been calibrated, the position of the joystick handle can be associated with known screen positions. The joystick can then be programmed to perform useful functions within a programming application.

Example 10.5 Programming a Joystick

The following QuickBASIC program is similar to the program shown in the previous example. However, this program incorporates the calibration data obtained in the last example. Hence, the position of the joystick handle can now be associated with a screen location. Pressing joystick button 0 (the top button) will now cause a special character (a smiling face) to be displayed at the indicated screen location.

```
' *** JOYSTICK DEMO ***

ON STRIG(0) GOSUB Display
STRIG(0) ON

ON STRIG(4) GOSUB Terminate
STRIG(4) ON

CLS
LET face$ = CHR$(2)          'define the display character
LET xmin = 40: xmax = 213    'x calibration values
LET ymin = 40: ymax = 194    'y calibration values
LET flag = 1

'main loop

DO WHILE flag = 1
   LET x = STICK(0)
   LET y = STICK(1)
   LET row = INT(24 * (y - ymin) / (ymax - ymin)) + 1
   LET col = INT(79 * (x - xmin) / (xmax - xmin)) + 1
   LOCATE row, col
LOOP

Display:          'display a character
   PRINT face$;
RETURN

Terminate:        'end the computation
END
```

Notice that the calibration values obtained from the previous program are now assigned to xmin, xmax, ymin and ymax, respectively. These values are utilized within the main loop. In particular, the statements

```
LET row = INT(24 * (y - ymin) / (ymax - ymin)) + 1
LET col = INT(79 * (x - xmin) / (xmax - xmin)) + 1
```

cause the joystick coordinate values to be translated into integer quantities that range from 1 to 25, for the row number, and 1 to 80 for the column number. Note that the LOCATE statement positions the cursor to the current row and column positions as these values are determined.

Whenever the top joystick button is pressed during program execution, the special character ☺ is displayed at the selected screen location. The program execution can be terminated at any time by pressing the lower joystick button.

10.3 USE OF COLOR AND SOUND

All personal computers utilize some type of TV display unit as a primary output device. In Chap. 7 we discussed the QuickBASIC CLS and LOCATE statements, which are used to clear the screen and to position the cursor, respectively (see Secs. 7.4 and 7.5). We now consider the use of color and sound as enhancements to text displays. We will consider the use of color graphics in the next chapter.

Most personal computers now support the use of color monitors, thus allowing text of one color to be displayed against a background of different color. Moreover, many monochrome monitors now display different colors as various shades of gray.

QuickBASIC allows colors to be selected by means of the COLOR statement. This statement generally includes three parameters, specifying the foreground (text) color, the background color and the "border" (that is, the background area along the outer edges of the screen). The foreground parameter can take on any of the following 16 values, each representing the indicated foreground color.

0	black	8	gray
1	blue	9	light blue
2	green	10	light green
3	cyan	11	light cyan
4	red	12	light red
5	magenta	13	light magenta
6	brown	14	yellow
7	white	15	high intensity white

Any of the first eight colors (0 through 7) may also be selected for the background or the border. Thus, the statement COLOR 7,0,0 indicates white text on a black background and a black border; COLOR 0,7,7 selects black text against a white background and a white border; COLOR 14,1,4 indicates yellow text against a blue background with a red border, and so on. The value of the parameters can be modified at any time during the execution of a program, thus causing the colors to change as desired.

The COLOR statement is often preceded by the SCREEN statement, which specifies the *mode* (text vs. graphics). For example, the statement SCREEN 0 specifies text mode, whereas SCREEN 9 specifies one of several different graphics modes (more about this in Chap. 11).

Example 10.6 Multicolored Text

To illustrate the use of colored text, we present a QuickBASIC program that fills the screen with the same line of text in a given color. Each line of text will actually scroll from the bottom to the top of the screen, though this will not be apparent to the user unless the screen colors are changed. Initially, the text will be displayed in white against a black background and border.

The foreground or background/border colors can be changed at any time during program execution by pressing function key F1 or F2, respectively. Also, the computation can be ended at any time by pressing function key F3. A message instructing the user in the use of the function keys will be generated at the bottom of the screen (line 25).

```
'*** COLOR TEXT DEMO ***

SCREEN 0

ON KEY(1) GOSUB ForegroundColor
KEY(1) ON

ON KEY(2) GOSUB BackgroundColor
KEY(2) ON

ON KEY(3) GOSUB Terminate
KEY(3) ON

LOCATE 25, 1                                   'display instructions
COLOR 0, 7
PRINT "F1: Change FOREGROUND Color    ";
PRINT "F2: Change BACKGROUND Color    ";
PRINT "F3: END                ";

LET Foreground = 1
LET Background = 0                             'select initial colors
LET Flag = 1

'main loop

DO WHILE Flag = 1
   COLOR Foreground, Background, Background
   PRINT "Programming with BASIC is lots of fun!"
LOOP

ForegroundColor:                              'change the foreground color
   LET Foreground = (Foreground + 1) MOD 16
RETURN

BackgroundColor:                              'change the background color
   LET Background = (Background + 1) MOD 8
RETURN

Terminate:
   COLOR 7, 0, 0                              'end the computation
END
```

The program begins with the SCREEN command, followed by three groups of statements that activate the function keys F1, F2 and F3, respectively. The function key activation statements are similar to those shown in Example 10.1.

The next group of statements generates the following message at the bottom of the screen.

```
F1: Change FOREGROUND Color    F2: Change BACKGROUND Color    F3: END
```

On many computers, this bottom line (i.e., line 25) is a nonscrolling line that is normally used to display prompts and messages of this type. Such messages are often displayed in colors that contrast with the remainder of the screen (in this case, black text on white background) to distinguish the message from whatever else may appear on the screen.

The initial foreground and background colors are then defined by assigning integer values to the variables `Foreground` and `Background`. This is followed by an infinite loop that specifies the current set of screen colors and then displays the following single line of text.

```
Programming with BASIC is lots of fun!
```

The foreground or background colors will change whenever function keys F1 or F2 are pressed, while the loop continues to execute.

At the bottom of the program are the three event-trapping subroutines associated with the function keys F1, F2 and F3. The first of these, labeled `ForegroundColor`, changes the foreground color and returns control to the main loop. Note that the variable `Foreground` takes on values ranging from 0 to 15. Its value increases by 1 each time function key F1 is pressed. The sequence continues indefinitely, with 0 following 15.

Similarly, the second subroutine, labeled `BackgroundColor`, changes the background/border color and returns control to the main loop. The variable `Background` takes on values ranging from 0 to 7, with 0 following 7. Its value increases by 1 each time function key F2 is pressed.

The last subroutine, labeled `Terminate`, restores the colors to a standard color scheme (white text against a black background). It then terminates the computation.

You should actually run this program on a computer equipped with a color monitor if at all possible. This will provide you with a greater appreciation of the dynamic effect that is created by this program.

Let us now turn our attention to the use of sound in a BASIC program. Most personal computers include an internal speaker that can be activated under program control. Though these speakers are typically small, they are capable of producing a remarkable variety of sounds. Many BASIC programs can be enhanced through the use of such program-generated sounds.

In QuickBASIC, for example, there is a BEEP statement that simply "beeps" the speaker, producing a short, high-pitched sound of constant frequency. Such beeps are useful for drawing the user's attention to some specific event that may occur during program execution.

Example 10.7

Let us modify the QuickBASIC program shown in the last example so that the speaker beeps whenever the foreground or background color is changed (i.e., whenever function key F1 or F2 is pressed). This can be accomplished very easily by adding a BEEP statement to subroutines `ForegroundColor` and `BackgroundColor`. Thus, the subroutines would appear as

```
ForegroundColor:                             'change the foreground color
    LET Foreground = (Foreground + 1) MOD 16
    BEEP
RETURN

BackgroundColor:                             'change the background color
    LET Background = (Background + 1) MOD 8
    BEEP
RETURN
```

You should make this change and execute this program, if at all possible, to experience the effect that is created.

QuickBASIC also includes the SOUND statement, which is used to create a tone with a frequency and duration specified by the programmer. The higher the frequency, the higher the tone. Similarly, the greater the duration, the longer the tone. For example, the statement SOUND 5000,1 will produce a relatively high-pitched, short tone whereas SOUND 100,2000 generates a low, long tone. (The first parameter represents frequency, and the second represents duration.)

A certain amount of experimentation with the SOUND statement can be very revealing, as many interesting sounds can be produced for the creative use of this statement. This is particularly true if the statement is included within a loop with changing values for the frequency and duration parameters. Some of these effects are illustrated in the next two examples.

Example 10.8 Programming the Speaker (A Siren)

Here is a QuickBASIC program that causes the computer's internal speaker to generate a siren sound. Essentially, the program consists of a FOR - NEXT loop that is repeated an indefinite number of times. Each complete execution of the loop produces one "wail" of the siren. This characteristic siren sound is repeated each time the loop is executed. The siren will continue indefinitely, until function key F1 is pressed.

```
'*** SOUND DEMO (SIREN) ***

ON KEY(1) GOSUB Terminate
KEY(1) ON

CLS
LOCATE 12, 32
PRINT "Press F1 to STOP"
LET duration = .1
LET flag = 1

'main loop

DO WHILE flag = 1
    FOR frequency = 400 TO 1000 STEP 5
        SOUND frequency, duration
    NEXT frequency
LOOP

Terminate:
END
```

The program begins by associating function key F1 activation with the subroutine labeled Terminate. The program then activates the event trapping associated with F1.

The next group of statements clears the screen and displays the following message in the center of the screen.

```
Press F1 to STOP
```

Numerical values are then assigned to the variables duration and flag. Note that the value assigned to duration will result in a very short duration for each tone.

The main loop consists of an infinite number of FOR - NEXT loops. A series of brief tones is generated within each FOR - NEXT loop. Each tone has a frequency higher than the previous tone. It is the melding of these individual tones that generates the siren sound.

At the end of the program we see the now-familiar subroutine labeled Terminate. This subroutine terminates the computation whenever function key F1 is pressed during program execution.

Once again, you are urged to run this program in order to appreciate what happens. Experiment with the program by varying the values assigned to the variables frequency and duration.

The next example illustrates the combined use of the COLOR, BEEP and SOUND statements to enhance a BASIC program that generates a simple display of text. The program is intended to be run on a color monitor.

Example 10.9 Programming a TV Display (Nothing Can Go Wrong, Go Wrong, Go Wrong . . .)

Shown below is a variation of the program originally presented in Example 7.11, which causes a line of text to appear repeatedly and scroll vertically off the screen. Each line of text now appears in a different color and is accompanied by sound enhancements. Color and sound are also used to enhance the opening displays and the final display, adding interest to the program.

```
'*** COLOR/SOUND DEMO (NOTHING CAN GO WRONG - VERSION 2) ***

BEEP: COLOR 15, 1: CLS
LOCATE 10, 28: PRINT "Welcome to the Wonderful"
LOCATE 12, 27: PRINT "World of Personal Computing"
FOR i = 1 TO 160000: NEXT i                              'time delay


BEEP
LOCATE 16, 18: PRINT "Just relax, enjoy yourself and remember that"
FOR i = 1 TO 160000: NEXT i                              'time delay


COLOR 14, 1
LOCATE 18, 25: PRINT "NOTHING CAN POSSIBLY GO WRONG!"
FOR i = 1 TO 160000: NEXT i                              'time delay


CLS                                                      'main loop
LOCATE 24
FOR m = 1 TO 2
   FOR j = 9 TO 15
      COLOR j, 1
      FOR k = 1 TO 7
         PRINT "GO WRONG! ";
      NEXT k
      PRINT "GO WRONG  "
      PRINT
      SOUND 50, 1: SOUND 32767, 1
      FOR i = 1 TO 30000: NEXT i                         'time delay
   NEXT j
NEXT m


CLS : COLOR 14, 1
LOCATE 12, 37: PRINT "DARN!"
FOR i = 1 TO 18
   SOUND 50, 1: SOUND 32767, 1
NEXT i


COLOR 15, 1
LOCATE 15, 30: PRINT "Something went wrong!"
END
```

The program logic is similar to that used in Example 7.11. However, this version of the program is enhanced by various COLOR, BEEP and SOUND statements. Thus, the program begins with a beep from the speaker. The first three lines of the opening message are then displayed in bright white against a blue background (COLOR 15, 1). The last line is displayed in bright yellow (COLOR 14, 1), for emphasis. Note the use of time delays between displays, to provide time to read each line of text. Also, note the use of a second beep just before the last two lines are displayed.

After a brief delay, the initial display disappears and the scrolling message

GO WRONG! GO WRONG! GO WRONG! GO WRONG! GO WRONG! GO WRONG! GO WRONG! GO WRONG

begins at the bottom of the screen. A total of 14 lines appear, each in a different color (COLOR j, 1). A blank line follows each line of text to enhance the scrolling effect. Also, the appearance of each new line is accompanied by a frog-like croaking sound (SOUND 50, 1: SOUND 32767, 1) and a brief time delay. The croaking sound was obtained as a result of experimenting with the SOUND command.

After the scrolling message is concluded, the screen clears and the final display appears. Note that the first line appears in bright yellow against a blue background (COLOR 14, 1), whereas the last line appears in bright white against the same blue background (COLOR 15, 1). A repeated croaking sound accompanies the first line of text. Thus, the use of color and sound emphasize the message that is conveyed by the first line (DARN!).

You are again encouraged to actually run this program, in order to appreciate fully the various visual and sound effects that are created.

Remember that the features discussed in this chapter are specific to Microsoft QuickBASIC and QBASIC. They may be implemented differently, or they may not be available, in other versions of personal computer BASIC. You should consult the programmer's reference manual for your particular version of BASIC for information concerning hardware-specific features.

Review Questions

10.1   Describe the major groups of keys on a typical personal computer keyboard. What is the purpose of each major group?

10.2   Does the version of BASIC available on your particular PC include a provision for programming the function keys? If so, how is this accomplished?

10.3   What is meant by event trapping? What is its purpose?

10.4   Is event trapping available with your particular version of BASIC? If so, how is event trapping carried out?

10.5   What is a light pen? For what kinds of applications is this device useful?

10.6   Does the version of BASIC available on your particular PC include a provision for programming a light pen? If so, how is this accomplished?

10.7   What is a mouse? For what kinds of applications is this device useful?

10.8   Does the version of BASIC available on your particular PC include a provision for programming a mouse? If so, how is this accomplished?

10.9   What is a joystick? For what kinds of applications is this device useful?

10.10 Does the version of BASIC available on your particular PC include a provision for programming a joystick? If so, how is this accomplished?

10.11 How can the screen be cleared during execution of a BASIC program?

10.12 How can the cursor be placed at a specified position on the screen during execution of a BASIC program?

10.13 Why are time delays useful in an interactive BASIC program? How can such time delays be generated?

10.14 What is the purpose of the COLOR statement? What is the purpose of each parameter?

10.15 What is the purpose of the SCREEN statement? What is the purpose of each parameter?

10.16 Does your particular version of BASIC include the COLOR and SCREEN statements? If not, are there other statements that accomplish the same thing?

10.17 What is the purpose of the BEEP statement?

10.18 What is the purpose of the SOUND statement? What is the purpose of each parameter?

10.19 How can the COLOR, BEEP and SOUND statements enhance a BASIC program that displays only text?

Problems

10.20 Answer the following questions as they apply to the particular version of BASIC used with your PC.

  (*a*) Does your PC keyboard include cursor movement keys and/or function keys? If so, are there special BASIC statements that allow these keys to be programmed?

  (*b*) Does your PC support the use of special peripheral devices, such as a light pen, mouse or joystick? If so, are there special BASIC statements that allow these devices to be programmed?

  (*c*) What is the maximum number of lines that can be displayed on your monitor? What is the maximum number of characters per line?

  (*d*) How can the screen be cleared within your version of BASIC?

  (*e*) How can the cursor be positioned when a program is being executed?

  (*f*) How can vertical scrolling be initiated and controlled within your version of BASIC?

  (*g*) Does your PC support colored text? If so, how is the color specified in BASIC? Can the background color be specified separately? Is there a separate border color?

  (*h*) Is there a special command to "beep" the speaker in your version of BASIC?

  (*i*) Does your version of BASIC allow various sounds to be generated under program control? If so, what command is used to do this? How are the frequency and the duration specified?

Programming Problems

10.21 Modify the program for generating Fibonacci numbers and searching for primes (Example 7.8) so that the prime numbers appear in a color that is different from the remaining text. Have the computer "beep" whenever a prime number is displayed.

10.22 Problem 5.35 asks you to calculate student exam scores, including the class average and the deviation of each student's average about the class average. Solve this problem using the enhanced features available in your version of PC BASIC. In particular:

  (*a*) Use the function keys F1 and F2 to display the class average and the deviation of each student's average about the class average, respectively.

  (*b*) Display all of the text in the same color except the student averages, the class average and the deviation of each student's average about the class average. Display the student averages in a second color and the class average in a third color. Display the student deviations in the same color as the individual student averages.

10.23 Modify the pig Latin generator given in Example 6.22 so that it can accommodate several additional features, such as multiline text, punctuation marks, uppercase and lowercase letters, and double-letter sounds (see Prob. 7.34). Display the English text (i.e., the input data) in one color and the pig Latin (the corresponding output) in another color. Add a "beep" at the start of each pig Latin translation (each new block of output). Utilize the functions keys F1 through F3 to change the colors of the English text, the pig Latin text and the background, respectively. Use function key F4 to switch the beeping on and off.

10.24 Modify the program shown in Example 4.24 (Calculating Depreciation) so that each column of numbers is shown in a different color. Use the function keys to select the method used to calculate the depreciation (e.g., use F1 to select straight-line depreciation, F2 to select the double-declining-balance method, etc.). Display a brief menu at the bottom of the screen, indicating the purpose of each function key. Show the results of each calculation on a separate screen (i.e., clear the screen between calculations).

10.25 Modify the "greeting" program given in Example 10.2 (Programming a Light Pen) to include the use of color. In particular, display the list of languages in one color and the corresponding greeting in another. Have the computer "beep" whenever a greeting is displayed.

10.26 Rewrite the program given in Example 10.2 so that a language can be selected with the function keys rather than a light pen. Include the use of color, as described in Problem 10.25.

10.27 Rewrite the program given in Example 10.2 so that a language can be selected with a joystick rather than a light pen. Include the use of color, as described in Problem 10.25.

10.28 Solve Problem 5.36 (currency conversion) using function keys F1 and F2 to select the source and target currencies, respectively. Enhance the program by utilizing color and sound.

10.29 Repeat Problem 10.28 using each of the following programmable input devices to select a source or a target currency.

  (*a*) Light pen   (*b*) Mouse   (*c*) Joystick

Enhance your program through the effective use of color and sound.

10.30 Solve Problem 5.37 (matching countries with their capitals) using function keys F1 and F2 to select a country or a capital, respectively. Enhance the program by utilizing color and sound, as described in Problem 10.25.

10.31 Repeat Problem 10.30 using each of the following programmable input devices to select either a country or a capital.

    (*a*) Light pen   (*b*) Mouse   (*c*) Joystick

Enhance your program through the effective use of color and sound.

10.32 Modify the program given in Example 10.5 (Programming a Joystick) so that the function keys F1 and F2 can be used to select different foreground and background colors. Design the program in such a manner that different colored faces can be displayed against a uniform background. Allow the background color to be changed at any time.

10.33 Repeat Problem 10.32 using a mouse rather than a joystick.

10.34 Modify the program given in Example 10.8 so that an "up-and-down" siren sound is generated. Include a provision that automatically changes the foreground and background colors each time the siren sound is generated.

10.35 Write a BASIC program that will generate a musical scale in the key of C. Include provisions for selecting an ascending scale, a descending scale or both (i.e., a scale that does up and then down). Allow the choice to be made by selecting an appropriate function key. Display a brief menu at the bottom of the screen indicating the purpose of each available function key. (Consult your programmer's reference manual to determine the frequencies required in order to generate musical tones.)

10.36 Write a BASIC program that will play a simple melody on your computer's speaker. (Consult your programmer's reference manual to determine how musical notes can be generated with your particular computer.)

Chapter 11

Introduction to Computer Graphics

Practically all personal computers allow information to be displayed graphically as well as textually. Such displays permit the generation of many different kinds of graphs and drawings. Most PCs support multicolored graphic displays, and some allow certain types of graphic objects to be animated. The ability to generate colored, animated displays, enhanced with sound effects, provides the foundation for the wide variety of computer games that have become so popular in recent years.

Most versions of personal computer BASIC include special graphics statements that allow a variety of graphic displays to be created easily. For example, individual instructions are available for generating common shapes, such as dots, lines, rectangles, circles and ellipses. These shapes can be used to create a variety of sophisticated graphic displays that include the use of color and sound. Special statements are also available to generate animated displays. Moreover, the animation can be controlled by auxiliary input devices, such as joysticks and mice. This chapter illustrates the use of these special BASIC instructions for a number of representative graphics applications.

As in the last chapter, our emphasis will be on the use of Microsoft QuickBASIC and QBASIC as implemented on MS-DOS (i.e., IBM-compatible) PCs. It should be understood, however, that other PCs utilize Microsoft BASIC in one form or another, and therefore support features that are essentially the same as those described in this chapter.

11.1 GRAPHICS FUNDAMENTALS

We have already seen that text displays are made up of words, which are made up of individual characters (i.e., letters, symbols, etc.). Therefore we can think of characters as the fundamental elements of text displays. A similar situation exists with graphic displays, where the fundamental elements are small dots called *pixels (picture elements)*. These pixels can be combined to form more complex shapes, just as characters are combined to form words, sentences and paragraphs.

The level of detail (i.e., the *resolution*) of a graphic display is measured in terms of the largest number of horizontal and vertical pixels that can be displayed at any one time. These values will be determined by the computer's hardware. Personal computers typically support graphic displays of 640 (horizontal) by 350 (vertical) or 640 by 480 pixels. These values will vary from one computer to another. Higher resolutions (e.g., 1024 by 1024, or 4096 by 4096) can be obtained with more expensive equipment.

The maximum available number of colors is also determined by the computer's hardware. Most personal computers support at least 16 colors and some support as many as 256 different colors. A larger number of colors can be obtained with more expensive equipment. If multiple levels of resolution are available with the same equipment, then the higher the resolution, the fewer the colors.

QuickBASIC supports several different graphic modes (i.e., several different levels of resolution). Each mode is specified via the SCREEN statement. (Recall that SCREEN 0 refers to the text mode, as discussed in Sec. 10.3.) We will utilize mode 9, which is commonly referred to as *EGA graphics*. This mode provides a display of 640 (horizontal) by 350 (vertical) pixels in 16 different colors. It is commonly available on most MS-DOS PCs.

The EGA graphics mode is activated by the statement SCREEN 9. This statement must precede the generation of any graphic displays. The use of this statement requires that the computer be equipped with an EGA-compatible display adapter and an EGA-compatible monitor.

The choice of colors is specified by the COLOR statement. This statement is interpreted in a manner that is similar to the text mode, as described in Sec. 10.3. In particular, the COLOR statement can include two parameters, the first of which specifies the foreground color and the second of which specifies the background color. Border colors are not specified. Each parameter must be any integer value between 0 and 15, thus providing a choice of 16 different colors. The individual colors and their corresponding numerical parameters are the same as those used in the text mode.

0	black	8	gray
1	blue	9	light blue
2	green	10	light green
3	cyan	11	light cyan
4	red	12	light red
5	magenta	13	light magenta
6	brown	14	yellow
7	white	15	high intensity white

The foreground colors can be modified with the PALETTE statement, though this is beyond the scope of our present discussion.

The choice of a foreground color can be overridden by the individual graphics shape statements, e.g., PSET or PRESET for a point (pixel), LINE for a line or rectangle and CIRCLE for a circle or an ellipse. We will say more about the use of these statements later in this chapter.

Example 11.1

Suppose we wish to generate an EGA graphic display in QuickBASIC, with high intensity white as a foreground color and black as a background color. Then our BASIC program must contain the following statements.

```
SCREEN 9
COLOR 15, 0
```

The first instruction (SCREEN 9) specifies the EGA graphics mode (i.e., 640 horizontal pixels, 350 vertical pixels). The second instruction (COLOR 15, 0) specifies high intensity white as a foreground color and black as a background color.

11.2 POINTS AND LINES

QuickBASIC includes two statements, PSET and PRESET, that generate single points at any specified location on the screen and in any color. The first of these, PSET, can be used with a specified color, thus overriding the foreground color that is specified in the COLOR statement.

To use this statement, the word PSET must be followed by a pair of parameters, enclosed in parentheses and separated by a comma, e.g., PSET (320, 175). These parameters indicate the x and y coordinates of the point. In the EGA mode, the first parameter may range from 0 to 639 and the second parameter from 0 to 349. Point (0, 0) represents the upper-left corner of the screen, and the point (639, 349) represents the lower-right corner.

Following the pair of coordinates is an optional third parameter which indicates the color of the point, e.g., PSET (320, 175), 2. This parameter may range from 0 to 15 in mode 9. If this last parameter is not explicitly included in the PSET statement, the color will be the foreground color selected in the COLOR statement.

Example 11.2

A QuickBASIC program contains the following statements.

```
SCREEN 9
COLOR 14, 1
PSET (320, 175), 4
```

The first statement specifies EGA graphics and the second specifies a yellow foreground against a blue background. The third statement causes a red point to be generated at the center of the screen.

Example 11.3

Here is a QuickBASIC program that generates 1000 different points at random locations on the screen. EGA graphics is used. Each point is displayed in a color that is selected at random.

```
'*** RANDOM POINTS ***

CLS
SCREEN 9
COLOR 15, 0
RANDOMIZE TIMER                 'initialize the random number generator

FOR I = 1 TO 1000
    LET X = INT(640 * RND)      'generate a random x coordinate
    LET Y = INT(350 * RND)      'generate a random y coordinate
    LET CLR = 1 + INT(15 * RND) 'generate a random color
    PSET (X, Y), CLR
NEXT I

END
```

The first three lines clear the screen, set the graphics mode and establish foreground and background colors, respectively. The fourth line initializes the random number generator, using the computer's internal clock. This statement causes a different sequence of random numbers to be generated whenever the program is executed (without this last statement, the *same* sequence of random numbers would always be obtained).

The individual points are generated by the FOR - NEXT loop. The first two LET statements generate a random pair of coordinates whereas the last LET statement selects a random color. The PSET statement generates the actual point, using the current randomly assigned values.

The displays generated by graphics programs must be seen to be appreciated. Run this program and observe what happens.

Let us now turn our attention to PRESET, which is the second of the QuickBASIC statements that will generate a single point. This statement is identical to PSET except in the interpretation of the default color (i.e., the color that is automatically selected if the color parameter is not explicitly shown). Whereas the PSET statement will automatically select the foreground color specified in the COLOR statement, the PRESET statement will automatically select the background color. Thus, in some applications it may be convenient to use PSET to generate a set of points and PRESET to "erase" the points, by regenerating the same points in the background color.

Example 11.4

Consider the following statements, which are included in a QuickBASIC program.

```
SCREEN 9
COLOR 15, 1


. . . . .

PSET (320, 175), 14
FOR I=1 TO 2000 : NEXT I
PRESET (320, 175)
```

The first two statements specify EGA graphics with a high intensity white foreground and a blue background. The PSET statement causes a yellow point to be generated at the center of the screen. (Note that the color specification overrides the foreground color specified in the COLOR statement.) A brief time delay is then generated by the empty FOR - NEXT loop. Following this time delay, the yellow point is erased (i.e., it is regenerated in the blue background color) with the PRESET statement.

Many interesting and creative effects can be achieved by generating and later erasing various graphic objects within a loop. The following example illustrates a simple application of this type.

Example 11.5 Random Points

Here is a more comprehensive QuickBASIC program that draws upon some of the ideas presented in earlier examples. This program generates 1000 different points at random locations on the screen, using EGA graphics. The location and color of each point are selected at random. However, the points remain visible for only a limited period of time. Eventually, each point disappears (is "erased") and is replaced by a new point, at some other location on the screen. The overall effect is a screen that is always filled with colored, randomly spaced points, but changes constantly as old points vanish and new ones appear.

```
'*** CHANGING RANDOM POINTS ***

ON KEY(1) GOSUB BackgroundColor
KEY(1) ON

ON KEY(2) GOSUB Terminate
KEY(2) ON

DIM X(1000), Y(1000)

SCREEN 0: COLOR 15, 0: CLS
LOCATE 11, 20: PRINT "F1: Change BACKGROUND Color"
LOCATE 12, 20: PRINT "F2: END"
LOCATE 14, 20: INPUT ; "Press any key to continue", ans$

SCREEN 9: CLS
RANDOMIZE TIMER                        'initialize the random number generator
LET I = 1
```

```
DO WHILE I > 0
    PRESET (X(I), Y(I))                  'erase the old point
    LET X(I) = INT(640 * RND)            'generate a random x coordinate
    LET Y(I) = INT(350 * RND)            'generate a random y coordinate
    LET Foreground = 1 + INT(15 * RND)   'generate a random color
    PSET (X(I), Y(I)), Foreground        'generate the new point
    LET I = I + 1
    IF I > 1000 THEN I = 1               'start over
LOOP

BackgroundColor:
    LET Background = (Background + 1) MOD 16
    COLOR 15, Background
RETURN

Terminate:
END
```

The program uses function keys F1 and F2 to change the background color and to terminate the computation, respectively, as in Example 10.6. The first few statements set up the function key event traps, dimension the arrays X and Y, and generate an opening menu with instructions for the user. The program then switches to the EGA graphics mode and initializes the random number generator and the iteration counter.

The heart of the program is the infinite loop that follows. The first statement causes the current point (i.e., the Ith point) to be erased. We then obtain a new set of coordinates and a new color for the Ith point. The Ith point is then regenerated with these new parameters.

Note that the new coordinates will be stored in the X and Y arrays. This allows the current point to be recalled and erased at some later time. The erasure will not occur, however, until an additional 999 points have been generated.

The counter is incremented and its value reset to 1, if necessary, at the end of the loop. This procedure allows the loop to execute indefinitely. Remember that the computation can be terminated at any time by pressing function key F2.

Following the main loop are the two subroutines that indicate the actions to be taken when either of the function keys is pressed. The first subroutine reassigns the background color and the second terminates the computation, as in Example 10.6.

We again recommend that you execute this program and observe what happens, in order to gain a heightened appreciation for the dynamic graphic effect that is created.

QuickBASIC includes a LINE statement that allows a straight line to be drawn between any two points on the screen. Both points can be specified explicitly, or one of them can be the last point specified in a previous graphics statement.

In its first form, the keyword LINE is followed by two pairs of parameters, where each pair represents the x and y coordinates of one of the points. The coordinates are enclosed in parentheses and separated by a comma. The two points must be separated by a dash (that is, a minus sign); for example, LINE (20, 50)-(300, 150). The permissible values of the coordinates are dependent upon the particular graphics mode selected, as described earlier in this section.

The coordinates can be followed by an optional parameter indicating the color of the line, such as LINE (20, 50)-(300, 150), 1. This value will override the foreground color specified in the COLOR statement.

Example 11.6

A QuickBASIC program includes the following statements.

```
SCREEN 9
COLOR 15, 1
LINE (20, 50)-(620, 300), 14
```

The first two statements specify EGA graphics with a high intensity white foreground and a blue background. The LINE statement generates a yellow diagonal line running from upper left, i.e., point (20, 50), to lower right, i.e., point (620, 300). Note that the last parameter (14) overrides the foreground color in the COLOR statement, thus generating a line that is yellow rather than white.

The second form of the LINE statement allows the initial pair of coordinates to be omitted; e.g., LINE -(620, 300). This statement causes a line to be drawn from the point that was last referenced (in a previous statement) to the point currently specified. This form of the LINE statement is useful when drawing a sequence of interconnected lines, as illustrated in the following example.

Example 11.7 A Lightning Bolt

Here is a short QuickBASIC program that causes a red "lightning bolt" to be displayed on the screen.

```
'*** LIGHTNING BOLT ***

SCREEN 9
COLOR 15, 0
CLS

LINE (80, 30)-(270, 140), 12
LINE -(190, 140), 12
LINE -(490, 330), 12
LINE -(350, 180), 12
LINE -(450, 180), 12
LINE -(310, 30), 12
LINE -(80, 30), 12

END
```

The first two statements specify EGA graphics with a high intensity white foreground and a black background. The screen is then cleared in preparation for drawing the graphic object. These statements are followed by several LINE statements that generate seven interconnected lines to form the lightning bolt. Notice that both forms of the LINE statement are used. The first form must be used to generate the first line. Once an end point is established, however, the second form of the LINE statement is used to generate the remaining lines.

Execution of the program results in the graphic display shown in Fig. 11.1, with bright red lines against a black background.

Some versions of BASIC support other forms of the LINE statement that allow such features as the specification of a line *relative* to a previous point rather than from one absolute point to another, or the generation of a dashed line. We will not discuss these features, since they are used less often than the features described above. Consult the BASIC programming manual that accompanies your particular computer for additional information on these features.

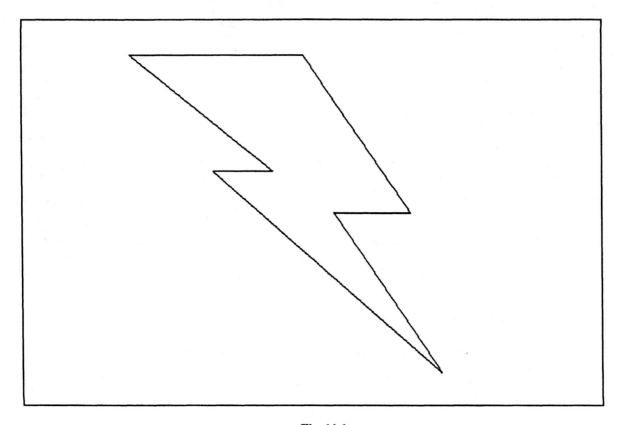

Fig. 11.1

A single LINE statement can be used to generate a complete rectangle rather than a single line. We shall see how this is accomplished in Section 11.3. First, however, let us consider some more comprehensive examples involving use of the LINE statement.

Example 11.8 Moving Lines (Kinetic Art)

We now turn our attention to a QuickBASIC program based upon the same general idea as the program shown in Example 11.5, but which generates displays that are much more dramatic.

This program generates a sequence of colored lines located randomly about the screen. The successive lines will not be generated independently of one another. Rather, the end points of successive lines will differ only by small displacements. This will result in groups of lines that form definitive patterns. Each group of lines will be displayed in a single color, selected randomly. The values selected for the end-point displacements and the foreground color will change periodically as the program continues to execute. In addition, we will include a provision so that the background color can be changed by pressing a function key.

The same number of lines will always be displayed on the screen, but each line will eventually be erased and a new line generated. Thus, the lines will appear to move around the screen in random but related patterns, with colors that change periodically. Intricate geometric patterns will be created as new lines intersect existing lines.

Here is the complete QuickBASIC program.

```
'*** MOVING LINES ***

ON KEY(1) GOSUB BackgroundColor
KEY(1) ON
```

```
ON KEY(2) GOSUB Terminate
KEY(2) ON

DEFINT A-Z
DIM X1(150), Y1(150), X2(150), Y2(150)

'opening menu (text mode)

SCREEN 0: COLOR 15, 0: CLS
LOCATE 11, 20: PRINT "F1: Change BACKGROUND Color"
LOCATE 12, 20: PRINT "F2: END"
LOCATE 14, 20: INPUT ; "Press any key to continue", ans$

'initialization (switch to graphics mode)

SCREEN 9: CLS
RANDOMIZE TIMER
LET X1 = 240: Y1 = 120: X2 = 400: Y2 = 220
LET Background = 0: ColorCount = 0: PointCount = 0: I = 1

'main loop

DO WHILE I > 0

    'erase the old line

    LINE (X1(I), Y1(I))-(X2(I), Y2(I)), Background

    IF ColorCount = 0 THEN
       LET ColorCount = 5 * (1 + INT(10 * RND))   'generate new color
       DO
          LET Foreground = 1 + INT(15 * RND)
       LOOP UNTIL Foreground <> Background
    END IF

    IF PointCount = 0 THEN                         'generate new pt increments
       LET PointCount = 5 * (1 + INT(10 * RND))
       LET DX1 = INT(19 * RND) - 9
       LET DY1 = INT(19 * RND) - 9
       LET DX2 = INT(19 * RND) - 9
       LET DY2 = INT(19 * RND) - 9
    END IF

    'generate end points for the new line

    LET X1 = X1 + DX1: IF X1 < 0 OR X1 > 639 THEN LET X1 = X1 - 2 * DX1
    LET Y1 = Y1 + DY1: IF Y1 < 0 OR Y1 > 349 THEN LET Y1 = Y1 - 2 * DY1
    LET X2 = X2 + DX2: IF X2 < 0 OR X2 > 639 THEN LET X2 = X2 - 2 * DX2
    LET Y2 = Y2 + DY2: IF Y2 < 0 OR Y2 > 349 THEN LET Y2 = Y2 - 2 * DY2

    'display the new line, then save the end points
```

```
        LINE (X1, Y1)-(X2, Y2), Foreground
        LET X1(I) = X1: Y1(I) = Y1: X2(I) = X2: Y2(I) = Y2

        FOR J = 1 TO 5000: NEXT J                    'time delay

        'adjust the counters and repeat

        LET ColorCount = ColorCount - 1: PointCount = PointCount - 1
        LET I = I + 1
        IF I > 150 THEN I = 1
    LOOP

    BackgroundColor:
        LET Background = (Background + 1) MOD 16
        COLOR Foreground, Background
    RETURN

    Terminate:
    END
```

The program begins much like the simpler program shown in Example 11.5, with function key activations and an opening menu. Notice the DEFINT statement, which causes all variables to be integer variables. Also, notice the DIM statement, which defines the integer arrays X1, Y1, X2 and Y2. These variables represent the end points of the 150 lines that will be displayed on the screen at any one time.

Following the opening menu we see an initialization block that first switches to the EGA graphics mode and then initializes the random number generator, the initial end points, the background color and the program control parameters ColorCount, PointCount and I.

The last parameter, I, is simply a line counter that is incremented during each pass through the main loop. This counter ranges from 1 to 150 and is reset to 1 when its value exceeds 150. The other two counters require some additional explanation.

ColorCount is a counter that determines when a different foreground color will be selected. ColorCount is initially set to zero, so that a new, nonzero value will be generated randomly during the first pass through the main loop. This is accompanied by a new, randomly generated value for the foreground color, represented by the variable Foreground. During each pass through the loop, ColorCount will be decreased by 1. When ColorCount has returned to zero, a new value will be generated and a new color selected, and so on.

Similarly, PointCount is a counter that determines when different values are selected for altering the displacement of successive lines. PointCount is initially set to zero so that a new, nonzero value will be generated during the first pass through the main loop. In addition, a new set of values for DX1, DY1, DX2 and DY2 will be determined when the value of PointCount is reset. These four parameters determine the displacement of the successive pairs of end points, which in turn define the locations of the successive lines. During each pass through the loop, PointCount will be decreased by 1. Once PointCount has returned to zero, a new value will be generated and a new set of displacements will be determined.

Within the main loop, the initial LINE statement erases the line defined by the Ith set of end points, which is currently stored in the array elements X1(I), Y1(I), X2(I) and Y2(I). (Note, however, that there will be no such end points during the first 150 passes through the loop.) We then test to see if ColorCount is equal to zero. If so, a new value, ranging from 5 to 50, is selected randomly. In addition, a new value, ranging from 1 to 15, is randomly assigned to Foreground, thus changing the line color. This color will remain unchanged until ColorCount again becomes equal to zero.

We then encounter a similar test for PointCount. If PointCount equals zero, a new value, ranging from 5 to 50, is generated randomly and a new set of values is selected for the displacement parameters. Each of these parameters will be assigned a separate value, ranging from −9 to +9. The displacement parameters will remain unchanged until PointCount again becomes equal to zero.

A new pair of end points for the current line, relative the previous line, is then generated. Each of the new coordinates is checked to determine if its new value is too large or too small (thus causing the end point to be located beyond the bounds of the screen). If so, the value of the coordinate is adjusted accordingly.

The new line is then generated in the current foreground color and its end points stored within the appropriate arrays. This allows the current line to be recalled and erased at some later time. The erasure will not occur, however, until an additional 149 lines have been generated. At the end of the loop are adjustments for the values of `ColorCount`, `PointCount` and `I`.

The main loop is followed by two brief subroutines that indicate the actions to be taken when either of the function keys F1 or F2 is pressed. Note that the background color will change whenever the user presses function key F1. Also, note that the loop will continue to execute indefinitely, until the user presses function key F2.

When the program is executed, random patterns are generated in a display that continuously moves about the screen. A typical pattern is shown in Fig. 11.2. You should actually run the program in order to appreciate the interesting effects that are created.

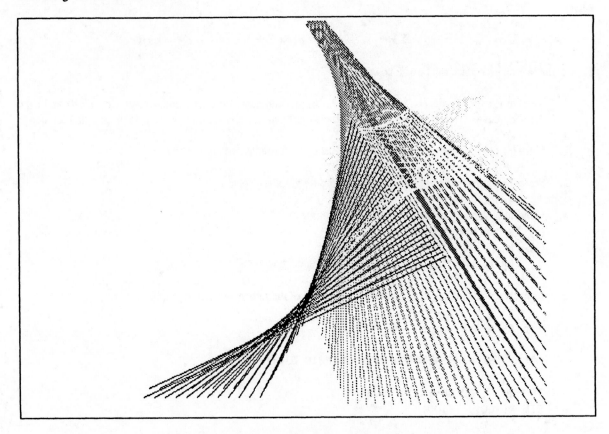

Fig. 11.2

Until now, the examples presented in this chapter have been oriented toward the use of graphic effects that are entertaining or artistic. However, graphics can also be used very effectively to generate displays that are useful in business and technical applications. This is illustrated in the next example.

Example 11.9 Linear Regression with Graphic Display

Let us now consider the problem of fitting a straight line to a given set of data points using the method of least squares, as described in Example 9.30. (This problem is often referred to as *linear regression*, though linear regression is not restricted to straight-line curve fits — it includes all of the curves discussed in Example 9.30.) We will present a

QuickBASIC program that first carries out the necessary mathematical calculations and then generates a graphic display of both the individual data points and the regression line. The graphic display will be scaled so that all of the data points are shown and the entire screen is filled, regardless of the magnitudes of the given data.

Essentially, the problem is that of fitting the linear equation

$$y = ax + b$$

to a set of data points $(x_1, y_1), (x_2, y_2), \ldots, (x_n, y_n)$ by minimizing the sum of the square errors, as discussed in Example 9.30. The unknown quantities are the values of the coefficients a and b. These values are obtained using the following formulas.

$$a = (n\, d_2 - c_1\, d_1) / (n\, c_2 - c_1^2) \qquad\qquad b = (d_1 - a\, c_1)/n$$

where

$$c_1 = \Sigma\, x_i \qquad\qquad c_2 = \Sigma\, x_i^2 \qquad\qquad d_1 = \Sigma\, y_i \qquad\qquad d_2 = \Sigma\, x_i\, y_i$$

Hence, the overall procedure will be as follows.

1. Read in the data points $(x_1,\ y_1), (x_2,\ y_2), \ldots, (x_n,\ y_n)$ and generate the cumulative sums c_1, c_2, d_1 and d_2, as defined above. While doing so, determine the largest and smallest values of x and y, in preparation for step 3.

2. Solve for the unknown coefficients a and b, using the formulas presented above.

3. Scale the data points so that they will fill the entire graphic display area.

4. Generate the actual graphic display, in three phases:
   (a) Plot and label the axes.
   (b) Plot the individual (scaled) data points.
   (c) Plot the corresponding (scaled) regression line.

5. Print the calculated regression equation at the top of the screen, above the graphic display.

The complete QuickBASIC program is shown below.

```
'*** LINEAR REGRESSION WITH GRAPHIC DISPLAY ***

SCREEN 0: COLOR 15, 0: CLS
DIM X(100), Y(100)

LOCATE 1, 20: PRINT "Straight-Line Linear Regression"
LOCATE 3, 20: PRINT "Press ENTER after last data point"
LET I = 1: C1 = 0: C2 = 0: D1 = 0: D2 = 0     'initialization
LET XMAX = -100000: YMAX = -100000: XMIN = 100000: YMIN = 100000

'data entry loop

LOCATE 6, 1
DO WHILE I > 0
    PRINT "X("; I; ") = "; : INPUT "", ans$
    LET X(I) = VAL(ans$)
```

```
        IF ans$ = "" THEN
           LET N = I - 1
           EXIT DO
        END IF

        LOCATE CSRLIN - 1, 20: PRINT "Y("; I; ") = "; : INPUT "", Y(I)
        IF X(I) > XMAX THEN XMAX = X(I)
        IF X(I) < XMIN THEN XMIN = X(I)
        IF Y(I) > YMAX THEN YMAX = Y(I)
        IF Y(I) < YMIN THEN YMIN = Y(I)

        LET C1 = C1 + X(I)
        LET C2 = C2 + X(I) ^ 2
        LET D1 = D1 + Y(I)
        LET D2 = D2 + X(I) * Y(I)
        LET I = I + 1
LOOP

'determine the unknown constants

LET A = (N * D2 - C1 * D1) / (N * C2 - C1 ^ 2)
IF ABS(A) < 1E-08 THEN A = 0
LET B = (D1 - A * C1) / N
IF ABS(B) < 1E-08 THEN B = 0

'scale the X's and Y's

FOR I = 1 TO N
   LET X(I) = 69 + INT(520 * (X(I) - XMIN) / (XMAX - XMIN))
   LET Y(I) = 284 - INT(230 * (Y(I) - YMIN) / (YMAX - YMIN))
NEXT I

LET X1 = 69                          'regression line end points
LET X2 = 589
LET Y1 = 284 - INT(230 * ((A * XMIN + B) - YMIN) / (YMAX - YMIN))
LET Y2 = 284 - INT(230 * ((A * XMAX + B) - YMIN) / (YMAX - YMIN))

'plot the graphic display

SCREEN 9
LINE (49, 299)-(589, 299)            'x-axis
FOR IX = 79 TO 569 STEP 30
   LINE (IX, 299)-(IX, 295)
NEXT IX
LOCATE 23, 39: PRINT "x";

LINE (49, 49)-(49, 299)              'y-axis
FOR IY = 74 TO 274 STEP 25
   LINE (49, IY)-(54, IY)
NEXT IY
LOCATE 13, 3: PRINT "y";
```

```
FOR I = 1 TO N                          'plot the data points
   PSET (X(I), Y(I))
   LINE (X(I), Y(I) - 2)-(X(I) - 4, Y(I) + 2)
   LINE -(X(I) + 4, Y(I) + 2)
   LINE -(X(I), Y(I) - 2)
NEXT I

LINE (X1, Y1)-(X2, Y2)                  'plot the regression line

LOCATE 5, 15: PRINT "y ="; A; "* x "; 'display the regression equation
IF B >= 0 THEN
   PRINT "+"; B
ELSE
   PRINT "-"; ABS(B)
END IF

END
```

The first six statements clear the screen, generate a program heading, define the required arrays and initialize key variables. The data input routine is provided by the DO - LOOP structure that follows. The program allows an unspecified number of data points to be entered. The data entry procedure continues until the user presses the RETURN (i.e., the ENTER) key when prompted for X(I), thus entering an empty (null) string. The individual data points are scanned as they are entered to determine the largest and smallest values of X(I) and Y(I).

The slope (*a*) and the y-intercept (*b*) of the desired regression line are determined in the block of statements following the DO - LOOP structure. The data points are then scaled so that they, together with the derived regression line, will be plotted in the center of the graphic display area. A scaled set of end points for the calculated regression line is also determined. Note that the largest and smallest values of X(I) and Y(I), determined within the data entry procedure, are used to carry out the scaling.

The actual graphic display is then generated in three different sections. First the axes, and their corresponding tick marks, are generated. The individual data points are then plotted, followed by the resulting regression line. Notice that each data point is enclosed in a small triangle so that it is clearly visible on the screen. Hence, the PSET and LINE statements are both used.

Finally, the equation for the calculated regression line is displayed in the upper-left portion of the screen. (Note that this is a *text* display, though it is being generated in the graphics mode.)

Now suppose the program is used to process the following set of data.

i	x_i	y_i
1	10	225
2	20	287
3	30	429
4	40	542
5	50	587
6	60	744
7	70	831
8	80	880

When the program is executed, the following data-entry screen appears. The input data provided by the user have been underlined for clarity. Notice the position of the flashing cursor following the prompt for X(9). Since all of the data have been entered at this point, the user simply presses the RETURN (i.e., the ENTER) key in response to the prompt, thus ending the data-entry phase.

Straight-Line Linear Regression

Press ENTER after last data point

```
X( 1 ) = 10          Y( 1 ) = 225
X( 2 ) = 20          Y( 2 ) = 287
X( 3 ) = 30          Y( 3 ) = 429
X( 4 ) = 40          Y( 4 ) = 542
X( 5 ) = 50          Y( 5 ) = 587
X( 6 ) = 60          Y( 6 ) = 744
X( 7 ) = 70          Y( 7 ) = 831
X( 8 ) = 80          Y( 8 ) = 880
X( 9 ) = __
```

Figure 11.3 shows the corresponding graphic display. We see that the equation for the calculated regression line is $y = 9.875\,x + 121.25$. The line that is drawn through the given data points is generated by this equation, though the displayed line has been scaled to fill the screen. The graphic display illustrates the accuracy with which the calculated regression line represents the given data points.

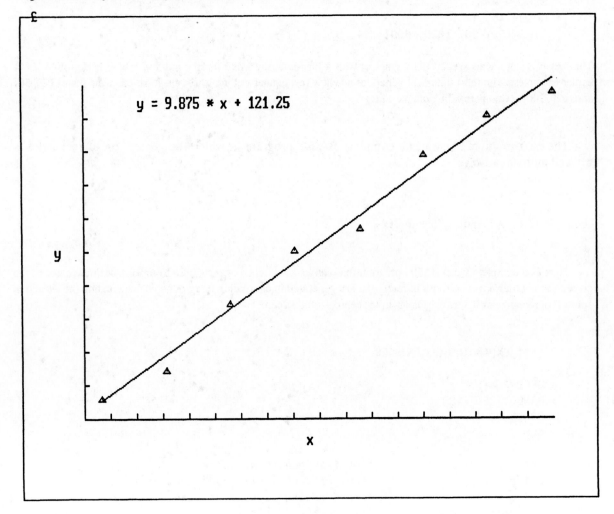

Fig. 11.3

11.3 SHAPES

Most versions of BASIC implemented on personal computers include statements that allow simple shapes to be drawn. For example, QuickBASIC includes a special form of the LINE statement that will generate rectangles and a CIRCLE statement that can generate circles and ellipses. These objects can be filled with an available color if desired. Many interesting graphic effects can be created by combining these objects in different ways.

Consider, for example, the LINE statement discussed in the last section. If the statement ends with the letter B, e.g., LINE (20, 50)-(620, 300), 14, B, then the two pairs of coordinates will be interpreted as the opposite corners of a rectangle (i.e., a "box"). Hence, a rectangle whose diagonal connects these two points will be drawn in the indicated color.

Example 11.10

A QuickBASIC program contains the following statements.

```
SCREEN 9
COLOR 15, 1
LINE (20, 50)-(620, 300), 14, B
```

The first two statements specify EGA graphics with a high-intensity white foreground and a blue background, as in earlier examples. The third statement generates a yellow rectangular outline whose diagonal connects points (20, 50) and (620, 300). (Compare with Example 11.6.)

The next example illustrates a complete BASIC program in which the generation of rectangles is utilized more creatively.

Example 11.11 Expanding Rectangles

Here is a complete QuickBASIC program that causes a sequence of rectangles to move from the center of the screen to the outer edges. Groups of rectangles are generated in alternating foreground colors, creating the illusion of "pulses" of rectangular shapes originating at the center of the screen.

```
'*** EXPANDING RECTANGLES ***

DEFINT A-Z
RANDOMIZE TIMER
SCREEN 9
CLS

LET clr = 15            'initial foreground color
LET p = 0               'draw rectangle size constant
LET q = -60             'erase rectangle size constant
LET delay = 20000       'time delay constant
```

```
'main loop

DO WHILE p >= 0
    LET x1 = 320 - 3 * p: LET y1 = 175 - 1.7 * p
    LET x2 = 320 + 3 * p: LET y2 = 175 + 1.7 * p
    LINE (x1, y1)-(x2, y2), clr, B                  'draw a rectangle
    FOR i = 1 TO delay: NEXT i                      'time delay

    IF q >= 0 THEN
        LET u1 = 320 - 3 * q: LET v1 = 175 - 1.7 * q
        LET u2 = 320 + 3 * q: LET v2 = 175 + 1.7 * q
        LINE (u1, v1)-(u2, v2), 0, B                'erase a rectangle
        FOR i = 1 TO delay: NEXT i                  'time delay
    END IF

    LET p = p + 5
    IF p > 100 THEN
        LET p = 0                                   'reset the draw offset
        LET clr = 1 + INT(15 * RND)                 'reset the color
    END IF

    LET q = q + 5
    IF q > 100 THEN LET q = 0                       'reset the erase offset
LOOP

END
```

The first group of statements defines all variables to be integer-type variables, initializes the random number generator, sets the graphics mode and clears the screen. The following group of statements initializes various program parameters, as explained by the accompanying comments.

The main loop begins by generating a rectangle screen whose size is determined by the value assigned to p. Initially $p = 0$, causing the first rectangle to appear as a dot at the center of the screen. The color of each rectangle is determined by the value assigned to clr (initially 15, which corresponds to high-intensity white). The generation of the rectangle is followed by an empty FOR - NEXT loop so that the newly drawn rectangle can be viewed before the screen again changes.

Another rectangle is then generated, provided q is not assigned a negative value. Now, however, the rectangle will be generated in the background color (black). The size of this rectangle will be determined by the value assigned to q. (Note that q is initially assigned a negative value in order to delay the generation of this second rectangle. Thereafter, q increases and remains nonnegative.) Since p and q will always differ in magnitude, this later rectangle will not coincide with the first rectangle generated in the current pass through the loop. The effect will be to erase one of the rectangles drawn in a previous pass through the loop. The erasure is followed by another empty FOR - NEXT loop, so that the screen can be viewed before it is again altered. Note that the loop will continue to execute indefinitely.

We then increment the values assigned to p and q, resetting each parameter to zero if its value exceeds 100. In addition, a new foreground color is generated randomly whenever p is reset to zero.

Figure 11.4 illustrates the type of graphic display that is generated once the program begins execution. As with other programs of this type, however, you are encouraged to run the program in order to fully appreciate the dynamic effects that are created.

Now suppose that a LINE statement ends with the letters BF rather than simply B, for example, LINE (20, 50)-(620, 300), 14, BF. The last letter, F, represents "fill." This parameter causes the rectangle (generated by the parameter B) to be filled with the specified foreground color.

Fig. 11.4

Example 11.12

A QuickBASIC program contains the following statements.

```
SCREEN 9
COLOR 15, 1
LINE (20, 50)-(620, 300), 14, BF
```

The first two statements specify EGA graphics with a high-intensity white foreground and a blue background, as in Examples 11.6 and 11.10. The third statement generates a solid yellow rectangle whose diagonal connects the points (20, 50) and (620, 300). (Compare with Examples 11.6 and 11.10.)

Example 11.13 Random Blocks

In this example we will generate objects that appear and later vanish at random locations in space, as in Example 11.5. Now, however, we will use small, randomly colored blocks (i.e., rectangles) rather than dots. The size, the color and the location of each block will be generated randomly.

The basic idea is the same as that used in Example 11.5. Thus, the end points of each block will be stored in a set of arrays. This will allow each block to be "erased" (i.e., redrawn in the current background color) once 999 additional blocks have been generated. We will also include provisions for changing the background color by pressing function key F1 and for terminating the computation by pressing function key F2, as in Example 11.5.

Here is the complete QuickBASIC program.

```
'*** CHANGING RANDOM BLOCKS ***

ON KEY(1) GOSUB BackgroundColor
KEY(1) ON

ON KEY(2) GOSUB Terminate
KEY(2) ON

DIM X1(1000), Y1(1000), X2(1000), Y2(1000)

SCREEN 0: COLOR 15, 0: CLS
LOCATE 11, 20: PRINT "F1: Change BACKGROUND Color"
LOCATE 12, 20: PRINT "F2: END"
LOCATE 14, 20: INPUT ; "Press any key to continue", ans$

SCREEN 9: CLS
RANDOMIZE TIMER                      'initialize the random number generator
LET MaxWidth = 10
LET MaxHeight = 8
LET I = 1

DO WHILE I > 0
    LINE (X1(I), Y1(I))-(X2(I), Y2(I)), Background, BF        'erase old rect

    LET X = INT((640 - MaxWidth) * RND) + MaxWidth / 2        'new x coordinate
    LET Y = INT((350 - MaxHeight) * RND) + MaxHeight / 2      'new y coordinate
    LET f = RND
    LET X1(I) = X - f * MaxWidth / 2: Y1(I) = Y - f * MaxHeight / 2
    LET X2(I) = X + f * MaxWidth / 2: Y2(I) = Y + f * MaxHeight / 2
    DO
        LET Foreground = INT(16 * RND)                        'new color
    LOOP UNTIL Foreground <> Background

    LINE (X1(I), Y1(I))-(X2(I), Y2(I)), Foreground, BF        'draw new rect
    LET I = I + 1
    IF I > 1000 THEN I = 1                                    'start over
LOOP

BackgroundColor:
    LET Background = (Background + 1) MOD 16
    COLOR 15, Background
RETURN

Terminate:
END
```

The similarity between this program and that shown in Example 11.5 should be readily apparent. Now, however, we use LINE statements rather than PSET and PRESET. Note the appearance of the symbols BF at the end of each LINE statement. This enables each LINE statement to generate a filled block in the specified color.

Notice also that the width of each block is given by f * Maxwidth, where f is a randomly generated value between 0 and 1. Similarly, the height of each block is given by f * Maxheight. In addition, the location of each block (i.e., the values for X and Y) and the color of each block (as specified by Foreground) are generated randomly. Though the foreground color is selected randomly, it is required to be different than the current background color.

Execution of the program results in a display similar to that shown in Fig. 11.5.

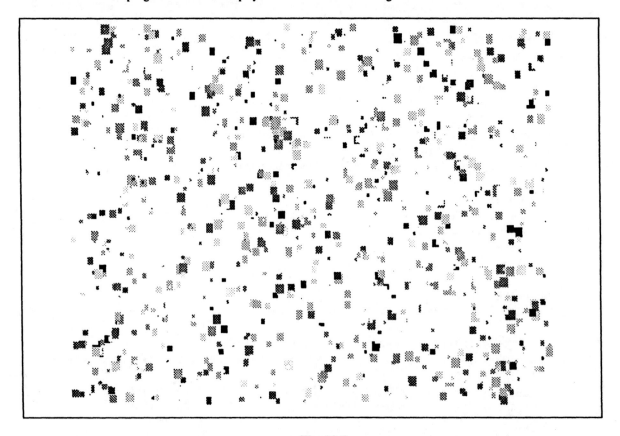

Fig. 11.5

As with other programs of this type, you are urged to run this program to appreciate the dynamic patterns that are created.

QuickBASIC includes a CIRCLE statement, which permits circles, arcs and ellipses to be drawn. In its simplest form, this statement consists of the word CIRCLE, followed by a pair of coordinates enclosed in parentheses and separated by a comma. The coordinates must be followed by a value for the radius; for example, CIRCLE (320, 175), 80. An integer indicating the choice of color may appear after the radius as an option, e.g., CIRCLE (320, 175), 80, 14.

Example 11.14

A QuickBASIC program contains the following statements.

```
SCREEN 9
COLOR 15, 1
CIRCLE (320, 175), 80, 14
```

The first two statements specify EGA graphics with a high-intensity white foreground and a blue background. The third statement generates a yellow circle, centered at the middle of the screen with a radius of 80 pixels.

Example 11.15 Expanding Circles

We now present a QuickBASIC program that causes a sequence of expanding circles to be generated. Each circle starts at the center of the screen and moves radially outward toward the edge. Each circle will be drawn in a different color that is selected at random. As successive circles are generated, the new circles create interference with the previous circles, thus forming interesting and colorful patterns.

As in other examples of this type, we will include a provision for changing the background color by pressing function key F1. Similarly, we will allow the computation to be terminated by pressing function key F2. The random foreground colors will be generated in such a manner that they always differ from the current background color.

The complete QuickBASIC program is shown below.

```
'*** EXPANDING CIRCLES ***

ON KEY(1) GOSUB BackgroundColor
KEY(1) ON

ON KEY(2) GOSUB Terminate
KEY(2) ON

SCREEN 0: COLOR 15, 0: CLS
LOCATE 11, 20: PRINT "F1: Change BACKGROUND Color"
LOCATE 12, 20: PRINT "F2: END"
LOCATE 14, 20: INPUT ; "Press any key to continue", ans$

SCREEN 9: CLS
RANDOMIZE TIMER
LET Foreground = 1: Background = 0
LET flag = 1
LINE (82, 0)-(558, 349), 15, B                 'rectangular outline

DO WHILE flag > 0
   FOR Radius = 1 TO 235
      CIRCLE (320, 175), Radius, Foreground     'draw circle
   NEXT Radius

   DO
      LET Foreground = INT(16 * RND)            'new foreground color
   LOOP UNTIL Foreground <> Background
LOOP

BackgroundColor:
   LET Background = (Background + 1) MOD 16
   LINE (84, 2)-(556, 347), Background, BF      'new background in rectangle
RETURN

Terminate:
END
```

The overall program logic is very straightforward. The initial groups of statements consist of event-trapping (function key) activations, an opening text menu and a block of initialization statements. Notice the LINE statement that creates a rectangular outline (actually, a square outline) in high-intensity white against a black background. The two x-values (82 and 558) are selected so that the rectangle will appear as a square on the screen. (The number of horizontal pixels, $558 - 82 = 476$, is 4/3 the number of vertical pixels, $349 - 0 = 349$. This value is known as the *aspect ratio*.)

The main loop has two components: a FOR - NEXT loop that draws the expanding circles in the stated foreground colors, and a DO - LOOP structure that resets the foreground color to something other than the current background color after each expanding circle has been drawn. Notice the maximum value of the radius used in the CIRCLE statement (235 pixels). This value is obtained by multiplying the maximum y-value (175 pixels) by the aspect ratio (4/3).

The program ends with the two subroutines that are required for the function key event trapping. Note that the subroutine labeled BackgroundColor contains a LINE statement rather than a COLOR statement, as in the programs presented in previous examples. The LINE statement includes the symbols BF, which results in a rectangle (actually, a square) filled with the current background color. The idea here is to change the background color only of the square containing the expanding circles rather than the entire screen.

Figure 11.6 indicates the type of patterns that are generated by this program. Remember, however, that the circles expand constantly as the program executes. Thus, you should observe the program in execution in order to appreciate what happens.

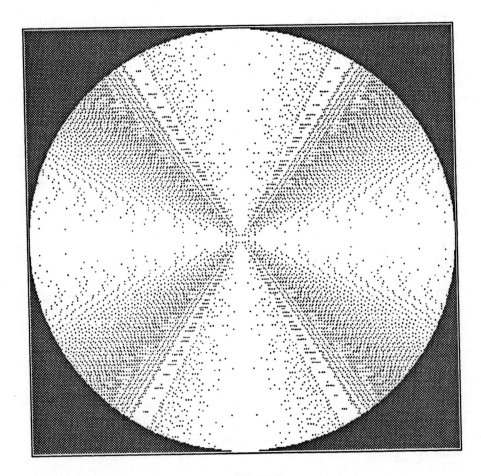

Fig. 11.6

The CIRCLE statement, unlike the LINE statement, does not include a provision for filling the circle with a color other than the background color. However, QuickBASIC also includes the PAINT statement, which allows any closed shape (including circles, ellipses and rectangles) to be filled with other colors. This statement consists of the word PAINT, followed by a pair of coordinates enclosed in parentheses and separated by a comma, e.g., PAINT (320, 175). The coordinates can represent any enclosed point within the shape that is to be filled.

The coordinates may be followed by two integers that specify the fill color and the outline color, respectively; for example, PAINT (320, 175), 14, 15. If these colors are not specified, the current foreground color will automatically be selected.

Example 11.16 A Filled Lightning Bolt

Let us again examine the program shown in Example 11.7, which generates a "lightning bolt" (see Fig. 11.1). Suppose that we now want the lightning bolt to appear in yellow against a blue background. To do so, we change the COLOR statement to COLOR 15, 1, remove the color specifications from the LINE statements and add the following PAINT statement to the program.

```
PAINT (100, 40), 14, 15
```

The coordinates for the PAINT statement represent a point that is known to be enclosed within the closed figure. (Any other enclosed point would be equally satisfactory.)

The complete QuickBASIC program is shown below.

```
'*** FILLED LIGHTNING BOLT ***

SCREEN 9
COLOR 15, 1
CLS

LINE (80, 30)-(270, 140)
LINE -(190, 140)
LINE -(490, 330)
LINE -(350, 180)
LINE -(450, 180)
LINE -(310, 30)
LINE -(80, 30)

PAINT (100, 40), 14, 15

END
```

Figure 11.7 shows the figure that is generated by this program (compare with Fig. 11.1). Remember, however, that the figure will appear in yellow against a blue background when the program is run on a computer with a color monitor.

The object to be filled in must match the boundary color specified in the PAINT statement. Thus, if the point specified by the PAINT statement is contained within more than one object and each object has a different color, the boundary color will determine which object will be filled.

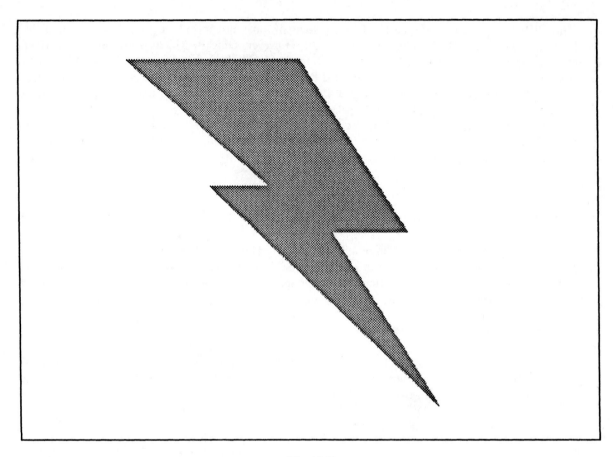

Fig. 11.7

Example 11.17

Now suppose that a QuickBASIC program contains the following five statements.

```
SCREEN 9
COLOR 15, 0
CIRCLE (320, 175), 80, 3
CIRCLE (320, 175), 60, 5
PAINT (320, 175), 14, 3
```

The CIRCLE statements cause two concentric circles to be generated. The outer circle will be cyan with a radius of 80, and the inner circle will be magenta with a radius of 60. The PAINT statement will cause the *outer* circle to be filled with color number 14 (yellow), since the boundary color in the PAINT statement (i.e., color number 3) coincides with the color specified in the first CIRCLE statement.

The CIRCLE statement can be used to generate *portions* of circles (arcs) as well as full circles. To do so, the color parameter must be followed by two additional parameters: a starting angle, and an ending angle. These angles are measured in the traditional geometric sense, increasing in the counterclockwise direction from the right half of the horizontal axis (i.e., the right half of the abscissa). Both angles must be expressed in *radians*, and therefore must fall within the range of 0 to 2π; for example, the semicircle
CIRCLE (320, 175), 80, 14, 0, 3.14.

If a value for the color parameter is not included in the CIRCLE statement but the starting and ending angles are included, then the value for the radius must be followed by two commas, for example, CIRCLE (320, 175), 80,, 0, 3.14. The two consecutive commas denote an empty color parameter.

Example 11.18

The following statements are included in a QuickBASIC program.

```
SCREEN 9
COLOR 15, 1
CIRCLE (160, 100), 80, 14, 0, 3.14
```

The first two statements specify EGA graphics with a high-intensity white foreground and a blue background. The third statement generates the top half of a yellow circle, with a radius of 80 pixels. Note that the starting and ending angles are 0 and π radians, respectively.

If the last statement is replaced with

```
CIRCLE (320, 175), 80, 14, 3.14, 0
```

then the *bottom* half of a yellow circle would be generated, since the starting and ending angles are π and 2π, respectively (0 is equivalent to 2π). This same effect could be achieved by writing

```
CIRCLE (320, 175), 80, 14, 3.14, 6.28
```

Now suppose that the original CIRCLE statement is replaced with

```
CIRCLE (320, 175), 80,, 0, 3.14
```

This statement would generate the top half of a circle but in high-intensity white rather than yellow, since a value for the color parameter is not explicitly specified.

The starting and ending angles in the CIRCLE statement can be negative as well as positive; for example, CIRCLE (320, 175), 80, 14, -3.14, -6.28. Negative angles will be interpreted as though they are positive, in the geometric sense. Now, however, each end point will be connected to the center of the circle, thus forming a pie-shaped sector.

Example 11.19

Now suppose that the QuickBASIC program described in the last example contained the statements

```
SCREEN 9
COLOR 14, 1
CIRCLE (320, 175), 80, 14,- 3.14,- 6.28
```

The CIRCLE statement will now generate the bottom half of a yellow circle, with a horizontal line connecting the two end points.

Example 11.20

The following statements will generate a figure that is familiar to many video-game buffs.

```
SCREEN 9
COLOR 13, 1
LET PI = 3.14159
CIRCLE (320, 175), 80, , -PI / 4, -2 * PI
CIRCLE (340, 136), 8
PAINT (320, 180), 13
END
```

Note that the figure will be bright magenta against a blue background.

Example 11.21 A Pie Chart Generator

A "pie chart" is a circular graph that is generally used to represent data expressed in the form of percentages. Each piece of information (i.e., each percentage) is represented in terms of a "pie-shaped" circular sector. The circumference of each sector is proportional to the value of the corresponding data point. Hence, the value 40 would be represented by a circular sector whose circumference is 40 percent of the entire circle.

Shown below is a complete pie chart generation program written in QuickBASIC. The data are entered as sets, where each data set consists of a title and a numeric value for the percentage. Hence, each sector within the pie chart will be labeled by an appropriate title.

This program will generate a pie chart containing as many as six sectors. The program consists of five main sections: a heading and initialization section, two data-entry sections, a high-resolution graphics section that generates the actual pie chart and a section that labels each of the sectors.

```
'*** PIE CHART GENERATOR ***

DIM title$(6), percent(6), angle(6)
SCREEN 0: COLOR 15, 0: CLS
LET pi = 3.14159
LET flag = 1

'enter number of sectors (1 - 6)

DO WHILE flag > 0
   PRINT "Pie Chart Generator"
   INPUT "Enter number of sectors (1-6): ", n
   IF n > 0 AND n < 7 THEN
      PRINT
      EXIT DO
   END IF
   BEEP: CLS
   'LOCATE 2, 32: PRINT " "
LOOP
```

```
'enter data for each sector

DO WHILE flag > 0
    LET sum = 0
    FOR i = 1 TO n
        PRINT "Sector"; i; SPC(8);
        INPUT "Title: ", title$(i)
        LOCATE CSRLIN - 1, 40: INPUT "Percent: ", percent(i)
        LET sum = sum + percent(i)
    NEXT i
    IF sum > 99.9 AND sum < 100.1 THEN EXIT DO
    BEEP: CLS
    PRINT "Percentages do not sum to 100 - Please try again"
    PRINT
LOOP

'generate the pie chart

SCREEN 9: COLOR 15, 1
LET a1 = 0
FOR i = 1 TO n
    LET a2 = a1 + 2 * pi * percent(i) / 100
    LET angle(i) = (a1 + a2) / 2
    CIRCLE (320, 175), 200, 15, -a1, -a2
    LET a1 = a2
NEXT i

'label the sectors

FOR i = 1 TO n
    LET col = (320 + 80 * COS(angle(i))) \ 8
    IF angle(i) > pi / 2 AND angle(i) < 3 * pi / 2 THEN LET col = col - 6
    LET row = (96 - 32 * SIN(angle(i))) \ 8
    IF angle(i) >= pi THEN row = row + 2
    LOCATE row, col: PRINT percent(i); "%"

    LET col = (320 + 160 * COS(angle(i))) \ 8 + 6
    IF angle(i) > pi / 2 AND angle(i) < 3 * pi / 2 THEN LET col = col - 22
    LET row = (96 - 80 * SIN(angle(i))) \ 8
    IF angle(i) >= pi THEN LET row = row + 3
    LOCATE row, col: PRINT title$(i);
NEXT i

END
```

The first section of the program defines several arrays, specifies the mode (text) and the color scheme (high-intensity white against black) and initializes two variables. The second section creates the dialog necessary to enter the number of sectors — a value between 1 and 6. Note that this routine contains a simple error trap, so that the user is repeatedly prompted for the same information until a value is entered that falls within the proper range.

The third section creates the dialog required to enter the data for each sector. This routine also creates a simple error trap, requiring the user to enter percentages that sum (approximately) to 100 percent. The user is repeatedly prompted for this information until a satisfactory set of values is entered.

The pie chart is generated in the fourth section. This section first switches to EGA graphics, with high-intensity white against a blue background. The FOR - NEXT loop then generates the individual sectors of the pie chart. The starting angle, a1, will always be known. Hence, the ending angle, a2, is then calculated and a representative average angle, angle(i), is determined. This last value is stored in an array, for later use when the pie chart is labeled, and the sector itself is generated. (Note that the last two parameters in the CIRCLE statement have negative starting and ending values, thus creating the pie-shaped sectors. The value of the starting angle is then reassigned, in preparation for the next sector.

The last section causes the pie chart to be labeled. This is carried out while the program remains in the graphics mode. The location of each percentage is determined, making use of the average angles calculated in the previous section, and the corresponding percentage is displayed. Similarly, the location of each sector title is determined and the corresponding sector is displayed. The entire pie chart will have been generated, with appropriate labels, upon completion of this section.

Now suppose that the program is executed using the following input data, which represent the sources of revenue for a large, state-related university.

Source of Revenue	_Percentage_
Tuition	45
State aid	25
Research	15
Gifts	8
Other	7

The input dialog is illustrated below. The user's responses are underlined.

```
Pie Chart Generator
Enter number of sectors (1-6): 5

Sector 1        Title: Tuition      Percent: 45
Sector 2        Title: State Aid    Percent: 25
Sector 3        Title: Research     Percent: 15
Sector 4        Title: Gifts        Percent: 8
Sector 5        Title: Other        Percent: 7
```

Figure 11.8 shows the resulting pie chart.

There is one additional parameter associated with the CIRCLE statement which has not been discussed. This is the *aspect* parameter. It is used to create ellipses and elliptical arcs rather than circles and circular arcs.

The aspect parameter must follow the starting and ending angles in the CIRCLE statement; for example, CIRCLE (320, 175), 80, 14, 0, 3.14, 2. It must be a positive number (not necessarily an integer) or an expression resulting in a positive numerical value. The default value results in a figure that is circular, or very nearly so. (The value required to produce a perfect circle will vary from one graphics mode to another.) A smaller value will generate a horizontal ellipse, whereas a larger value will generate a vertical ellipse. The more the aspect parameter differs from the default value, the greater the eccentricity.

When the CIRCLE statement is used to generate an ellipse or an elliptical arc, the radius parameter refers to the length of the major axis (i.e., the largest axis).

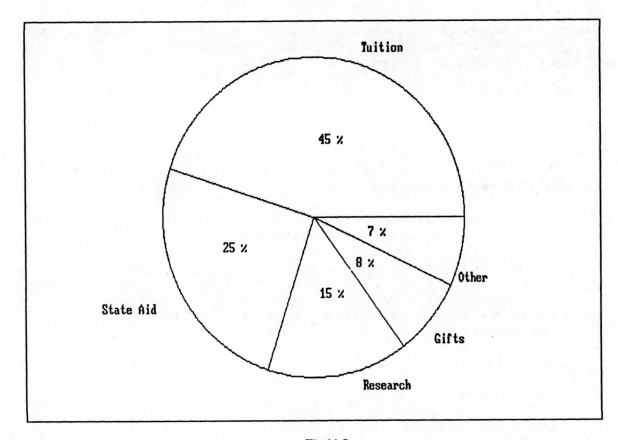

Fig 11.8

Example 11.22

The following statements are included in a QuickBASIC program.

```
SCREEN 9
COLOR 15, 1
LET PI=3.14159
CIRCLE (320, 175), 80, 14, 0, PI, .5
```

This group of statements generates a yellow elliptical arc that ranges from 0 to π. The value of the aspect parameter in the CIRCLE statement is less than the default (which is 4/3 x 350/640 = 0.729). Hence, the major axis of the elliptical arc will be horizontal, with a length of 80 pixels.

Example 11.23

Now suppose that a QuickBASIC program contains the following statements.

```
SCREEN 9
COLOR 15, 0
CIRCLE (320, 175), 100, , , , .5
```

These statements generate a high-intensity white horizontal ellipse at the center of the screen (note that high-intensity white is the default color, corresponding to a value of 15). The major axis will be 100 units long.

Suppose the CIRCLE statement is changed to

```
CIRCLE (320, 175), 100, , , , 2
```

The ellipse will now be vertical rather than horizontal.

Example 11.24 Blimp with Animated Text

Here is a QuickBASIC program that generates a drawing of a blimp. At the center of the blimp is an area that displays an animated message (in this case, *READ SCHAUM'S OUTLINES*).

```
'*** ANIMATED BLIMP ***

SCREEN 9: COLOR 15, 1: CLS
LET text$ = "R E A D   S C H A U M ' S   O U T L I N E S"
LET message$ = SPACE$(26) + text$ + SPACE$(22)
LET delay = 12000
LET flag = 1

'draw the blimp

CIRCLE (280, 175), 270, , , , .35      'body
PAINT (280, 175), 7, 15
CIRCLE (280, 175), 270, , , , .25
CIRCLE (280, 175), 270, , , , .15

LINE (460, 105)-(500, 65)              'top vertical fin
LINE -(629, 65)
LINE -(550, 175)
PAINT (500, 100), 7, 15
                                       'bottom vertical fin
LINE (460, 245)-(500, 285)
LINE -(629, 285)
LINE -(550, 175)
PAINT (500, 250), 7, 15


LINE (460, 174)-(629, 175), 15, BF     'horizontal fin

LINE (220, 268)-(235, 288)             'gondola
LINE -(325, 288)
LINE -(340, 268)
CIRCLE (255, 278), 5, , , , .5
CIRCLE (280, 278), 5, , , , .5
CIRCLE (305, 278), 5, , , , .5
PAINT (300, 286), 7, 15
PAINT (255, 278), 1, 15
PAINT (280, 278), 1, 15
PAINT (305, 278), 1, 15
```

```
LINE (180, 165)-(380, 185), 15, B      'message area

'generate the message

DO WHILE flag > 0
   FOR i = 1 TO 70
      LOCATE 13, 24: PRINT MID$(message$, i, 24);
      FOR count = 1 TO delay: NEXT count              'time delay
      LOCATE 13, 24: PRINT SPACE$(24);
   NEXT i
LOOP

END
```

The program begins by invoking EGA graphics with a high-intensity white foreground against a blue background. This is followed by several initialization statements. The body of the blimp is then created by three CIRCLE statements that generate three concentric ellipses. Several LINE statements then generate the tail section (i.e., the fins) and the undercarriage (the gondola). Three additional CIRCLE statements generate the portholes within the undercarriage. The last LINE statement generates a rectangle, within which the moving message will be displayed.

Note that several PAINT statements are interspersed within the CIRCLE and LINE statements. These statements cause the various objects that comprise the blimp to be displayed in white (actually, a light gray). This provides contrast for the objects that are outlined in high-intensity white and displayed against a blue background.

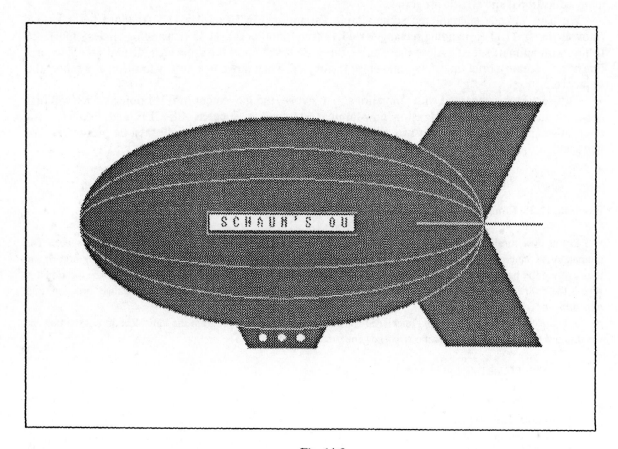

Fig. 11.9

The DO - LOOP structure at the end of the program generates the animated message. Note that this group of statements involves the use of the MID$ function within a FOR - NEXT loop. The essential idea is to display 24 characters of the message at any one time. However, each pass through the loop will result in the group of characters being shifted one character to the right. Following the printing of each group of characters there is a short time delay. The display area is then cleared in preparation for the next group of characters. The overall DO - LOOP structure causes the FOR - NEXT loop to be repeated, thus causing the animated message to continue indefinitely.

Figure 11.9 illustrates a typical display. Remember, however, that the display is constantly in motion when the program is executed.

QuickBASIC also includes the DRAW statement, which allows a complex shape to be defined in terms of a string. For example, the statement DRAW "R100 D50 L100 U50" defines a horizontal rectangle, by moving right 100 units, down 50 units, left 100 units and then up 50 units. Execution of this statement will automatically generate the rectangle.

We will not discuss the DRAW statement in any detail within this book, as the rules for defining the shape strings are relatively complex. For more information on this subject, the reader is referred to the BASIC reference manual that is available for your particular computer.

11.4 ANIMATIONS

One of the most interesting and entertaining applications of personal computers is that of animated displays. Such applications provide a basis for many computer games and they are an important part of many educational and artistic programs.

We have already encountered some simple animations, in Examples 11.5 (random points), 11.8 (moving lines), 11.11 (expanding rectangles), 11.13 (random blocks), 11.15 (expanding circles) and 11.24 (blimp with animated text). All of these animations are based upon the same idea: display an object or a line of text, create a brief time delay, and erase the object. Then move to a nearby location and repeat the sequence.

This section is concerned with animations that involve the movement of filled objects. We will first see how this is accomplished using now-familiar statements, such as CIRCLE and PAINT. An alternative approach, based upon two new statements — GET and PUT — will then be presented. We will see that the second approach offers some distinct advantages over the first one.

Example 11.25 Simulation of a Bouncing Ball

Let us now consider a simple animation in which a ball is allowed to move freely within a confined space. The animation is created by first displaying the ball at some particular location, filling it with a color, pausing briefly, and then erasing the ball (i.e., redisplaying the ball using the background color). We then move to a nearby location and repeat the entire procedure. Whenever a barrier (i.e., a "wall") is encountered, the ball will change direction, thus appearing to "bounce" off the wall.

A complete program, written in QuickBASIC is shown below. In this program the initial location of the ball and the distance between successive locations will be generated randomly.

```
'*** BOUNCING BALL ***

DEFINT A-Z
RANDOMIZE TIMER
LET delay = 5000
LET flag = 1
```

```
      SCREEN 9: COLOR 15, 1: CLS
      LINE (0, 0)-(639, 349), , B          'border
      LINE (10, 7)-(629, 342), , B
      PAINT (5, 2)

                                           'define an initial position

      LET x = 20 + INT(600 * RND)
      LET y = 20 + INT(310 * RND)
      LET dx = INT(21 * RND) - 10
      LET dy = INT(21 * RND) - 10


      'main loop

      DO WHILE flag > 0
         CIRCLE (x, y), 12, 1              'erase the ball
         PAINT (x, y), 1

         LET x1 = x + dx                   'new coordinates
         LET y1 = y + dy

         IF x1 < 23 THEN                   'hit the left wall
            LET x1 = 23
            LET dx = -dx
         ELSEIF x1 > 616 THEN              'hit the right wall
            LET x1 = 616
            LET dx = -dx
         END IF

         IF y1 < 18 THEN                   'hit the top
            LET y1 = 18
            LET dy = -dy
         ELSEIF y1 > 331 THEN              'hit the bottom
            LET y1 = 331
            LET dy = -dy
         END IF

         CIRCLE (x1, y1), 12               'redraw the ball
         PAINT (x1, y1)
         LET x = x1
         LET y = y1
         FOR i = 1 TO delay: NEXT i        'time delay
      LOOP

      END
```

The program begins in the usual manner, by declaring all variables to be integers, initializing the random number generator and several variables and then switching to the EGA graphics mode with a high-intensity white foreground and a blue background. The program then draws a solid white rectangle around the edge of the screen. This rectangle serves as the wall for the bouncing ball. A random starting point (x and y) and a random set of values for changing location (dx and dy) are then generated.

The program then enters a large loop. First, the ball is erased from its current location (that is, the ball is drawn in the background color). A new location (x1 and y1) is then generated. The two IF - ELSEIF - END IF structures test the new location to determine if it will cause the ball to be drawn beyond the confines of walls. If so, the direction of motion is altered, creating the illusion that the ball bounces off the walls and back into the confined interior space. The ball is then displayed at the new location, followed by a brief time delay. Finally, the values of the new coordinates are assigned to the variables x and y. These two variables will be used to erase the ball during the next pass through the loop.

Figure 11.10 illustrates the type of output that is created when the program is run. Remember, however, that the ball is constantly in motion when the program is executing.

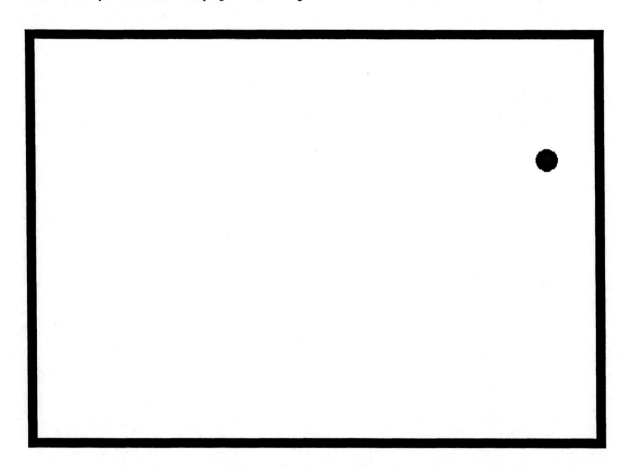

Fig 11.10

Though the preceding animation technique works reasonably well, the animation is relatively slow and it may be accompanied by an annoying flicker. Faster, flicker-free animations can be generated through the use of the GET and PUT statements. With this method, the moving object is generated only once. The GET statement then transfers the object from the screen to an array. Thereafter, the PUT statement will transfer the object from the array back to the screen, at a selected location. If the object is placed directly over itself, it will appear in a color that is opposite to the previous color (e.g., black replacing white). Thus, by executing a pair of PUTs at the same location, the object can automatically be displayed and then erased. (*Note:* The GET and PUT statements, when used in this manner, should not be confused with the GET and PUT statements that are used in conjunction with direct data files, as described in Sec. 8.5.)

The overall procedure, then, is to generate the object that will move about the screen and place it in an array, using the GET statement. This is carried out only once. The program then enters a loop in which the object is erased from its old location (via the PUT statement), a new location is determined, and the object is redisplayed at this new location (again via PUT). The animation is created by repeated passes through the loop.

The GET statement consists of the word GET, followed by two pairs of coordinates. Each pair of coordinates must be enclosed in parentheses and separated by a comma. These coordinates define the opposite corners of a rectangle which contains the object. A dash (minus sign) separates the two pairs of coordinates. The second pair of coordinates is followed by the name of the array that will contain the object; for example, GET (x, y)-(x + 20, y + 20), figure.

The dimensionality of the array depends on both the size of the object (actually, the size of the enclosing rectangle) and the level of resolution. There is a rather involved formula for calculating the required dimensionality that makes use of these two factors. Consult the user's reference manual for more information on this topic.

Once the object is stored in the required array, it is redisplayed by means of the PUT statement. This statement consists of the word PUT, followed by a single pair of coordinates, enclosed in parentheses and separated by a comma. These coordinates represent the upper-left corner of the rectangle containing the object. The coordinates are then followed by the name of the array; for example, PUT (x, y), figure.

Example 11.26 The Bouncing Ball Revisited

Let us again consider the animation of a ball within an enclosure, as described in Example 11.25. Now, however, we will generate the animation by means of the GET and PUT statements.

The complete QuickBASIC program is shown below.

```
'*** BOUNCING BALL ***

DEFINT A-Z
DIM ball(202)
RANDOMIZE TIMER
LET delay = 5000
LET flag = 1

SCREEN 9: COLOR 15, 1: CLS
LINE (0, 0)-(639, 349), , B         'border
LINE (10, 7)-(629, 342), , B
PAINT (5, 2)
                                    'define an initial position
LET x = 20 + INT(600 * RND)
LET y = 20 + INT(310 * RND)
LET dx = INT(21 * RND) - 10
LET dy = INT(21 * RND) - 10

CIRCLE (x, y), 12, 15
PAINT (x, y), 15
GET (x - 12, y - 12)-(x + 12, y + 12), ball

'main loop

DO WHILE flag > 0
    LET x1 = x + dx                 'new coordinates
    LET y1 = y + dy
```

```
        IF x1 < 23 THEN                'hit the left wall
           LET x1 = 23
           LET dx = -dx
        ELSEIF x1 > 616 THEN           'hit the right wall
           LET x1 = 616
           LET dx = -dx
        END IF

        IF y1 < 18 THEN                'hit the top
           LET y1 = 18
           LET dy = -dy
        ELSEIF y1 > 331 THEN           'hit the bottom
           LET y1 = 331
           LET dy = -dy
        END IF

        PUT (x - 12, y - 12), ball     'erase the ball
        PUT (x1 - 12, y1 - 12), ball   'redraw the ball
        LET x = x1
        LET y = y1
        FOR i = 1 TO delay: NEXT i     'time delay
     LOOP

     END
```

This program is similar to that shown in the previous example, though there are some important differences. Notice, for example, the addition of the DIM statement, which defines ball to be a 202-element array. Also, the CIRCLE and PAINT statements appear only once in the current program. These two statements define the initial shape of the ball. The following GET statement then causes this shape definition to be stored in ball.

The loop portion of the program is also somewhat different than the earlier version. The pairs of CIRCLE and PAINT statements in the earlier program are now replaced by PUT statements. The first of these erases the ball from its previous location whereas the second displays the ball at its new location. The erasure and redraw statements are placed next to each other in order to minimize flicker.

When the program is executed, the screen will again appear as shown in Figure 11.10 but the motion will now be considerably faster and smoother. You are urged to run both programs, in order to appreciate the differences in the resulting animations.

Animations that are created in this manner need not be limited to a single moving object. Multiple objects can also be moved about the screen, by means of multiple pairs of PUT statements. Each object must, however, be stored in a separate array. The technique is illustrated in the next example.

Example 11.27 A Game of Paddleball

Here is a simple version of a popular video game, commonly referred to as "paddleball." A ball is enclosed by three walls. A small moveable "paddle" is located where the fourth wall would normally be placed. This paddle can move up and down in response to the setting of some control device, such as a joystick (we are assuming that the missing wall is vertical). The ball will be deflected back into the playing area if it is hit by the paddle. Otherwise, the ball will pass through the opening and disappear.

The object of the game is to anticipate the ball's trajectory as it moves toward the open area and to position the paddle so that it hits the ball, knocking it back into the playing area. The player will receive one point for each hit and lose one point for each miss. The ball will automatically reappear at some random location within the playing area after each miss.

A complete QuickBASIC program for this game is shown below. It includes the use of EGA graphics, a function key, joystick control statements and sound enhancements to accompany the movement of the ball. Thus, the program contains several features described in Chap. 10 as well as an animation technique.

```
'*** PADDLEBALL GAME ***

DEFINT A-Z
DIM ball(202), paddle(246)
RANDOMIZE TIMER

ON KEY(1) GOSUB Terminate
KEY(1) ON

'opening text screen

SCREEN 0: COLOR 15, 1: CLS
LOCATE 4, 30: PRINT "Welcome to PADDLEBALL"
LOCATE 6, 32: PRINT "Press F1 to END"
LOCATE 10, 27: PRINT "Rules: 1 point for each hit"
LOCATE 11, 33: PRINT "-1 point for each miss"
LOCATE 15, 27: PRINT "Press any key to continue"
LET ans$ = INPUT$(1)

SCREEN 9: COLOR 15, 1: CLS
LET dx = INT(11 * RND) + 5
LET dy = INT(21 * RND) - 10
LET p = 10
LET hit = 1: miss = 2: flag = hit
LET score = 0

'draw the border

LINE (0, 0)-(639, 7), 15, BF
LINE (0, 329)-(639, 322), 15, BF
LINE (629, 6)-(639, 321), 15, BF
LOCATE 25, 20: PRINT "SCORE: "; score;
LOCATE 25, 45: PRINT "Press F1 to END";

'define the moving objects

LET x = 320 + INT(220 * RND): y = 175 + INT(100 * RND)
CIRCLE (x, y), 12
PAINT (x, y)
GET (x - 12, y - 12)-(x + 12, y + 12), ball

LINE (0, p)-(10, p + 60), 15, BF
GET (0, p)-(10, p + 60), paddle
```

```
'main loop

DO WHILE flag > 0
    LET x1 = x + dx: y1 = y + dy              'new ball position

    LET dummy = STICK(0)
    LET f! = (STICK(1) - 40) / 140
    IF f! < 0 THEN f! = 0
    IF f! > 1 THEN f! = 1
    LET p1 = 8 + 253 * f!                     'new paddle position

    IF x1 < 23 THEN
        IF y1 > p1 - 3 AND y1 < p1 + 57 THEN 'hit the paddle
            LET x1 = 23: dx = -dx
            LET score = score + 1
            SOUND 1000, 2
            LOCATE 25, 28: PRINT score;
        ELSE                                 'missed the paddle
            LET x1 = 320 + INT(220 * RND)    'generate a new location
            LET y1 = 175 + INT(100 * RND)
            LET dx = INT(11 * RND) + 5
            LET dy = INT(21 * RND) - 10
            LET flag = miss
            LET score = score - 1
            LOCATE 25, 28: PRINT score;
        END IF

    ELSE
        IF x1 > 615 THEN                      'hit the right wall
            LET x1 = 615: dx = -dx
            SOUND 1000, 2
        END IF

        IF y1 < 17 THEN                       'hit the top
            LET y1 = 17: dy = -dy
            SOUND 1000, 2
        END IF

        IF y1 > 311 THEN                      'hit the bottom
            LET y1 = 311: dy = -dy
            SOUND 1000, 2
        END IF
    END IF

    PUT (x - 12, y - 12), ball                'erase the ball
    IF flag = miss THEN
        FOR i = 1 TO 18
            SOUND 50, 1: SOUND 32767, 1
        NEXT i
        LET flag = hit
    END IF
    PUT (x1 - 12, y1 - 12), ball              'redraw the ball
```

```
      PUT (0, p), paddle                         'erase the paddle
      PUT (0, p1), paddle                        'redraw the paddle

      LET x = x1: y = y1: p = p1                  'update the old coordinates
LOOP

Terminate:
END
```

In general, this program is an extension of the program shown in Example 11.26. The program begins by declaring all variables to be integers, defining two arrays that store the animated objects, and initializing the random number generator. Event trapping is then activated for function key F1, thus providing a means of ending the program execution. This is followed by a group of statements that create an opening text display, informing the user how the game is played.

The program then switches into the EGA graphics mode with a high-intensity white foreground and a blue background. Initial values are assigned to several variables, including dx and dy, which determine the speed and direction of the ball. Note that these two values are determined randomly. The program then generates the three fixed walls and displays some text at the bottom of the screen. The text consists of the score and a prompt indicating how the game is ended.

The next group of statements begins by randomly generating an initial location for the ball. The ball itself is then defined and assigned to the array ball. This is followed by a definition for the paddle, which is then assigned to the array paddle.

The main loop, in which the animation is created, is contained within the large DO - LOOP structure. Each pass through the loop begins by determining a new position for the ball and the paddle (x1 and y1 represent the center of the ball, and p1 represents the top of the paddle). This is followed by an IF - ELSE - END IF structure that tests whether the ball has either hit or missed the paddle.

If the ball has hit the paddle, the horizontal motion is reversed, thus "bouncing" the ball back into the playing area. This is accompanied by an increase in the score and a brief, high-pitched "beep." If, on the other hand, the ball has missed the paddle, new values are generated for the location, direction and speed of the ball. A flag is then set to indicate a miss (for later use in the program) and the score is decreased.

The main loop contains three additional IF blocks that adjust the motion of the ball if the ball hits any of the three fixed walls. Each block causes the direction of motion to be reversed, thus "bouncing" the ball off the surface. This is accompanied by a high-pitched "beep."

The ball and the paddle are then erased from their old locations and redrawn at their new locations. If the ball has just missed the paddle, as indicated by the value of the flag, there is a brief time delay in which the ball does not appear on the screen. A sound enhancement is generated during this time delay. Finally, the new coordinates of the ball and the paddle are saved, in preparation for the next pass through the loop.

When the program is executed, the following text display appears.

```
            Welcome to PADDLEBALL

            Press F1 to END




        Rules: 1 point for each hit
              -1 point for each miss




        Press any key to continue
```

Once any key is pressed, the screen switches to the graphics mode and the ball appears at some random location on the screen, enclosed by the three fixed walls. The ball remains in constant motion, bouncing off whatever surface it happens to touch, unless it wanders off to the left and misses the paddle. The location of the paddle is adjusted by manipulating the joystick up or down.

Each time the paddle hits the ball, the cumulative score increases by 1; similarly, the cumulative score decreases by 1 whenever the paddle misses the ball. The current value of the cumulative score is always displayed at the bottom of the screen. The game continues until the player presses function key F1.

Figure 11.11 illustrates the appearance of the screen as the ball approaches the paddle from the lower right.

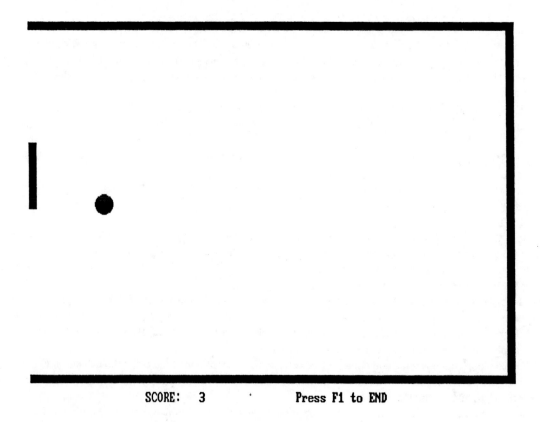

SCORE: 3   ˙   Press F1 to END

Fig. 11.11

You are urged to run this program in order to appreciate what actually happens.

11.5 CHARACTER GRAPHICS

Certain graphic effects can often be achieved through the clever manipulation of text characters. Such effects include animated message displays as well as the creation of simple graphs and shapes. We have already seen some examples of animated message displays, with vertical scrolling in Examples 7.11 and 10.9, and a horizontal animation included as a part of Example 11.24.

As a rule, graphic effects that are created in this manner are less effective than graphic effects created in a graphics mode. Nevertheless they do serve a purpose, particularly for computers that do not support separate text and graphics modes, or for applications that are primarily textual in nature.

The following example illustrates the use of character-type graphics to represent numeric data.

Example 11.28 A Bar Chart Generator

Suppose we have a group of numeric values that we want to display in graphic form, emphasizing the magnitude of each value. One way to do this is to construct a *bar chart*, in which each value is represented by a rectangle whose height is directly proportional to its corresponding value. Usually the rectangles are displayed vertically, with all of them visible at the same time.

Shown below is a QuickBASIC program that generates a bar chart for as many as 12 numeric values. Each value is assumed to be nonnegative (i.e., greater than or equal to zero). The actual values will be displayed above each of their respective rectangles (i.e., above each "bar"). Each value will have a corresponding label, which will be displayed at the bottom of the bar. The bars themselves will be comprised of clusters of asterisks (*).

```
'*** BAR CHART GENERATOR ***

SCREEN 0: COLOR 15, 1: CLS
DIM label$(12), y(12)
LOCATE 1, 30: PRINT "BAR CHART GENERATOR"
LET ymax = 0
LET flag = 1

'enter data and find the largest y-value

LOCATE 3, 1: INPUT "Title: ", title$
DO WHILE flag > 0
   LOCATE 5, 1: INPUT "How many data items? (1-12) ", ans$
   LET n = VAL(ans$)
   IF n > 0 AND n < 13 THEN EXIT DO
   BEEP
   LOCATE 5, 29: PRINT SPACE$(6)                'data error - try again
LOOP

FOR i = 1 TO n                                  'enter individual y-values
   LOCATE i + 7, 1: PRINT "i ="; i

   DO WHILE flag > 0
      LOCATE i + 7, 15: INPUT "Value: ", ans$:
      LET y(i) = VAL(ans$)
      IF LEFT$(ans$, 1) = "0" OR y(i) > 0 THEN EXIT DO
      BEEP
      LOCATE i + 7, 21: PRINT SPACE$(6)          'data error - try again
   LOOP

   LOCATE i + 7, 35: INPUT "Label: ", label$(i)

   IF y(i) > ymax THEN ymax = y(i)
NEXT i                                          'tag largest y-value

'generate and display the bar chart

CLS
LET w = 60 \ n
```

```
FOR i = 1 TO n
   LET r = 20 - 18 * y(i) \ ymax
   IF r < 20 THEN
      FOR row = r TO 20
         FOR col = (i - 1) * w + 11 TO i * w + 8
            LOCATE row, col: PRINT "*"              'generate bar
         NEXT col
      NEXT row
   END IF
NEXT i

'label the bar chart

FOR i = 1 TO n
   LET row = 19 - 18 * y(i) \ ymax
   LET col = 9 + (i - 1) * w + (w - LEN(STR$(y(i)))) / 2
   LOCATE row, col: PRINT y(i)                    'display value above bar
   LET col = 10 + (i - 1) * w + (w - LEN(label$(i))) / 2
   LOCATE 21, col: PRINT label$(i)
NEXT i                                             'display label beneath bar

LET col = 10 + (n * w - LEN(title$)) / 2
LOCATE 23, col: PRINT title$; : LOCATE 23, 1      'display title at bottom
END
```

The opening block of statements establishes the mode and color, defines the arrays label$ and y, and initializes the variables ymax and flag. The program then prompts for the bar chart title and the number of data items to be entered. The latter includes an error trap, so that the user cannot enter a nonnumeric character or an improper numeric value (less than 1 or greater than 12) for the number of data items.

The FOR - NEXT loop then prompts the user for each numeric value and its accompanying label. This loop includes an error trap that prevents a nonnumeric character or a negative number from being entered. The loop ends by tagging the largest input value, for later use when constructing the bar chart.

The actual bar chart is generated next. First the screen is cleared and the width of each bar is calculated. (The greater the number of bars, the smaller the width of each bar.) A triple loop is then used to generate the bars. The outermost loop generates the successive bars. (Notice that the top row of each bar is based upon the ratio of the given value to the maximum value. This value is recalculated during each pass through the outer loop.) The middle loop generates the rows that make up each bar and the inner loop generates the columns within each row.

The remaining statements label the bar chart. The FOR - NEXT loop causes each numeric data value to be displayed on the line above the corresponding bar and the accompanying label to appear beneath each bar. The title of the bar chart is then displayed at the bottom of the screen, centered horizontally.

Now suppose the program is executed, using the following set of input data.

Annual Sales Increases

Increase (%)	Year
5.2	1992
7.8	1993
8.2	1994
6.7	1995
10.6	1996
12.3	1997

The dialog generated by the data-input portion of the program is shown below. The user's responses are again underlined.

BAR CHART GENERATOR

Title: <u>Annual Sales Increases</u>

How many data items? (1-12) <u>6</u>

i = 1	Value: <u>5.2</u>	Label: <u>1992</u>
i = 2	Value: <u>7.8</u>	Label: <u>1993</u>
i = 3	Value: <u>8.2</u>	Label: <u>1994</u>
i = 4	Value: <u>6.7</u>	Label: <u>1995</u>
i = 5	Value: <u>10.6</u>	Label: <u>1996</u>
i = 6	Value: <u>12.3</u>	Label: <u>1997</u>

The resulting bar chart is shown below.

```
                                                              12.3
                                                            *******
                                                            *******
                                                   10.6     *******
                                                 *******    *******
                                                 *******    *******
                                      8.2        *******    *******
                            7.8     *******      *******    *******
                          *******   *******  6.7 *******    *******
                          *******   *******  *******  *******    *******
                          *******   *******  *******  *******    *******
                 5.2      *******   *******  *******  *******    *******
               *******    *******   *******  *******  *******    *******
               *******    *******   *******  *******  *******    *******
               *******    *******   *******  *******  *******    *******
               *******    *******   *******  *******  *******    *******
               *******    *******   *******  *******  *******    *******
               *******    *******   *******  *******  *******    *******
               *******    *******   *******  *******  *******    *******
               *******    *******   *******  *******  *******    *******

                1992      1993      1994      1995      1996      1997


                          Annual Sales Increases
```

Many personal computers include a special graphics character set, in addition to the 128 standard ASCII characters. For example, IBM-compatible personal computers support 256 different characters, including 128 special characters. Several of these are graphics characters (as well as mathematical symbols and characters used in foreign languages). We have already used certain of these graphics characters to create blocks of light (in Examples 10.2 and 10.3) and to display "smiling faces" (in Example 10.5). The use of these graphics characters generally results in a significant improvement in character-based graphic displays.

Example 11.29 An Improved Bar Chart Generator

Here is another QuickBASIC program that generates a bar chart, as described in Example 11.28. Now, however, we make use of the special graphics characters available on an IBM-compatible personal computer.

```
'*** BAR CHART GENERATOR ***

SCREEN 0: COLOR 15, 1: CLS
DIM label$(12), y(12)
LOCATE 1, 30: PRINT "BAR CHART GENERATOR"
LET bar1$ = CHR$(177): bar2$ = CHR$(178)          'graphics characters
LET ymax = 0
LET flag = 1


'enter data and find the largest y-value

LOCATE 3, 1: INPUT "Title: ", title$
DO WHILE flag > 0
   LOCATE 5, 1: INPUT "How many data items? (1-12) ", ans$
   LET n = VAL(ans$)
   IF n > 0 AND n < 13 THEN EXIT DO
   BEEP: LOCATE 5, 29: PRINT SPACE$(6)            'data error - try again
LOOP

FOR i = 1 TO n                                    'enter individual y-values
   LOCATE i + 7, 1: PRINT "i ="; i

   DO WHILE flag > 0
      LOCATE i + 7, 15: INPUT "Value: ", ans$:
      LET y(i) = VAL(ans$)
      IF LEFT$(ans$, 1) = "0" OR y(i) > 0 THEN EXIT DO
      BEEP: LOCATE i + 7, 21: PRINT SPACE$(6)     'data error - try again
   LOOP

   LOCATE i + 7, 35: INPUT "Label: ", label$(i)

   IF y(i) > ymax THEN ymax = y(i)
NEXT i                                            'tag largest y-value
```

```
'generate and display the bar chart

CLS
LET w = 60 \ n
FOR i = 1 TO n
   LET r = 20 - 18 * y(i) \ ymax
   IF r < 20 THEN
      FOR row = r TO 20
         FOR col = (i - 1) * w + 11 TO i * w + 8
            LOCATE row, col
               IF i MOD 2 = 0 THEN PRINT bar1$ ELSE PRINT bar2$     'generate bar
         NEXT col
      NEXT row
   END IF
NEXT i

'label the bar chart

FOR i = 1 TO n
   LET row = 19 - 18 * y(i) \ ymax
   LET col = 9 + (i - 1) * w + (w - LEN(STR$(y(i)))) / 2
   LOCATE row, col: PRINT y(i)                    'display value above bar
   LET col = 10 + (i - 1) * w + (w - LEN(label$(i))) / 2
   LOCATE 21, col: PRINT label$(i)
NEXT i                                            'display label beneath bar

LET col = 10 + (n * w - LEN(title$)) / 2
LOCATE 23, col: PRINT title$; : LOCATE 23, 1      'display title at bottom
END
```

Notice that the characters CHR$(177) and CHR$(178) are now assigned to the variables **bar1$** and **bar2$** in the opening block of statements. These variables appear in the PRINT statement contained within the triple loop, thus causing the rectangular bars to be composed of partially shaded rectangular blocks rather than asterisks. The effect of is shown below. Note that alternate bars are shown in different shadings.

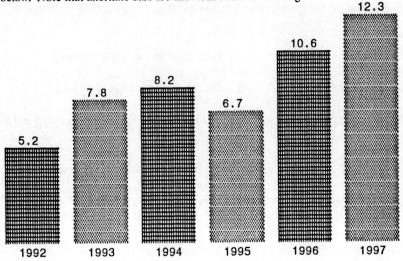

Annual Sales Increases

It is interesting to compare this bar graph with that shown in the previous example. The special graphics characters used in the present bar graph greatly improve the appearance of the display. Thus, we see that a small amount of additional programming effort results in a much better-looking display.

Review Questions

11.1   Determine whether or not the version of BASIC available for your particular computer includes special graphics statements. If so, are they the same as those described in this chapter?

11.2   What level of resolution is provided by the graphics features on your particular computer? Are multiple graphics modes available? If so, what are they?

11.3   Is color available on your particular computer? If so, how many different colors are available in the text mode? How many are available in each of the various graphics modes?

11.4   What is a pixel? What are pixels used for?

11.5   What is the purpose of the SCREEN statement? Summarize the rules that apply to its use.

11.6   What is the purpose of the PSET statement? Summarize the rules that apply to its use.

11.7   What is the purpose of the PRESET statement? Summarize the rules that apply to its use. How does it differ from the PSET statement?

11.8   How can individual points be generated in your version of BASIC?

11.9   What is the purpose of the LINE statement? Summarize the rules that apply to its use.

11.10   How can individual lines be generated in your version of BASIC?

11.11   Explain how a display consisting entirely of individual points or lines (not shapes) can be animated; that is, how can points or lines be displayed and later erased, as in the "moving lines" program?

11.12   How can the LINE statement be used to generate a closed rectangle? How can this rectangle be filled with a specified color?

11.13   What is the purpose of the CIRCLE statement? Summarize the rules that apply to its use.

11.14   What is the purpose of the PAINT statement? Summarize the rules that apply to its use.

11.15   How can the CIRCLE and PAINT statements be used to generate circular shapes that are filled with a specified color?

11.16   Can closed circles be generated in your version of BASIC? If so, how is this accomplished?

11.17   How can the CIRCLE statement be used to generate arcs rather that entire circles? How can these arcs be connected to the origin, thus creating "pie-shaped" objects?

11.18   How can the CIRCLE statement be used to generate ellipses? How can the size and orientation (i.e., horizontal or vertical) of an ellipse be specified?

11.19 Can elliptical arcs be generated in your version of BASIC? If so, how is this accomplished?

11.20 Explain how a text display can be animated in the horizontal direction within a fixed, confined space.

11.21 How can simple shapes be animated in your version of BASIC?

11.22 What is the purpose of the GET statement when used in the graphics mode? Summarize the rules that apply to its use.

11.23 What is the purpose of the PUT statement when used in the graphics mode? Summarize the rules that apply to its use.

11.24 When creating an animation, what is the advantage in using the GET and PUT statements rather than simply generating the shape in alternate colors (first foreground, then background)?

11.25 What is meant by character graphics? How does the quality of character-type graphics compare with other types of graphic displays?

11.26 Does your version of BASIC include special graphics characters? If so, what are they? What are their ASCII codes?

Problems

The following questions are concerned with information gathering rather than actual problem solving. Answer the questions as they apply to your particular version of BASIC.

11.27 Does your computer include a graphics capability? If so, can graphic displays be created within a BASIC program? How many graphics modes are available? What level of resolution is available within each mode?

11.28 Is color available? If so, how many colors can be displayed at any one time within each graphics mode? What are these colors? Is there a distinction between foreground and background colors?

11.29 Determine how each of the following features can be implemented in your particular version of BASIC.

(a) How is each graphics mode accessed?

(b) How are individual colors specified?

(c) How are individual points generated? How are they erased?

(d) How are lines generated?

(e) Can a rectangle be generated with a single statement? If so, can the rectangle be filled with a solid color?

(f) Can a circle be generated with a single statement? If so, can the circle be filled with a solid color?

(g) Can an ellipse be generated with a single statement? If so, can the ellipse be filled with a solid color?

(h) Can a circular or elliptical arc be generated with a single statement?

(i) Are special statements available for carrying out animations? If so, what are they and how do they work?

(j) Can text be generated within the graphics modes?

(k) Are there other special graphics features that were not described in this chapter? If so, what are they and how do they work?

(l) Does your computer include special graphics characters? If so, what are they? How are these characters accessed in BASIC?

Programming Problems

11.30 Modify the following programs so that the foreground and background colors can be changed at any time by pressing function keys F1 and F2. Be certain that the foreground and background colors are always different. In addition, add a provision for terminating the computation by pressing function key F4.

(a) Expanding rectangles (Example 11.11)

(b) Linear regression with graphic display (Example 11.9)

(c) Blimp with animated text (Example 11.24)

(d) Simulation of a bouncing ball (Examples 11.25 and 11.26)

(e) A game of paddleball (Example 11.27)

11.31 Modify the pie chart generation program given in Example 11.21 so that the background and the pie chart sectors (and corresponding labels) are displayed in color. Be sure that adjacent sectors are displayed in different colors, and that the background color is different than any of the foreground colors.

11.32 Repeat problem 11.31 for the bar chart generation program given in Example 11.29.

11.33 Alter some of the numerical values included in the moving lines program given in Example 11.8. Experiment with different values until you find a set of values that you like.

11.34 Modify the random blocks program given in Example 11.13 so that the screen is filled with a larger number of blocks. Reduce the size of the blocks to compensate for the greater number.

11.35 Modify the linear regression program given in Example 11.9 so that the x- and y-axes are labeled. Include a provision for generating a title near the top of the graph.

11.36 Modify the linear regression program given in Example 11.9 so that the new features suggested in Problems 11.30 (*b*) and 11.35 are all included in one program.

11.37 Expand the linear regression program given in Example 11.9 so that power functions, exponentials and polynomials can be fitted to a set of input data and then plotted. Use closely spaced points to represent curves when plotting the graphs. (Example 9.30 gives the appropriate equations for fitting each type of curve, based upon the method of least squares.) Include a menu that will allow the user to select the desired type of curve. Be sure to include appropriate prompts and error checks for both the numerical data and the menu selections.

11.39 Modify the bar chart generator given in Example 11.29 so that one, two or three different data sets can be displayed simultaneously, provided all of the data sets have the same number of bars. Place the corresponding bars next to one another with no intervening space (i.e., place the first bar for each data set in one cluster, then the second bar for each data set, etc.). Use either a different color or a different pattern for each data set.

11.40 Write a single BASIC program that will read a set of data into the computer and then generate either a pie chart or a bar chart (see Examples 11.21 and 11.29). Include a menu that will allow the user to select the desired type of graph. Include color enhancements, as suggested in Problems 11.31 and 11.32. In addition, include appropriate prompts and error checks for both the numerical data and the menu selections.

11.41 Modify the program given in Example 11.24 (blimp with animated text) so that the user may specify the message that moves across the display area. Include a prompt for the desired message at the start of the program, before the blimp is drawn.

11.42 Alter some of the numerical values included in the bouncing ball program given in Example 11.26. Experiment with different values until you find a set of values that you like. Compare the program's performance with that obtained using the original values.

11.43 Modify the paddleball game given in Example 11.27 so that the user may specify the degree of difficulty before the game begins. For a more difficult game, make the paddle smaller and make the ball move faster. Include a menu, with appropriate prompts and error checks, to assist the user in selecting the desired degree of difficulty.

11.44 Extend the program given in Example 10.5 (programming a joystick) so that several different graphics characters can be utilized. Include a menu that allows the user to select the graphics characters. Also, allow the user to change the color of the background or the color of each new character by pressing an appropriate function key. Include the function key choices in the menu. (*Suggestion:* Reserve the rightmost 20 columns of the screen for the menu. Allow the remainder of the screen to be used as the graphics area.)

11.45 Solve Problem 11.44 utilizing a mouse rather than a joystick.

11.46 Write a BASIC program, similar to the one given in Example 10.5, that will allow a mouse or a joystick to generate individual pixels in the graphics mode. Include a provision for changing the color of the background or the color of each new pixel by pressing an appropriate function key. Provide a small menu at the bottom of the screen explaining the use of the function keys.

11.47 Extend the program described in Problem 11.46 so that lines, rectangles and circles can be drawn, in addition to individual pixels. Include a provision for filling each solid shape with a color that the user can select from a menu. Also, allow the user to change the color of the background or the color of each new object by pressing an appropriate function key.

11.48 Write a BASIC program that will generate a full-screen display of your school emblem or company logo. Include color if it is available.

11.49 Write a BASIC program that will generate a full-screen display of the flag of each of the following countries (listed in the order of increasing difficulty).

(*a*) Japan
(*b*) France
(*c*) Denmark
(*d*) Norway
(*e*) United States
(*f*) United Kingdom
(*g*) Canada
(*h*) Saudi Arabia

11.50 Write a BASIC program that will generate an x-axis and a y-axis that divides the screen into four equal quadrants. Then display a graph of the equation

$$y = c_1 + c_2 x + c_3 x^2 + c_4 x^3 + c_5 x^4$$

using values of your own choice for c_1, c_2, c_3, c_4 and c_5. (Note that it is possible to plot straight lines, quadratics, cubics, etc. by setting certain of these constants equal to zero.)

Write the program in such a manner that it can be executed repeatedly, with different values for c_1, c_2, c_3, c_4 and c_5 entered from the keyboard at the beginning of each run.

11.51 Write a BASIC program that will generate a graphic display of the equation

$$y = 2 e^{-0.1 x} \sin (0.5 x + c)$$

for values of x varying from 0 to 60, and $c = 0$. Include the x- and y-axes in the graphic display. Label the axes.

11.52 Extend Problem 11.51 so that the generation of the graphic display occurs within a loop, with a different (increasing) value assigned to c during each pass.

11.53 A variety of interesting graphic displays can be generated by the equations that represent *Archimedes' spiral*; namely,

$$x = ar \cos r$$

$$y = br \sin r$$

where a and b are positive constants and r represents an angle, in radians.

Write a BASIC program that will generate a graphic display of Archimedes' spiral. Let the constants a and b be input parameters. Generate a sequence of values for r (and hence a sequence of x- and y- values) by embedding the above formulas within a FOR - NEXT loop that includes a STEP parameter. Enter the value of the STEP parameter from the keyboard, along with the values of a and b, at the start of each run. (*Note:* Many different graphic displays can be generated by specifying different values for a, b and the STEP parameter.)

11.54 Extend the craps game given in Example 6.11 to include a graphic display of the dice after every throw. (This problem can be solved using either pixel-type graphics or character graphics.)

11.55 Extend the tic-tac-toe program described in Problem 6.66 to include a graphic display showing the players' moves. Use the customary Xs and Os to indicate the moves. (This problem can be solved using either pixel-type graphics or character graphics.)

11.56 Extend the roulette program described in Problem 6.68 to include a graphic display of the roulette wheel (in color, if possible). Show where the marble comes to rest after each spin.

11.57 Extend the BINGO program described in Problem 6.69 to include a graphic display of the master BINGO card. (This card will contain all 75 possible letter-number combinations in five columns, labeled B, I, N, G, O, respectively.) Use character graphics to generate the display. Identify each letter-number combination as it is drawn (e.g., shade in the location on the card, or change the color).

11.58 One of the earliest of the popular video games is a game called *brickout*. This game is similar to the paddleball game described in Example 11.27, except that there is a "brick wall" located near the right side of the playing area, as illustrated in Figure 11.12.

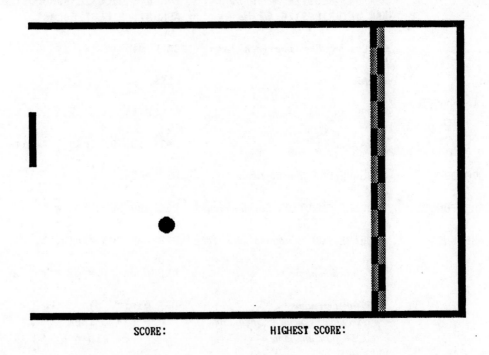

SCORE: HIGHEST SCORE:

Fig. 11.12

If the ball hits a brick, the brick disappears and the player receives one point. If the ball passes through a channel created by missing bricks, then the ball can continue to bounce within the right portion of the playing area, hitting and removing bricks, until it again passes through a channel to the left portion of the playing area. The game continues until all of the bricks are gone or else the player misses the ball with the paddle. The player is allowed five balls during each game.

Write a BASIC program to play successive games of brickout. Make each successive game more difficult, by making the paddle smaller and making the ball move more rapidly. Begin a new score for each game, but maintain a record of the highest score.

Appendix A

Summary of True BASIC Statements

True BASIC follows the 1987 ANSI standard very closely. The True BASIC statements described in this book are summarized below. True BASIC also includes other statements. Consult your programmer's reference manual for more definitive information.

Statement	General Form	Example
ASK	ASK	ASK MARGIN mval ASK COLOR fcolor ASK BACKGROUND COLOR bcolor ASK PIXELS xval, yval ASK WINDOW left, right, bottom, top
ASK #n	ASK #n: RECSIZE *record size* ASK #n: FILESIZE *file size*	ASK #1: RECSIZE RecordSize ASK #1: FILESIZE Last
CALL	CALL *subroutine name* (*actual args*)	CALL min (x, y, z)
CLEAR	CLEAR	CLEAR
CLOSE	CLOSE #n	CLOSE #1
DATA	DATA *data list*	DATA (3, 0, "red", "white", "blue")
DECLARE DEF	DECLARE DEF *function name*	DECLARE DEF w
DECLARE FUNCTION	DECLARE FUNCTION *function name*	DECLARE FUNCTION w
DECLARE SUB	DECLARE SUB *subroutine name* (*args*)	DECLARE SUB min(a, b, c)
DEF	DEF *function name* = . . .	DEF area(r) = pi * r ^ 2

	DEF *function name*
	   executable statements, including
	   LET *function name* = . . .
	END DEF
		DEF min(a, b)
		  IF a < b THEN
		    LET min = a
		  ELSE
		    LET min = b
		  END IF
		END DEF

DIM	DIM *array list*	DIM a(100), b(50, 100), names$(100) DIM table(0 TO 10, -10 TO 0) *or* DIM table(0 : 10, -10 : 0)

358

Statement	*General Form*	*Example*

DO WHILE - LOOP	DO WHILE *logical expression*
	    executable statements
	LOOP
		LET count = 1
		DO WHILE count <= 10
		   PRINT count
		   LET count = count + 1
		LOOP

DO UNTIL - LOOP	DO UNTIL *logical expression*
	    executable statements
	LOOP
		LET count = 1
		DO UNTIL count > 10
		   PRINT count
		   LET count = count + 1
		LOOP

DO - LOOP WHILE	DO
	    executable statements
	LOOP WHILE *logical expression*
		LET count = 1
		DO
		   PRINT count
		   LET count = count + 1
		LOOP WHILE count <= 10

DO - LOOP UNTIL	DO
	    executable statements
	LOOP UNTIL *logical expression*
		LET count = 1
		DO
		   PRINT count
		   LET count = count + 1
		LOOP UNTIL count > 10

END	END	END

EXIT DEF	EXIT DEF	DEF min(a, b)
		   IF a < 0 OR b < 0 THEN
		     EXIT DEF
		   ELSEIF a < b THEN
		     LET min = a
		   ELSE
		     LET min = b
		   END IF
		END DEF

EXIT DO	EXIT DO	INPUT x
		DO UNTIL x = 0
		   LET sum = sum + x
		   IF sum >= 100 THEN EXIT DO
		   INPUT x
		LOOP

EXIT FOR	EXIT FOR	FOR count = 1 TO n
		   LET sum = sum + count
		   IF sum > 100 THEN EXIT FOR
		NEXT count

Statement	*General Form*	*Example*
| EXIT FUNCTION | EXIT FUNCTION | ```
FUNCTION min(a, b)
   IF a < 0 OR b < 0 THEN
      EXIT FUNCTION
   ELSEIF a < b THEN
      LET min = a
   ELSE
      LET min = b
   END IF
END FUNCTION
``` |
| EXIT SUB | EXIT SUB | ```
SUB min (a, b, c)
   IF a < 0 OR b < 0 THEN
      EXIT SUB
   ELSEIF a < b THEN
      LET c = a
   ELSE
      LET c = b
   END IF
END SUB
``` |
| EXTERNAL DEF<br>(*see* DEF, FUNCTION) | EXTERNAL DEF *function name*<br>   *executable statements, including*<br>   LET *function name* = . . .<br>END DEF | ```
EXTERNAL DEF min(a, b)
   IF a < b THEN
      LET min = a
   ELSE
      LET min = b
   END IF
END DEF
``` |
| FOR - NEXT | FOR *index = val1* TO *val2* STEP *val3*<br>   *executable statements*<br>NEXT *index* | ```
FOR count = 0 TO 3 STEP 0.5
   LET sum = sum + count
NEXT count
``` |
GET KEY	GET KEY *numeric variable*	GET KEY v
IF - THEN	IF *logical expr.* THEN *exec. statement*	IF x < 0 THEN PRINT x
IF - THEN - ELSE	IF *log. expr.* THEN *stmt1* ELSE *stmt2*	IF x < y THEN PRINT x ELSE PRINT y
|  | IF *logical expression* THEN<br>   *executable statements*<br>ELSE<br>   *executable statements*<br>END IF | ```
IF (form$ = "circle") THEN
   INPUT radius
   LET area = pi * radius ^ 2
ELSE
   INPUT length, width
   LET area = length * width
END IF
``` |
```

Statement	*General Form*	*Example*

IF - THEN - ELSE	IF *logical expression 1* THEN
	    executable statements
	ELSEIF *logical expression 2* THEN
	    executable statements
	    . . . .
	ELSE
	    executable statements
	END IF
		IF d > 0 THEN
		    LET x1 = (-b + SQR(d)) / (2 * a)
		    LET x2 = (-b - SQR(d)) / (2 * a)
		ELSEIF d = 0 THEN
		    LET x = -b / (2 * a)
		ELSE
		    LET real = -b / (2 * a)
		    LET imag = SQR(-d) / (2 * a)
		END IF

INPUT	INPUT *input list*	INPUT a, b, c, name$, title$
INPUT #n	INPUT #*n*: *input list*	INPUT #1: AcctNo, OldBalance
INPUT PROMPT	INPUT PROMPT *prompt string*: *input list*	INPUT PROMPT "Enter a value: ": x
LET	LET *variable* = *expression*	LET area = pi * radius ^ 2
LINE INPUT	LINE INPUT *input string*	LINE INPUT city$
MAT *assignment*	MAT *variable* = *expression* MAT *array1* = *array2*	MAT name$ = "Santa Claus" MAT C = A
MAT *addition*	MAT *array1* = *array2* + *array3*	MAT C = A + B
MAT *subtraction*	MAT *array1* = *array2* - *array3*	MAT C = A - B
MAT *const mult*	MAT *array1* = *value* * *array2*	MAT C = (2 * X + Y) * A
MAT *matrix mult*	MAT *array1* = *array2* * *array3*	MAT C = A * B
MAT INPUT	MAT INPUT *array* MAT INPUT *array(?)*	MAT INPUT A MAT INPUT A(?)
MAT INPUT #n	MAT INPUT #*n*: *array*	MAT INPUT #1: A
MAT INPUT PROMPT	MAT INPUT PROMPT *prmpt str*: *array*	MAT INPUT PROMPT "Values: ": A
MAT LINE INPUT	MAT LINE INPUT *string array*	MAT LINE INPUT "Names: ": Names$
MAT LINE INPUT #n	MAT LINE INPUT #*n*: *strng array*	MAT LINE INPUT #1: Names$
MAT PRINT	MAT PRINT *array list*	MAT PRINT A, B, C
MAT PRINT #n	MAT PRINT #*n*: *array*	MAT PRINT #2: C

Statement	_General Form_	_Example_
MAT READ	MAT READ *array list*	DIM A(2, 3) MAT READ A DATA 3, 1, -5, 5, 0, 2
MAT READ #n	MAT READ #*n*: *array*	MAT READ #1: A
MAT REDIM	MAT REDIM *array list*	DIM A(100), B(2 TO 5, -6 TO 0) . . . . REDIM A(40), B(20 TO 100, 8)
MAT WRITE #n	MAT WRITE #*n*: *array*	MAT WRITE #2: C

OPEN	OPEN #*n*: NAME *filename*,
	   ACCESS *access*, CREATE *status*,
	   ORGANIZATION *type*,
	   RECSIZE *record size*
		OPEN #1: NAME "SCORES.DAT",
		   ACCESS INPUT, CREATE OLD

PAUSE	PAUSE	PAUSE
PRINT	PRINT *output list*	PRINT a, b, c, name$, title$
PRINT #n	PRINT #*n*: *output list*	PRINT #2: AcctNo, NewBalance
PRINT USING	PRINT USING *format string*: *output list*	PRINT USING "##.##": const
RANDOMIZE	RANDOMIZE	RANDOMIZE
READ	READ *data list*	READ u, v, x, y, z DATA (3, 6, 9, 12, 15)
READ #n	READ #*n*: *input list*	READ #1: State$, Capital$
REM	REM *remarks*	REM calculate the unknown constants
RESTORE	RESTORE	READ x, y, z RESTORE READ a, b, c, d

SELECT CASE	SELECT CASE *expression*
	CASE *value1*
	   executable statements
	CASE *value2*
	   executable statements
	  . . . .
	CASE ELSE
	   executable statements
	END SELECT
		SELECT CASE n
		CASE 1
		   PRINT "x ="; x
		CASE 2
		   PRINT "x squared ="; x ^ 2
		CASE 3
		   PRINT "x cubed ="; x ^ 3
		CASE ELSE
		   PRINT "ERROR - Please try again"
		END SELECT

Statement	*General Form*	*Example*
SET	SET	SET MARGIN 55 SET COLOR 15 SET BACKGROUND COLOR backgrnd SET WINDOW 0.25, 0.75, 0.2, 0.8
SET #n	SET #n: RECORD *record number* SET #n: POINTER *pointer loc*	SET #1: RECORD RecNo SET #1: POINTER SAME
SET CURSOR	SET CURSOR *row, column*	SET CURSOR 12, 30
STOP	STOP	STOP

SUB	SUB *subroutine name* (*args*)
	    executable statements
	END SUB
		SUB min (a, b, c)
		    IF a < b THEN
		        LET c = a
		    ELSE
		        LET c = b
		    END IF
		END SUB

UNSAVE	UNSAVE *filename*	UNSAVE "SCORES.DAT"
WRITE #n	WRITE #n: *output list*	WRITE #2: State$, Capital$

Operators (listed hierarchically)

1.	Exponentiation	^
2.	Multiplication and division	* /
3.	Addition and subtraction	+ —
4.	Relationals	< <= > >= = <>
5.	Logical NOT	NOT
6.	Logical AND	AND
7.	Logical OR	OR
	String concatenation	&

Other Punctuation

Exclamation mark(!)   Designates comments at the end of a statement line

Example :   CLEAR   !clear the screen

Substrings   *string name* [*first character* : *last character*]

Example :   message$[3:6]

Appendix B

Summary of True BASIC Functions

True BASIC follows the 1987 ANSI standard very closely. Several commonly used True BASIC library functions are summarized below. True BASIC also includes other library functions. Consult your programmer's reference manual for more definitive information.

Function	*Purpose*	*Example*
ABS	Absolute value	`LET Y = ABS(X)`
ACOS	Arccosine	`LET Y = ACOS(X)`
ASIN	Arcsine	`LET Y = ASIN(X)`
ATN	Arctangent	`LET Y = ATN(X)`
CEIL	Round up	`LET Y = CEIL(X)`
CHR$	Single character	`LET B$ = CHR$(N)`
CON	Constant array	`DIM A(10, 20)` `MAT A = CON`
COS	Cosine	`LET Y = COS(X)`
COSH	Hyperbolic cosine	`LET Y = COSH(X)`
COT	Cotangent	`LET Y = COT(X)`
CSC	Cosecant	`LET Y = CSC(X)`
DEG	Radians to degrees	`LET Y = DEG(X)`
DET	Determinant	`DIMENSION A(10, 10)` `LET Y = DET(A)`
DOT	Dot product	`DIMENSION A1(10), A2(10)` `LET Y = DOT(A1, A2)`
EXP	Exponential	`LET Y = EXP(X)`
IDN	Identity matrix	`DIM A(10, 10)` `MAT A = IDN`
INT	Truncate down	`LET Y = INT(X)`

Function	_Purpose_	_Example_
INV	Inverse matrix	DET A(10, 10), B(10, 10) MAT B = INV(A)
IP	Truncate toward zero	LET Y = IP(X)
LCASE$	Lowercase conversion	LET B$ = LCASE$(A$)
LEN	String length	LET N = LEN(A$)
LOG	Natural logarithm	LET Y = LOG(X)
LOG10	Logarithm (base 10)	LET Y = LOG10(X)
LTRIM$	Remove leading blanks	LET B$ = LTRIM$(A$)
MAX	Larger of two numbers	LET Y = MAX(X1, X2)
MAXNUM	Largest value permitted	LET Y = MAXNUM
MIN	Smaller of two numbers	LET Y = MIN(X1, X2)
MOD	Modulo remainder	LET Y = MOD(X1, X2)
NUL$	Null array	DIM A$(20) MAT A$ = NUL$
ORD	Character code	LET Y = ORD("a")
PEEK	Contents of an address	LET Y = PEEK(N)
PI	3.14159...	LET A = PI * R ^ 2
POKE (subroutine)	Change contents of an address	CALL POKE(N, X)
POS	Character location	LET Y = POS("a", "c")
RAD	Degrees to radians	LET Y = RAD(X)
REPEAT$	Repeat a string	LET B$ = REPEAT$(A$, N)
RND	Random number	LET Y = RND
ROUND	Round to _n_ decimals	LET Y = ROUND(X, N)
RTRIM$	Remove trailing blanks	LET B$ = RTRIM$(A$)
SEC	Secant	LET Y = SEC(X)
SGN	Sign	LET Y = SGN(X)

Function	*Purpose*	*Example*
SIN	Sine	`LET Y = SIN(X)`
SINH	Hyperbolic sine	`LET Y = SINH(X)`
SIZE	Determine array size	`DIM A(10, 20)` `LET Y = SIZE(A)`
SQR	Square root	`LET Y = SQR(X)`
STR$	Number-to-string conversion	`LET A$ = STR$(X)`
TAB	Tab (Print line)	`PRINT TAB(N); X`
TAN	Tangent	`LET Y = TAN(X)`
TANH	Hyperbolic tangent	`LET Y = TANH(X)`
TRIM$	Remove leading and trailing blanks	`LET B$ = TRIM$(A$)`
TRN	Transpose an array	`DIM A(10, 20), B(20, 10)` `MAT B = TRN(A)`
TRUNCATE	Truncate to *n* decimals	`LET Y = TRUNCATE(X, N)`
UCASE$	Uppercase conversion	`LET B$ = UCASE$(A$)`
VAL	String-to-number conversion	`LET Y = VAL(A$)`
ZER	Zero array	`DIM A(10, 20)` `MAT A = ZER`

Appendix C

Summary of QuickBASIC Statements

The QuickBASIC/QBASIC statements described in this book are summarized below. Note that QuickBASIC and QBASIC include additional statements. Consult your programmer's reference manual for more definitive information.

Statement	*General Form*	*Example*
BEEP	BEEP	BEEP
CALL	CALL *subroutine name* (*actual args*)	CALL min (x, y, z)
CIRCLE	CIRCLE (*x, y*), *radius, color*	CIRCLE (320, 175), 80, 14
	CIRCLE (*x, y*), *radius, color,* *angle1, angle2*	CIRCLE (320, 175), 80, 14, 0, 3.14
	CIRCLE (*x, y*), *radius, color,* *angle1, angle2, aspect*	CIRCLE (50, 85), 30, 7, 0, 3.14, .5
CLOSE	CLOSE #*n*	CLOSE #1
CLS	CLS	CLS
COLOR	COLOR *foreground, background*	COLOR 15, 0
DATA	DATA *data list*	DATA (3, 0, "red", "white", "blue")
DECLARE FUNCTION	DECLARE FUNCTION *function name*	DECLARE FUNCTION w *or* DECLARE FUNCTION w(x)
DECLARE SUB	DECLARE SUB *subroutine name* (*args*)	DECLARE SUB min(a, b, c)
DEF	DEF *function name* = . . .	DEF FNa(r) = pi * r ^ 2

	DEF *function name*
	   executable statements, including
	   LET *function name* = . . .
	 END DEF
		DEF FNmin(a, b)
		   IF a < b THEN
		     LET min = a
		   ELSE
		     LET min = b
		   END IF
		 END DEF

DEF SEG	DEF SEG *beginning address*	DEF SEG 32768

Statement	*General Form*	*Example*
DEFINT	DEFINT *letters*	DEFINT M, N
	DEFINT *range*	DEFINT A - Z
DEFSNG	DEFSNG *letters*	DEFSNG A, B, C
	DEFSNG *range*	DEFSNG W - Z
DIM	DIM *array list*	DIM a(100), b(50, 100), names$(100) DIM table(0 TO 10, -10 TO 0)

DO WHILE - LOOP	DO WHILE *logical expression*
	    executable statements
	LOOP
		LET count = 1
		DO WHILE count <= 10
		   PRINT count
		   LET count = count + 1
		LOOP

DO UNTIL - LOOP	DO UNTIL *logical expression*
	    executable statements
	LOOP
		LET count = 1
		DO UNTIL count > 10
		   PRINT count
		   LET count = count + 1
		LOOP

DO - LOOP WHILE	DO
	    executable statements
	LOOP WHILE *logical expression*
		LET count = 1
		DO
		   PRINT count
		   LET count = count + 1
		LOOP WHILE count <= 10

DO - LOOP UNTIL	DO
	    executable statements
	LOOP UNTIL *logical expression*
		LET count = 1
		DO
		   PRINT count
		   LET count = count + 1
		LOOP UNTIL count > 10

END	END	END

EXIT DEF	EXIT DEF	DEF min(a, b)
		  IF a < 0 OR b < 0 THEN
		    EXIT DEF
		  ELSEIF a < b THEN
		    LET min = a
		  ELSE
		    LET min = b
		  END IF
		END DEF

Statement	_General Form_	_Example_

EXIT DO	EXIT DO	```INPUT x```
		 ```DO UNTIL x = 0```
		 ``` LET sum = sum + x```
		 ``` IF sum >= 100 THEN EXIT DO```
		 ``` INPUT x```
		 ```LOOP```

EXIT FOR	EXIT FOR	```FOR count = 1 TO n```
		 ``` LET sum = sum + count```
		 ``` IF sum > 100 THEN EXIT FOR```
		 ```NEXT count```

EXIT FUNCTION	EXIT FUNCTION	```FUNCTION min(a, b)```
		 ``` IF a < 0 OR b < 0 THEN```
		 ``` EXIT FUNCTION```
		 ``` ELSEIF a < b THEN```
		 ``` LET min = a```
		 ``` ELSE```
		 ``` LET min = b```
		 ``` END IF```
		 ```END FUNCTION```

EXIT SUB	EXIT SUB	```SUB min (a, b, c)```
		 ``` IF a < 0 OR b < 0 THEN```
		 ``` EXIT SUB```
		 ``` ELSEIF a < b THEN```
		 ``` LET c = a```
		 ``` ELSE```
		 ``` LET c = b```
		 ``` END IF```
		 ```END SUB```

FOR - NEXT	FOR _index_ = _val1_ TO _val2_ STEP _val3_
	 executable statements
	 NEXT _index_
		```FOR count = 0 TO 3 STEP 0.5```
		 ``` LET sum = sum + count```
		 ```NEXT count```

FUNCTION
 (_see_ DEF, EXTERNAL)
	FUNCTION _function name_
	 executable statements, including
	 LET _function name_ = . . .
	 END FUNCTION
		```FUNCTION min(a, b)```
		 ``` IF a < b THEN```
		 ``` LET min = a```
		 ``` ELSE```
		 ``` LET min = b```
		 ``` END IF```
		 ```END FUNCTION```

GET	GET (_x1_, _y1_)-(_x2_, _y2_), _array_	```GET (x, y)-(x + d, y + d), ball```
GET #n	GET #_n_, _record number_, _record_	```GET #1, RecNo, Record```
IF - THEN	IF _logical expr._ THEN _exec. statement_	```IF x < 0 THEN PRINT x```

Statement	_General Form_	_Example_
IF - THEN - ELSE	IF _log. expr._ THEN _stmt1_ ELSE _stmt2_	IF x < y THEN PRINT x ELSE PRINT y

```
IF logical expression THEN            IF (form$ = "circle") THEN
    executable statements                 INPUT radius
ELSE                                      LET area = pi * radius ^ 2
    executable statements             ELSE
END IF                                    INPUT length, width
                                          LET area = length * width
                                      END IF
```

```
IF logical expression 1 THEN          IF d > 0 THEN
    executable statements                 LET x1 = (-b + SQR(d)) / (2 * a)
ELSEIF logical expression 2 THEN          LET x2 = (-b - SQR(d)) / (2 * a)
    executable statements             ELSEIF d = 0 THEN
    . . . . . .                           LET x = -b / (2 * a)
ELSE                                  ELSE
    executable statements                 LET real = -b / (2 * a)
END IF                                    LET imag = SQR(-d) / (2 * a)
                                      END IF
```

Statement	General Form	Example
INPUT	INPUT _input list_	INPUT a, b, c, name$, title$
	INPUT _prompt string, input list_	INPUT "Enter a value for x: ", x
	INPUT _prompt string; input list_	INPUT "x = "; x
INPUT #n	INPUT #_n, input list_	INPUT #1, AcctNo, OldBalance
KEY (_see_ ON KEY - GOSUB)	KEY(_n_) ON _or_ KEY(_n_) OFF	KEY(1) ON
KILL	KILL _filename_	KILL "SCORES.DAT"
LET	LET _variable = expression_	LET area = pi * radius ^ 2
LINE	LINE (_x1, y1_)-(_x2, y2_), _color_	LINE (20, 50)-(300, 150), 14
	LINE -(_x2, y2_), _color_	LINE -(80, 30), 14
	LINE (_x1, y1_)-(_x2, y2_), _color_, B	LINE (20, 50)-(620, 300), 14, B
	LINE (_x1, y1_)-(_x2, y2_), _color_, BF	LINE (20, 50)-(620, 300), 14, BF
LINE INPUT	LINE INPUT _input string_	LINE INPUT city$
LOCATE	LOCATE _row, column_	LOCATE 12, 30
LPRINT	LPRINT _output list_	LPRINT a, b, c
LPRINT USING	LPRINT USING _format string; output list_	LPRINT USING "##.##"; a, b, c

Statement	*General Form*	*Example*
NAME - AS	NAME *filename1* AS *filename2*	NAME "UPDATE.DAT" AS "SCORES.DAT"
ON KEY - GOSUB	ON KEY(*n*) GOSUB *label*	ON KEY(1) GOSUB Reverse KEY(1) ON
ON PEN GOSUB	ON PEN GOSUB *label*	ON PEN GOSUB Greetings PEN ON
ON STRIG - GOSUB	ON STRIG(*n*) GOSUB *label*	ON STRIG(0) GOSUB Display STRIG(0) ON
OPEN	OPEN *filename* FOR *access* AS #*n*	OPEN "SCORES.DAT" FOR INPUT AS #1
PAINT	PAINT (*x, y*), *color1, color2*	PAINT (100, 40), 14, 15
PEN (*see* ON PEN GOSUB)	PEN ON *or* PEN OFF	PEN ON
PRINT	PRINT *output list*	PRINT a, b, c, name$, title$
PRINT #n	PRINT #*n*, *output list*	PRINT #2, AcctNo, NewBalance
PRINT USING	PRINT USING *format string*; *output list*	PRINT USING "##.##"; const
POKE	POKE *value, address*	POKE 200, 65
PRESET	PRESET (*x, y*)	PRESET (320, 175)
PSET	PSET (*x, y*), *color*	PSET (320, 175), 15
PUT	PUT (*x, y*), *array*	PUT (x, y), ball
PUT #n	PUT #*n*, *record number*, *record*	PUT #2, RecNo, Record
RANDOMIZE	RANDOMIZE *expression*	RANDOMIZE TIMER
READ	READ *data list*	READ u, v, x, y, z DATA (3, 6, 9, 12, 15)
REM	REM *remarks*	REM calculate the unknown constants
RESTORE	RESTORE	READ x, y, z RESTORE READ a, b, c, d
RETURN	RETURN	RETURN
SCREEN	SCREEN *n*	SCREEN 0

Statement	*General Form*	*Example*

SELECT CASE	SELECT CASE *expression*
	CASE *value1*
	   executable statements
	CASE *value2*
	   executable statements
	  . . . . . .
	CASE ELSE
	   executable statements
	END SELECT
		SELECT CASE n
		CASE 1
		   PRINT "x ="; x
		CASE 2
		   PRINT "x squared ="; x ^ 2
		CASE 3
		   PRINT "x cubed ="; x ^ 3
		CASE ELSE
		   PRINT "ERROR - Please try again"
		END SELECT

SOUND	SOUND *frequency*, *duration*	SOUND 32767, 1
STOP	STOP	STOP
STRIG (*see* ON STRIG - GOSUB)	STRIG(*n*) ON *or* STRIG(*n*) OFF	STRIG(0) ON

SUB	SUB *subroutine name* (*args*)
	   executable statements
	END SUB
		SUB min (a, b, c)
		  IF a < b THEN
		    LET c = a
		  ELSE
		    LET c = b
		  END IF
		END SUB

TYPE	TYPE
	  record items
	END TYPE
		TYPE
		  State AS STRING * 15
		  Capital AS STRING * 15
		END TYPE

WHILE - WEND	WHILE *logical expression*
	   executable statements
	WEND
		INPUT x
		WHILE x <> 0
		  LET sum = sum + x
		  INPUT x
		WEND

Operators (listed hierarchically)

1.	Exponentiation	^
2.	Negation	−
3.	Multiplication and division	* /
4.	Integer division	\
5.	Integer remainder	MOD
6.	Addition and subtraction	+ −
7.	Relationals	< <= > >= = <>
8.	Logical NOT	NOT
9.	Logical AND	AND
10.	Logical OR	OR
11.	Logical XOR (exclusive OR)	XOR
12.	Logical EQV (equivalence)	EQV
13.	Logical IMP (implication)	IMP
	String concatenation	+

Other Punctuation

Colon (:)   Separates statements on the same line

Example: `SCREEN 0: COLOR 15, 0: CLS`

Apostrophe (')   Designates comments at the end of a statement line

Example: `CLS    'clear the screen`

Appendix D

Summary of QuickBASIC Functions

Several commonly used QuickBASIC/QBASIC library functions are summarized below. QuickBASIC and QBASIC also include other library functions. Consult your Programmer's Reference Manual for more definitive information.

Function	_Purpose_	_Example_
ABS	Absolute value	LET Y = ABS(X)
ASC	ASCII code of a single character	LET Y = ASC(A$)
ATN	Arctangent	LET Y = ATN(X)
CDBL	Convert to double precision	LET Y = CDBL(X)
CHR$	Single character	LET B$ = CHR$(N)
CINT	Convert to integer (round)	LET Y = CINT(X)
CLNG	Convert to long integer (round)	LET Y = CLNG(X)
COS	Cosine	LET Y = COS(X)
CSNG	Convert to single precision	LET Y = CSNG(X)
CSRLIN	Cursor row position	LET N = CSRLIN
EOF	End of file	DO UNTIL EOF(1)
EXP	Exponential	LET Y = EXP(X)
FIX	Truncate toward zero	LET Y = FIX(X)
FRE	Available memory	PRINT FRE(0)
INKEY$	Enter a character from the keyboard	DO: LOOP WHILE INKEY$ = ""
INPUT$	Enter a string of characters	LET B$ = INPUT$(N)
INSTR	Character location	LET Y = INSTR(A$, "c")
INT	Truncate down	LET Y = INT(X)
LCASE$	Lowercase conversion	LET B$ = LCASE$(A$)

Function	*Purpose*	*Example*
LEFT$	Left-most characters within a string	LET B$ = LEFT$(A$, N)
LEN	String length	LET N = LEN(A$)
LOC	Current position within a file	LET P = LOC(1)
LOF	File length	LET N = LOF(1)
LOG	Natural logarithm	LET Y = LOG(X)
LTRIM$	Remove leading blanks	LET B$ = LTRIM$(A$)
MID$	*N* characters within a string	LET B$ = MID$(A$, 3, N)
PEEK	Contents of an address	LET Y = PEEK(N)
POINT	*x*- or *y*-coordinate of a pixel	LET X = POINT(0): Y = POINT(1)
POS	Current horizontal cursor position	LET N = POS(0)
RIGHT$	Right-most characters within a string	LET B$ = RIGHT$(A$, N)
RND	Random number	LET Y = RND
RTRIM$	Remove trailing blanks	LET B$ = RTRIM$(A$)
SEEK	Next record number	LET N = SEEK(1)
SGN	Sign	LET Y = SGN(X)
SIN	Sine	LET Y = SIN(X)
SPACE$	String of blank spaces	PRINT SPACE$(5)
SPC	Skip spaces when printing	PRINT X; SPC(5); Y
SQR	Square root	LET Y = SQR(X)
STICK	*x*- or *y*-coordinate of a joystick	LET X = STICK(0): Y = STICK(1)
STR$	Number-to-string conversion	LET A$ = STR$(X)
STRING$	String of *N* ASCII characters	PRINT STRING$(N, 65)
TAB	Tab (Print line)	PRINT TAB(N); X
TAN	Tangent	LET Y = TAN(X)
TIMER	Number of seconds since midnight	LET N = TIMER

Function	*Purpose*	*Example*
UCASE$	Uppercase conversion	LET B$ = UCASE$(A$)
VAL	String-to-number conversion	LET Y = VAL(A$)

The ASCII Character Set

ASCII Value	Character	ASCII Value	Character	ASCII Value	Character	ASCII Value	Character
0	NUL	32	(blank)	64	@	96	`
1	SOH	33	!	65	A	97	a
2	STX	34	"	66	B	98	b
3	ETX	35	#	67	C	99	c
4	EOT	36	$	68	D	100	d
5	ENQ	37	%	69	E	101	e
6	ACK	38	&	70	F	102	f
7	BEL	39	'	71	G	103	g
8	BS	40	(	72	H	104	h
9	HT	41	)	73	I	105	i
10	LF	42	*	74	J	106	j
11	VT	43	+	75	K	107	k
12	FF	44	,	76	L	108	l
13	CR	45	-	77	M	109	m
14	SO	46	.	78	N	110	n
15	SI	47	/	79	O	111	o
16	DLE	48	0	80	P	112	p
17	DC1	49	1	81	Q	113	q
18	DC2	50	2	82	R	114	r
19	DC3	51	3	83	S	115	s
20	DC4	52	4	84	T	116	t
21	NAK	53	5	85	U	117	u
22	SYN	54	6	86	V	118	v
23	ETB	55	7	87	W	119	w
24	CAN	56	8	88	X	120	x
25	EM	57	9	89	Y	121	y
26	SUB	58	:	90	Z	122	z
27	ESC	59	;	91	[	123	{
28	FS	60	<	92	\	124		
29	GS	61	=	93	]	125	}
30	RS	62	>	94	^	126	~
31	US	63	?	95	_	127	DEL

Note: The first 32 characters and the last character are control characters. Usually, they are not printed. However, some versions of BASIC (some computers) support special graphics characters for these ASCII values. For example, 001 often represents the character ☺, 002 often represents ●, and so on.

The Extended ASCII Character Set

ASCII Value	Character	ASCII Value	Character	ASCII Value	Character	ASCII Value	Character
128	Ç	160	á	192	└	224	α
129	ü	161	í	193	┴	225	β
130	é	162	ó	194	┬	226	Γ
131	â	163	ú	195	├	227	π
132	ä	164	ñ	196	─	228	Σ
133	à	165	Ñ	197	┼	229	σ
134	å	166	a	198	╞	230	μ
135	ç	167	o	199	╟	231	τ
136	ê	168	¿	200	╚	232	Φ
137	ë	169	⌐	201	╔	233	Θ
138	è	170	¬	202	╩	234	Ω
139	ï	171	½	203	╦	235	δ
140	î	172	¼	204	╠	236	∞
141	ì	173	¡	205	═	237	φ
142	Ä	174	«	206	╬	238	ε
143	Å	175	»	207	╧	239	∩
144	É	176	░	208	╨	240	≡
145	æ	177	▒	209	╤	241	±
146	Æ	178	▓	210	╥	242	≥
147	ô	179	│	211	╙	243	≤
148	ö	180	┤	212	╘	244	⌠
149	ò	181	╡	213	╒	245	⌡
150	û	182	╢	214	╓	246	÷
151	ù	183	╖	215	╫	247	≈
152	ÿ	184	╕	216	╪	248	°
153	Ö	185	╣	217	┘	249	·
154	Ü	186	║	218	┌	250	·
155	¢	187	╗	219	█	251	√
156	£	188	╝	220	▄	252	η
157	¥	189	╜	221	▌	253	²
158	₧	190	╛	222	▐	254	■
159	ƒ	191	┐	223	▀	255	

There are several different extended ASCII character sets. This one is known as the *IBM Extended ASCII Character Set*, or the *PC-8 Extended ASCII Character Set*. It is commonly used with most programming languages, particularly on personal computers.

Answers to Selected Problems

Chapter 1

1.26 (a) Calculate the sum of five numbers.

(b) Calculate the area of a rectangle whose length and width are known.

(c) Calculate the area of several triangles whose base and height are known. Continue until a nonpositive value is entered for the base.

(d) Calculate values for x_1 and x_2 from the formulas

$$x_1 = [-b + (b^2 - 4ac)^{1/2}] / 2a$$

$$x_2 = [-b - (b^2 - 4ac)^{1/2}] / 2a$$

where the values for a, b and c are specified.

(e) Evaluate the formulas

$$w = u + v, \quad x = u - v, \quad y = u v, \quad z = u / v$$

where the values of u and v are specified.

(f) Calculate the area of a series of rectangles whose length and width are known. Continue until a nonpositive value is entered for the length.

(g) Evaluate the formula

$$y = 1 + x + x^2 / 2 + x^3 / 6$$

repeatedly, for a specified value of x. Continue as long as a positive value is entered for x.

1.27
```
REM PROGRAM TO CALCULATE THE AREA OF A CIRCLE - VERSION 3
PRINT "AREAS OF CIRCLES - To STOP, Enter 0 for the Radius"
PRINT "Radius = ";
INPUT radius
DO WHILE radius > 0                           'begin loop
   LET area = 3.14159 * radius ^ 2
   PRINT "Area ="; area
   PRINT
   PRINT "Radius = ";
   INPUT radius
LOOP                                          'end loop
PRINT "GOODBYE, Have a Nice Day!"
END
```

1.28 (a) Since $a = \pi r^2$ we can solve for r, which yields

$$r = (a / \pi)^{1/2}$$

Hence, a very simple version of the desired program is

```
PRINT "Area = ";
INPUT A
LET R = (A / 3.14159) ^ .5
PRINT "Radius ="; R
END
```

(b)
```
PRINT "Enter values for A, B, C, D and E below:"
INPUT A, B, C, D, E
LET P = A * B * C * D * E
PRINT "P =";P
END
```

(c)
```
PRINT "Area = ";
INPUT A
PRINT "Width = ";
INPUT W
LET L = A / W
PRINT "Length ="; L
END
```

1.29   The second line contains multiple statements.
The keyword LET is missing in the third line.
The variable X in the fourth line is undefined.
The END statement is missing.

Chapter 2

2.39   (a)   7350, 7.35E3, etc.

    (b)   -12

    (c)   1000000, 1E6, etc.

    (d)   -2053180, -2.05318E6, etc.

    (e)   0.00008291, 8.291E-5, etc.

    (f)   9.563E12

    (g)   0.1666667

2.40   (a)   Comma not allowed.

    (b)   Double sign not allowed.

    (c)   Exponent may be too large.

    (d)   Too many significant figures (excess digits will be ignored).

      (e)   Exponent cannot contain a decimal point.

2.41   *(a)*   Correct.

      (b)   Correct.

      (c)   The string is not enclosed in quotation marks.

      (d)   Correct.

      (e)   Single quotation marks are not allowed within a string constant.

      (f)   Correct.

      (g)   Trailing quotation mark is missing.

2.42   *(a)*   Correct.

      (b)   Correct.

      (c)   Blank spaces are not allowed.

      (d)   Correct (most versions of BASIC).

      (e)   First character must be a letter.

      (f)   May be correct (some versions of BASIC).

      (g)   Question mark is not allowed.

      (h)   Correct.

      (i)   `Input` is a reserved word.

      (j)   Correct.

2.43   *(a)*   Correct.

      (b)   Dollar sign is missing.

      (c)   Last character must be a dollar sign.

      (d)   Correct.

      (e)   Correct (though `input` is a reserved word).

2.44   *(a)*   `3 * x + 5`

      (b)   `i + j - 2`

      (c)   `x ^ 2 + y ^ 2`

(d)   (x + y) ^ 2

(e)   (u + v) ^ (k - 1)

(f)   (4 * t) ^ (1 / 6) or (4 * t) ^ 0.1666667

(g)   t ^ (n + 1)

(h)   (x + 3) ^ (1 / k)

2.45   (a)   5.666667   (g)   5.461539

(b)   5   (h)   7

(c)   2   (i)   0

(d)   4.333334   (j)   3.944445

(e)   4   (k)   3

(f)   0   (l)   1

2.46   (a)   A$ & B$ & C$ or   A$ + B$ + C$

(b)   name$ & " " & address$ & " " & city$ or

name$ + " " + address$ + " " + city$

(c)   "Hello, " & NAME$

2.47   (a)   LET C = 2.54

(b)   LET xmin = 12

(c)   LET NSTAR = N

(d)   LET DATE$ = "January 31"

(e)   LET TSTR$ = STR$

(f)   LET squares = A ^ 2 + B ^ 2 + C ^ 2

(g)   LET count = count + 0.01

(h)   LET I = I + J

(i)   LET city$ = "PITTSBURGH, PA."

(j)   LET F_STAR = X / (A + B - C)

(k)   LET K = K - 2

   (*l*) `LET prize = 2 * prize`

2.48 (*a*) `LET z = x / y + 3`

   (*b*) `LET z = x / (y + 3)`

   (*c*) `LET w = (u + v) / (s + t)`

   (*d*) `LET f1 = 2 * a * b / (c + 1)`
      `LET f2 = t / (3 * (p + q))`
      `LET f = (f1 - f2) ^ 0.3333333`

   (*e*) `LET y1 = a1 - a2 * x + a3 * x ^ 2 - a4 * x ^ 3 + a5 * x ^ 4`
      `LET y2 = c1 - c2 * x + c3 * x ^ 2 - c4 * x ^ 3`
      `LET y = y1 / y2`

   (*f*) `LET P = A * i * (1 + i) ^ n / ((1 + i) ^ n - 1)`

2.49 If the value of Y is less than the value of Z, there will be a problem because a negative number cannot be raised to a fractional power.

2.50 -16

2.51 16

2.52 (*a*) `INPUT A, B, C, HEADING$`

   (*b*) `INPUT A, B, C`
      `INPUT HEADING$`

   (*c*) `INPUT A, B`
      `INPUT C, HEADING$`

   (*d*) `PRINT C1, C2, C3, C4, C5`

   (*e*) `PRINT A, B, C`
      `PRINT`
      `PRINT X, Y, Z`

   (*f*) `PRINT A; B; C; X; Y; Z`

   (*g*) `PRINT "X ="; X, "Y ="; Y, "Z ="; Z` or

      `PRINT "X ="; X; "Y ="; Y; "Z ="; Z`

   (*h*) `PRINT N$; N; A ^ 2 + B ^ 2` or `120 PRINT N$; N, A ^ 2 + B ^ 2`

   (*i*) `PRINT "LEFT",,,,"RIGHT"`

   (*j*) `PRINT "Enter NUMBER OF ITEMS and COST PER ITEM below:"`
      `INPUT Items, Cost`

(k) PRINT, "Roots of Simultaneous Equations"

(l) PRINT "Const = ";
     INPUT Const

(m) PRINT "NAME: "; NAME$
     PRINT
     PRINT "SOCIAL SECURITY NUMBER: "; SSN$

2.53 (a) ?<u>4.83E-3,-537,941.55,Boston</u> or ?<u>.00483,-537,941.55,Boston</u>

(b) ?<u>Boston,4.83E-3</u>
     ?<u>-537,941.55</u>

(c) ?<u>"Boston, MA",-8.05,350</u>   (the string must be enclosed in quotation marks)

(d) ?<u>"New York","Chicago","San Francisco"</u>   (New York and San Francisco must be enclosed in quotation marks; Chicago is optional.)

(e) ?<u>2770543,"July 4, 1776",48.8E9,"Philadelphia, PA"</u>

2.54 (a) Name: George Smith 7000   1500   5500

(b) Name: George Smith 7000 1500 5500

(c) 3   6   9   12
     5   10   15   20

(d) 3 6 9 12 5 10 15 20

(e) 9   1.333333   .1666667

2.55 (a) REM AREA AND CIRCUMFERENCE OF A CIRCLE

(b) REM AVERAGING OF AIR POLLUTION DATA

(c) LET A = PI * R ^ 2   !AREA
     LET C = 2 * PI * R   !CIRCUMFERENCE

     or

     LET A = PI * R ^ 2   'AREA
     LET C = 2 * PI * R   'CIRCUMFERENCE

(d) REM LOOP TO CALCULATE CUMULATIVE SUM

(e) LET avg = sum / n   !CALCULATE AN AVERAGE VALUE

     or

     LET avg = sum / n   'CALCULATE AN AVERAGE VALUE

2.57   (a)   LET W = LOG(V)

        (b)   LET P = Q * EXP(-Q * T) or 20 LET P = Q / EXP(Q * T)

        (c)   LET W = ABS(ABS(U - V) - ABS(U + V))

        (d)   LET R = (P + Q) ^ 0.5 or 40 LET R = SQR(P + Q)

        (e)   LET Y = A * EXP(B * X) * SIN(C * X)

        (f)   LET Y = SQR(ABS(SIN(X) - COS(X)))

2.58   (a)   LET Y = SGN((A * B - C * D) / (F + G))

        (b)   LET M = N / 2 - INT(N / 2)   or   10 LET M = N / 2 - IP(N / 2)

              If the value of M is zero, N is even; otherwise, N is odd.

        (c)   The method still works properly.

        (d)   I = INT(X ^ 2 - Y ^ 2)

        (e)   -34

        (f)   PRINT TAB(4); "X= "; X; TAB(28); "Y= "; Y; TAB(52); "Z= "; Z

        (g)   PRINT TAB(10); X$; X; TAB(50); Y$; Y

2.59   (a)   24

        (b)   1600 PENNSYLVANIA AVENUE

        (c)   1600 pennsylvania avenue

        (d)   0.2

        (e)   1.25

Chapter 4

4.33   (a)   IF sum > 100 THEN LET sum = 100

        (b)   IF sum > 100 THEN
                  PRINT sum
                  LET sum = 100
                  PRINT sum
              END IF

        (c)   IF sum <= 100 THEN
                  LET sum = sum + v
                  PRINT sum

```
            ELSE
                PRINT sum
                LET sum = 100
                PRINT sum
            END IF
```

4.34   (a) IF hours > 40 THEN LET pay = 6.25

        (b) IF hours <= 40 THEN
                LET pay = 4.50
                LET status$ = "REGULAR"
            ELSE
                LET pay = 6.25
                LET status$ = "OVERTIME"
            END IF

4.35   IF FLAG$ = "TRUE" THEN
                LET count = 0
                PRINT "RESETTING THE COUNTER"
                IF Z > ZMAX THEN
                    PRINT "MAXIMUM VALUE EXCEEDED"
                    LET Z = ZMIN
                ELSE
                    LET Z = Z + W
                    PRINT Z
                END IF
            ELSE
                LET count = count + 1
                PRINT count
                IF TYPE$ = "A" THEN
                    LET Z = Z + U
                ELSEIF TYPE$ = "B" THEN
                    LET Z = Z + V
                ELSE
                    LET Z = Z + W
                END IF
                PRINT TYPE$, Z
                LET FLAG$ = "TRUE"
            END IF

4.36   (a) LET sum = 0
            FOR i = 2 TO 99 STEP 3
                LET sum = sum + i
            NEXT i

        (b) LET sum = 0
            LET i = 2
            DO WHILE (i < 100)
                LET sum = sum + i
                LET i = i + 3
            LOOP
```
```

(c)
```
LET sum = 0
LET i = 2
DO UNTIL (i >= 100)
   LET sum = sum + i
   LET i = i + 3
LOOP
```

(d)
```
LET sum = 0
LET i = 2
DO
   LET sum = sum + i
   LET i = i + 3
LOOP WHILE (i < 100)
```

(e)
```
LET sum = 0
LET i = 2
DO
   LET sum = sum + i
   LET i = i + 3
LOOP UNTIL (i >= 100)
```

4.37 (a)
```
LET sum = 0
FOR i = nstart TO nstop STEP n
   LET sum = sum + i
NEXT i
```

(b)
```
LET sum = 0
LET i = nstart
DO WHILE (i <= nstop)
   LET sum = sum + i
   LET i = i + n
LOOP
```

(e)
```
LET sum = 0
LET i = nstart
DO
   LET sum = sum + i
   LET i = i + n
LOOP UNTIL (i >= nstop + 1)
```

4.38 (a)
```
LET sum = 0
FOR i = nstart TO nstop STEP n
   LET sum = sum + i
   IF sum > maxsum THEN EXIT FOR
NEXT i
```

(b)
```
LET sum = 0
LET i = nstart
DO WHILE (i <= nstop)
   LET sum = sum + i
   IF sum > maxsum THEN EXIT DO
   LET i = i + n
LOOP
```

```
(e)  LET sum = 0
     LET i = nstart
     DO
         LET sum = sum + i
         IF sum > maxsum THEN EXIT DO
         LET i = i + n
     LOOP UNTIL (i >= nstop + 1)
```

4.39 (a) FOR j = 2 TO 13
```
         LET sum = 0
         FOR i = 2 TO 99 STEP j
             LET sum = sum + i
         NEXT i
         PRINT j, i, sum
     NEXT j
```

(b) FOR j = 2 TO 13
```
         LET sum = 0
         LET i = 2
         DO WHILE (i < 100)
             LET sum = sum + i
             LET i = i + j
         LOOP
         PRINT j, i, sum
     NEXT j
```

(e) FOR j = 2 TO 13
```
         LET sum = 0
         LET i = 2
         DO
             LET sum = sum + i
             LET i = i + j
         LOOP UNTIL (i >= 100)
         PRINT j, i, sum
     NEXT j
```

4.40 LET sum = 0
```
      LET i = 2
      DO WHILE (i < 100)
          IF (i / 5 - INT(i / 5) = 0) THEN LET sum = sum + i
          LET i = i + 3
      LOOP
```

4.41 LET sum = 0
```
      LET i = nstart
      DO WHILE (i <= nstop)
          IF (i / k - INT(i / k) = 0) THEN LET sum = sum + i
          LET i = i + n
      LOOP
```

4.42   This solution uses the MID$ function (found in QuickBASIC/QBASIC). The original string is called **a$**.

```
LET letters = 0
LET digits = 0
LET blanks = 0
LET others = 0
FOR i = LEN(a$) TO 1 STEP -1
   LET c$ = MID$(a$, i, 1)
   IF (UCASE$(c$) >= "A" AND UCASE$(c$) <= "Z") THEN
      LET letters = letters + 1
   ELSEIF (c$ >= "0" AND c$ <= "9") THEN
      LET digits = digits + 1
   ELSEIF (c$ = " ") THEN
      LET blanks = blanks + 1
   ELSE
      LET others = others + 1
   END IF
NEXT i
PRINT a$
PRINT letters, digits, blanks, others
```

4.43   This solution uses the MID$ function (found in QuickBASIC/QBASIC). The original string is called **a$**.

```
LET vowels = 0
LET consonants = 0
FOR i = LEN(a$) TO 1 STEP -1
   LET c$ = UCASE$(MID$(a$, i, 1))
   IF (c$ >= "A" AND c$ <= "Z") THEN          'character is a letter
      IF (c$ = "A" OR c$ = "E" OR c$ = "I" OR c$ = "O" OR c$ = "U") THEN
         LET vowels = vowels + 1
      ELSE
         LET consonants = consonants + 1
      END IF
   END IF
NEXT i
PRINT a$
PRINT vowels, consonants
```

4.44   This solution uses the MID$ function (found in QuickBASIC/QBASIC). The original string is called **a$**.

```
FOR i = LEN(a$) TO 1 STEP -1
   PRINT MID$(a$, i, 1);
NEXT i
```

4.45
```
SELECT CASE flag
CASE 1
   PRINT "HOT"
CASE 2
   PRINT "LUKE WARM"
CASE 3
   PRINT "COLD"
CASE ELSE
```

```
            PRINT "OUT OF RANGE"
        END SELECT

4.46    SELECT CASE color$
        CASE IS = "r", IS = "R"
            PRINT "RED"
        CASE IS = "g", IS = "G"
            PRINT "GREEN"
        CASE IS = "b", IS = "B"
            PRINT "BLUE"
        CASE ELSE
            PRINT "BLACK"
        END SELECT
```

4.47   Yes, SELECT CASE can be used.

```
        SELECT CASE TEMP
        CASE IS < 0
            PRINT "ICE"
        CASE 0 TO 100
            PRINT "WATER"
        CASE IS > 100
            PRINT "STEAM"
        END SELECT
```

4.48   (a)   0   5   15   30

        (b)   1   2   3   4

        (c)   1   2   3   4   5

        (d)   1   4   9   16   25

        (e)   1   0   3   2   7   6   13   12   21   20

        (f)   1

        (g)   0   1   3   5   8   12   15   19   24   30

        (h)   0   1   3   6

        (i)   0

        (j)   0   0   2   4   5   9   10   14   14   20

        (k)   1   3   5   7   9   12   14   17   20   23

Chapter 5

5.20   (a)   cost is a 100-element, one-dimensional numeric array; items$ is a 100 x 3, two-dimensional string array.

(b)   P is a one-dimensional numeric array; Q is a two-dimensional numeric array.

(c)   A$ is a one-dimensional string array.

(d)   X$ is a one dimensional string array; Y is a one-dimensional numeric array; Z is a two-dimensional numeric array.

(e)   message$ is a one-dimensional string array.

(f)   k is a one-dimensional numeric array; m$ is a one-dimensional string array.

5.21   (a)
```
LET sum = 0
FOR i = 1 TO n
   LET sum = sum + costs(i)
NEXT i
```

(b)
```
LET sum = 0
FOR i = 1 TO 60
   LET sum = sum + values(i, 3)
NEXT i
```

(c)
```
LET sum = 0
FOR j = 1 TO 20
   LET sum = sum + values(5, j)
NEXT j
```

(d)
```
LET sum = 0
FOR i = 1 to m
   FOR j = 1 TO n
      LET sum = sum + values(i, j)
   NEXT j
NEXT i
```

(e)
```
FOR i = 2 TO 60 STEP 2
   PRINT names$(i)
NEXT i
```

(f)
```
LET city$ = "Philadelphia, Pennsylvania"
LET n = LEN(city$)
FOR i = 1 TO n STEP 2
   PRINT city$[i:i]
NEXT i
```

In Microsoft QuickBASIC, the solution is

```
LET city$ = "Philadelphia, Pennsylvania"
LET n = LEN(city$)
FOR i = 1 TO n STEP 2
   PRINT(MID$(city$, i, 1)
NEXT i
```

(g)
```
LET sum = 0
FOR i = 1 TO 199 STEP 2
    LET sum = sum + X(i) ^ 2
NEXT i
LET root = sqr(sum)
```

(h)
```
DIM h(8, 12)
. . . . .
FOR i = 1 TO 8
   FOR j = 1 TO 12
       LET h(i, j) = 1 / (i + j - 1)
   NEXT j
NEXT i
```

(i)
```
PRINT I, K(I)
FOR I = 1 TO N
    IF (K(I) <= KMAX) PRINT I, K(I)
NEXT I
```

(j)
```
LET PROD = 1
FOR I = 1 TO K
   LET PROD = PROD * W(I, I)
NEXT I
```

5.22 (a)
```
DIM C(12)
DATA 1, 4, 7, 10, 13, 16, 19, 22, 25, 28, 31, 34
. . . . .
FOR i = 1 TO 12
   READ C(i)
NEXT i
```

(b)
```
DIM directions$(4)
DATA NORTH, SOUTH, EAST, WEST
. . . . .
FOR i = 1 TO 4
   READ directions$(i)
NEXT i
```

(c)
```
DIM player1$(4), player2$(4)
DATA NORTH, SOUTH, EAST, WEST
. . . . .
FOR i = 1 TO 4
   READ player1$(i)
NEXT i
RESTORE
FOR i = 1 TO 4
   READ player2$(i)
NEXT i
```

    (d)
```
DIM cities$(4)
DATA "New York", "St. Louis", "San Francisco", "Los Angeles"
. . . . .
FOR i = 1 TO 4
   READ cities$(i)
NEXT i
```

    (e)
```
DIM consts(3, 4)
DATA 10, 12, 14, 16, 20, 22, 24, 26, 30, 32, 34, 36
. . . . .
FOR i = 1 TO 3
   FOR j = 1 TO 4
      READ consts(i, j)
   NEXT j
NEXT i
```

5.23 (a)
```
DATA WHITE, YELLOW, ORANGE, RED
DATA 2.5E5, 6.1E-9, 1.3E12, RESTART
DATA 1, -3, 5, -7, -2, 4, -6, 8
. . . . .
FOR i = 1 TO 4
   READ COLOR$(i)
NEXT i
READ P, Q, R, H$
FOR i = 1 TO 2
   FOR j = 1 TO 4
      READ T(i, j)
   NEXT j
NEXT i
```

    (b)
```
DATA WHITE, YELLOW, ORANGE, RED
DATA 2.5E5, 6.1E-9, 1.3E12, RESTART
DATA 1, -3, 5, -7, -2, 4, -6, 8
. . . . .
FOR i = 1 TO 4
   READ COLOR$(i)
NEXT i
READ P, Q, R, H$
FOR i = 1 TO 2
   FOR j = 1 TO 4
      READ T(i, j)
   NEXT j
NEXT i
. . . . .
RESTORE
READ A1$, A2$, A3$, A4$
```

5.24 (a) 60

    (b) 75

    (c) 75

(d)   3   (smallest value)

(e)   3   15   27   (smallest value within each row)

(f)   12   24   36   (largest value within each row)

(g)   27   30   33   36   (largest value within each column)

(h)   The entire string is displayed, alternating upper- and lowercase characters. Every other character is uppercase, beginning with the second. (QuickBASIC.)

(i)   The entire string is displayed, alternating upper- and lowercase characters. Every other character is uppercase, beginning with the first. (ANSI standard BASIC / True BASIC.)

Chapter 6 (Solutions are written in QuickBASIC unless the problem states otherwise.)

6.46   (a)   `DEF fnz(u, v, x, y) = (u / v + x / y) / 2`

(b)   `DEF FNY(X) = .01 * INT(100 * (X + .005))`

(c)   `DEF fny(a, b, x) = a * x ^ b`

(d)   `DEF fnq(r) = c0 + c1 * r + c2 * r ^ 2 + c3 * r ^ 3 + c4 * r ^ 4`

(e)   `DEF fni(j, k) = (j + k) ^ (j + k)`

6.47   (a)   `PRINT "f ="; fnz(a, b, c, d)`

(b)   `PRINT "v ="; INT(t) + FNY(t - INT(t))`

(c)   `PRINT "t ="; fny((c1 + c2), 3, (x + y))`

(d)   `PRINT "q ="; fnq(log(x))`

(e)   `PRINT "f ="; fni((a - b), c)`

6.48   (a)
```
DEF fnp(t, a)
    IF (t ^ 2 > a) THEN
        LET fnp = LOG(t ^ 2 - a)
    ELSE
        LET fnp = LOG(t ^ 2)
    END IF
END DEF
```

(b)
```
DEF fnsum(a, n)
    LET total = 0
    FOR i = 1 TO n
        LET total = total + a(i)
    NEXT i
    LET fnsum = total
END DEF
```

```
(c)  DEF FNtwo$(M$, N$)
         IF (M$ <= N$) THEN
             LET FNtwo$ = M$ + N$
         ELSE
             LET FNtwo$ = N$ + M$
         END IF
     END DEF

(d)  DEF fnavg(a, b)
         LET r1 = a + (b - a) * RND
         LET r2 = a + (b - a) * RND
         LET fnavg = (r1 + r2) / 2
     END DEF

(e)  DEF FNMESSAGE$(X)
         IF (X < 0) THEN
             LET FNMESSAGE$ = "NEGATIVE"
         ELSEIF (X > 0) THEN
             LET FNMESSAGE$ = "POSITIVE"
         ELSE
             LET FNMESSAGE$ = "ZERO"
         END IF
     END DEF

(f)  DEF fnfirst$ (word$)
         LET c$ = "z"
         FOR i = 1 TO LEN(word$)
             LET w$ = MID$(word$, i, 1)
             IF (w$ < c$) THEN LET c$ = w$
         NEXT i
         LET fnfirst$ = c$
     END DEF
```

6.49 (a)
```
     FUNCTION p (t, a)
         IF (t ^ 2 > a) THEN
             LET p = LOG(t ^ 2 - a)
         ELSE
             LET p = LOG(t ^ 2)
         END IF
     END FUNCTION
```

(b)
```
     FUNCTION sum (a(), n)
         LET total = 0
         FOR i = 1 TO n
             LET total = total + a(i)
         NEXT i
         LET sum = total
     END FUNCTION
```

(c)
```
     FUNCTION two$ (M$, N$)
         IF (M$ <= N$) THEN
             LET two$ = M$ + N$
```

```
        ELSE
            LET two$ = N$ + M$
        END IF
    END FUNCTION
```

(d) ```
    FUNCTION avg (a, b)
        LET r1 = a + (b - a) * RND
        LET r2 = a + (b - a) * RND
        LET avg = (r1 + r2) / 2
    END FUNCTION
```

(e)  ```
    FUNCTION MESSAGE$ (X)
        IF (X < 0) THEN
            LET MESSAGE$ = "NEGATIVE"
        ELSEIF (X > 0) THEN
            LET MESSAGE$ = "POSITIVE"
        ELSE
            LET MESSAGE$ = "ZERO"
        END IF
    END FUNCTION
```

(f) ```
    FUNCTION first$ (word$)
        LET c$ = "z"
        FOR i = 1 TO LEN(word$)
            LET w$ = MID$(word$, i, 1)
            IF (w$ < c$) THEN LET c$ = w$
        NEXT i
        LET first$ = c$
    END FUNCTION
```

6.50  (a)  ```
    PRINT "q ="; fnp((a + b), c)
```

(b) ```
    PRINT "Difference ="; fnsum(a, m) - fnsum(a, n)
```

(c)  ```
    PRINT UCASE$(FNtwo$(c$, d$))
```

(d) ```
    PRINT fnavg(1, 10)
```

(e)  ```
    FOR i = 1 TO 100
        PRINT FNMESSAGE$(list(i))
    NEXT i
```

6.51 (a) ```
    SUB LARGEST (X(), N, BIG, K)
        LET BIG = -1E+38
        FOR I = 1 TO N
            IF (X(I) > BIG) THEN
                LET BIG = X(I)
                LET K = I
            END IF
        NEXT I
    END SUB
```
```

```
(b)  SUB MESSAGE (X)
         IF (X < 0) THEN
             PRINT "NEGATIVE"
         ELSEIF (X > 0) THEN
             PRINT "POSITIVE"
         ELSE
             PRINT "ZERO"
         END IF
     END SUB




(c)  SUB STRINGCHARS (A$, VOWELS, CONSONANTS, DIGITS, OTHER)
         LET VOWELS = 0
         LET CONSONANTS = 0
         LET DIGITS = 0
         LET OTHER = 0
         FOR I = 1 TO LEN(A$)
             LET C$ = UCASE$(MID$(A$, I, 1))
             IF (C$ = "A" OR C$ = "E" OR C$ = "I" OR C$ = "O" OR C$ = "U") THEN
                 LET VOWELS = VOWELS + 1
             ELSEIF (C$ >= "B" AND C$ <= "Z") THEN
                 LET CONSONANTS = CONSONANTS + 1
             ELSEIF (C$ >= "0" AND C$ <= "9") THEN
                 LET DIGITS = DIGITS + 1
             ELSE
                 LET OTHER = OTHER + 1
             END IF
         NEXT I
     END SUB




(d)  SUB STRINGCHARS (A$, LETTERS, DIGITS)
         LET LETTERS = 0
         LET DIGITS = 0
         FOR I = 1 TO LEN(A$)
             LET C$ = UCASE$(MID$(A$, I, 1))
             IF (C$ >= "A" AND C$ <= "Z") THEN
                 LET LETTERS = LETTERS + 1
             ELSEIF (C$ >= "0" AND C$ <= "9") THEN
                 LET DIGITS = DIGITS + 1
             ELSE
                 PRINT "CHARACTER ENCOUNTERED THAT IS NOT A LETTER OR A DIGIT"
                 EXIT SUB
             END IF
         NEXT I
     END SUB
```

(e) ```
     DIM a(10, 20), b(20, 10)
       . . . . .
     SUB transpose (a(), b(), m, n)
        FOR i = 1 TO m
           FOR j = 1 TO n
              LET b(j, i) = a(i, j)
           NEXT j
        NEXT i
     END SUB
     ```

6.52  (a)  ```
           DECLARE SUB LARGEST (X(), N, BIG, K)
             . . . . .
           CALL LARGEST(X(), 8, BIG, K)
           ```

      (b) ```
           DECLARE SUB MESSAGE (X)
             . . . . .
           CALL MESSAGE(X)
           ```

      (c)  ```
           DECLARE SUB STRINGCHARS (A$, VOWELS, CONSONANTS, DIGITS, OTHER)
             . . . . .
           CALL STRINGCHARS(A$, VOWELS, CONSONANTS, DIGITS, OTHER)
           ```

      (d) ```
           DECLARE SUB STRINGCHARS (A$, LETTERS, DIGITS)
             . . . . .
           CALL STRINGCHARS(A$, LETTERS, DIGITS)
           ```

      (e)  ```
           DECLARE SUB transpose (a(), b(), m, n)
             . . . . .
           CALL transpose(a(), b(), 3, 5)
           ```

6.53 (a) 'Hello, There!'

      (b) 11

      (c) 146

      (d) 25

      (e) Ifmmp-!Uifsf"
           (*Note:* asc is a library function that returns the ASCII value corresponding to a specified character.
           Also, chr$ is a library function that returns the character corresponding to a specified ASCII value.)

      (f) 55

      (g) 55

      (h) 0

      (i) 15

      (j) 0

(k)   36

(l)   0

(m)   1600 Pennsylvania Avenue NW, Washington, DC 20500
      1600 pENNSYLVANIA aVENUE nw, wASHINGTON, dc 20500
      1600 Pennsylvania Avenue NW, Washington, DC 20500

(n)   1   2   3
         4   5   6
         7   8   9

         1   0   0
         4   5   0
         7   8   9

         1   0   0
         0   5   0
         0   0   9

         1   2   3
         0   5   6
         0   0   9

         1   2   3
         4   5   6
         7   8   9

(o)   1600 Pennsylvania Avenue NW, Washington, DC 20500
      00502 CD ,notgnihsaW ,WN eunevA ainavlysnneP 0061

6.54   (a) $y_1 = x_1$ and $y_n = x_n + y_{n-1}$ for $n > 1$

       (b) $y_0 = 1$ and $y_n = (-1)^n x^n / n! + y_{n-1}$ for $n > 0$

       (c) $p_1 = f_1$ and $p_t = f_t * p_{t-1}$ for $t > 1$

Chapter 7

7.19   (a)   Integer.

       (b)   Double-precision.

       (c)   Real (fixed-point).

       (d)   Long-integer.

       (e)   Real (fixed-point).

       (f)   Double-precision.

(g) Real (fixed-point).

(h) Real (floating-point).

(i) Double-precision.

(j) Real (floating-point).

(k) Double-precision.

(l) Double-precision.

(m) Double-precision.

(n) Double-precision.

7.20 (a) X%

(b) X&

(c) X!

(d) X#

(e) X$

7.21 (a) DEFDBL r, t, u-z

(b) DEFINT i-n

(c) DEFSNG c, e, g

(d) DEFLNG p-r

(e) DEFSTR s

7.22 (a) .25

(b) 55.5555555

(c) 3703703.817171961

(d) 33.48333330596046

(e) 2777777.865656749

(f) 123456794

(g) 18518524.08585981

7.23 (a) 1526

    (*b*)   1526.25

    (*c*)   1526.25

    (*d*)   (overflow)

    (*e*)   150000

    (*f*)   150000

    (*g*)   150000

    (*h*)   0

    (*i*)   0.0012

    (*j*)   0.0012

    (*k*)   21

    (*l*)   21

    (*m*) 21

7.24   (*a*)   INPUT "Name: ", name$ (QuickBASIC)

             INPUT "Name: ": name$ (True BASIC)

    (*b*)   INPUT "What is your name "; name$ (QuickBASIC)

            In True BASIC, the question mark is *always* suppressed when a prompt string is present. Hence, one must write

```
PRINT "What is your name ";
INPUT name$
```

7.25   (*a*)   1.56   30,287

    (*b*)   2   ****

    (*c*)   .15556e+01

    (*d*) $30,287

    (*e*) $ 30,287

    (*f*) $ 30,287

    (*g*) $0,030,287

    (*h*)   ****

    (i)   BOSTON

    (j)   BOSTON

    (k) BOSTON

    (l) $1.5556 $ 30,287   BOSTON

7.26 *(a)* 1.56   30,287

    (b)   2   %30287   (Note: the percent sign (%) indicates a field-width overflow.)

    (c) .15556E+01

    (d) $30,287

    (e) $ 30,287

    (f) $30,287

    (g) *****30,287

    (h) BOSTON

    (i) $1.5556 $ 30,287   BOSTON

7.27 *(a)* PRINT USING "$####,###   .#####"; x; y   (QuickBASIC)
          PRINT USING "$-###,###   .#####": x, y   (True BASIC)

    (b) PRINT USING "#.#####^^^^   .#####^^^^"; x; y   (QuickBASIC)
          PRINT USING "-.#####^^^^   .#####^^^^": x, y   (True BASIC)

    (c) PRINT USING "####^^^^ ###.#^^^^"; x; y   (QuickBASIC)
          PRINT USING "-###^^^^ ##.#^^^^": x, y   (True BASIC)

    (d) PRINT USING "##.#^^^^ ##.#^^^^"; x; y   (QuickBASIC)
          PRINT USING "-#.#^^^^ #.#^^^^": x, y   (True BASIC)

7.28 *(a)* PRINT USING "$#,###,###"; c   (QuickBASIC)
          PRINT USING "$#,###,###": c   (True BASIC)

    (b) PRINT USING ".###^^^^"; c   (QuickBASIC)
          PRINT USING ".###^^^^": c   (True BASIC)

    (c) PRINT USING ".#######^^^^"; c   (QuickBASIC)
          PRINT USING ".#######^^^^": c   (True BASIC)

    (d) PRINT USING "$####,###,###"; c   (QuickBASIC)
          PRINT USING "$####,###,###": c   (True BASIC)

Chapter 8

8.24 (*a*) New text file called SAMPLE.001, opened as an output file on data channel 1.

(*b*) Existing direct file whose name is given by `filename$`, with a maximum record size of 48 characters, opened on data channel 2.

(*c*) New direct file whose name is given by `newfile$`, with a maximum record size given by `nchars`, opened on data channel 3.

(*d*) Existing text file called BACKUP.DAT, opened as an input file on data channel 4.

(*e*) Printer file (for directing output to the printer), opened on data channel 5.

8.25 (*a*) Existing sequential file called DEMO.DAT, opened as an input file on data channel 3.

(*b*) New sequential file whose name is given by `datafile$`, opened as an output file on data channel 5.

(*c*) Direct data file whose name is given by `datafile$`, with a record size given by `recname`, opened on data channel 2.

(*d*) Existing sequential file called `customers.dat`, opened as an append file (i.e., an output file set for writing new data at the end of the file) on data channel 1.

8.26 (*a*) OPEN #3: NAME "students.dat", ACCESS INPUT, CREATE OLD, ORG TEXT

(*b*) OPEN #5: NAME "grades.dat", ACCESS OUTPUT, CREATE NEW, ORG TEXT

(*c*) OPEN #2: NAME "orders.dat", CREATE NEW, ORG RANDOM, RECSIZE 72

(*d*) OPEN #4: NAME filename$, CREATE OLD, ORG RANDOM, RECSIZE recsize

(*e*) OPEN #9: PRINTER

8.27 (*a*) OPEN "students.dat" FOR INPUT AS #3

(*b*) OPEN "grades.dat" FOR OUTPUT AS #5

(*c*) OPEN filename$ FOR APPEND AS AS #2

(*d*) OPEN "orders.dat" FOR RANDOM AS #1 LEN = 72

(*e*) OPEN filename$ FOR RANDOM AS #2 LEN = LEN(recsize)

8.28 (*a*) True BASIC:

```
OPEN #1: NAME "oldrecs.dat", CREATE OLD, ORG TEXT
OPEN #2: NAME "newrecs.dat", CREATE NEW, ORG TEXT

DO UNTIL END #1
    INPUT #1: name$, salary, taxes, netpay

    . . . . .           'update the data

    PRINT #2: name$, salary, taxes, netpay
LOOP

CLOSE #1
CLOSE #2
END
```

(*b*) QuickBASIC:

```
OPEN "oldrecs.dat" FOR INPUT AS #1
OPEN "newrecs.dat" FOR OUTPUT AS #2

DO UNTIL EOF(1)
    INPUT #1, name$, salary, taxes, netpay

    . . . . .           'update the data

    PRINT #2, name$, salary, taxes, netpay
LOOP

CLOSE
END
```

8.29 (*a*) True BASIC:

```
OPEN #1: NAME "salaries.dat", ORG RANDOM
ASK #1: RECSIZE RecordSize
ASK #1: FILESIZE Last

LET Count = 1
DO
    READ #1: name$, salary, taxes, netpay

    . . . . .           'update the data

    SET #1: POINTER SAME
    WRITE #1: name$, salary, taxes, netpay
    LET Count = Count + 1
LOOP UNTIL Count > Last

CLOSE #1
END
```

(*b*) QuickBASIC:

```
TYPE RecordType
   Name    AS STRING * 20
   Salary AS SINGLE
   Taxes  AS SINGLE
   Netpay AS SINGLE
END TYPE

DIM Employee AS RecordType

OPEN "salaries.dat" FOR RANDOM AS #1 LEN = LEN(Employee)

LET Last = LOF(1) / LEN(Employee)
LET RecNo = 1
DO
   GET #1, RecNo, Employee

   . . . . .          'update the data

   PUT #1, RecNo, Employee
   LET RecNo = RecNo + 1
LOOP UNTIL RecNo > Last

CLOSE
END
```

8.30   (*a*)   True BASIC:

```
OPEN #1: NAME "oldrecs.dat", CREATE OLD, ORG TEXT
OPEN #2: PRINTER

DO UNTIL END #1
   INPUT #1: name$, salary, taxes, netpay
   PRINT     name$, salary, taxes, netpay
   PRINT #2: name$, salary, taxes, netpay
LOOP
CLOSE #1
CLOSE #2
END
```

(*b*)   QuickBASIC:

```
OPEN "oldrecs.dat" FOR INPUT AS #1

DO UNTIL EOF(1)
   INPUT #1, name$, salary, taxes, netpay
   PRINT     name$, salary, taxes, netpay
   LPRINT    name$, salary, taxes, netpay
LOOP
CLOSE
END
```

8.31 (*a*)   True BASIC:

```
OPEN #1: NAME "oldrecs.dat", CREATE OLD, ORG TEXT
OPEN #2: NAME "newrecs.dat", CREATE NEW, ORG RANDOM
SET  #2: RECSIZE 50

DO UNTIL END #1
   INPUT #1: name$, salary, taxes, netpay
   PRINT     name$, salary, taxes, netpay
   WRITE #2: name$, salary, taxes, netpay
LOOP
CLOSE #1
CLOSE #2
END
```

(*b*)   QuickBASIC:

```
TYPE RecordType
   name   AS STRING * 20
   salary AS SINGLE
   taxes  AS SINGLE
   netpay AS SINGLE
END TYPE
DIM Employee AS RecordType

OPEN "oldrecs.dat" FOR INPUT AS #1
OPEN "newrecs.dat" FOR RANDOM AS #2 LEN = LEN(Employee)

LET RecNo = 1
DO UNTIL EOF(1)
   INPUT #1, Employee.name, Employee.salary, Employee.taxes, Employee.netpay
   PRINT     Employee.name, Employee.salary, Employee.taxes, Employee.netpay
   PUT #2,   RecNo, Employee
   LET RecNo = RecNo + 1
LOOP
CLOSE
END
```

8.32 (*a*)   True BASIC:

```
OPEN #1: NAME "oldrecs.dat", ORG RANDOM
OPEN #2: NAME "newrecs.dat", CREATE NEW, ORG TEXT
ASK #1: RECSIZE RecordSize
ASK #1: FILESIZE Last

LET Count = 1
DO
   READ #1:  name$, salary, taxes, netpay
   PRINT     name$, salary, taxes, netpay
   PRINT #2: name$, salary, taxes, netpay
   LET Count = Count + 1
LOOP UNTIL Count > Last
```

```
CLOSE #1
CLOSE #2
END
```

(b)   QuickBASIC:

```
TYPE RecordType
    name    AS STRING * 20
    salary AS SINGLE
    taxes  AS SINGLE
    netpay AS SINGLE
END TYPE

DIM Employee AS RecordType

OPEN "oldrecs.dat" FOR RANDOM AS #1 LEN = LEN(Employee)
OPEN "newrecs.dat" FOR OUTPUT AS #2

LET Last = LOF(1) / LEN(Employee)
LET RecNo = 1
DO
    GET #1,   RecNo, Employee
    PRINT       Employee.name, Employee.salary, Employee.taxes, Employee.netpay
    PRINT #2, Employee.name, Employee.salary, Employee.taxes, Employee.netpay

    LET RecNo = RecNo + 1
LOOP UNTIL RecNo > Last
CLOSE
END
```

8.33   (a)   True BASIC:

```
OPEN #1: NAME "oldrecs.dat", ORG RANDOM
ASK #1:   RECSIZE RecordSize
INPUT PROMPT "Record No. ": RecNo
DO UNTIL RecNo = 0
    SET #1: RECORD
    READ #1: name$, salary, taxes, netpay
    PRINT name$, salary, taxes, netpay
    INPUT PROMPT "Record No. ": RecNo
LOOP
CLOSE #1
END
```

(b)   Quick BASIC:

```
TYPE RecordDef
    name    AS STRING * 20
    salary AS SINGLE
    taxes  AS SINGLE
    netpay AS SINGLE
END TYPE
```

```
DIM Employee AS RecordDef

OPEN "oldrecs.dat" FOR RANDOM AS #1 LEN = LEN(Employee)

INPUT "Record No. ", RecNo
DO UNTIL RecNo = 0
    GET #1, RecNo, Employee
    PRINT Employee.name, Employee.salary, Employee.taxes, Employee.netpay
    INPUT "Record No. ", RecNo
LOOP
CLOSE #1
END
```

Chapter 9

9.44 (a) Assigns the value 0.3 to each element of C and each element of D, and assigns the string "Hello, there!" to each element of A$ and each element of B$.

(b) Carries out matrix addition, matrix subtraction and multiplication by a constant. The resulting output is

10	12	14	16
18	20	22	24
26	28	30	32
34	36	38	40

```
36  40  44  48
52  56  60  64

16  16  16  16
16  16  16  16

32  32  32  32
32  32  32  32
```

(c) Carries out matrix multiplication, resulting in a 2 x 2 matrix. The resulting output is

```
1704      1808
2728      2896
```

(d) Forms a dot product of two vectors, resulting in a scalar (single-valued) quantity. The resulting output is

```
C = 800
```

(e) Assigns fractional elements to the elements of a matrix and displays the elements in a formatted form. The resulting output is

```
1.111e-01   2.222e-01   3.333e-01
2.222e-01   3.333e-01   4.444e-01
3.333e-01   4.444e-01   5.556e-01
```

9.45
```
DIM X(100)
MAT INPUT X(?)
```

Input data: <u>5, 10, 15, 20, 25, 30,</u>
              <u>35, 40, 45, 50, 55, 60</u>   (Notice the comma at the end of the first line of data.)

9.46   `MAT INPUT PROMPT "Please enter six values per line :": X(?)`

9.47   `MAT LINE INPUT cities$`

Input data: <u>Boston, MA</u>
              <u>Chicago, IL</u>
              <u>Denver, CO</u>
              <u>Honolulu, HI</u>
              <u>New York, NY</u>
              <u>Pittsburgh, PA</u>
              <u>San Diego, CA</u>
              <u>Seattle, WA</u>

9.48   `MAT LINE INPUT PROMPT "Please enter each city on a new line: ": cities$`

Input data: Please enter each city on a new line: <u>Boston, MA</u>
              ?<u>Chicago, IL</u>
              ?<u>Denver, CO</u>
              ?<u>Honolulu, HI</u>
              ?<u>New York, NY</u>
              ?<u>Pittsburgh, PA</u>
              ?<u>San Diego, CA</u>
              ?<u>Seattle, WA</u>

9.49
```
DIM X(100)
OPEN #1: NAME "VALUES.DAT", CREATE OLD, ORG TEXT
. . . . .
MAT INPUT #1: X
MAT PRINT X
. . . . .
CLOSE #1
END
```

9.50
```
DIM X(100)
OPEN #1: NAME "VALUES.DAT", CREATE NEW, ORG TEXT
. . . . .
MAT INPUT X
MAT PRINT #1: X
. . . . .
CLOSE #1
END
```

9.51
```
DIM cities$(100)
OPEN #1: NAME "CITIES.DAT", CREATE OLD, ORG TEXT
 .  .  .  .  .
MAT LINE INPUT #1: cities$
MAT PRINT cities$
 .  .  .  .  .
CLOSE #1
END
```

9.52
```
DIM cities$(100)
OPEN #1: NAME "CITIES.DAT", CREATE NEW, ORG TEXT
 .  .  .  .  .
MAT LINE INPUT cities$
MAT PRINT #1: cities
 .  .  .  .  .
CLOSE #1
END
```

9.53
```
DIM A(20, 30)
OPEN #1: NAME "MATRIX.DAT", CREATE OLD, ORG RANDOM, RECSIZE 6000
 .  .  .  .  .
MAT READ #1: A
MAT PRINT A
 .  .  .  .  .
CLOSE #1
END
```

9.54
```
DIM A(20, 30)
OPEN #1: NAME "MATRIX.DAT", CREATE NEW, ORG RANDOM, RECSIZE 6000
 .  .  .  .  .
MAT INPUT A
MAT WRITE #1: A
 .  .  .  .  .
CLOSE #1
END
```

9.55   (a)
```
MAT Z = TRN(X)          or          MAT Z = TRN(X)
MAT B = Z * A                       MAT C = A * X
MAT Y = B * X                       MAT Y = Z * C
```

The result of this expression is a single value. Hence, Y will be an ordinary variable, not an array.

(b)
```
MAT A = INV(F)
MAT B = A * G
MAT C = V * B
MAT T = C + H          T will be a 50 x 50 matrix.
```

(c)
```
MAT B = INV(A)
MAT C = B * A
MAT I = IDN
MAT D = I - C
```

(*d*) `MAT PRINT D;`

(*e*) `MAT READ A, C`
       `MAT B = TRN(C)`   Note that A and C are each read row-by-row.

(*f*) `MAT PRINT P, T, X`

(*g*) `MAT PRINT P; T; X;`

(*h*) `MAT E = A * C`
       `MAT F = B * D`
       `MAT G = E - F`
       `LET DETG = DET(G)`
       `PRINT "Determinant of G ="; DETG`

(*i*) `MAT E = A * C`
       `MAT F = B * D`
       `MAT G = E - F`
       `LET H = INV(G)`
       `LET DETG = DET(G)`
       `MAT PRINT G; H;`
       `PRINT "Determinant of G ="; DETG`

(*j*) `MAT A = ZER(12, 8)`

(*k*) `MAT SYMBOLS$ = NUL$(12, 12)`

(*l*) `MAT READ A(8, 12), B(6, 15)`

The data block must contain the elements of A in row-by-row order, followed by the elements of B, row-by-row.

(*m*)
```
FOR I = 1 TO 8          !A-matrix
   FOR J = 1 TO 12
      PRINT A(I, J);
   NEXT J
   PRINT
NEXT I
PRINT                   !blank line
FOR I = 1 TO 6          !B-matrix
   FOR J = 1 TO 15
      PRINT B(I, J);
   NEXT J
   PRINT
NEXT I
```

The explicit FOR - NEXT loops are required because the variable dimension feature is not available with the MAT PRINT statement.

Here is another approach:

```
REDIM A(8, 12), B(6, 15)
MAT PRINT A, B
```

This approach is simpler, but will result in the loss of those array elements that are not displayed (for A, rows 9 through 20 and columns 13 through 30; for B, rows 7 through 20 and columns 16 through 30).

Index

Access type, file, 215
Addition, matrix, 250
Advantages of BASIC, 12
Air, mass of, 60
Algebraic equation, solution of, 79, 100, 177
Algol, 8
Allen, Paul, 9
Americal National Standards Institute, 9
American flag, generation of, 179
American presidents, 125
AND operator, 63
Animated text, 336
Animation, 338, 340
ANSI, 9
Answers to selected problems, 379-412
Arc, elliptical, 334
Archimedes' spiral, 356
Argument, 31, 132
    formal, 131
Arithmetic operators, 18, 19
Array, 105
Array argument:
    external function, 147, 149
    subroutine, 152
Array:
    dimensionality, 105
    initialization, 113
    variable size, 271
Art, kinetic, 314
ASCII character set, 377
ASCII characters, extended, 350
ASK statement, 204, 230, 233
Aspect, 334
Assignment, 22
    matrix, 248, 249
Auxiliary storage device, 4
Average:
    deviations about, 108
    geometric, 101, 178
    of a list of numbers, 71, 73, 76, 78, 128
    weighted, 101, 178
Bacteria culture, growth of, 61
Ball, bouncing, 338, 341
Bank loan, 102, 178
Bar chart generator, 347, 350
Baseball team records, 238, 243, 244
BASIC, 742
    advantages of, 12
    definition, 1

introduction to, 8
structured, 1, 9
BASIC program:
    structure of, 10
    writing, 44
BASICA, 9
Batch processing, 5
BEEP statement, 301
Binary digit, 3
Binary file, 214
Binary search, 230, 234
BINGO, game of, 180, 357
Bit, 3
Blackjack, game of, 179
Blimp, 336
Blocks, random, 324
Bottom-up programming, 43
Bouncing ball, simulation of, 338, 341
Breakpoint, 52
Brickout, game of, 357
Built-in functions, 31
Byte, 3
C, 7
Calculating factorials, 161
Calculator, simulation of, 103, 178
Calibration, joystick, 297
CALL statement, 151, 126, 179, 307
CASE ELSE statement, 86
CASE statement, 86
Changing dimensions, 270
Channel number, 215
Character data, 2
Character graphics, 346
Characters:
    ASCII, 377
    extended ASCII, 378
CIRCLE statement, 326, 330, 334
Circles, expanding, 327
CLEAR statement, 186
CLOSE statement, 215
CLS statement, 186
COBOL, 8
COLOR statement, 290, 299, 308
Color, use of, 299, 308
Command area, True BASIC, 55
Comments, 29, 30
Compilation, 8
Compilation errors, 49
Compiler, 8

Compound interest, 61, 195
Compound interest factors, 125, 245
Computer:
  characteristics, 2
  keyboard, 288
  mainframe, 1
  memory, 3
  mini, 1
  modes of operation, 5
  personal, 1, 288
  program, 2
  reliability, 4
  speed, 4
  super, 1
  word, 4
  workstations, 1
Computing, interactive, 6
Concatenation, 22
Conditional execution, 62, 65
Conditional looping, 62, 74, 77
Constant:
  numeric, 16
  string, 17
Control statements, line-oriented, 92
Control structures, nested, 78
Convergence, iterative procedure, 79
Conversational program, 7
Correcting errors, 51
Countries and their capitals, 126
Craps, game of, 140, 145, 244, 357
Creating a direct data file, 228, 229
Creating a sequential data file, 217, 218
CSMP, 8
Currency conversions, 126, 179, 245, 246, 306
Cursor keys, 288
Cursor, positioning, 186
Curve fitting, least squares method, 272, 317
Data block, rules, 114
Data file, 214
  direct, 227
  processing, 215
  random access, 227
  sequential, 216
DATA statement, 113
Data type, conversions, 184
Data types, 181
  memory requirements, 182
Data:
  character, 2
  graphic, 2
  input, 188
  input, 2

  numeric, 2
  output, 2
  rereading, 118
  types, 2
Date conversion, 103, 178
Debugger, QuickBASIC, 52
Debugging:
  aids, 52
  logical, 50
Declaration:
  external function, 144
  external subroutine, 159
  subroutine, 155
DECLARE DEF statement, 144
DECLARE FUNCTION statement, 144
Decoding a line of text, 130, 179, 246
DEF SEG statement, 205
DEF statement, 131, 136
DEFDBL statement, 183
DEFINT statement, 183
DEFLNG statement, 183
DEFSNG statement, 183
DEFSTR statement, 183
Depreciation, calculation of, 88, 306
DET function, 266
Detecting errors, 50
Determinant, 266
Deviations about an average, 108, 128
Device output, file-directed, 227
Diagnostics, 48
DIM statement, 105
  omission of, 106
Dimensionality, of an array, 105
Dimensions, variable, 270
Direct data file, 214, 227
  creating, 228, 229
  reading, 230, 234
  updating, 238
Displaying output data, 25
Division, integer, 19
DO - LOOP structures, 74
DOT function, 254
Double-precision data, 181
Double-precision variables, 182
DRAW statement, 338
Drop-down menu, QuickBASIC, 45
Duration, sound, 301
Editing area, True BASIC, 55
Editor:
  program, 45
  text, 247
EGA graphics, 308

Elementary functions, 31
Ellipse, 334
Embedded control structures, 78
Emulation, light pen, 294
Encoding a line of text, 130, 179, 246
END DATA, 114
END DEF statement, 136
END FUNCTION statement, 136
END statement, 30
END SUB statement, 150
Entering a program into the computer, 45
Equations, graphs of, 356
EQV operator, 63, 183
Error diagnostics, 48
Error:
    compilation, 49
    correcting, 51
    detecting, 50
    execution, 49
    logical, 50
    syntactic, 48
Event trapping, 288
Exam scores, 103, 126, 178, 217, 218, 220, 222,
    223, 226, 242, 243, 306
Executing a program, 47
Execution errors, 49
Execution, conditional, 62, 65
EXIT DEF statement, 139
EXIT DO statement, 76
EXIT FOR statement, 73
EXIT FUNCTION statement, 145
EXIT SUB statement, 153
Expanding circles, 327
Expanding rectangles, 322
Exponent, 16, 21
Exponential notation, 16
Exponentiation, 18, 19, 21
Exponentiation operator, 18
Expression:
    logical, 62
    mixed data, 184
    numeric, 18, 183
    string, 22
Extended ASCII character set, 378
Extended ASCII characters, 350
External function, 131, 143
    array argument, 147, 149
    declaration, 144
EXTERNAL FUNCTION statement, 144
External subroutine, 131, 150, 159
    declaration, 159
Factorials, calculation of, 161

Fibonacci numbers, 82, 185, 245, 306
Field (data), 193
Field (file), 214
File, 214
    access type, 215
    channel number, 215
    file number, 215
    mode, 215
status, 215
File directed device output, 227
File number, 215
Fixed-point constant, 16
Flags, of countries, 356
Floating-point constant, 16
FOR - NEXT structure, 70
    rules, 72
Formal argument, 131
Formal parameter, 131
Format string, 192
Formatted file, 214
Formatted output, 192
Fortran, 7, 8
Frequency, sound, 301
Function keys, 288
    programming, 289
Function, 131
    DET, 266
    DOT, 254
    external, 143
    INKEY$, 189
    INPUT$, 190
    INT, 32
    LEFT$, 236
    LEN, 236
    LOC, 230
    LOF, 230, 236
    LOG, 32
    MAT CON, 263, 271
    MAT IDN, 264, 271
    MAT INV, 265
    MAT NUL$, 270, 271
    MAT TRN, 265
    MAT ZER, 263, 271
    multi-line, 136
    PEEK, 205
    PEN, 293
    programmer-defined, 131
    RND, 140
    single-line, 131
    SIZE, 271
    SPC, 292
    SQR, 32

STICK, 297
TAB, 33
UCASE$, 234
Functions, library, 31
Game of chance, 140, 145, 244, 357
Gates, William, 9
General-purpose languages, 7
Geometric average, 101, 178
GET KEY statement, 191
GET statement, 236, 340, 341
GOSUB statement, 92, 157
GOTO statement, 92
Grammatical errors, 48
Graphic data, 2
Graphics:
    character, 346
    EGA, 308
    fundamentals, 308
Graphs, of equations, 356
GW-BASIC, 9
Hanoi, towers of, 163
Hierarchy of operations, 19, 64
High-level languages, 7
Identity matrix, 264
IF - THEN - ELSE block, 65
IF - THEN statement, 65, 92
IMP operator, 63, 183
Index (FOR - NEXT structure), 70
INKEY$ function, 189
INPUT #n statement, 216, 222
Input data, 2, 188
    rules for entering, 24
    strings, 24
Input devices, programmable, 290
Input prompts, 188, 259
INPUT statement, 188
Input statement, 23
INPUT$ function, 190
Input, matrix, 255
INT function, 32
Integer constant, 16
Integer data, 181
Integer division, 19
Integer remainder, 19, 182
Interactive computing, 6
Interest factors, 125
Interest, compound, 61, 195
Internal functions, 131
Internal subroutine, 131, 150
Interpolation, Lagrangian, 129, 179
Interpretation, 8
Interpreter, 8

Introduction to BASIC, 8
Inverse, matrix, 265
Iterative procedure, 79
Joystick, 290, 296, 298, 307
    calibration, 297
Kemeny, John, 8, 54
KEY INPUT, 190
KEY ON statement, 290
Key words, 17
Keyboard:
    function keys, 288
    personal computer, 288
KILL statement, 225
Kinetic art, 314
Kurtz, Thomas, 8, 54
Label, line, 93
Lagrangian interpolation, 129, 179
Language:
    general-purpose, 7
    high-level, 7
    machine, 7
    simulation, 8
    special-purpose, 7
Least squares, method of, 272, 317
LEFT$ function, 236
LEN function, 236
LET statement, 22
Library functions, 31
    list of, 31
    QuickBASIC, 374-376
    True BASIC, 364-366
    use of, 34
Library, mouse, 296
Light pen, 290, 291
    emulation, 294
Lightning bolt, 313, 329
LINE INPUT statement, 191
Line label, 93
Line numbers, 10, 11
Line spacing, output data, 25
LINE statement, 312, 313, 322, 323
Line-oriented control statements, 92
Line-oriented subroutine calls, 157
Line-oriented text editor, 247
Linear regression, 317
Lines, 309
    moving, 314
LISP, 8
List of names, reordering, 125
List of numbers:
    average of, 71, 73, 76, 78, 128
    reordering, 115, 124, 245

standard deviation, 128
variance, 128, 179
Loans, 102, 178
LOC function, 230
LOCATE statement, 186
Locations, record, 230
LOF function, 230, 236
LOG function, 32
Logical debugging, 50
Logical errors, 50
Logical expressions, 62
Logical operators, 63, 183
Long-integer data, 181
Long-integer variables, 182
Looping, 62
conditional, 62, 74, 77
unconditional, 62, 70
LPRINT statement, 203
LPRINT USING statement, 203
Machine independence, 8
Machine language, 7
Magnitude, numeric constant, 16
Mainframes, 1
MAT CON function, 263, 271
MAT IDN function, 264, 271
MAT INPUT #n statement, 261
MAT INPUT statement, 258, 271
MAT INV function, 265
MAT LINE INPUT #n statement, 262
MAT LINE INPUT statement, 260
MAT NUL$ function, 270, 271
MAT PRINT #n statement, 261
MAT PRINT statement, 256
MAT PRINT USING statement, 257
MAT READ #n statement, 262
MAT READ statement, 255, 271
MAT REDIM statement, 271
MAT TRN function, 265
MAT WRITE #n statement, 262, 263, 271
Matrices, special, 263
Matrix addition, 250
Matrix assignment, 248, 249
Matrix file input/output, 261
Matrix input/output, 255
Matrix multiplication, 127, 179, 253
by a constant, 251
Matrix operations, 248
Matrix statements, 248
Matrix subtraction, 250
Matrix, identity, 264
Matrix, inverse, 265
Matrix, singular, 266

Matrix, transpose, 265
Maximum, search for, 133
Memory, 3
Menu bar:
QuickBASIC, 45
True BASIC, 55
Microsecond, 4
Microsoft Corp., 9
Minicomputers, 1
Minimizing a function ,177
Mixed data types, 184
MOD operator, 19, 183
Mode:
file, 215
screen, 299
Modem, 6
Module, program, 150
Monitor, 2
MORE DATA, 114
Mouse, 45, 290, 293
library, 296
Moving lines, 314
Multi-line function, 136
Multicolored text, 299
Multiple statements per line, 184
Multiplication by a constant, matrix, 251
Multiplication, matrix, 253
Music, programming, 307
NAME AS statement, 225
Names and addresses, 246
Nanosecond, 4
Nested control structures, 78
NOT operator, 63
Notation, exponential, 16
Null string, 270
Numbers:
Fibonacci, 82, 185
prime, 82, 185
Numeric constant, 16
fixed-point, 16
floating-point, 16
integer, 16
magnitude of, 16
significant figures, 16
Numeric data, 2
Numeric expression, 18
special rules, 20
Numeric quantity:
precision, 3
type, 3
Object program, 8
ON - GOSUB statement, 157, 288, 289

ON - GOTO statement, 92
ON KEY statement, 290
ON PEN statement, 292
ON STRIG statement, 297
OPEN statement, 215, 216, 228, 229
Operand, 62
Operations:
    hierarchy of, 19, 64
    matrix, 248
    modes of, 5
    vector, 248
Operators:
    arithmetic, 18, 19
    logical, 63, 183
    QuickBASIC, 373
    relational, 62
    True BASIC, 363
OR operator, 63
Output data, 2
    line spacing, 25
    significant figures, 26
    spacing, 27
Output:
    displaying, 25
    formatted, 192
    matrix, 255
Overflow, field, 193
Paddleball, game of, 342
PAINT statement, 329
PALETTE statement, 309
Parameter, formal, 131
Parentheses, use of, 20, 64
Pascal, 7
PAUSE statement, 205
PCs, 1
PEEK function, 205
PEN function, 293
PEN ON statement, 292
Personal computer, 1, 2, 288
    keyboard, 288
Personal finance calculations, 195
Phone numbers, 246, 332
Pig Latin generator, 155, 244, 306
Piggy bank problem, 60
Pixel, 308
Planning a BASIC program, 42
POINTER SAME, 237
Pointer, record, 230
Points and lines, 309
Points, random, 311
POKE statement, 205
PRESET statement, 310

Presidents, American, 125
Prime numbers, 82, 185, 245, 306
PRINT #n statement, 216, 226
Print files, 227
PRINT statement, 25
    special rules, 25
PRINT USING statement, 192
Procedure, iterative, 79
Program, 2
    comments, 29, 30
    entering into the computer, 45
    executing, 47
    object, 8
    source, 8
Program module, 150
Programmable input devices, 290
Programmer-defined function, 131
Programming languages, types of, 7
Programming the function keys, 289
Programming:
    bottom-up, 43
    top-down, 42
Programs, conversational, 7
Prompts, input, 188, 259
PSET statement, 309
PUT statement, 230, 340, 341
QBASIC, 9
Quadratic equation, roots of, 42, 44, 46, 47, 53,
    55, 68
QuickBASIC, 9, 45, 47
    debugger, 52
    command summary, 367-372
    library functions, 374-376
    operators, 373
    punctuation, 373
Random access data files, 214, 227
Random blocks, 324
Random points, 311
RANDOMIZE statement, 140
READ #n statement, 233
READ statement, 113
Reading a direct data file, 230, 234
Reading a sequential data file, 220, 222
Reading input, 23
Real data, 181, 182
Record, 214
    composition, 214
    definition, 230
    variable, 230
Record file, 214
Record locations, 230
Rectangles, expanding, 322

Recursion, 161
Regression, linear, 317
Relational operators, 62
Reliability, 4
REM statement, 29
Remainder, integer, 19
Reordering a list of names, 125
Reordering a list of numbers, 115, 124, 245
Rereading data, 118
Reserved words, 17, 18
Resolution, 308
RESTORE statement, 118
RETURN statement, 157, 290
RND function, 140
Roots of an algebraic equation, 79, 100
Roots, quadratic equation, 42, 44, 46, 47, 53, 55,
    68
Roulette, game of, 179, 357
Screen mode, 299
SCREEN statement, 299, 308
Screen-movement keys, 288
Scrolling, vertical, 187
Search for a maximum, 133
SEEK statement, 230
SELECT CASE structure, 85
Selection, 62, 85
Sequential data file, 214, 215
    creating, 217, 218
    reading, 220, 222
    updating, 223, 226
SET CURSOR statement, 186
SET statement, 204, 230, 233
Shapes, 322
Significant figures:
    numeric constant, 16
    output data, 26
SIMAN, 8
Simulation languages, 8
Simultaneous equations, solution of, 267, 268
Sine function, 102, 178
Single-line function, 131
Singular matrix, 266
Siren, 302, 307
SIZE function, 271
Size, of an array, 105
Solution of an algebraic equation, 79, 100, 177
Solution of simultaneous equations, 267, 268
Sound, 2, 299, 301
SOUND statement, 301
Source program, 8
Spacing of output data items, 27
SPC function, 292

Special matrices, 263
Special-purpose languages, 7
Speed, 4
Sphere, volume and area, 60
Split bar, True BASIC, 55
SQR function, 32
Stack, 163
Standard deviation, 128
Standard functions, 31
State capitals, 228, 229, 230, 234, 243
Statement, 10
    ASK, 204, 230, 233
    BEEP, 301
    CALL, 151
    CIRCLE, 326, 330, 334
    CLEAR, 186
    CLOSE, 215
    CLS, 186
    COLOR, 290, 299, 308
    DATA, 113
    DECLARE DEF, 144
    DECLARE FUNCTION, 144
    DEF, 131, 136
    DEF SEG, 205
    DEFDBL, 183
    DEFINT, 183
    DEFLNG, 183
    DEFSNG, 183
    DEFSTR, 183
    DIM, 105
    DRAW, 338
    END, 30
    END DEF, 136
    END FUNCTION, 136
    END SUB, 150
    EXIT DEF, 139
    EXIT DO, 76
    EXIT FOR, 73
    EXIT FUNCTION, 145
    EXIT SUB, 153
    EXTERNAL FUNCTION, 144
    GET, 236, 340, 341
    GET KEY, 191
    GOSUB, 92, 157
    GOTO, 92
    IF - THEN, 65, 92
    IF - THEN - ELSE, 65
    INPUT, 23, 188
    INPUT #n, 216, 222
    KEY ON, 290
    KILL, 225
    LET, 22

LINE, 312, 313, 322, 323
LINE INPUT, 191
LOCATE, 186
LPRINT, 203
LPRINT USING, 203
MAT INPUT, 258, 271
MAT INPUT #n, 261
MAT LINE INPUT, 260
MAT LINE INPUT #n, 262
MAT PRINT, 256
MAT PRINT #n, 261
MAT PRINT USING, 257
MAT READ, 255, 271
MAT READ #n, 262
MAT REDIM, 271
MAT WRITE #n, 262
matrix addition, 250
matrix assignment, 248, 249
matrix constant multiplication, 251
matrix multiplication, 253
matrix subtraction, 250
NAME AS, 225
ON - GOSUB, 157, 288, 289
ON - GOTO, 92
ON KEY, 290
ON PEN, 292
ON STRIG, 297
OPEN, 215, 216, 228, 229
PAINT, 329
PALETTE, 309
PAUSE, 205
PEN ON, 292
POKE, 205
PRESET, 310
PRINT, 25
PRINT #n, 216, 226
PRINT USING, 192
PSET, 309
PUT, 230, 340, 341
RANDOMIZE, 140
READ, 113
READ #n, 233
REM, 29
RESTORE, 118
RETURN, 157, 290
SCREEN, 299, 308
SEEK, 230
SET, 204, 230, 233
SET CURSOR, 186
SOUND, 301
STOP, 30
STRIG ON, 297

SUB, 150
UNSAVE, 227
WRITE #n, 248
Statements:
    multiple per line, 184
    QuickBASIC, 367-372
    True BASIC, 358-363
Status, file, 215
STICK function, 297
STOP statement, 30
Storage device, auxiliary, 4
Stream file, 214
STRIG ON statement, 297
String:
    constant, 17
    expressions, 17, 22
    format, 192
    null, 270
    part of, 112
    variables, 182
Structure:
    BASIC program, 10
    DO - LOOP, 74
    FOR - NEXT, 70
    SELECT CASE, 85
    WHILE - WEND, 77
Structured BASIC, 9
Student exam scores, 103, 126, 178, 217, 218, 220, 222, 223, 226, 242, 243, 306
SUB statement, 150
Subprogram, 150
Subroutine calls, line-oriented, 157
Subroutine declaration, 155
Subroutine, 131, 150
    array argument, 152
    external, 150
    external, 159
    internal, 150
Subscript, 105, 107
Subscripted variables, 107
Substring, 112
Subtraction, matrix, 250
Suffixes, 182
Supercomputer, 1
Syntactic error, 48
TAB function, 33
Table manipulation, 154, 179
Table of numbers, sums, 125, 179
Table of transcendental functions, 125
Temperature conversion, 60
Text editor, line-oriented, 247
Text file, 214

Text:
    animated, 336
    encoding and decoding, 130, 179, 246
    multicolored, 299
Tic-tac-toe, game of, 179, 357
Timesharing, 5
TO, 106
Top-down programming, 42
Towers of Hanoi, 163
Tracing, 51
Transcendental functions, table of, 125
Transpose, matrix, 265
Triangle, properties of , 60
True BASIC, 54
    and the 1987 ANSI standard, 54
    command summary, 358-363
    library functions, 364-366
    operators, 363
    punctuation, 363
UCASE$ function, 234
Unconditional looping, 62, 70
Unformatted file, 214
UNSAVE statement, 227
Updating a direct data file, 236, 238
Updating a sequential data file, 223, 226
Variable name, size of, 17
Variable, 17, 182
    double-precision, 182
    integer, 182
    long-integer, 182
    real, 182
    record, 230
    string, 17, 182
    subscripted, 107
Variance, 128, 179
Vector operations, 248
Vertical scrolling, 187
Watch expression, 52
Watch variable, 52
Watchpoint, 52
Weighted average, 101, 178
WHILE - WEND structure, 77
Word, 4
Word unscrambling, 109
Workstations, 1
WRITE #n statement, 228
Writing a BASIC program, 44
XOR operator, 63, 183